SIXTH EDITION

MANAGEMENT MISTAKES AND SUCCESSES

Robert F. Hartley
Cleveland State University

JOHN WILEY & SONS, INC.

New York • Chichester • Weinheim
Brisbane • Toronto • Singapore

Acquisitions Editor	Brent Gordon
Marketing Manager	Carlise Paulson
Senior Production Editor	Patricia McFadden
Cover Designer	David Levy
Illustration Editor	Anna Melhorn
Production Management	Hermitage Publishing Services

This book was set in New Caledonia by Hermitage Publishing Services, and printed and bound by Courier Westford. The cover was printed by Lehigh Press.

This book is printed on acid-free paper. ∞

Library of Congress Cataloging in Publication Data:

ISBN 0-471-33311-5

Printed in the United States of America

10 9 8 7 6 5 4 3 2 1

PREFACE

Once again, I would like to welcome back past users of *Management Mistakes.* I hope you will find this sixth edition with its new and updated cases a worthwhile change from earlier editions. It is always difficult to abandon interesting cases that have stimulated student discussions and provided good learning experiences. But newer case possibilities are ever competing for inclusion. Examples of good and bad handling of problems and opportunities are always emerging.

For new users, I hope the book will meet your full expectations and be an effective instructional tool. Although case books abound, you and your students may find this somewhat unique and very readable, a book that can help transform dry and rather remote concepts into practical reality, and lead to lively class discussions, and even debates amid the arena of decision making.

NEW TO THIS EDITION

In contrast to the early editions, which examined only notable mistakes, and based on your favorable comments about the last edition, I have again included a number of well-known successes. The hypothesis is that while we can learn from mistakes, we can also learn from successes, and we can learn by comparing the unsuccessful with the successful.

I have again given prominent placement to cases dealing with great comebacks, the truly inspiring examples of firms coming back from adversity. I have also continued cases dealing with the challenges and great satisfaction that can come from entrepreneurship. From polls of my students, interest in entrepreneurship has never been greater.

A number of you have asked that I identify which cases would be most appropriat for the traditional coverage of topics as organized in most management texts. With many cases it is not possible to truly compartmentalize the mistake or success strictly according to each topic. The patterns of success or failure tend to be more pervasive. Still, I think you will find the following classification of cases by subject matter to be helpful. I thank those of you who make this and other suggestions.

TABLE 1   Classification of Cases by Major Management Topics

Topics	Most Relevant Cases
Great Comebacks	Continental Airlines, Harley Davidson, IBM
Planning	Coca-Cola, Euro Disney, Southwest Airlines
	Scott Paper, Sunbeam, Saturn, Boston Beer, OfficeMax, Boston Chicken, Planet Hollywood

(continues)

TABLE 1 **(Continued)**

Topics	Most Relevant Cases
Organizing	Saturn, Wal-Mart, United Way, OfficeMax, McDonald's, Maytag
Leadership/Execution	Continental Airlines, Harley Davidson, IBM, Nike, Southwest Airlines, Boeing, Toys Я Us, Wal-Mart, Boston Beer, Archer-Daniels-Midland, OfficeMax, Johnson & Johnson
Control	United Way, Met Life, Maytag, McDonald's, Boeing
Crisis Management	Johnson & Johnson, Met Life, Maytag, United Way, Scott Paper, Sunbeam, Archer-Daniels-Midland, R. J. Reynolds, Philip Morris, Boeing, Boston Chicken, Planet Hollywood
Customer Service	Continental Airlines, Saturn, Harley Davidson, OfficeMax, Met Life, Toys Я Us
Nonprofit/Nonproduct	United Way, Euro Disney
Global Applications	Saturn, Euro Disney, Archer-Daniels-Midland, Harley Davidson, R. J. Reynolds, Philip Morris, Maytag, McDonald's, Nike
Entrepreneurial	Boston Beer, Boston Chicken, OfficeMax, Planet Hollywood
Social and Ethical	Met Life, United Way, Archer-Daniels-Midland, Johnson & Johnson, R. J. Reynolds, Philip Morris, Scott Paper and Sunbeam

TARGETED COURSES

As a supplemental text, this book can be used in a great variety of courses, both under-graduate and graduate, ranging from principles of management to strategic manage-ment. It can also be used in courses in business ethics and organizational theory.

TEACHING AIDS

As in the previous editions, this edition presents a number of teaching aids within and at the end of each chapter. Some of these will be common to several cases, and illus-trate that certain successful and unsuccessful practices tend to cross company lines.

Updated Information Boxes and Issue Boxes are included within every chapter to highlight relevant concepts and issues. Learning insights help students see how certain practices—both errors and successes—cross company lines and are prone to be either traps for the unwary or success modes. Discussion Questions and Hands-On Exercises encourage and stimulate student involvement. A recent pedagogical feature is the Team Debate Exercises, in which formal sides and options can be debated regarding various decisions and issues within the respective cases. Invitation to Research suggestions allow students to take the cases a step further, to investigate what has happened since the case was written. In the final chapter, the various learn-ing insights are summarized and classified into general conclusions.

An Instructor's Manual accompanies this text to provide possible answers and considerations for the pedagogical material within and at the ends of chapters.

ACKNOWLEDGMENTS

A number of persons have provided encouragement, information, advice, and constructive criticism. I thank in particular Barnett Helzberg, Jr. of the Shirley and Barnett Helzberg Foundation. Andrew J. Deile, Mercer University, Glenna Asbury Dod, Wesleyan College, Samuel Hazen, Tarleton State University, Micheal B. McCormick, Jacksonville State University. Finally, I express my appreciation to Brent Gordon, editor at John Wiley & Sons, for his kind assistance and support.

I really welcome your suggestions, criticisms, and other comments. In particular I would like to hear how you have used this book in your classes. Please feel free to contact me.

Robert F. Hartley
James J. Nance College of Business Administration
Cleveland State University
Cleveland, Ohio 44115

CONTENTS

CHAPTER ONE

Introduction

*I*n this sixth edition, we have added seven new cases, with the rest revamped and updated, and in some instances, reclassified. Many of these cases are as recent as today's headlines; some have still not come to complete resolution.

In accordance with your expressed preferences, we have continued the format of the last several editions by examining not only notable mistakes but also some notable successes. We continue to seek what can be learned—insights that are transferable to other firms, other times, and other situations. What key factors brought monumental mistakes for some firms and resounding successes for others? Through such evaluations and studies of contrasts, we may learn to improve the "batting average" in the intriguing, ever-challenging art of decision making.

We will encounter examples of the phenomenon of organizational life cycles, with an organization growing and prospering, then failing (just as humans do), but occasionally resurging. Success rarely lasts forever, but even the most serious mistakes can be (but are not always) overcome.

As in previous editions, a variety of firms, industries, mistakes, and successes are presented. You will be familiar with most of the organizations, although probably not with the details of their situations.

We are always on the alert for particular cases that bring out certain points or caveats in the art of decision making, and that give a balanced view of the spectrum of management problems. We have sought to present examples that provide somewhat different learning experiences, where at least some aspect of the mistake or success is unique. Still, we see similar mistakes occurring time and again. The prevalence of some of these mistakes makes us wonder how much decision making has really improved over the decades.

Let us then consider what learning insights we can gain, with the benefit of hindsight, from examining these examples of successful and unsuccessful management practices.

LEARNING INSIGHTS

Analyzing Mistakes

In looking at sick companies, or even healthy ones that have experienced difficulties with certain parts of their operations, we are tempted to be unduly critical. It is easy to criticize with the benefit of hindsight. Mistakes are inevitable, given the present state of the art of decision making and the dynamic environment facing organizations.

Mistakes can be categorized as errors of omission and of commission. *Mistakes of omission* are those in which no action was taken and the status quo was contentedly embraced amid a changing environment. Such errors, which often typify conservative or stodgy management, are not as obvious as the other category of mistakes. They seldom involve tumultuous upheaval; rather, the company's fortunes and competitive position slowly fade, until management at last realizes that mistakes having monumental impact have been allowed to happen. The firm's fortunes often never regain their former luster. But sometimes they do, and we have devoted Part I to the intriguing and inspiring topic of Great Comebacks, describing the cases of Continental Airlines, Harley Davidson, and IBM, all of which fought back successfully from adversity.

Mistakes of commission are more spectacular. They involve bad decisions, wrong actions taken, misspent or misdirected expansion, and the like. Although the costs of the erosion of competitive position coming from errors of omission are difficult to calculate precisely, the costs of errors of commission are often fully evident. For example, the costs associated with the misdirected efforts of Met Life in fines and restitution totaled nearly a hundred million dollars. With Euro Disney, in 1993 alone the loss was $960 million; it improved in 1994 with only a $366 million loss. With Maytag's overseas Hoover Division, the costs of an incredibly bungled sales promotion eventually approached $100 million.

Although they may make mistakes, organizations with alert and aggressive management show certain actions or reactions when reviewing their own problem situations:

1. Looming problems or present mistakes are quickly recognized.

2. The causes of the problem(s) are carefully determined.

3. Alternative corrective actions are evaluated in view of the company's resources and constraints.

4. Corrective action is prompt. Sometimes this requires a ruthless axing of the product, the division, or whatever is at fault.

5. Mistakes provide learning experiences. The same mistakes are not repeated, and future operations are consequently strengthened.

Being slow to recognize emerging problems leads us to think that management is lethargic and incompetent or that controls have not been established to provide prompt feedback at strategic control points. For example, a declining competitive position in one or a few geographical areas should be a red flag to management that something is amiss. To wait months before investigating or taking action may mean a permanent loss of business. Admittedly, signals sometimes get mixed, and complete information may be lacking, but procrastination cannot be easily defended.

Just as problems should be quickly recognized, the causes of these problems—the "why" of the unexpected results—must be determined as quickly as possible. It is premature, and rash, to take action before knowing where the problems really lie. To go back to the previous example, the loss of competitive position in one or a few areas may reflect circumstances beyond the firm's immediate control, such as an aggressive new competitor who is drastically cutting prices to "buy sales." In this situation, all competing firms will likely lose market share, and little can be done except to stay as competitive as possible with prices and servicing. However, closer investigation may reveal that the erosion of business was due to unreliable deliveries, poor quality control, uncompetitive prices, or incompetent sales staff.

With the cause(s) of the problem defined, various alternatives for dealing with it should be identified and evaluated. This may require further research, such as obtaining feedback from customers or from field personnel. Finally the decision to correct the situation should be made as objectively and prudently as possible. If drastic action is needed, there usually is little rationale for delaying. Serious problems do not go away by themselves: They tend to fester and become worse.

Finally, some learning experience should result from the misadventure. The president of one successful firm told me

> I try to give my subordinates as much decision-making experience as possible. Perhaps I err on the side of delegating too much. In any case, I expect some mistakes to be made, some decisions that were not for the best. I don't come down too hard usually. This is part of the learning experience. But God help them if they make the same mistake again. There has been no learning experience, and I question their competence for higher executive positions.

Analyzing Successes

Successes deserve as much analysis as mistakes, although admittedly the urgency is less than with an emerging problem that requires remedial action lest it spread.

Any analysis of success should seek answers to at least the following questions:

Why were such actions successful?
- Was it because of the nature of the environment, and if so, how?
- Was it because of particular research, and if so, how?
- Was it because of particular engineering and/or production efforts, and if so, can these be adapted to other aspects of our operations?
- Was it because of any particular element of the strategy—such as service, promotional activities, or distribution methods—and if so, how?
- Was it because of the specific elements of the strategy meshing well together, and if so, how was this achieved?

Was the situation unique and unlikely to be encountered again?
- If not unique to the situation, how can we use these successful techniques in the future or in other operations at the present time?

ORGANIZATION OF THIS BOOK

In this sixth edition we have kept the same format as the fifth edition. This includes two changes introduced then that many of you approved of: Great Turnarounds (Comebacks), and Entrepreneurial Adventures. The learning insights where great adversity was finally turned to success seem fertile enough to deserve a prominent place in the book. Polls of students show that interest in entrepreneurship has never been greater, and Entrepreneurial Adventures gives us four intriguing cases with their problems, challenges, and triumphs. Otherwise, we have categorized cases under traditional management functions of planning and control but have combined the organization and leadership functions under "execution." Finally, of course, we can hardly ignore social and ethical concerns in the closer scrutiny of business practices today.

Great Comebacks

The comeback of Continental Airlines from extreme adversity and devastated employee morale to become one of the best airlines in the country is an achievement of no small moment. New CEO Gordon Bethune brought human relations skills to one of the most rapid turnarounds ever, after a decade of raucous adversarial relations.

In the early 1960s, Harley Davidson dominated a static motorcycle industry. Suddenly, Honda burst on the scene and Harley's market share dropped from 70 percent to 5 percent in only a few years. It took Harley nearly three decades to revive, but now it has created a mystique for heavy motorcycles and a new type of biker.

In a previous edition, I classified IBM as a prime example of a giant firm that had failed to cope with changing technology. Along with many other analysts, I thought the behemoth could never rouse itself enough to again be a major player. But we were wrong, and IBM resurrected itself to become a premier growth company again.

Planning Blunders and Successes

The classic miscalculation of Coca-Cola in changing the flavor and tampering with the heritage of its major product showed flawed planning, despite the use of extensive research. Although the situation eventually worked out, embarrassed executives had to make a major improvisation.

In April 1992, just outside Paris, Disney opened its first European theme park. It had high expectations and supreme self-confidence (critics would say arrogance). The earlier Disney parks in California, Florida, and more recently, Japan, were spectacular successes. But the rosy expectations soon became a delusion as a variety of planning miscues finally showed Disney that Europeans, and particularly the French, were not carbon copies of visitors elsewhere.

Albert Dunlap had gained a well-deserved reputation of being the premier hatchet man, the one who would come into a sick organization and fire enough people to make it temporarily profitable—they called him "Chainsaw Al." Somehow, with Sunbeam this seemingly proven downsizing strategy did not work. Dunlap himself was fired by the board of directors.

Last in this section we examine the outstanding success of Southwest Air. It found a window of opportunity in being the lowest-cost and lowest-price airline. Now its strategic plan threatens major airlines in all their domestic routes.

Execution Flaws and Accomplishments

Nike, the dominant athletic-shoe firm, found its success threatened by bad publicity about sweatshop conditions in foreign factories, by customer disenchantment with the high-priced athletes it sponsored, and also by what many thought were its exorbitant prices. Somehow, the successful strategy was crumbling.

Boeing represents an interesting dilemma: too much business. It was unable to cope with a deluge of orders in the mid- and late 1990s. Months, and then years went by, as it tried to make its production more efficient.

A major category-killer retail chain, Toys Я Us, found its past successful strategy eroding. It failed to keep in the vanguard with inventory control, state-of-the-art stores, and enhanced customer service.

General Motors' Saturn seemed to represent a new tomorrow in U.S. automaking. Relying on a motivated workforce, Saturn produced cars matching Japanese cars in quality and often priced better, and it achieved the highest customer-satisfaction ratings of any U.S. car. When it turned its attention to Japan, however, it fell flat. What caused a successful format to strike out in Japan?

The last case in this section describes Sam Walton and his Wal-Mart empire, now the biggest retailer of all. Walton believed in frugality and a lean but efficient organization. The story of one man's rise to the pinnacle of his chosen field in just a few decades is inspiring. Despite his wealth and prestige, his was the common touch. Yet, the juggernaut of Wal-Mart is not without its critics.

Control Weaknesses and Strengths

United Way of America is a not-for-profit organization. The man who led it to prominence as the nation's largest charity came to perceive himself as virtually beyond authority. Exorbitant spending, favoritism, conflicts of interest—these went uncontrolled and uncriticized until investigative reporters from the *Washington Post* publicized the scandalous conduct. Amid the hue and cry, charitable contributions nationwide drastically declined.

Met Life, the huge insurance firm, whether through loose controls or tacit approval, permitted an agent to use deceptive selling tactics on a grand scale, and enrich himself in the process. Investigations of several state attorneys general forced the company to cough up almost $100 million in fines and restitutions.

The problems of Maytag's Hoover subsidiary in Great Britain almost defy belief. The subsidiary, acting under very loose reins from corporate Maytag, planned a promotional campaign so generous that it was overwhelmed with takers; it was unable either to supply the products or to grant the prizes. In a control miscue of multimillion-dollar consequences, Maytag had to foot the bills while trying to appease irate customers and stockholders.

Although it would seem that maintaining high standards and controls for independent franchises is more difficult than controlling company-owned outlets, McDonald's refutes this notion. Since its beginning, McDonald's had been the epitome of tightly controlled operations, with the highest standards of cleanliness, product quality and freshness, and customer service. As such, its growth pattern continued almost unabated for nearly four decades. Now it seems to have encountered difficulties, and is no longer the same paragon.

Entrepreneurial Adventures

Boston Beer burst upon the microbrewery scene with Samuel Adams beers, higher priced even than most imports. Notwithstanding this—or maybe because of it—Boston Beer became the largest microbrewer. The experience shows that a small entrepreneur can compete successfully against the giants in the industry, and do this on a national scale.

The next case describes two concept restaurant chains: Boston Chicken and Planet Hollywood. Both went public with great publicity and hype, and the offering price was quickly bid up. Unfortunately, their popularity with customers, and with investors, proved short-lived, and their very viability became jeopardized. How could their entrepreneurs and the investors who bought in the hype of their initial public offerings (IPOs) have been so mistaken?

The third chapter in this section describes OfficeMax, a business that grew to $2.5 billion in sales in only a few years. The dedication and creative efforts of its founder can serve as a model for any would-be entrepreneur who aspires to make it big.

Ethical Challenges

ADM presents a paradox. It is a successful firm, but with its success tarnished by unethical practices and even illegal price-fixing schemes. A dictatorial CEO also fostered political cronyism.

The tobacco industry continues to be beleaguered but defiant as it pursues its profit-maximizing strategy. A November 1998 deal with state attorneys general in which it will pay some $200 billion over 25 years may give it relief from lawsuits, but force it to raise the price of cigarettes. But the industry is finding other opportunities.

Johnson & Johnson (J & J) exemplifies a superb example of crisis management under the most severe circumstances: loss of life directly connected to its flagship product, Tylenol. J & J became a role model of how to "keep the faith" with its customers, putting their best interests ahead of the firm's and in the process enhancing a public image as a responsive and caring firm. Of late, however, the steadfastness of this philosophy is in question.

GENERAL WRAP-UP

When possible, we have depicted the major personalities involved in these cases. Imagine yourself in their positions, confronting the problems and facing choices at their points of crisis or just-recognized opportunities. What would you have done differently, and why? We invite you to participate in the discussion questions, the hands-on exercises, and, yes, the debates appearing at the ends of chapters. There are also discussion questions for the various boxes within chapters. We urge you to consider the pros and cons of alternative actions.

In so doing you may feel the excitement and challenge of decision making under conditions of uncertainty. Perhaps you may even become a better future executive and decision maker.

QUESTIONS

1. Do you agree that it is impossible for a firm to avoid mistakes? Why or why not?

2. How can a firm speed up its awareness of emerging problems so that it can take corrective action? Be as specific as you can.

3. Large firms tend to err on the side of conservatism and are slower to take corrective action than smaller ones. Why do you suppose this is so?

4. Which do you think is likely to be more costly to a firm, errors of omission or errors of commission? Why?

5. So often we see the successful firm eventually losing its pattern of success. Why is success not more enduring?

PART ONE

GREAT COMEBACKS

CHAPTER TWO

Continental Airlines: From the Ashes

*I*n the fourth edition of *Mistakes,* published in 1994, we described massive management blunders at Continental Airlines as a "confrontational destruction of an organization." In only a few years, in a remarkable recovery under new management, Continental became a star of the airline industry. The changemaker, CEO Gordon Bethune, wrote a best-selling book about his efforts to turn around the moribund company, titled *From Worst to First.* In this chapter we will look first at the unfolding scenario leading to the difficulties of Continental, and then examine the ingredients of the great comeback.

THE FRANK LORENZO ERA

Lorenzo was a consummate manipulator, parlaying borrowed funds and little of his own money to build an airline empire. By the end of 1986, he controlled the largest airline network in the non-Communist world: only Aeroflot, the Soviet airline, was larger. Lorenzo's network was a leveraged amalgam of Continental, People Express, Frontier, and Eastern, with $8.6 billion in sales—all this from a small investment in Texas International Airlines in 1971. In the process of building his network, Lorenzo defeated unions and shrewdly used the bankruptcy courts to further his ends. When he eventually departed, his empire was swimming in red ink, had a terrible reputation, and was burdened with colossal debt and aging planes.

The Start

After getting an MBA from Harvard, Lorenzo's first job was as a financial analyst at Trans World Airlines. In 1966, he and Robert Carney, a buddy from Harvard, formed an airline consulting firm, and in 1969 the two put up $35,000 between them to form an investment firm, Jet Capital. Through a public stock offering they were able to raise an additional $1.15 million. In 1971 Jet Capital was called in to fix ailing Texas International and wound up buying it for $1.5 million, and Lorenzo became CEO. He restructured the debt as well as the airline's routes, found funds to upgrade the almost obsolete planes, and brought Texas International to profitability.

In 1978, acquisition-minded Lorenzo lost out to Pan Am in a bidding war for National Airlines, but he made $40 million on the National stock he had acquired. In 1980 he created nonunion New York Air and formed Texas Air as a holding company. In 1982 Texas Air bought Continental for $154 million.

Lorenzo's Treatment of Continental

In 1983 Lorenzo took Continental into bankruptcy court, filing for Chapter 11. This permitted the corporation to continue to operate but spared its obligation to meet heavy interest payments and certain other contracts while it reorganized as a more viable enterprise. The process nullified the previous union contracts, and this prompted a walkout by many union workers.

Lorenzo earned the lasting enmity of organized labor and the reputation of union-buster as he replaced strikers with nonunion workers at much lower wages. (A few years later, he reinforced this reputation when he used the same tactics with Eastern Airlines.)

In a 1986 acquisition achievement that was to backfire a few years later, Lorenzo struck deals for a weak Eastern Airlines and a failing People Express/Frontier Airlines. That same year Continental emerged out of bankruptcy. Now Continental, with its nonunion workforce making it a low-cost operator, was Lorenzo's shining jewel. The low bid accepted for Eastern reinforced Lorenzo's reputation as a visionary builder.

What kind of executive was Lorenzo? Although he was variously described as a master financier and visionary, his handling of day-to-day problems bordered on the inept.[1] One former executive was quoted as saying, "If he agreed with one thing at 12:15, it would be different by the afternoon."[2] Inconsistent planning and poor execution characterized his lack of good operational strength. Furthermore, his domineering and erratic style alienated talented executives. From 1983 to 1993, nine presidents left Continental.

But Lorenzo's treatment of his unions brought the most controversy. He became the central figure of confrontational labor-management relations, to a degree perhaps unmatched by any other person in recent years. Although he won the battle with Continental's unions and later with Eastern's, he was burdened with costly strikes and the residue of ill feeling that impeded any profitable recovery during his time at the helm.

The Demise of Eastern Airlines

In an environment of heavy losses and its own militant unions, Eastern in 1986 accepted the low offer of Lorenzo. With tough contract demands and the stockpiling

---

[1]See, for example, Todd Vogel, Gail DeGeorge, Pete Engardio, and Aaron Bernstein, "Texas Air Empire in Jeopardy," *Business Week* (March 27, 1989), p. 30.

[2]Mark Ivey and Gail DeGeorge, "Lorenzo May Land a Little Short of the Runway," *Business Week* (February 5, 1990), p. 48.

of $1 billion in cash as strike insurance, Lorenzo seemed eager to precipitate a strike that he might crush. He instituted a program of severe downsizing, and in 1989, after 15 months of fruitless talks, some 8,500 machinists and 3,800 pilots went on strike. Lorenzo countered the strike at Eastern by filing for Chapter 11 bankruptcy, and replaced many of the striking pilots and machinists within months.

At first Eastern appeared to be successfully weathering the strike, while Continental benefited with increased business. But soon revenue dropped drastically with Eastern planes flying less than half full amid rising fuel costs. Fares were slashed in order to regain business, and a liquidity crisis loomed. Then, on January 16, 1990, an Eastern jet sheared the top off a private plane in Atlanta. Even though the accident was attributed to air controller error, Eastern's name received the publicity.

Eastern creditors now despaired of Lorenzo's ability to pay them back in full and they pushed for a merger with Continental, which would expose it to the bankruptcy process. On December 3, 1990, Continental again tumbled into bankruptcy, burdened with overwhelming debt. In January 1991, Eastern finally went out of business.

CONTINENTAL'S EMERGENCE FROM BANKRUPTCY, AGAIN

Lorenzo was gone. The legacy of Eastern remained, however. Creditors claimed more than $400 million in asset transfers between Eastern and Continental, and Eastern still had $680 million in unfunded pension liabilities. The board brought in Robert Ferguson, veteran of Braniff and Eastern bankruptcies, to make changes. On April 16, 1993, the court approved a reorganization plan for Continental to emerge from bankruptcy, the first airline to have survived two bankruptcies. However, creditors got only pennies on the dollar.[3]

Still, despite its long history of travail and a terrible profit picture, Continental in 1992 was the nation's fifth largest airline, behind American, United, Delta, and Northwest, and it served 193 airports. Table 2.1 shows the revenues and net profits (or losses) of Continental and its major competitors from 1987 through 1991.

The Legacy of Lorenzo

Continental was savaged in its long tenure as a pawn in Lorenzo's dynasty-building efforts. He had saddled it with huge debts, brought it into bankruptcy twice, left it with aging equipment. Perhaps a greater detriment was a ravished corporate culture. The following information box discusses corporate culture.

A devastated reputation proved to be a major impediment. The reputation of a surly labor force had repercussions far beyond the organization itself. For years Continental had had a problem wooing the better-paying business travelers. Being on expense accounts, they wanted quality service rather than cut-rate prices. A reputa-

---

[3] Bridget O'Brian, "Judge Backs Continental Airlines Plan to Regroup, Emerge from Chapter 11," *The Wall Street Journal* (April 19, 1993), p. A4.

TABLE 2.1   **Performance Statistics, Major Airlines, 1987–1991**

	1987	1988	1989	1990	1991	Percent 5-Year Gain
Revenues:						
(Millions $)						
American	6,368	7,548	8,670	9,203	9,309	46.0%
Delta	5,638	6,684	7,780	7,697	8,268	46.6
United	6,500	7,006	7,463	7,946	7,850	20.8
Northwest	3,328	3,395	3,944	4,298	4,330	30.1
Continental	3,404	3,682	3,896	4,036	4,031	18.4
Income						
(Millions $)						
American	225	450	412	(40)	(253)	
Delta	201	286	467	(119)	(216)	
United	22	426	246	73	(175)	
Continental	(304)	(310)	(56)	(1,218)	(1,550)	

Source: Company annual reports.

Commentary: Note the operating performance of Continental relative to its major competitors during this period. It ranks last in sales gain. It far and away has the worst profit performance, having massive losses during each of the years in contrast to its competitors, who, while incurring some losses, had neither the constancy nor the magnitude of losses of Continental. And the relative losses of Continental are even worse than they at first appear: Continental is the smallest of these major airlines.

tion for good service is not easily or quickly achieved, especially when the opposite reputation is well entrenched.

On another dimension, Continental's reputation also hindered competitive parity. Surviving two bankruptcies does not engender confidence among investors, creditors, or even travel agents.

A Sick Airline Industry

Domestic airlines lost a staggering $8 billion in the years 1990 through 1992. Tense fare wars and excess planes proved to be albatrosses. Even when planes were filled, discount prices often did not cover overhead.

A lengthy recession was mostly to blame, inducing both firms and individuals to fly more sparingly. Business firms were finding teleconferencing to be a viable substitute for business travel, and consumers, facing diminished discretionary income and the threat of eventual layoffs or forced retirements, were hardly in an optimistic mood. The airlines suffered.

Part of the blame for the red ink lay directly with the airlines—they were reckless in their expansion efforts—yet they did not deserve total blame. In the late 1980s, passenger traffic climbed 10 percent per year, and in response the airlines ordered hun-

INFORMATION BOX

IMPORTANCE OF A POSITIVE CORPORATE CULTURE

A corporate or organizational culture can be defined as the system of shared beliefs and values that develops within an organization and guides the behavior of its members.[4] Such a culture can be powerful influence on performance results:

If employees know what their company stands for, if they know what standards they are to uphold, then they are much more likely to make decisions that will support those standards. They are also more likely to feel as if they are an important part of the organization. They are motivated because life in the company has meaning for them.[5]

Lorenzo had destroyed the former organizational climate as he beat down the unions. The replacement employees had little reason to develop a positive culture or esprit de corps given the many top management changes, the low pay relative to other airline employees, and the continuous possibility of corporate bankruptcy. Employees had little to be proud of. But this was to change abruptly under new management.

Can a corporate climate be too upbeat? Discuss.

[4]Edgar H. Schein, "Organizational Culture," *American Psychologist,* vol. 45 (1990), pp. 109–119.
[5]Terrence E. Deal and Alan A. Kennedy, *Corporate Cultures: The Rites and Rituals of Corporate Life* (Reading, MA: Addison-Wesley, 1982), p. 22.

dreds of jetliners.[6] The recession arrived just as the new planes were being delivered. The airlines greatly increased their debt structure in their expansion efforts; the big three, for example—American, United, and Delta—doubled their leverage in the four years after 1989, with debt by 1993 at 80 percent of capitalization.[7]

In such a climate, cost-cutting efforts prevailed. But how much can be cut without jeopardizing service and even safety? Some airlines found that hubs, heralded as the great strategy of the 1980s, were not as cost-effective as expected. With hub cities, passengers were gathered from outlying "spokes" and then flown to final destinations. Maintaining too many hubs, however, brought costly overheads. While the concept was good, some retrenchment seemed necessary to be cost effective.

Airlines such as Continental with heavy debt and limited liquidity had two major concerns: first, how fast the country could emerge from recession; second, the risk of fuel price escalation in the coming years. Despite Continental's low operating costs, external conditions impossible to predict or control could affect viability.

[6]Andrea Rothman, "Airlines: Still No Wind at Their Backs," *Business Week* (January 11, 1993), p. 96.
[7]*Ibid.*

THE GREAT COMEBACK UNDER GORDON BETHUNE

In February 1994, Gordon Bethune left Boeing and took the job of president and chief operating officer of Continental. He faced a daunting challenge. While it was the fifth largest airline, Continental was by far the worst among the nation's 10 biggest according to these quality indicators of the Department of Transportation:

- In on-time percentage (the percentage of flights that land within 15 minutes of their scheduled arrival)
- In number of mishandled-baggage reports filed per 1,000 passengers
- In number of complaints per 100,000 passengers
- In involuntarily denied boarding (i.e., passengers with tickets who are not allowed to board because of overbooking or other problems)[8]

In late October he became chief executive officer. Now he sat in the pilot's seat.

He made dramatic changes. In 1995, through a "renewed focus on flight schedules and incentive pay" he greatly improved on-time performance, along with lost-baggage claims, and customer complaints. Now instead of being dead last in these quality indicators of the Department of Transportation, Continental by 1996 was third best or better in all four categories.

Customers began returning, especially the higher-fare business travelers, climbing from 32.2 percent in 1994 to 42.8 percent of all customers by 1996. In May 1996, based on customer surveys Continental was awarded the J. D. Power Award as the best airline for customer satisfaction on flights of 500 miles or more. It also received the award in 1997, the first airline to win two years in a row. Other honors followed. In January 1997, it was named "Airline of the Year" by *Air Transport World*, the leading industry monthly. In January 1997, *Business Week* named Bethune one of its top managers of 1996.

Bethune had transformed the workforce into a happy one, as measured by these statistics:

- Wages up an average of 25 percent
- Sick leave down more than 29 percent
- Personnel turnover down 45 percent
- Workers compensation claims down 51 percent
- On-the-job injuries down 54 percent[9]

Perhaps nothing illustrates the improvement in employee morale as much as this: in 1995, not all that long after he became top executive, employees were so

---

[8]Gordon Bethune, *From Worst to First* (New York: Wiley, 1998), p. 4.

[9] *Ibid.*, pp. 7–8.

happy with their new boss's performance that they chipped in to buy him a $22,000 Harley-Davidson.[10]

Naturally such improvement in employee relations and customer service had major impact on revenues and profitability. See Table 2.2 for the trend since 1992.

Gordon Bethune

Bethune's father was a crop duster, and as a teenager Gordon helped him one summer and learned first hand the challenges of responsibility: in this case, preparing a crude landing strip for nightime landings, with any negligence disastrous. He joined the Navy at 17, before finishing high school. He graduated second in his class at the Naval Technical School to become an aviation electronics technician, and over 19 years worked his way up to lieutenant. After leaving the Navy he joined Braniff, then Western, and later Piedmont Airlines as senior vice president of Operations. He finally left Piedmont for Boeing as VP/general manager of Customer Service. There he became licensed as a 757 and 767 pilot: "An amazing thing happened. All the Boeing pilots suddenly thought I was a great guy," he writes. "I hope I hadn't given them any reason to think otherwise of me before that, but this really got their attention."[11]

TABLE 2.2 Continental Sales and Profits, Before and After Bethune, 1992–1997

	Before Bethune			After Bethune		
	1992	1993	1994	1995	1996	1997
Revenues						
(Millions $)	5,494	3,907	5,670	5,825	6,360	7,213
Net Income	−110	−39	−612	224	325	389
(Millions $)						
Earnings per Share ($)		−1.17	−11.88	3.60	4.25	5.03

Sources: Company annual reports.

Commentary: While the revenue statistics do not show a striking improvement, the net income certainly does. Most important to investors, the earnings per share show a major improvement.

These statistics suggest the fallacy of a low-price strategy at the expense of profitability in the 1992–1994 era. At the same time, we have to realize that the early 1990s were recession years, particularly for the airline industry.

[10] *Ibid.,* frontispiece.

[11] *Ibid.,* p. 268.

HOW DID HE DO IT?

Bethune stressed the human element in guiding the comeback of a lethargic, even bitter, organization, even by doing the simple things: "On October 24, 1994, I did a very significant thing in the executive suite of Continental Airlines. ... I opened the doors. ... [Before] the doors to the executive suite were locked, and you needed an ID to get through. Security cameras added to the feeling of relaxed charm. ... So the day I began running the company, I opened the doors. I wasn't afraid of my employees, and I wanted everybody to know it."[12] Still, he had to entice employees to the twentieth floor of headquarters, and he did this with open houses, supplying food and drink, and personal tours and chat sessions. "I'd take a group of employees into my office, open up the closet, and say, 'You see? Frank's not here.' Frank Lorenzo had left Continental years before; the legacy of cost cutting and infighting of that era was finally gone, and I wanted them to know it."[13]

Of course, the improved employee relations needed tangible elements to cement and sustain it, and to improve the morale. Bethune worked hard to instill a spirit of teamwork. He did this by giving on-time bonuses to all employees, not just pilots. He burned the employee procedure manual that bound them to rigid policies instead of being able to use their best judgment. He even gave the planes a new paint job to provide tangible evidence of a disavowal of the old and an embracing of new policies and practices. This new image impressed both employees and customers.

Better communications was also a key element in improving employee relationships and the spirit of teamwork. Information was shared with employees through newsletters, updates on bulletin boards, e-mail, voice-mail, and electronic signs over worldwide workplaces. To Bethune it was a cardinal sin for any organization if employees first heard of something affecting them through the newspaper or other media. The following Information Box contrasts the classic Theory X and Theory Y managers. Bethune was certainly a Theory Y manager, and Lorenzo Theory X.

Now Continental had to win back customers. Instead of the company's old focus on cost savings, efforts were directed to putting out a better product. This meant emphasis on on-time flights, better baggage handling, and the like. By giving employees bonuses for meeting these standards, the incentive was created.

Bethune sought to do a better job of designing routes with good demand, to "fly places people wanted to go." This meant, for example, cutting back on six flights a day between Greensboro, North Carolina and Greenville, South Carolina. It meant not trying to compete with Southwest's Friends Fly Free Fares, which "essentially allowed passengers to fly anywhere within the state of Florida for

---

[12] *Ibid.*, p. 14.
[13] *Ibid.*, p. 32.

INFORMATION BOX

THE THEORY X AND THEORY Y MANAGER

Douglas McGregor, in his famous book, *The Human Side of Enterprise*, advanced the thesis of two different types of managers, the traditional Theory X manager with rather low opinion of subordinates, and his new Theory Y manager, who we might call a human-relations type of manager.

Schermerhorn contrasts the two styles as follows:[14]

Theory X views subordinates as
- Disliking work
- Lacking in ambition
- Irresponsible
- Resistant to change
- Preferring to be led than to lead

Theory Y sees subordinates this way:
- Willing to work
- Willing to accept responsibility
- Capable of self-direction
- Capable of self-control
- Capable of imagination, ingenuity, creativity

Which is better? With the success of Bethune in motivating his employees for strong positive change in the organization, one would think Theory Y is the only way to go. McGregor certainly thought so and predicted that giving workers more participation, freedom, and responsibility would result in high productivity.[15]

So, is there any room for a Theory X manager today? If so, under what circumstances?

[14] John R. Schermerhorn, Jr., *Management*, 6th ed. (New York: John Wiley 1999), p. 79.

[15] Douglas McGregor, *The Human Side of Enterprise* (New York: McGraw-Hill), 1960.

$24.50.[16] The frequent flyer program was reinstated. Going a step further, the company apologized to travel agents, business partners, and customers and showed them how it planned to do better and earn their business back.

Continental queried travel agents about their biggest clients, the major firms that did the most traveling, asking how could it better serve their customers. As a result, more first-class seats were added, particular destinations were given more attention, discounts for certain volumes were instituted. Travel agents themselves were made members of the team and given special incentives beyond normal airline commissions.

[16] *Ibid.*, pp. 51–52.

TABLE 2.3 Competitive Position of Continental Before and After Bethune, 1992–1997

	Before Bethune			After Bethune		
	1992	1993	1994	1995	1996	1997
Revenues (Millions $):						
AMR (American)	14,396	15,701	16,137	16,910	17,753	18,570
UAR (United)	12,890	14,511	13,950	14,943	16,362	17,378
Delta	10,837	11,997	12,359	12,194	12,455	13,590
Northwest	NA	8,649	9,143	9,085	9,881	10,226
Continental	5,494	3,907	5,670	5,825	6,360	7,213
Continental's Market Share (Percent of total sales of Big Five Airlines):		7.1%	9.9%	9.9%	10.1%	10.8%

Sources: Company annual reports. NA = information not available.

Commentary: Most significant is the gradual increase in market share of Continental over its four major rivals. This is an improving competitive position.

This still left financial considerations. Bethune was aggressive in renegotiating loans and poor airplane lease agreements, and in getting supplier financial cooperation. Controls were set up to monitor cash flow and stop waste. Tables 2.3 and 2.4 show the results of Bethune's efforts from the dark days of 1992–94, and how the competitive position of Continental changed. Remember, Bethune joined the firm in February 1994 and did not become the top executive until late October of that year.

TABLE 2.4 Profitability Comparison of Big Five Airlines, 1992–1997

	Before Bethune			After Bethune		
	1992	1993	1994	1995	1996	1997
Net Income (Millions $):						
AMR	−474	−96	228	196	1,105	985
UAL	−416	−31	77	378	600	958
Delta	−505	−414	−408	294	156	854
Northwest	NA	−114	296	342	536	606
Continental	−110	−39	−696	224	325	389

Source: Company annual reports.

NA = information not available.

Commentary: Of interest is how the good and bad times for the airlines seem to move in lockstep. Still, the smallest of the Big Five, Continental, incurred the biggest loss of any airline in 1994. Under Bethune, it has seen a steady increase in profitability, but so have the other airlines, although AMR and Delta have been more erratic.

WHAT CAN BE LEARNED?

It is possible to quickly turn around an organization. This idea flies in the face of conventional wisdom. How can a firm's bad reputation with employees, customers, creditors, stockholders, and suppliers be overcome without years of trying to prove that it has changed for the better? This conventional wisdom is usually correct: a great comeback does not often occur easily or quickly. But it sometimes does, with a streetwise leader, and a bit of luck perhaps. Gordon Bethune is proof that negative attitudes can be turned around quickly.

This possibility of a quick turnaround should be inspiring to other organizations mired in adversity.

Still, reputation should be carefully guarded. In most cases, a poor image is difficult to overcome, with trust built up only over time. The prudent firm is careful to safeguard its reputation.

Give employees a sense of pride and a caring management. Bethune proved a master at changing employees' attitudes and their sense of pride. Few top executives ever faced such a negative workforce, reflecting the Lorenzo years. But Bethune changed all this, and in such a short time. His open-door policy and open houses to encourage employees to interact with him and other top executives was such a simple gesture, but so effective, as was his opening wide the channels of communication about company plans. The incentive plans for improving performance, and the freeing up of employee initiatives by abolishing the rigidity of formal policies, were further positives. He engendered an atmosphere of teamwork and a personal image of an appreciative CEO. What is truly remarkable is how quickly such simple actions could turn around the attitudes of a workforce from adversarial with morale in the pits to pride and an eagerness to build an airline.

Contradictory and inconsistent strategies are vulnerable. Lorenzo was often described as mercurial and subject to knee-jerk planning, and poor execution.[17] Clearly focused objectives and strategies mark effective firms. They bring stability to an organization and give customers, employees, and investors confidence in undeviating commitments. Admittedly, some objectives and strategies may have to be modified occasionally to meet changing environmental and competitive conditions, but the spirit of the organization should be resolute, provided it is a positive influence and not a negative one.

The dangers of competing mostly on low price. Bethune inherited one of the lowest-cost air carriers, and it was doing badly. He says "you can make an airline so cheap nobody wants to fly it," [just as] "you can make a pizza so cheap nobody wants to eat it." "Trust me on this—we did it. ... In fact, it was making us lousy, and people didn't want to buy what we offered."[18]

---

[17] For example, Ivey and DeGeorge, *op. cit.*, p. 48.

[18] Bethune, *op. cit.*, p. 50.

ISSUE BOX

SHOULD AN ORGANIZATION BE NURTURED OR CONFRONTED?

Lorenzo used a confrontational and adversarial approach to his organization and the unions. He was seemingly successful in destroying the unions and hiring nonunion replacements at lower pay scales. This resulted in Continental becoming the lowest-cost operator of the major carriers, but there were negatives: service problems, questionable morale, diminished reputation, and devastated profitability.

Bethune used the opposite tack. It is hard to argue against nurturing and supporting an existing organization, avoiding the adversarial mindset of "them or us" if at all possible. Admittedly this may sometimes be difficult—sometimes impossible, at least in the short-run—but it is worth trying. It should result in better morale, motivation, and commitment to the company's best interest. (See Chapter 8 for Southwest Airlines' approach to organizational relations.)

We might add here that competing strictly on a price basis usually leaves any firm vulnerable. Low prices can easily be matched or countered by competitors if such low prices are attracting enough customers. On the other hand, competition based on such nonprice factors as better service, quality of product, a good public image or reputation, are not so easily matched, and can be more attractive to many customers.

In Chapter 8, again with Southwest Airlines, we find a firm competing ever so successfully with a low-price strategy. But Southwest has operational efficiency unmatched in the industry.

CONSIDER

Can you add any other learning insights?

QUESTIONS

1. Could Lorenzo's confrontation with the unions of Continental have been more constructively handled? How?

2. Do you see any limitations to Bethune's employee relations, especially in the areas of discipline and acceptance of authority?

3. Compare Bethune's handling of employees with that of Kelleher of Southwest Airlines in Chapter 8. Are there commonalities? Contrasts?

4. Compare Bethune's management style with that of Lorenzo. What conclusions can you draw?

5. Bethune gave great credit to his open-door policy when he became CEO. Do you think this was a major factor in the turnaround? How about changing the paint of the planes?

6. How do you motivate employees to give a high priority to customer service?

7. Evaluate the causes and the consequences of frequent top executive changes such as Continental experienced in the days of Lorenzo?

8. How can replacement workers—in this case pilots and skilled maintenance people hired at substantially lower salaries than their unionized peers at other airlines—be sufficiently motivated to provide top-notch service and a constructive esprit de corps?

HANDS-ON EXERCISES

1. It is 1994 and Bethune has just taken over. As his staff adviser he has asked you to prepare a report on improving customer service as quickly as possible. He has also asked you to design a program to inform both business and nonbusiness potential passengers of this new commitment. Be as specific as possible in your recommendations.

2. You are the leader of the machinists' union at Eastern. It is 1986 and Lorenzo has just acquired your airline. You know full well how he broke the union at Continental, and rumors are flying that he has similar plans for Eastern. Describe your tactics under two scenarios:
   (a) You decide to take a conciliatory stance.
   (b) You plan to fight him every step of the way.

How successful do you think you will be in saving your union?

TEAM DEBATE EXERCISE

In this case we have a great contrast in management styles. While the participative approach of Bethune seems the winner in this particular case, such is not always so. There are good arguments for the autocratic style, and indeed, Lorenzo made himself a wealthy man by so doing. Debate the general issue of autocratic versus participative management from as many aspects as you can.

INVITATION TO RESEARCH

What is the situation with Continental today? Is Bethune still CEO? Whatever happened to Lorenzo?

CHAPTER THREE

Harley Davidson: At Last

*I*n the early 1960s, a staid and unexciting market was shaken up, was rocked to its core, by the most unlikely invader. This intruder was a smallish Japanese firm that had risen out of the ashes of World War II, and was now trying to encroach on the territory of a major U.S. firm, a firm that had in the space of 60 years destroyed all of its U.S. competitors, and now had a solid 70 percent of the motorcycle market.

Yet, almost inconceivably, in half a decade this market share was to fall to 5 percent, and the total market was to expand many times over what it had been for decades. A foreign invader had furnished a textbook example of the awesome effectiveness of carefully crafted marketing efforts. In the process, this confrontation between Honda and Harley Davidson was a harbinger of the Japanese invasion of the auto industry.

Eventually, by the late 1980s, Harley was to make a comeback. But only after more than two decades of travail and mediocrity.

THE INVASION

Sales of motorcycles in the United States were around 50,000 per year during the 1950s, with Harley Davidson, Britain's Norton and Triumph, and Germany's BMW accounting for most of the market. By the turn of the decade, Honda began to penetrate the U.S. market. In 1960 less than 400,000 motorcycles were registered in the United States. While this was an increase of almost 200,000 from the end of World War II, 15 years before, it was far below the increase in other motor vehicles. But by 1964, only four years later, the number had risen to 960,000; two years later it was 1.4 million; and by 1971 it was almost 4 million.

In expanding the demand for motorcycles, Honda instituted a distinctly different strategy. The major elements of this strategy were lightweight cycles and an advertising approach directed toward a new customer. Few firms have ever experienced such a shattering of market share as did Harley Davidson in the 1960s. (Although its market share declined drastically, its total sales remained nearly constant, indicating that it was getting none of the new customers for motorcycles.)

Reaction of Harley Davidson to the Honda Threat

Faced with an invasion of its staid and static U.S. market, how did Harley react to the intruder? They did not react! At least not until far too late. Harley Davidson considered themselves the leader in full-size motorcycles. While the company might shudder at the image tied in with their product's usage by the leather jacket types, it took solace in the fact that almost every U.S. police department used its machines. Perhaps this is what led Harley to stand aside and complacently watch Honda make deep inroads into the American motorcycle market. The management saw no threat in Honda's thrust into the market with lightweight machines. The attitude was exemplified in this statement by William H. Davidson, the president of the company and son of the founder:

> Basically, we don't believe in the lightweight market. We believe that motorcycles are sport vehicles, not transportation vehicles. Even if a man says he bought a motorcycle for transportation, it's generally for leisure-time use. The lightweight motorcycle is only supplemental. Back around World War I, a number of companies came out with lightweight bikes. We came out with one ourselves. They never got anywhere. We've seen what happens to these small sizes.[1]

Eventually Harley recognized that the Honda phenomenon was not an aberration, and that there was a new factor in the market. The company attempted to fight back by offering an Italian-made lightweights in the mid-1960s. But it was far too late; Honda was firmly entrenched. The Italian bikes were regarding in the industry to be of lower quality than the Japanese. Honda, and toward the end of the 1960s other Japanese manufacturers, continued to dominate what had become a much larger market than ever dreamed.

AFTERMATH OF THE HONDA INVASION: 1965–1981

In 1965, Harley Davidson made its first public stock offering. Soon after, it faced a struggle for control. The contest was primarily between Bangor Punta, an Asian company, and AMF, an American company with strong interests in recreational equipment including bowling. In a bidding war, Harley Davidson's stockholders chose AMF over Bangor Punta, even though the bid was $1 less than Bangor's $23 a share offer. Stockholders were leery of Bangor's reputation of taking over a company, squeezing it dry, and then scrapping it for the remaining assets. AMF's plans for expansion of Harley Davidson seemed more compatible.

But the marriage was troubled: Harley Davidson's old equipment was not capable of the expansion envisioned by AMF. At the very time that Japanese manufacturers—Honda and others—were flooding the market with high-quality motorcycles,

---

[1] Tom Rowan, "Harley Sets New Drive to Boost Market Share," *Advertising Age* (January 29, 1973), pp. 34–35.

Harley was falling down on quality. One company official noted that "quality was going down just as fast as production was going up."[2] Indicative of the depths of the problem at a demoralized Harley Davidson, quality-control inspections failed 50–60 percent of the motorcycles produced. This compared to 5 percent of Japanese motorcycles that failed their quality-control checks.

AMF put up with an average $4.8 million operating loss for eleven years. Finally, it called quits and put the division up for sale in 1981. Vaughan Beals, vice president of motorcycle sales, still had faith in the company: he led a team that used $81.5 million in financing from Citicorp to complete a leveraged buyout. All ties with AMF were severed.

VAUGHAN BEALS

Beals was a middle-aged Ivy Leaguer, a far cry from what one might think of as a heavy motorcycle aficianado. He had graduated from MIT's Aeronautical Engineering School, and was considered a production specialist.[3] But he was far more than that. His was a true commitment to motorcycles, personally as well as professionally. Deeply concerned with AMF's declining attention to quality, he achieved the buyout from AMF.

The prognosis for the company was bleak. Its market share, which had dominanted the industry before the Honda invasion, now was 3 percent. In 1983, Harley Davidson would celebrate its eightieth birthday; some doubted it would still be around by then. Tariff protection seemed Harley's only hope. And massive lobbying paid off. In 1983, Congress passed a huge tariff increase on Japanese motorcycles. Instead of a 4 percent tariff, now Japanese motorcycles would be subject to a 45 percent tariff for the coming five years.

The tariff gave the company new hope, and it slowly began to rebuild market share. Key to this was restoring confidence in the quality of its products. And Beals took a leading role in this. He drove Harley Davidsons to rallies where he met Harley owners. There he learned of their concerns and their complaints, and he promised changes. At these rallies a core of loyal Harley Davidson users, called HOGs (for Harley Owners Group), were to be trailblazers for the successful growth to come.

Beals had company on his odyssey: Willie G. Davidson, grandson of the company's founder, and the vice president of design. Willie was an interesting contrast to the more urbane Beals. His was the image of a middle-age hippie. He wore a Viking helmet over his long, unkempt hair, while a straggly beard hid some of his wind-burned face. An aged leather jacket was compatible. Beals and Davidson fit in nicely at the HOG rallies.

---

[2] Peter C. Reid, *Well Made in America—Lessons from Harley Davidson on Being the Best* (New York: McGraw-Hill, 1990), p. 10.

[3] Rod Willis, "Harley Davidson Comes Roaring Back," *Management Review* (March 1986), pp. 20–27.

THE STRUGGLE BACK

In December 1986, Harley Davidson asked Congress to remove the tariff barriers, more than a year earlier than originally planned. The confidence of the company had been restored and it believed it could now compete with the Japanese head to head.[4]

Production Improvements

Shortly after the buyout, Beals and other managers visited Japanese plants both in Japan and Honda's assembly plant in Marysville, Ohio. They were impressed that they were being beaten not by "robotics, or culture, or morning calisthenics and company songs, [but by] professional managers who understood their business and paid attention to detail."[5] As a result, Japanese operating costs were as much as 30 percent lower than Harley's.

Beals and his managers tried to implement some of the Japanese management techniques. Each plant was divided into profit centers, with managers assigned total responsibility within their particular area. Just-in-time (JIT) inventory and materials-as-needed (MAN) systems sought to control and minimize all inventories both inside and outside the plants. Quality circles (QCs) were formed to increase employee involvement in quality goals and to improve communication between management and workers. See the following box for further discussion of quality circles. Another new program called statistical operator control (SOC) gave employees the responsibility for checking the quality of their own work and making proper correcting adjustments. Efforts were made to improve labor relations by more sensitivity to employees and their problems as well as better employee assistance and benefits. Certain product improvements were also introduced, notably a new engine and mountings on rubber to reduce vibration. A well-accepted equipment innovation was to build stereo sytems and intercoms into the motorcycle helmets.

The production changes between 1981 and 1988 resulted in:[6]

- Inventory reduced by 67 percent
- Productivity up by 50 percent
- Scrap and rework down two-thirds
- Defects per unit down 70 percent

In the 1970s, the joke among industry experts was, "If you're buying a Harley, you'd better buy two—one for spare parts."[7] Now this had obviously changed, but the change still had to be communicated to consumers, and believed.

---

[4] "Harley Back in High Gear," *Forbes* (April 20, 1987), p. 8.

[5] Dexter Hutchins, "Having a Hard Time with Just-in-Time," *Fortune* (June 19, 1986), p. 65.

[6] Hutchins, *op. cit.* p. 66.

[7] *Ibid.*

INFORMATION BOX

QUALITY CIRCLES

Quality circles were adopted by Japan in an effort to rid its industries of poor quality control and junkiness after World War II. Quality circles are worker-management committees that meet regularly, usually weekly, to talk about production problems, plan ways to improve productivity and quality, and resolve job-related gripes on both sides. They have been described as "the single most significant explanation for the truly outstanding quality of goods and services produced in Japan."[8] For example, Mazda had 2,147 circles with more than 16,000 employees involved. They usually consisted of seven to eight volunteer members who met on their own time to discuss and solve the issues they were concerned with. In addition to making major contributions to increased productivity and quality, they provided employees an opportunity to participate and gain a sense of accomplishment.[9]

The idea—like so many ideas adopted by the Japanese—did not originate with them: it came from two American personnel consultants. The Japanese refined the idea and ran with it. Now, American industry had rediscovered quality circles. Some firms have found them a desirable way to promote teamwork and good feelings, and to avoid at least some of the adversarial relations stemming from collective bargaining and union grievances that must be negotiated.

Despite sterling claims for quality circles, they have not always worked out well. Some workers claim they smack of "tokenism," and are more a facade than anything practical. Questions are also raised as to how much lasting benefits such circles have, once the novelty has worn off. Others doubt that the time invested in quality circles by management and workers is that productive. And few U.S. workers accept the idea of participating in quality circles on their own time.

How would you feel about devoting an hour or more to quality circle meetings every week or so, on your own time? If your answer is, "No Way," do you think this is a fair attitude on your part? Why or why not?

---

[8] "A Partnership to Build the New Workplace," *Business Week* (June 30, 1980), p. 101.

[9] As described in a Mazda ad in *Forbes* (May 24, 1982), p. 5.

Marketing Moves

Despite its bad times and its poor quality, Harley had a cadre of loyal customers almost unparalleled. Company research maintained that 92 percent of its customers remained with Harley.[10] Despite such hard-core loyalists, the company had always had a serious public image problem. It was linked to an image of the pot-smoking, beer-drinking,

---

[10] Mark Marvel, "The Gentrified HOG," *Esquire* (July 1989), p. 25.

woman-chasing, tattoo-covered, leather-clad biker: "When your company's logo is the number-one requested in tattoo parlors, it's time to get a licensing program that will return your reputation to the ranks of baseball, hot dogs, and apple pie."[11]

Part of Harley's problem had been with bootleggers ruining the name by placing it on unlicensed goods of poor quality. Now the company began to use warrants and federal marshalls to crack down on unauthorized uses of its logo at motorcycle conventions. And it began licensing its name and logo on a wide variety of products, from leather jackets to cologne to jewelry—even to pajamas, sheets, and towels. Suddenly retailers realized that these licensed goods were popular, and were even being bought by a new customer segment, undreamed of until now: bankers, doctors, lawyers, and entertainers. This new breed of customers soon expanded their horizons to include the Harley Davidson bikes themselves. They joined the HOGs, only now they became known as Rubbies—the rich urban bikers. And high prices for bikes did not bother them in the least.

Beals was quick to capitalize on this new market with an expanded product line with expensive heavyweights. In 1989 the largest motocycle was introduced, the Fat Boy, with 80 cubic inches of V-twin engine and capable of a top speed of 150 mph. By 1991, Harley had 20 models, ranging in price from $4,500 to $15,000.

The Rubbies brought Harley back to a leading position in the industry by 1989, with almost 60 percent of the super-heavyweight motorcycle market; by the first quarter of 1993, this had become 63 percent. See Figure 3.1. The importance of this customer to Harley could be seen in the demographic statistics supplied by *The Wall*

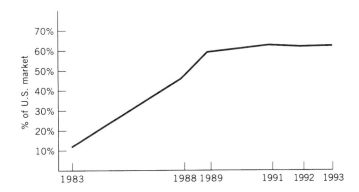

Figure 3.1. Harley Davidson's Share of the U.S. Heavyweight Motorcycle Market, Selected Years, 1983–1993.

Sources: Company reports; R. L. Polk & Company; Gary Slutsker, "Hog Wild," *Forbes* (May 24, 1993), pp. 45–46.

---

[11] "Thunder Road," *Forbes* (July 18, 1983), p. 32.

Street Journal in 1990: "One in three of today's Harley Davidson buyers are professionals or managers. About 60 percent have attended college, up from only 45 percent in 1984. Their median age is 35, and their median household income has risen sharply to $45,000 from $36,000 five years earlier."[12]

In 1989, Beals stepped down as CEO, turning the company over to Richard Teerlink, who was chief operating officer of the Motorcycle Division. Beals, however, retained his position as chairman of the board. The legacy of Beals in the renaissance of Harley led management writer John Schermerhorn to call him a visionary leader.[13] The information box discusses visionary leadership.

INFORMATION BOX

VISIONARY LEADERSHIP

Vision has been identified as an essential ingredient of effective leadership. Having vision characterizes someone who has a clear sense of the future environment and the actions needed to thrive in it.

Undoubtedly, a visionary leader is an asset in a dynamic environment. Such a leader can help a firm grasp opportunities ahead of competitors, revitalize itself, pull itself up from adversity. Schermerhorn states that a visionary begins with a clear vision, communicates that vision to all concerned, and motivates and inspires people in pursuit of that vision. He proposes these five principles of visionary leadership:

1. **Challenge the process.** Be a pioneer—encourage innovation and people with ideas.

2. **Be enthusiastic.** Inspire others through personal example to share in a common vision.

3. **Help others to act.** Be a team player, and support the efforts and talents of others.

4. **Set the example.** Provide a consistent model of how others should act.

5. **Celebrate achievements.** Bring emotion into the workplace and rally "hearts" as well as "minds."[14]

Can you name any visionary leaders? What makes you think they were visionary? Could some of our acclaimed visionary leaders have been merely lucky rather than prophetic?

---

[14] John R. Schermerhorn, Jr., *Management,* 6th ed. (New York: Wiley, 1999) pp. 262–263.

---

[12] Robert L. Rose, "Vrooming Back," *The Wall Street Journal* (August 31, 1990), p. 1.

[13] John R. Schermerhorn, Jr., *Management for Productivity,* 4th ed. (New York: Wiley, 1993), pp. 410–411.

SUCCESS

By 1993 Harley Davidson had a new problem, one born of success. Now it could not even come close to meeting demand. Customers faced empty showrooms, except perhaps for rusty trade-ins or antiques. Waiting time for a new bike could be six months or longer, unless the customer was willing to pay a 10 percent or higher premium to some gray marketer advertising in biker magazines.

Some of the 600 independent U.S. dealers worried that these empty showrooms and long waiting lists would induce their customers to turn to foreign imports, much as they had several decades before. But other dealers recognized that somehow Beals and company had engendered a brand loyalty unique in this industry, and perhaps in all industries. Assuaging the lack of big bike business, dealers were finding other sources of revenues. Harley's branded line of merchandise, available only at Harley dealers and promoted through glossy catalogs, had really taken off. Harley black leather jackets were bought eagerly at $500; fringed leather bras went for $65; even shot glasses brought $12—all it seemed to take was the Harley name and logo. So substantial was this ancillary business, that in 1992 non-cycle business generated $155.7 million in sales, up from $130.3 million in 1991.

Production

In one sense, Harley's production situation was enviable: it had far more demand than production capability. More than this, it had such a loyal body of customers that delays in product gratification were not likely to turn many away to competitors. The problem, of course, was that full potential was not being realized.

Richard Teerlink, the successor of Beals, expressed the corporate philosophy to expanding quantity to meet the demand: "Quantity isn't the issue, quality is the issue. We learned in the early 1980s you do not solve problems by throwing money at them."[15]

The company increased output slowly. In early 1992 it was making 280 bikes a day; by 1993, this had risen to 345 a day. With increased capital spending, goals were to produce 420 bikes a day, but not until 1996.

Export Potential

Some contrary concerns with the conservative expansion plans of Teerlink surfaced regarding international operations. The European export market beckoned. Harleys had become very popular in Europe. But the company had promised its domestic dealers that exports would not go beyond 30 percent of total production, until the North American market was fully satisfied. Suddenly the European big-bike market grew by an astounding 33 percent between 1990 and 1992. Yet, because of its production constraints, Harley could only maintain a 9 to 10 percent share of this market. In other words, it was giving away business to foreign competitors.

---

[15] Gary Slutsker, "Hog Wild," *Forbes* (May 24, 1993), p. 46.

To enhance its presence in Europe, Harley opened a branch office of its HOG club in Frankfurt, Germany, for its European fans.

Specifics of the Resurgence of Harley Davidson

Table 3.1 shows the trend in revenues and net income of Harley since 1982. The growth in sales and profits did not go unnoticed by the investment community. In 1990, Harley Davidson stock sold for $7; in January of 1993, it hit $39. Its market share of heavyweight motorcycles (751 cubic centimeters displacement and larger) had soared from 12.5 percent in 1983, to 63 percent by 1993. Let the Japanese have the lightweight bike market! Harley would dominate the heavyweights.

Harley acquired Holiday Rambler in 1986. As a wholly owned subsidiary, this manufacturer of recreational and commercial vehicles was judged by Harley management to be compatible with the existing motorcycle business as well as moderating some of the seasonality of the motorcycle business. The diversification proved rather mediocre. In 1992, it accounted for 26 percent of total corporate sales, but only 2 percent of profits.[16]

TABLE 3.1 Harley Davidson's Growth in Revenue and Income 1983–1994 (Millions of $)

Year	Revenue	Net Income
1982	$ 210	def. $25.1
1983	254	1.0
1984	294	2.9
1985	287	2.6
1986	295	4.3
1987	685	17.7
1988	757	27.2
1989	791	32.6
1990	865	38.3
1991	940	37.0
1992	1,100	54.0
1993	1,210	68.0
1994	1,537	83.0

Source: Company annual reports.

Commentary: The steady climb in sales and profits, except for a pause in 1985, is noteworthy. The total gain in revenues over these years was 631.9%, while income rose more than eightyfold since 1983.

[16] Company annual reports.

Big motorcycles, made in America by the only U.S. manufacturer, continued the rage. Harley's ninetieth anniversary was celebrated in Milwaukee on June 12, 1993. As many as 100,000 people, including 18,000 HOGS, were there to celebrate. Hotel rooms were sold out for a 60-mile radius. Harley Davidson was up and doing real well.

ANALYSIS

One of Vaughan Beals's first moves after the 1981 leveraged buyout was to improve production efficiency and quality control. This became the foundation for the strategic regeneration moves to come. In this quest, he borrowed heavily from the Japanese, in particular in cultivating employee involvement.

The cultivation of a new customer segment for the big bikes had to be a major factor in the company's resurgence. To some, that more affluent consumers embraced the big, flashy Harley motorcycles was a surprise of no small moment. After all, how could you have two more incompatible groups than the stereotyped black-jacketed cyclists, and the Rubbies? Perhaps part of the change was due to high-profile people such as Beals and some of his executives frequently participating at motorcycle rallies and charity rides. Technological and comfort improvements in motorcycles and their equipment added to the new attractiveness. Dealers were also coaxed to make their stores more inviting.

Along with this, expanding the product mix not only made such Harley-branded merchandise a windfall for company and dealers alike, but also piqued the interest of upscale customers in motorcycles themselves. The company was commendably aggressive in running with the growing popularity of the ancillary merchandise, and making this well over a $100 million revenue booster.

Some questions remained. How durable was this popularity, both of the big bikes and the complementary merchandise, with this affluent customer segment? Would it prove to be only a passing fad? If so, then Harley needed to seek diversifications as quickly as possible, even though the Holiday Rambler Corporation had brought no notable success by 1992. Diversifications often bring disappointed earnings compared with a firm's core business.

Another question concerned Harley's slowness in expanding production capability. Faced with a burgeoning demand, was it better to go slowly, to be carefully protective of quality, and to refrain from heavy debt commitments? This had been Harley's most recent strategy, but it raised the risk of permitting competitors to gain market share in the United States and especially in Europe. The following issue box discusses aggressive versus conservative planning.

UPDATE, 1993–1998

The 1990s have continued to be kind to Harley. Demand continued to grow, with the mystique as strong as ever. The company significantly increased its motorcycle production capacity with a new engine plant in Milwaukee completed in 1997 and a new assembly plant in Kansas City in 1998. It expected that demand in the United States would still exceed the supply of Harley bikes.

ISSUE BOX

SHOULD WE BE AGGRESSIVE OR CONSERVATIVE IN OUR PLANNING?

The sales forecast—the estimate of sales for the periods ahead, serves a crucial role because it is the starting point for all detailed planning and budgeting. A volatile situation presents some high-risk alternatives: Should we be optimistic or conservative?

On one hand, with conservative planning in a growing market, a firm risks underestimating demand and being unable to expand its resources sufficiently to handle the potential. It may lack the manufacturing capability and sales staff to handle growth potential, and it may have to abdicate a good share of the growing business to competitors who are willing and able to expand their capability to meet the demands of the market.

On the other hand, a firm facing burgeoning demand should consider whether the growth is likely to be a short-term fad or a more permanent situation. A firm can easily become overextended in the buoyancy of booming business, only to see the collapse of such business jeopardizing its viability.

Harley's conservative decision was undoubtedly influenced by concerns about expanding beyond the limits of good quality control. The decision was probably also influenced by management's belief that Harley Davidson had a loyal body of customers who would not switch despite the wait.

Do you think Harley Davidson made the right decision to expand conservatively? Why or why not? Defend your position.

The following numbers show how motorcycle shipments increased from 1993 to 1997, both domestically and export, in thousands of units:

	U.S.	Exports
1997	96.2	36.1
1993	57.2	24.5

Despite continuous increases in production, U.S. consumers still had to wait to purchase a new Harley Davidson bike, but the waits only added to the mystique.

The following shows the growth in revenues and income from 1993 to 1997:

(Millions $)		
	Revenues	Net Income
1997	1,763	174.0
1993	1,217	18.4

Indicative of the popularity of the Harley Davidson logo, Wolverine World Wide, maker originally of Hush Puppies, but now the largest manufacturer of footwear in the United States, entered into a licensing agreement with Harley to use its "sexy" name for a line of boots and fashion shoes to come out in late 1998.[17]

WHAT CAN BE LEARNED?

Again, a firm can come back from adversity. The resurrection of Harley Davidson almost from the point of extinction proves that adversity can be overcome. It need not be fatal or forever. This should be encouraging to all firms facing difficulties, and to their investors. Noteworthy, however, in comparing Harley with the previous case of Continental Air, is the great difference in time these two firms took to turn around. Continental under Bethune achieved spectacular results in only months; it took Harley decades before a Vaughan Beals came on the scene as changemaker. We will find another changemaker in the next case, IBM.

What does a turnaround require? Above all, it takes a leader who has the vision and confidence that things can be changed for the better. The change may not necessitate anything particularly innovative. It may involve only a rededication to basics, such as better quality control or an improved commitment to customer service brought about by a new positive attitude of employees. But such a return to basics requires that a demoralized or apathetic organization be rejuvenated and remotivated. This calls for leadership of a high order. If the core business has still been maintained, it at least provides a base to work from.

Preserve the core business at all costs. Every viable firm has a basic core or distinctive position—sometimes called an "ecological niche"—in its business environment. This unique position may be due to its particular location, or to a certain product. It may come from somewhat different operating methods or from the customers served. Here, a firm is better than its competitors. This strong point is the basic core of a company's survival. Though it may diversify and expand far beyond this area, the firm should not abandon its main bastion of strength.

Harley almost did this. Its core—and indeed, only—business was its heavyweight bikes sold to a limited and loyal, thought not at the time particularly savory, customer segment. Harley almost lost this core business by abandoning reasonable quality control to the point that its motorcycles became the butt of jokes. To his credit, upon assuming leadership Beals acted quickly to correct the production and employee motivation problems. By preserving the core, Beals could pursue other avenues of expansion.

The power of a mystique. Few products are able to gain a mystique or cult following. Coors beer did in the 1960s and early 1970s, when it became the brew of celebrities and the emblem of the purity and freshness of the West. In the cigarette industry, Marlboro rose to become the top seller from a somewhat similar advertising and image thrust: the Marlboro man. The Ford Mustang had a mys-

[17] Carleen Hawn, "What's in a Name? Whatever You Make It," *Forbes* (July 27, 1998), p. 88.

tique at one time. Somehow the big bikes of Harley Davidson developed a mystique. Harleys appealed to the HOGS and to the Rubbies: two disparate customer segments, but both loyal to their Harleys. The mystique led to "logo magic": Simply put the Harley Davidson name and logo on all kinds of merchandise, and watch the sales take off.

How does a firm develop (or acquire) a mystique? There is no simple answer, no guarantee. Certainly a product has to be unique, but though most firms strive for this differentiation, few achieve a mystique. Image-building advertising, focusing on the target buyer, may help. Perhaps even better is image-building advertising that highlights the people customers might wish to emulate. But what about the black leather-jacketed, perhaps bearded, cyclist?

Perhaps in the final analysis, acquiring a mystique is a more accidental and fortuitous success than something that can be deliberately orchestrated. Two lessons, however, can be learned about mystiques. First, they do not last forever. Second, firms should run with them as long as possible and try to expand the reach of the name or logo to other goods, even unrelated ones, through licensing.

CONSIDER

What additional learning insights can you see coming from this Harley Davidson resurgence?

QUESTIONS

1. Do you think Beals' rejuvenation strategy for Harley Davidson was the best policy? Discuss and evaluate other strategies that he might have pursued.

2. How durable do you think the Rubbies' infatuation with the heavyweight Harleys will be? What leads you to this conclusion?

3. A Harley Davidson stockholder criticizes present management: "It is a mistake of the greatest magnitude that we abdicate a decent share of the European motorcycle market to foreign competitors, simply because we do not gear up our production to meet the demand." Discuss.

4. Given the resurgence of Harley Davidson in the 1990s, would you invest money in the company? Discuss, considering as many factors bearing on this decision as you can.

5. "Harley Davidson's resurgence is only the purest luck. Who could have predicted, or influenced, the new popularity of big bikes with the affluent?" Discuss.

6. "The tariff increase on Japanese motorcycles in 1983 gave Harley Davidson badly needed breathing room. In the final analysis, politics is more important than management in competing with foreign firms." What are your thoughts?

HANDS-ON EXERCISES

1. As a representative of a mutual fund with a major investment in Harley Davidson, you are particularly critical of Vaughn Beals's visible presence at motorcycle rallies and his hobnobbing with black-jacketed cycle gangs. He maintains this is a fruitful way to maintain a loyal core of customers. Playing the devil's advocate (a person who opposes a position to establish its merits and validity), argue against Beals's practices.

2. As a vice president at Harley Davidson, you believe the recovery efforts should have gone well beyond the heavyweight bikes into lightweights. What arguments would you present for this change in strategy, and what specific recommendations would you make for such a new course of action? What contrary arguments would you expect? How would you counter them?

3. As a staff assistant to Vaughan Beals, you have been charged to design a strategy to bring a mystique to the Harley Davidson name. How would you propose to do this? Be as specific as you can, and defend your reasoning.

TEAM DEBATE EXERCISE

A major schism has arisen in the executive ranks of Harley Davidson. Many executives believe that a monumental mistake is being made not to gear up production to match the burgeoning worldwide demand for Harleys. The other side believes the present go-slow approach to increasing production is more prudent. Persuasively support your position and attack the opposing view.

INVITATION TO RESEARCH

What is the situation with Harley Davidson today? Two new U.S. competitors were expected to introduce their own cruisers in late 1998. They are Victory Motorcycles and Excelsior-Henderson, both based in Minnesota. Have they had any early competitive impact on Harley?

CHAPTER FOUR

IBM: A Recovered Giant

IBM exhibited similar rollercoaster fortunes as did Continental Air and Harley Davidson, with the major difference that it was so much bigger and had so many years of industry domination. The common notion is that the bigger the firm, the more difficult it is to turn it around, just as the grand ship needs far more room to maneuver to avoid catastrophe than a smaller vessel.

THE REALITY AND THE FLAWED ILLUSION

On January 19, 1993, International Business Machines Corporation reported a record $5.46 billion loss for the fourth quarter of 1992, and a deficit for the entire year of $4.97 billion, the biggest annual loss in American corporate history. (General Motors recorded a 1991 loss of $4.45 billion, after huge charges for cutbacks and plant closings. And Ford Motor Company reported a net loss of more than $6 billion for 1992, but that was a noncash charge to account for the future costs for retiree benefits.) The cost in human lives, as far as employment was concerned, was also consequential, as some 42,900 had been laid off during 1992, with an additional 25,000 planned to go in 1993. In its fifth restructuring, seemingly endless rounds of job cuts and firings had eliminated 100,000 jobs since 1985. Not surprisingly, IBM's share price, which was above $100 in the summer of 1992, closed at an 11-year low of $48.375. And yet IBM had long been the ultimate blue-chip company, reigning supreme in the computer industry. How could its problems have surfaced so suddenly and so violently?

THE ROAD TO INDUSTRY DOMINANCE

"They hired my father to make a go of this company in 1914, the year I was born," said Thomas J. Watson, Jr. "To some degree I've been a part of IBM ever since."[1] Watson took over his father's medium-sized company in 1956 and built it into a technological giant. Retired for almost 19 years by 1992, he was now witnessing the company in the throes of its greatest adversity.

[1] Michael W. Miller, "IBM's Watson Offers Personal View of the Company's Recent Difficulties," *The Wall Street Journal* (December 21, 1992), p. A3.

IBM had become the largest computer maker in the world. With its evergrowing revenues, since 1946 it had become the bluest of blue-chip companies. It had 350,000 employees worldwide and was one of the largest U.S.-based employers. Its 1991 revenues had approached $67 billion, and while profits had dropped some from the peak of $6.5 billion in 1984, its common stock still commanded a price/earnings ratio of over 100, making it a darling of investors. In 1989, it ranked first among all U.S. firms in market value (the total capitalization of common stock, based on the stock price and the number of shares outstanding), fourth in total sales, and fourth in net profits.[2]

During the days of the younger Watson, IBM was known for its centralized decision making. Decisions affecting product lines were made at the highest levels of management. Even IBM's culture was centralized and standardized, with strict behavioral and dress codes. For example, a blue suit, white shirt, and dark tie was the public uniform, and IBM became widely known as "Big Blue."

One of IBM's greatest assets was its research laboratories, by far the largest and costliest of their kind in the world, with staffs that included three Nobel Prize winners. IBM treated its research and development (R & D) function with loving care, regularly budgeting 10 percent of sales for this forward-looking activity: in 1991, for example, the R & D budget was $6.6 billion.

The past success of IBM and the future expectations for the company, with a seeming stranglehold over the technology of the future, made it a favorite of consultants, analysts, and market researchers. Management theorists from Peter Drucker to Tom Peter (of *In Search of Excellence* fame) lined up to analyze what made IBM so good. And the business press regularly produced articles in praise and awe of IBM.

Alas, the adulation was to change abruptly by 1992. Somehow, insidiously, IBM had gotten fat and complacent over the years. (In Chapter 3, the case on Harley Davidson, we encounter a similar situation of complacency stemming from long-standing market dominance.) IBM's problems, however, went deeper, as we will explore in the next section.

CHANGING FORTUNES

Perhaps the causes of the great IBM debacle of 1992 started in the early 1980s with a questionable management decision. Perhaps the problems were more deep-rooted than any single decision; perhaps they were a consequence of the bureaucracy that often typifies giant organizations (Sears and General Motors faced somewhat similar problems), growing layers of policies, and entrenched interests.

In the early 1980s, two little firms, Intel and Microsoft, were upstarts, just emerging in the industry dominated by IBM. Their success by the 1990s can be attributed largely to their nurturing by IBM. Each got a major break when it was "anointed" as a key supplier for IBM's new personal computer (PC). Intel was signed on to make the chips, and Microsoft, the software. The aggressive youngsters set stan-

---

[2] "Ranking the Forbes 500s," *Forbes* (April 30, 1990), p. 306.

dards for successive PC generations and in the process wrested from IBM control over the PC's future. And the PC was to become the product of the future, shouldering aside the giant mainframe that was IBM's strength.

As IBM began losing ground in one market after another, Intel and Microsoft were gaining dominance. In 1982, the combined market value of Intel's and Microsoft's stock amounted to about one-tenth of IBM's. By October 1992, their combined stock value surpassed IBM's; by the end of the year, they topped IBM's market value by almost 50 percent. See Table 4.1 for comparative operating statistics of IBM, Intel, and Microsoft. Table 4.2 shows the market valuation of IBM, Intel, and Microsoft from 1989 to 1992, the years before and during the collapse of investor esteem.

Defensive Reactions of IBM

As the problems of IBM became more visible to the investment community, chairman John Akers sought to institute reforms to turn the behemoth around. His problem—and need—was to uproot a corporate structure and culture that had developed when IBM had no serious competition.

A cumbersome bureaucracy stymied the company from being innovative in a fast-moving industry. Major commitments still went to high-margin mainframes, but these were no longer necessary in many situations, given the computing power of desktop PCs. IBM had problems getting to market quickly with the technological

TABLE 4.1   Growth of IBM and the Upstarts, Microsoft and Intel 1983–1992 (in millions)

	1983	1985	1987	1989	1991	1992
IBM						
Revenues	$40,180	$50,056	$54,217	$62,710	$64,792	$67,045
Net income	5,485	6,555	5,258	3,758	(2,827)	(2,784)
% of revenue	13.6%	13.1%	9.7%	6.0%	—	—
Microsoft						
Revenues	$50	$140	$346	$804	$1,843	$2,759
Net income	6	24	72	171	463	708
% of revenue	12.0%	17.1%	20.8%	21.3%	25.1%	25.7%
Intel						
Revenues	$1,122	$1,365	$1,907	$3,127	$4,779	$5,192
Net income	116	2	176	391	819	827
% of revenue	10.3%	0.1%	9.2%	12.5%	17.1%	15.9%

Sources: Company annual statements. Figures from 1992 are estimates from "Annual Report of American Industry" *Forbes* (January 4, 1993), pp. 115–116.

Commentary: Note the great growth of the "upstarts" in recent years, both in revenues and in profits, compared with IBM. Also note the performance of Microsoft and Intel in profit as a percent of revenues.

TABLE 4.2 Market Value and Rank of IBM, Microsoft, and Intel among All U.S. Companies, 1989 and 1992

	Rank		Market Value ($ millions)	
	1989	1992	1989	1992
IBM	1	13	$60,345	$30,715
Microsoft	92	25	6,018	23,608
Intel	65	22	7,842	24,735

Source: "The Forbes Market Value 500," *Forbes* Annual Directory Issue (April 13, 1990), pp. 258–259; and *Forbes* (April 26, 1993), p. 242. The market value is the per-share price multiplied by the number of shares outstanding for all classes of common stock.

Commentary: The market valuation reflects the stature of the firms in the eyes of investors. Obviously, IBM has declined during this period, while Microsoft and Intel have more than tripled their market valuation, almost approaching that of IBM. Yet IBM's sales were $65.5 billion in 1992, against sales of $3.3 for Microsoft and $5.8 for Intel.

innovations that were revolutionizing the industry. In 1991 Akers warned an unbelieving group of IBM managers of the coming difficulties. "The business is in crisis."[3] He attempted to push power downward, to decentralize some of the decision making that for decades had resided at the top. His more radical proposal was to break up IBM, to divide it into 13 divisions and give each division more autonomy. He sought to expand the services business and make the company more responsive to customer needs. And, perhaps most important, he saw a crucial need to pare costs by cutting the fat from the organization.

The need for cost-cutting was evident to all but the entrenched bureaucracy. IBM's total costs grew 12 percent a year in the mid-1980s, but revenues were not keeping up with this growth.[4] Part of the plan for reducing costs involved cutting employees, which violated a cherished tradition dating back to Thomas Watson's father and the beginning of IBM: a promise never to lay off IBM workers for economic reasons.[5] (Most of the downsizing was indeed accomplished by voluntary retirements and attractive severance packages, but eventually outright layoffs became necessary.)

The changes decreed by Akers would leave the unified sales division untouched, but each of the new product group divisions would act as a separate operating unit, with financial reports broken down accordingly. Particularly troubling to Akers was the recent performance of the personal computer (PC) business. At a time when demand, as well as competition, was burgeoning for PCs, this division was languish-

[3] David Kirkpatrick, "Breaking up IBM," *Fortune* (July 27, 1992), p. 44.

[4] *Ibid.,* p. 53.

[5] Miller, *op. cit.,* p. A4.

ing. Early in 1992 Akers tapped James Cannavino to head the $11 billion Personal Systems Division, which also included workstations and software.

IBM PCS

PCs had been the rising star of the company, despite the fact that mainframes still accounted for about $20 billion in revenues. But in 1990, market share dropped drastically as new competitors offered PCs at much lower prices than IBM; many experts even claimed that these clones were at least equal to IBM's PCs in quality. Throughout 1992, IBM had been losing market share in an industry price war. Even after it attempted to counter Compaq's price cuts in June, IBM's prices still remained as much as one-third higher than its competitor's prices. Even worse, IBM had announced new fall models, and this development curbed sales of current models. At the upper end of the PC market, firms such as Sun Microsystems and Hewlett Packard were bringing out more powerful workstations that tied PCs together with mini- and mainframe computers. James Cannavino faced a major challenge in reviving the PC.

Cannavino planned to streamline operations by slicing off a new unit to focus exclusively on developing and manufacturing PC hardware. By doing so, he would cut PCs loose from the rest of Personal Systems and the workstations and software. This, he believed, would create a streamlined organization that could cut prices often, roll out new products several times a year, sell through any kind of store, and provide customers with whatever software they wanted, even if it was not IBM's.[6] Such autonomy was deemed necessary in order to respond quickly to competitors and opportunities, without having to deal with the IBM bureaucracy.

THE CRISIS

On January 25, 1993, John Akers announced that he was stepping down as IBM's chairman and chief executive. He had lost the confidence of the board of directors. Until mid-January, Akers seemed determined to see IBM through its crisis, at least until he would reach IBM's customary retirement of age 60, which would be December 1994. But the horrendous $4.97 billion loss in 1992 changed that, and investor and public pressure mounted for a top management change. The fourth quarter of 1992 was particularly shocking, brought on by weak European sales and a steep decline in sales of minicomputers and mainframes. Now IBM's stock sank to a 17-year low, below $46.

Other aspects of the operation also accentuated IBM's fall from grace: most notably, the decline of the jewel of its operation, IBM's mainframe processors and storage systems.

For 25 years IBM had dominated the $50 billion worldwide mainframe industry. In 1992, overall sales of such equipment grew at only 2 percent, but IBM experienced a 10 to 15 percent drop in revenue. At the same time, its major mainframe

---

[6] "Stand Back, Big Blue—And Wish Me Luck," *Business Week* (August 17, 1992), p. 99.

rivals, Amdahl Corporation and Unisys Corporation had respective sales gains of 48 percent and 10 percent.[7]

IBM was clearly lagging in developing new computers that could out-perform the old ones, such as IBM's old system/390. Competitors' models exceeded IBM's old computers not only in absolute power but in prices, selling at prices of a tenth or less of IBM's price per unit of computing. For example, with IBM's mainframe computers, customers paid approximately $100,000 for each MIPS, or the capacity to execute 1 million instructions per second, this being the rough gauge of computing power. Hewlett Packard offered similar capability at a cost of only $12,000 per MIPS, and AT&T's NCR unit could sell a machine for $12.5 million that outperformed IBM's $20 million ES/9000 processor complex.[8]

In a series of full-page advertisements appearing in such business publications as *The Wall Street Journal*, IBM defended the mainframe and attacked the focus on MIPS:

> One issue surrounding mainframes is their cost. It's often compared using dollars per MIPS with the cost of microprocessors systems, and on that basis mainframes lose. But ... dollars per MIPS alone is a superficial measurement. The real issue is function. Today's appetite for information demands serious network and systems management, around-the-clock availability, efficient mass storage and genuine data security. MIPS alone provides none of these, but IBM mainframes have them built in, and more fully developed than anything available on microprocessors.[9]

On March 24, 1993, 51-year-old Louis V. Gerstner, Jr., was named the new chief executive of IBM. The two-month search for a replacement for Akers had captivated the media, with speculation ranging widely. The choice of an outsider caught many by surprise: Gerstner was chairman and CEO of RJR Nabisco, a food and tobacco giant, but Nabisco was a far cry from a computer company. And IBM had always prided itself on promoting from within–for example, John Akers–with most IBM executives being life-long IBM employees. Not all analysts supported the selection of Gerstner. While most did not criticize the board for going outside IBM to find a replacement for Akers, some questioned going outside the computer industry or other high-tech industries. Geoff Lewis, senior editor of *Business Week*, fully supported the choice. He had suggested the desirability of bringing in some outside managers to Akers in 1988.

> Akers seemed shocked—maybe even offended—by my question. After a moment, he answered: "IBM had the best recruitment system anywhere and spends more than anybody training. Sometimes it might help to seek outsiders with unusual skills, but the company already had the best people in the world."[10]

See the following issue box for a discussion of promotion from within.

---

[7] John Verity, "Guess What: IBM Is Losing out in Mainframes, Too," *Business Week* (February 8, 1993), p. 106.

[8] *Ibid.*

[9] Taken from advertisement, *The Wall Street Journal* (March 5, 1993), p. B8.

[10] Geoff Lewis, "One Fresh Face at IBM May Not Be Enough," *Business Week* (April 12, 1993), p. 33.

ISSUE BOX

SHOULD WE PROMOTE FROM WITHIN?

A heavy commitment to promoting from within, as had long characterized IBM, is sometimes derisively called "inbreeding." The traditional argument against this stand maintains that an organization with such a policy is not alert to needed changes, that it is enamored with the status quo, "the way we have always done it." Proponents of promotion from within talk about the motivation and great loyalty it engenders, with every employee knowing that he or she has a chance of becoming a high-level executive.

However, the opposite course of action—that is, heavy commitment to placing outsiders in important executive positions—plays havoc with morale of trainees and lower-level executives and destroys the sense of continuity and loyalty. A middle ground seems preferable: filling many executive positions from within, promoting this idea to encourage both the achievement of current executives and the recruiting of trainees, and at the same time bringing the strengths and experiences of outsiders into the organization.

Do you think there are particular circumstances in which one extreme or the other regarding promotion policy might be best? Discuss.

ANALYSIS

In examining the major contributors to IBM's fall from grace, we will analyze the predisposing or underlying factors, resultants, and controversies.

Predisposing Factors

Cumbersome Organization

As IBM grew with its success, it became more and more bureaucratic. One author described it as big and bloated. Another called it "inward-looking culture that kept them from waking up on time."[11] Regardless of phraseology, by the late 1980s IBM could not bring new machines quickly into the market, nor was it able to make the fast pricing and other strategic decisions of its smaller competitors. Too many layers of management, too many vested interests, a tradition-ridden mentality, and a gradually emerging contentment with the status quo shackled it—this in an industry that some thought to be mature, but which in reality was gripped by burgeoning change in important sectors. As a huge ship requires considerable time and distance to turn or to stop, so the giant IBM found itself at a competitive disadvantage compared with smaller, hungrier, more aggressive, and above all, more nimble firms. And impeding

---

[11] Jennifer Reese, "The Big and the Bloated: It's Tough Being No. 1," *Fortune* (July 27, 1992), p. 49.

INFORMATION BOX

RESISTANCE TO CHANGE

People as well as organizations have a natural reluctance to embrace change. Change is disruptive. It can destroy accepted ways of doing things and familiar authority–responsibility relationships. It makes people uneasy because their routines will likely be disrupted; their interpersonal relationships with subordinates, coworkers, and superiors may well be modified. Positions that were deemed important before the change may be downgraded. And persons who view themselves as highly competent in a particular job may be forced to assume unfamiliar duties.

Resistance to change can be combatted by good communication with participants about forthcoming changes. Without such communication, rumors and fears can assume monumental proportions. Acceptance of change can be facilitated if managers involve employees as fully as possible in planning the changes, solicit and welcome their participation, and assure them that their positions will not be impaired, only changed. Gradual rather than abrupt changes also make a transition smoother, as participants can be initially exposed to the changes without drastic upheavals.

In the final analysis, however, needed changes should not be delayed or canceled because of their possible negative repercussions on the organization. If change is necessary, it should be initiated. Individuals and organizations can adapt to change, although it may take some time.

The worst change an employee may face is layoff. And when no one knows when the next layoff will occur or who will be affected, morale and productivity may both be devastated. Discuss how managers might best handle the necessity of upcoming layoffs.

all efforts to make major changes effective was the typical burden facing all large and mature organizations: resistance to change. The accompanying information box discusses this phenomenon.

Overly Centralized Management Structure

Often related to a cumbersome bureaucratic organization is rigid centralization of authority and decision making. Certain negative consequences may result when all major decisions have to be made at corporate headquarters rather than down the line. Decision making is necessarily slowed, since executives believe they must investigate fully all aspects, and not being personally involved with the recommendation, they may be not only skeptical but critical of new projects and initiatives. More than this, the enthusiasm and creativity of lower level executives may be curbed by the typical conservatism of a higher management team divorced from the intimacy of the problem or the opportunity. The motivation and morale needed for a climate of innovation and creativity is stifled under the twin bureaucratic attitudes "Don't take a chance" and "Don't rock the boat."

The Three C's Mindset of Vulnerability

Firms that have been well entrenched in their industry and that have dominated it for years tend to fall into a particular mindset that leaves them vulnerable to aggressive and innovative competitors.

The following "three C's" are detrimental to a frontrunner's continued success:

Complacency

Conservatism

Conceit

Complacency is smugness—a complacent firm is self-satisfied, content with the status quo, no longer hungry and eager for growth. *Conservatism* when excessive characterizes a management that is wedded to the past, to the traditional, to the way things have always been done. Conservative managers see no need to change because they believe nothing is different today (e.g., "Mainframe computers are the models of the industry and will always be"). Finally, *conceit* further reinforces the myopia of the mindset: conceit for current and potential competitors. The beliefs that "we are the best" and "no one else can touch us" can easily permeate an organization that has enjoyed success for years.

The three C's leave no incentive to undertake aggressive and innovative actions, causing growing disinterest in such important facets of the business as customer relations, service, and even quality control. Furthermore, they inhibit interest in developing innovative new products that may cannibalize—that is, take business away from—existing products or disrupt entrenched interests. (We will discuss cannibalization in more detail shortly.)

Resultants

Overdependence on High-Margin Mainframes

The mainframe computers had long been the greatest source of market power and profits for IBM. But the conservative and tradition-minded IBM bureaucracy could not accept the reality that computer power was becoming a desktop commodity. Although a market still existed for the massive mainframes, it was limited and had little growth potential; the future belonged to desktop computers and workstations. And thus IBM, in a lapse of monumental proportions, relinquished its dominance. The minicomputers first opened up a whole new industry, one with scores of hungry competitors. But the cycle of industry creation and decline started anew by the early 1980s as personal computers began to replace minicomputers in defining new markets and fostering new competitors. The mainframe was not replaced, but its markets became more limited, and cannibalization became the fear.

Neglect of Software and Service

At a time when software and service had become ever more important, IBM still had a fixation on hardware. In 1992 services made up only 9 percent of IBM's revenue. Criticisms flowed:

Technology is becoming a commodity, and the difference between winning and losing comes in how you deliver that technology. Service will be the differentiator.

As a customer, I want a supplier who's going to make all my stuff work together.

The job is to understand the customer's needs in detail.[12]

In the process of losing touch with customers, the sales force had become reluctant to sell low-margin open systems if it could push proprietary mainframes or minicomputers.

Bloated Costs

As indications of the fat that had insidiously grown in the organization, some 42,900 jobs were cut in 1992, thankfully all through early retirement programs. An additional 25,000 people were expected to be laid off in 1993, some without the benefit of early retirement packages. Health benefits for employees were also scaled down. Manufacturing capacity was reduced 25 percent, and two of three mainframe development labs were closed. But perhaps the greatest bloat was R & D.

The Diminishing Payoff of Massive R & D Expenditures

As noted earlier, IBM spent heavily on research and development, often as much as 10 percent of sales (see Table 4.3). Its research labs were by far the largest and costliest of their kind the world.

And IBM labs were capable of inventing amazing things. For example, they developed the world's smallest transistor, 1/75,000th the width of a human hair.

Somehow, with all these R & D resources and expenditures, IBM lagged in transferring its innovation to the marketplace. The organization lacked the ability to quickly translate laboratory prototypes into commercial triumphs. Commercial R & D is wasted without this translation.

TABLE 4.3   IBM Research and Development Expenditures as a Percent of Revenues, 1987–1991

	1987	1988	1989	1990	1991
Revenues ($ millions)	$54,217	$59,681	$62,710	$64,792	$67,045
Research, development, and engineering costs	5,434	5,925	6,827	6,554	6,644
Percent of revenues	10.0%	9.9%	10.9%	10.1%	9.9%

Source: Company annual reports.

Commentary: Where has been the significant contribution from such heavy investment in R & D?

[12] Kirkpatrick, *op. cit.*, pp. 49, 52.

INFORMATION BOX

CANNIBALIZATION

Cannibalization occurs when a company's new product takes some business away from an existing product. The new product's success consequently does not contribute its full measure to company revenues since some sales will be shifted from older products. The amount of cannibalization can range from virtually none to almost total. In the latter case, the new product simply replaces the older product, with no real sales gain achieved. If the new product is less profitable than the older one, the impact and the fear of cannibalization becomes all the greater.

For IBM, the PCs and the other equipment smaller than mainframes would not come close to replacing the bigger units. Still, some cannibalization was likely. And the profits on the lower-priced computers were many times less than those of mainframes.

The argument can justifiably be made that if a company does not bring out new products then competitors will, and that it is better to compete with one's own products. Still, the threat of cannibalization can cause a hesitation, a blink, in a full-scale effort to rush to market an internally competing product. This reluctance and hesitation needs to be guarded against, lest the firm find itself no longer in the vanguard of innovation.

Assume the role of a vocal and critical stockholder at the annual meeting. What arguments would you introduce for a crash program to rush the PC to market, despite possible cannibalization? What contrary arguments would you expect, and how would you counter them?

Controversies

Questionable Decisions

No executive has a perfect batting average of good decisions. Indeed, most executives do well to bat more than 500—that is, to have more good decisions than bad decisions. But, alas, decisions are all relative. Much depends on the importance, the consequences, of these decisions.

IBM made a decision of monumental long-term consequences in the early 1980s. At that time IBM designated two upstart West Coast companies to be the key suppliers for its new personal computer. Thus, it gave away its chances to control the personal computer industry. Over the next 10 years, each of the two firms would develop a near-monopoly—Intel in microprocessors and Microsoft in operating-systems software—by setting standards for successive PC generations. Instead of keeping such developments proprietary (that is, within its own organization) IBM, in an urge to save developmental time, gave these two small firms a golden opportunity, which both grasped to the fullest. By 1992, Intel and Microsoft had emerged as the computer industry's most dominant firms.

The decision still is controversial. It saved IBM badly needed time in bringing its PC to market, and as computer technology becomes ever more complex, not even an IBM can be expected to have the ability and resources to go it alone. Linking up with competitors offers better products and services and a faster flow of technology today, and it seems to be the way of the future.

Former IBM CEO Thomas Watson, Jr., has criticized his successors Frank Cary and John Opel for phasing out rentals and selling the massive mainframe computer outright. Originally, purchasers could only lease the machines, thus giving IBM a dependable cushion of cash each year ("my golden goose," Mr. Watson called it.)[13] Doing away with renting left IBM, and John Akers, a newly volatile business, just as the industry position began worsening. Akers, newly installed as CEO, was thus left with a hostile environment without the cushion or support of steady revenues from such rentals, according to Watson's argument. But the counterposition holds that selling brought needed cash quickly into company coffers. Furthermore, opponents say it is unlikely, given the competitive climate that was emerging in the 1980s, that big customers would continue to tolerate the leasing arrangement when they could buy their machines, if not from IBM, then from another supplier whose machines were just as good or better.

Breaking up IBM

The general consensus of management experts was to support Akers' reforms to break up Big Blue into 13 divisions and give them increasing autonomy—even to the point that shares of some of these new Baby Blues might be distributed to stockholders. The idea is not unlike that of Japan's *keiretsu,* in which alliances of companies with common objectives but with substantial independence seek and develop business individually.

The assumption in favor of such breaking up is that the sum of the parts is greater than the whole, that the autonomy and motivation will bring more total revenues and profits. But these hypothesized benefits are not guaranteed. At issue is whether the good of the whole would be better served by suboptimizing some business units—that is, by reducing the profit maximizing of some units in order to have the highest degree of coordination and cooperation. Giving disparate units of an organization goals of individual profit maximization lays the seeds for intense intramural competition, with cannibalization and infighting likely. IBM has embarked on a program of decentralization and internal competition. But will gross profit margins deteriorate even more with such competition? Is the whole better served by a less intensely competitive internal environment?

Intrapreneurship reinforced by *skunkworks* is an approach that some firms have found valuable in bringing an aura of entrepreneurship to large organizations, beset as they are with tendencies toward rigidity and bureaucratic malaise. The following box describes this plan for fostering innovation in large firms.

---

[13] Miller, *op. cit.,* p. A4.

INFORMATION BOX

INTRAPRENEURSHIP AND SKUNKWORKS—PURSUING INNOVATION

Intrapreneurship is the term used to describe the encouragement of entrepreneurial behavior within the large organization. Such a spirit of entrepreneurship—usually only the domain of smaller enterprises—is more conducive to innovative thinking, calculated risk-taking, and quick actions, qualities that are crucial as organizations grow to cumbersome size.

Skunkworks refers to the creation of smaller subunits within the larger corporate structure "where groups of people are allowed to work together in a setting that is highly creative and free of many of the restrictions of large organizations."[14]

As an example of the skunkworks concept, Ford Motor Company in late 1989 considered overhauling the Mustang, once a legend but by the 1980s only a fading star. "Team Mustang," a group of about 400 people, scrambled to save this beloved car "on a skinflint budget." In the process they broke rules that previously had governed product development in the rigidly disciplined corporation. They upset the status quo as they vigorously pursued their redesign goal. The result: The Mustang was redone in three years for about $700 million, 25 percent faster and for 30 percent less money than for any comparable new car program in recent years.[15]

In similar fashion, a small group of enthusiastic Apple Computer employees were given separate facilities and permitted to operate free from Apple's normal product development bureaucracy: They set their own norms, and worked without outside interference. They even raised a "jolly roger" over their building as a symbol of their independence. The result? The Macintosh Computer.[16]

Would intrapreneurship or confederations of entrepreneurs within IBM be a viable alternative to breaking up the company into a number of smaller divisions? Do you see any problems with skunkworks?

[14] John R. Schermerhorn, Jr., *Management* 6th ed. (New York: Wiley, 1999), p. 175.

[15] Joseph B. White and Oscar Suris, "How a 'Skunk works' Keeps Mustang Alive—On a Tight Budget," *The Wall Street Journal* (September 21, 1993), pp. A1, A12.

[16] For further information, see Apple Computer *Annual Report, 1991.*

THE COMEBACK UNDER GERSTNER

Louis Gerstner took command in March 1993. The company, as we have seen, was reeling. In a reversal of major proportions, he brought IBM back to record profitability. Table 4.4 shows the statistics of what appears to be a sensational turnaround. In 1994, the company earned $3 billion, its first profitable year since 1990. Perhaps of greater significance, compared with the previous year this represented a profit swing of $11 billion. And revenue grew for the first time since 1990. Annual expenses

TABLE 4.4   IBM's Resurgence Under Gerstner, 1993–1994

	1993	1994
	(millions of dollars)	
Revenue	$62,716	$64,052
Net earnings (loss)	(8,101)	3,021
Net earnings (loss) per share of common stock	(14.22)	5.02
Working capital	6,052	12,112
Total debt	27,342	22,118
Number of employees	256,207	219,839

Source: Company annual reports.

Commentary: In virtually all measures of performance, IBM has made a significant turnaround from 1993 to 1994. Note in particular the decrease in debt, the decrease in number of employees, and the great profit turnaround.

were reduced by $3.5 billion, about 15 percent. And 1994 finished with financial strength: IBM had more than $10 billion in cash; basic debt was reduced by $3.3 billion. Of greater importance to stockholders, IBM stock nearly tripled in price, racing from a 1993 low of 40 to a high of 114 on August 17, 1995.

By all such performance statistics, Gerstner had done an outstanding job of turning the giant around. Yet, there were still doubters. For the most part, their skepticism was rooted in the notion that Gerstner was not aggressive enough.

Gerstner did not tamper mightily with the organizational structure of IBM. Before he took over, IBM was moving toward a breakup into 13 independent units: one for mainframes, one for PCs, one for disk drives, and so on. But he saw IBM's competitive advantage to be offering customers a complete package, a one-stop shopping to all those seeking help in solving technological problems: a unified IBM— somehow, an IBM with a single, efficient team.

The critics persisted. *Fortune* questioned, "Is He Too Cautious to Save IBM?" The article said, "After running IBM for more than a year and a half, CEO Lou Gerstner has revealed himself to be something other than the revolutionary whom the directors of this battered and demoralized enterprise once seemed to want ... he seems to be attempting a conventional turnaround: deep-cleaning and redecorating the house rather than gutting and renovating it."[17] The article admitted the "surprisingly good" results, but attributed this to luck: "Unexpectedly high demand for mainframe computers has given the company temporary respite from the inevitable shift to less lucrative products."[18]

So, what do we have here? A turnaround of monumental proportions, or a dud? Is Gerstner a hero or a flop? Whatever, we do not have sensationalism here, nor a ransacking of the company in the process.

[17] Allison Rogers, "Is He Too Cautious to Save IBM?" *Fortune,* October 3, 1994, p. 78.
[18] *Ibid.*

The Quiet Revolution

The critics inclined toward revolutionary measures had to be disappointed. "Transforming IBM is not something we can do in one or two years," Gerstner had stated. "The better we are at fixing some of the short-term things, the more time we have to deal with the long-term issues."[19] His efforts were contrasted with those of Albert Dunlap, who overhauled Scott Paper at about the same time. Dunlap replaced 9 of the 11 top executives in the first few days and laid off one-third of the total workforce. Gerstner brought in only 8 top executives from outside IBM to sit on the 37-person Worldwide Management Council.

A nontechnical man, Gerstner's strengths were in selling: cookies and cigarettes at RJR, travel services during an 11-year career at American Express Company. Weeks after taking over, he talked to IBM's top 100 customers at a retreat in Chantilly, Virginia. He asked them what IBM was doing right and wrong. They were surprised and delighted: this was the first time the chairman of the 72-year-old company had ever polled its customers. The input was revealing:

> The customers told him IBM was difficult to work with and unresponsive to customers' needs. For example, customers who needed IBM's famed mainframe computers were being told that the machines were dinosaurs and that the company would have to consider getting out of the business.[20]

Gerstner told these customers that IBM was in mainframes to stay, and would aggressively cut prices and focus on helping them set up, manage, and link the systems. And IBM's hardware sales turned around also, rising from $30.6 billion in 1993 to $35.6 billion in 1995.

Perhaps the most obvious change Gerstner instituted was the elimination of a dress code that once kept IBM salespeople in blue suits and white shirts.

By the spring of 1997, *Fortune* magazine highlighted Gerstner on its cover with the feature article, "The Holy Terror Who's Saving IBM."[21] Total company sales for 1996 were $75.947 billion, up 5.6 percent from the previous year, and net profits gained 30 percent over 1995, to $5.429 billion.

The growth continued. Revenues in 1997 were $78.508 and net income $6.093. The first three quarters of 1998 showed surprisingly robust sales growth, with practically all the portfolios of businesses contributing to the sparkling performance. For example, third quarter earnings were up 10 percent, on an unexpectedly healthy sales growth of 8 percent. For the year, IBM shares were one of the leading gainers among the companies that make up the Dow Jones Industrial Average.[22] Gerstner's turnaround was no fluke.

---

[19] *Ibid.*, p. 78.

[20] "IBM Focuses on Sales," *Cleveland Plain Dealer* (September 10, 1996), p. 6-C.

[21] Betsy Morris, "He's Saving Big Blue," *Fortune* (April 14, 1997), pp. 68–81.

[22] *1998 Annual Report;* and Raju Narisetti, "IBM Profit Rose 10% in 3rd Period, Topping Estimates, Amid Robust Sales," *The Wall Street Journal* (October 21, 1998), p. A3.

WHAT CAN BE LEARNED?

Beware of cannibalization phobia. We have just set the parameters of the issue of cannibalization—that is, how far a firm should go in developing products and encouraging intramural competition that will take sales away from other products and other units of the business. The issue is particularly troubling when the part of business that is likely to suffer is the most profitable in the company. And yet cannibalization should not even be an issue. At stake is the forward-leaning of the company, its embracing of innovation and improved technology, and its competitive stance. Unless a firm has an assured monopoly position, it can expect competitors to introduce advances in technology and new efficiencies in productivity and customer service.

In general we can conclude that no firm should rest on its laurels, that firms must introduce improvements and change as soon as possible, hopefully ahead of competition—all without regard to any possible impairment of sales and profits of existing products and units.

Remember the need to be "lean and mean" (sometimes called "acting small"). The marketplace is uncertain, especially in high-tech industries. In such environments a larger firm needs to keep the responsiveness and flexibility of smaller firms. It must avoid layers of management, delimiting policies, and a tradition-bound mindset. Otherwise a big firm is like the enormous vessel that is unable to stop or change course without losing precious time and distance. But how can a big firm keep the maneuverability and innovative thinking of a small firm? How can it remain lean and mean with increasing size?

We can identify certain conditions, or factors, of lean and mean firms:

1. They have simple organizations. Typically, they are decentralized, with decision making moved lower in the organization. This decentralization discourages the buildup of cumbersome bureaucracy and staff, which tend to add both increasing overhead expenses and the red tape that stultifies fast reaction time.

   With a simple organization comes a relatively flat structure, with fewer levels of management than comparable firms. This tendency also has certain desirable consequences. Overhead is greatly reduced, with fewer executives and their expensive staffs. But communications is also improved, because higher executives are more accessible, and directions and feedback are less distorted because of more direct communications channels. Even morale is improved because of the better communications and accessibility to leaders of the organization.

2. They encourage new ideas. A major factor in the inertia of large firms is the vested interests of those who see their power threatened by new ideas and innovative directions. Consequently, real creativity is stymied by going unappreciated; often it is even discouraged.

A firm that wishes to be lean and mean must seek new ideas. To do so requires rewards and recognition for creativity but, even more, acting upon the worthwhile ideas. Few things thwart creativity in an organization more than pigeonholing good ideas of eager employees.

3. Participation in planning is moved as low in the organization as possible. Important employees and lower-level managers are involved in decisions concerning their responsibilities, and their ideas receive reasonable weight in final decisions. Performance goals and rewards should be moved to the lowest possible level in the organization. Such an organizational climate encourages innovation, improves motivation and morale, and can lead to the fast reaction time that characterizes small organizations and often eludes the large.

4. A characteristic of some highly successful, proactive large organizations, as well as small firms, is minimum frills—even austerity at the corporate level. Two of our most successful firms today, Wal-Mart and Southwest Airlines, evince this philosophy to the utmost. A nofrills management philosophy is the greatest corporate model for curbing frivolous costs throughout an organization.

5. A final factor is the regular use of periodic evaluations and housecleaning of products, operations, and staff. Those deemed to be contributing little now, or to be unlikely in the future to contribute, should be objectively phased out or reassigned.

Beware the "king-of-the-hill" three-C's mindset. As a firm gains dominance and maturity, it must guard against a natural mindset evolution toward conservatism, complacency, and conceit. Usually the C's insidiously move in at the highest levels and eagerly filter down to the rest of the organization. As discussed earlier, this mindset leaves a firm highly vulnerable to competitors who are smaller, hungrier, and anxious to topple the king of the hill.

Although top management usually initiates such a mindset, top management can also lead in inhibiting it. The lean and mean organization is anathema to the three-C's mindset. If managers can curb bureaucratic buildup, then the seeds are thwarted. Keys to preventing this mindset are encouragement of innovative thinking throughout the organization and introduction of fresh talent from outside the organization to fill some internal positions. A strict adherence to promotion from within is inhibiting.

The power of greater commitment to customers. One of the bigger contributions Gerstner may have made to the turnaround of IBM was his customer focus: putting the needs of customers first and relying on his in-house experts for the technology; asking, not merely talking—finding out what customers wanted, and seeing what could be done to best meet these needs as quickly as possible; at the same time, toning down the arrogance of an "elite" staff of sales representatives. Perhaps the style change from blue suits and white shirts was the visible sign of a change in culture and attitudes.

Many firms profess a great commitment to customers and service. So common are such statements that one wonders how much is mere lip service. It is so easy to say this, and then not really follow up. In so doing, the opportunity to develop a trusting relationship is lost.

We can overcome adversity! We saw this with Continental Air and Harley Davidson, and now with IBM. Such examples should be motivating and inspiring for any organization and the executives trying to turn them around. Firms and their managers should be capable of learning from mistakes. As such, mistakes should be valuable learning experiences, leading the way to better performance and decisions in the future.

CONSIDER

What additional learning insights do you see emerging from the IBM case?

QUESTIONS

1. Assess the pro and con arguments for the 1982 decision to offer Microsoft and Intel a foothold in software and operating systems. (Keep your perspective to that of the early 1980s; don't be biased with the benefit of hindsight.)

2. Do you see any way that IBM could have maintained its nimbleness and technological edge as it grew to a $60 billion company? Reflect on this, and be as creative as you can.

3. "Tradition has no place in corporate thinking today." Discuss this statement.

4. Playing devil's advocate (one who takes an opposing position for the sake of argument), can you defend the position that the problems besetting IBM were not its fault, that they were beyond its control?

5. Giant organizations are often plagued with cumbersome bureaucracies. Discuss how this tendency could be prevented as an organization grows to large size over many years.

6. Which of the 3 C's do you think was most to blame for IBM's problems? Why do you conclude this?

HANDS-ON EXERCISES

1. You are a management consultant reporting to the CEO in the late 1980s. IBM is still racking up revenue and profit gains. But you detect serious emerging weaknesses. What do you advise management to do at this time? (Make any assumptions you feel necessary, but state them clearly.) Persuasively explain your rationale.

2. You are the executive assistant to Gerstner. It is 2001 and the great growth in revenues and profits of the last seven years has slowed. The critics are

again demanding a drastic overhaul. Gerstner still stoutly maintains that customer service is the key, and that this has somehow slipped. He charges you to come up with concrete recommendations for improving the effectiveness of customer service. Be as specific as you can.

TEAM DEBATE EXERCISE

At issue, whether to break up the company into 10–15 semiautonomous units, or to keep basically the same organization. Debate the opposing views as persuasively as possible.

INVITATION TO RESEARCH

What is the current situation of IBM? Have any new problems arisen for IBM? Is Gerstner still the CEO?

PART TWO

PLANNING BLUNDERS AND SUCCESSES

Coca-Cola's Classic Planning Miscalculation

*I*n this classic case we see a vivid example of the challenges, and risks, of management decision making. Despite careful planning and seemingly ample research, the decision was a strikeout. Fortunately for Coca-Cola, the consequences were more an acute embarrassment than an operational disaster.

On April 23, 1985, Roberto C. Goizueta, chairman of Coca-Cola, made a momentous announcement. It was to lead to more discussion, debate, and intense feelings than perhaps ever before encountered from one business decision.

"The best has been made even better," he proclaimed. After 99 years, the Coca-Cola Company had decided to abandon its original formula in favor of a sweeter variation, presumably an improved taste, which was named "New Coke."

Less than three months later, public pressure brought the company to admit that it had made a mistake and that it was bringing back the old Coke under the name "Coca-Cola Classic." It was July 11, 1985. Despite $4 million and two years of research, the company had made a major planning miscalculation in its estimation of customer acceptance of a product change. How could this have happened with such an astute and successful firm? The story is intriguing and provides a number of sobering insights, as well as a happy ending for Coca-Cola.

THE HISTORY OF COCA-COLA

Early Days

Coca-Cola was invented by a pharmacist who rose to cavalry general for the Confederates during the Civil War. John Styth Pemberton settled in Atlanta after the war and began putting out patent medicines such as Triplex Liver Pills and Globe of Flower Cough Syrup. In 1885 he registered a trademark for French Wine Coca, "an Ideal Nerve and Tonic Stimulant." In 1886, Pemberton unveiled a modification of French Wine Coca, which he called Coca-Cola, and began distributing it to soda fountains in used beer bottles. He looked on the concoction less as a refreshment than as a headache cure, especially for people who had overindulged in food or drink.

By chance, one druggist discovered that the syrup tasted better when mixed with carbonated water.

As his health failed and Coca-Cola failed to bring in sufficient money to meet his financial obligations, Pemberton sold the rights to Coca-Cola to a 39-year-old pharmacist, Asa Griggs Candler, for a paltry $2,300. The destitute Pemberton died in 1888 and was buried in a grave that went unmarked for the next 70 years.

Candler, a small-town Georgia man born in 1851, had planned to become a physician but changed his mind after observing that druggists made more money than doctors. He struggled for almost 40 years until he bought Coca-Cola, but then his fortunes changed profoundly. In 1892 he organized the Coca-Cola Company; a few years later he downplayed the therapeutic qualities of the beverage and began emphasizing the pleasure-giving qualities. At the same time, he developed a bottling system that still exists, and for 25 years he almost single-handedly guided the drink's destiny.

Robert Woodruff and the Maturing of the Coca-Cola Company

In 1916 Candler left Coca-Cola to run for mayor of Atlanta. He left the company in the hands of his relatives, who, after only three years, sold it to a group of Atlanta businessmen for $25 million. Asa was not consulted, and he was deeply distraught. The company was then netting $5 million. By the time of his death in 1929, annual profits were approaching the $25 million sale price. The group who bought Coca-Cola was headed by Ernest Woodruff, an Atlanta banker. Coke today still remains in the hands of the Woodruff family. Under the direction of the son, Robert Winship Woodruff, Coca-Cola became not only a household word within the United States but one of the most recognized symbols the world over.

Robert Woodruff grew up in affluence but believed in the virtues of personal achievement and effort. As a young man, he ignored his father's orders to return to Emory College to complete the remaining years of his education. He wanted to earn his keep in the real world and not "waste" three years in school. Eventually in 1911 he joined one of his father's firms, the newly organized Atlantic Ice & Coal Company, as a salesman and buyer. But he and his father violently disagreed again, this time over Robert's purchases of trucks from White Motors to replace the horse-drawn carts and drays of the day. Ernest fired his son and told him never to return home. Robert promptly joined White Motors. At the age of 33, he had become the nation's top truck salesman and was earning $85,000 a year. But then he heeded his father's call to come home.

By 1920 the Coca-Cola Company was threatened by bankruptcy. An untimely purchase of sugar just before prices plummeted had resulted in a staggering amount of borrowing to keep the company afloat. Bottler relations were at an all-time low because the company had wanted to raise the price of syrup, thus violating the original franchise contracts in which the price had been permanently fixed. In April 1923 Robert was named president, and he cemented dealer relationships, stressing his conviction that he wanted everyone connected with Coca-Cola to make money. He instituted a quality control program and greatly expanded distribution: By 1930 Coca-Cola had 64 bottlers in 28 countries.

During World War II, Coke went with the GIs. Woodruff saw to it that every man in uniform could get a bottle of Coca-Cola for a nickel whenever he wanted, no matter what the cost to the company. Throughout the 1950s, 1960s, and early 1970s, Coca-Cola ruled the soft drink market, despite strong challenges by Pepsi. It outsold Pepsi two to one. But this was to change.

BACKGROUND OF THE DECISION

Inroads of Pepsi, 1970s and 1980s

By the mid-1970s the Coca-Cola Company was a lumbering giant, and performance reflected this. Between 1976 and 1979, the growth rate of Coca-Cola soft drinks dropped from 13 percent annually to a meager 2 percent. As the giant stumbled, Pepsi Cola was finding heady triumphs. First came the "Pepsi Generation." This advertising campaign captured the imagination of the baby boomers with its idealism and youth. Pepsi's association with youth and vitality greatly enhanced its image and firmly associated it with the largest consumer market for soft drinks.

Then came another management coup, the "Pepsi Challenge," in which comparative taste tests with consumers showed a clear preference for Pepsi. This campaign led to a rapid increase in Pepsi's market share, from 6 to 14 percent of total U.S. soft-drink sales.

Coca-Cola, in reaction, conducted its own taste tests. Alas, these tests had the same result—people liked the taste of Pepsi better, and market share changes reflected this. As Table 5.1 shows, by 1979 Pepsi had closed the gap on Coca-Cola, having 17.9 percent of the soft-drink market to Coke's 23.9 percent. By the end of 1984, Coke had only a 2.9 percent lead, and in the grocery store market it was now trailing 1.7 percent. Further indication of Coke's diminishing position relative to Pepsi was a study done by Coca-Cola's own marketing research department. This study showed that in 1972, 18 percent of soft-drink users drank Coke exclusively, whereas only 4 percent drank only Pepsi. In 10 years the picture had changed greatly: Only 12 percent now claimed loyalty to Coke, and the number of exclusive Pepsi drinkers almost matched, with 11 percent. Figure 5.1 shows this graphically.

The fact that Coca-Cola was outspending Pepsi in advertising by $100 million made Coke's deteriorating competitive performance all the more worrisome and frus-

TABLE 5.1   Coke and Pepsi Shares of Total Soft-Drink Market 1950s–1984

		1975		*1979*		*1984*	
	Mid-1950s Lead	% of Market	Lead	% of Market	Lead	% of Market	Lead
Coke	Better than 2 to 1	24.2	6.8	23.9	6.0	21.7	2.9
Pepsi		17.4		17.9		18.8	

Source: Thomas Oliver, *The Real Coke, The Real Story* (New York: Random House, 1986), pp. 21, 50; "Two Cokes Really Are Better Than One—For Now," *Business Week* (September 9, 1985), p. 38.

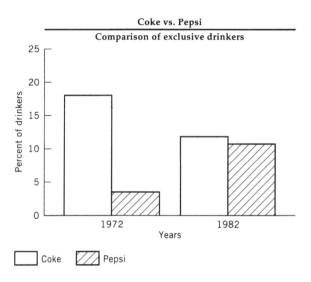

Figure 5.1 Coke versus Pepsi: Comparison of exclusive drinkers.

trating. Coca-Cola had twice as many vending machines, dominated fountains, had more shelf space, and was competitively priced. Why was it still losing market share?

The Changing of the Guard

J. Paul Austin, the chairman of Coca-Cola, was nearing retirement in 1980. Donald Keough, the president for Coca-Cola's American group, was expected to succeed him. But a new name, Roberto Goizueta, suddenly emerged.

Goizueta's background was far different from that of the typical Coca-Cola executive. He was not from Georgia, was not even Southern. Rather, he was the son of a wealthy Havana sugar plantation owner. He came to the United States at age 16 to enter an exclusive Connecticut preparatory school, Cheshire Academy. He spoke virtually no English when he arrived, but he quickly learned the language by using the dictionary and watching movies—and became the class valedictorian.

Goizueta graduated from Yale in 1955 with a degree in chemical engineering and returned to Cuba. Spurning his father's business, he went to work in Coke's Cuban research labs.

Goizueta's complacent life was to change in 1959 when Fidel Castro seized power and expropriated foreign facilities. He fled to the United States with his wife and their three children, arriving with $20. With Coca-Cola he soon became known as a brilliant administrator, and in 1968 he was brought to company headquarters. In 1980 Goizueta and six other executives were made vice chairpersons and began battling for top spots in the company.

Chief executive officer J. Paul Austin, soon to retire because of Alzheimer's disease, favored an operations man to become the next CEO. But he was overruled by

Robert Woodruff, the 90-year-old patriarch. In April 1980 the board of directors approved the recommendation of Goizueta for the president. When Goizueta moved on to become chairman of the board in March 1981, Donald Keough succeeded him as president.

Shortly after his promotion, Goizueta called a worldwide manager's conference in which he announced that nothing was sacred to the company anymore, that change was imminent, and that managers had to accept that situation. He also announced ambitious plans to diversify beyond the soft-drink industry.

In a new era of change announced by a new administration, the sacredness of the commitment to the original Coke formula became tenuous, and the ground was laid for the first flavor change in 99 years.

Marketing Research

With the market share erosion of the late 1970s and early 1980s, despite strong advertising and superior distribution, the company began to look at the product itself. Evidence was increasingly suggesting that taste was the single most important cause of Coke's decline. Perhaps the original secret formula needed to be scrapped. And so Project Kansas began.

Under Project Kansas in 1982 some 2,000 interviews in 10 major markets were conducted to investigate customers' willingness to accept a different Coke. People were shown storyboards and comic strip-style mock commercials and were asked series of questions. One storyboard, for example, said that Coke had added a new ingredient and tasted smoother; another said the same about Pepsi. Then consumers were asked about their reactions to the "change concept" (for example, "Would you be upset?" and "Would you try the new drink?"). Researchers estimated from the responses that 10 to 12 percent of Coke drinkers would be upset and that one-half of these would get over it, but one-half would not.

Although interviews showed a willingness to try a new Coke, other tests disclosed the opposite. Small consumer panels, or focus groups, revealed strong favorable and unfavorable sentiments. But the technical division persisted in trying to develop a new, more pleasing flavor. By September 1984 the division thought it had done so. The new version was a sweeter, less fizzy cola with a soft, sticky taste due to a higher sugar content from the exclusive use of corn syrup sweetener, which is sweeter than sucrose. This cola was introduced in blind taste tests in which consumers were not told what brand they were drinking. These tests were highly encouraging: The new flavor substantially outperformed Pepsi, whereas in previous blind taste tests Pepsi had always beaten Coke.

As a result researchers estimated that the new formula would boost Coke's share of the soft-drink market by one percentage point. This point would be worth $200 million in sales.

Before adopting the new flavor, Coca-Cola invested $4 million in the biggest taste test ever. Some 191,000 people in more than 13 cities participated in a comparison of unmarked various Coke formulations. The use of unmarked colas was intended to eliminate any bias toward brand names. Fifty-five percent of the participants favored New Coke over the original formula, and New Coke also beat Pepsi. The research results seemed to be conclusive in favor of the new formula.

The Go Decision

Even when the decision was made to introduce the new flavor, a number of ancillary decisions had to be made. For example, should the new flavor be added to the product line, or should it replace the old Coke? Executives thought that bottlers would be opposed to adding another cola. After considerable soul searching, top executives unanimously decided to change the taste of Coke and take the old Coke off the market.

In January 1985 the task of introducing the new Coke was given to the McCann-Erickson advertising agency. Bill Cosby was to be the spokesperson for the nationwide introduction of the new Coke, scheduled for April. All departments of this company were gearing their efforts for a coordinated introduction.

On April 23, 1985, Goizueta and Keough held a press conference at Lincoln Center in New York City in order to introduce the new Coke. Invitations had been sent to the media from all over the United States, and some 200 newspaper, magazine, and TV reporters attended the press conference. However, many of them came away unconvinced of the merits of the new Coke, and their stories were generally negative. In the days ahead, the news media's skepticism would exacerbate the public rejection of the new Coke.

The word spread quickly. Within 24 hours, 81 percent of the U.S. population knew of the change, and this was more people than were aware in July 1969 that Neil Armstrong had walked on the moon.[1] Early results looked good; 150 million people tried the new Coke—more people than had ever before tried a new product. Most comments were favorable. Shipments to bottlers rose to the highest percent in five years. The decision looked unassailable. But not for long.

AFTERMATH OF THE DECISION

The situation changed rapidly. Although some objections were expected, the protests quickly mushroomed. In the first four hours, the company received about 650 calls. By mid-May, calls were coming in at a rate of 5,000 a day, in addition to a barrage of angry letters. The company added 83 WATS lines and hired new staff to handle the responses. People were speaking of Coke as an American symbol and as a longtime friend that had suddenly betrayed them. Some threatened to switch to tea or water. Here is a sampling of the responses:[2]

> The sorrow I feel knowing not only won't I ever enjoy real Coke, but my children and grandchildren won't either. ... I guess my children will have to take my word for it.

[1] John S. Demott, "Fiddling with the Real Thing," *Time* (May 6, 1985), p. 55.

[2] Thomas Oliver, *The Real Coke, the Real Story* (New York: Random House, 1986), pp. 155–156.

It is absolutely TERRIBLE! You should be ashamed to put the Coke label on it. … This new stuff tastes worse than Pepsi.

It was nice knowing you. You were a friend for most of my 35 years. Yesterday I had my first taste of new Coke, and to tell the truth, if I would have wanted Pepsi, I would have ordered a Pepsi not a Coke.

In all, more than 40,000 such letters were received that spring and summer. In Seattle strident loyalists calling themselves Old Coke Drinkers of America laid plans to file a class action suit against Coca-Cola. People began stockpiling the old Coke. Some sold it at scalper's prices. When sales in June did not pick up as the company had expected, bottlers demanded the return of old Coke.

The company's research also confirmed an increasing negative sentiment. Before May 30, 53 percent of consumers said they liked the new Coke. In June the vote began to change: More than one-half of all people surveyed said they did not like the new Coke. By July only 30 percent of the people surveyed each week said that they liked the new Coke.

Anger spread across the country, fueled by media publicity. Fiddling with the formula for the 99-year-old beverage became an affront to patriotic pride. As Robert Antonio, a University of Kansas sociologist, stated, "Some felt that a sacred symbol had been tampered with."[3] Even Goizueta's father spoke out against the switch when it was announced. He told his son the move was a bad one and jokingly threatened to disown him. By now company executives began to worry about a consumer boycott.

Coca-Cola Cries "Uncle"

Company executives now began seriously thinking about how to recoup the fading prospects of Coke. In an executive meeting, the managers decided to take no action until after the Fourth of July weekend, when the sales results for this holiday weekend were in. Results were unimpressive. They decided to reintroduce Coca-Cola under the trademark of Coca-Cola Classic. The company would keep the new flavor and call it New Coke. Top executives announced the decision to the public on July 11, walking onto the stage in front of the Coca-Cola logo to make an apology to the public. They never admitted that New Coke had been a total mistake.

This presentation delivered two messages to American consumers. First, to those who were drinking New Coke and enjoying it, the company conveyed its thanks. To those who wanted the original Coke, the message was, "We heard you—the original taste of Coke is back."

The news spread fast. ABC interrupted its soap opera *General Hospital* on Wednesday afternoon to break the news. In the kind of saturation coverage normally reserved for disasters or diplomatic crises, the decision to bring back old Coke was prominently reported on every evening network news broadcast. The general feeling of soft-drink fans was joy. Democratic Senator David Pryor of Arkansas expressed his jubilation on the Senate floor: "A very meaningful moment

---

[3] John Greenwald, "Coca-Cola's Big Fizzle," *Time* (July 22, 1985), p. 48.

in the history of America, this shows that some national institutions cannot be changed."[4] Even Wall Street was happy. Old Coke's comeback drove Coca-Cola stock to its highest level in 12 years.

On the other hand, Roger Enrico, president of Pepsi-Cola USA, said, "Clearly this is the Edsel of the '80s. This was a terrible mistake. Coke's got a lemon on its hands and now they're trying to make lemonade."[5] Other critics labeled this decision to change Coke "the blunder of the decade."[6]

WHAT WENT WRONG?

The most convenient scapegoat, according to consensus opinion, was the marketing research that preceded the decision. Yet Coca-Cola spent about $4 million and devoted two years to the marketing research. About 200,000 consumers were contacted during this time. The error in judgment was surely not from want of trying. But when we dig deeper into the research efforts, some flaws become apparent.

Flawed Marketing Research

The major design of the marketing research involved taste tests by representative consumers. After all, the decision point involved a different-flavored Coke, so what could be more logical than to conduct blind taste tests to determine the acceptability of the new flavor, not only versus the old Coke but also versus Pepsi? And these results were significantly positive for the new formula, even among Pepsi drinkers. A "go" signal seemed clear.

But with the benefit of hindsight, some deficiencies in the research design were more apparent and should have caused concern at the time. The research participants were not told that by picking one cola, they would lose the other. This turned out to be a significant distortion: Any addition to the product line would naturally be far more acceptable to a loyal Coke user than would be a complete substitution, which meant the elimination of the traditional product.

While three to four new tastes were tested with almost 200,000 people, only 30,000 to 40,000 of these tests involved the specific formula for the new Coke. The research was geared more to the idea of a new, sweeter cola than to the final formula. In general a sweeter flavor tends to be preferred in blind taste tests. This is particularly true with youth, the largest drinkers of sugared colas, and the group that had been drinking more Pepsi in recent years. Furthermore, preferences for sweeter tasting products tend to diminish with use.[7]

Consumers were asked whether they favored change as a concept and whether they would likely drink more, less, or the same amount of Coke if there were a change. But such questions could hardly probe the depth of feelings and emotional

[4] *Ibid.*

[5] *Ibid.* p. 49.

[6] James E. Ellis and Paul B. Brown, "Coke's Man on the Spot," *Business Week* (July 29, 1985), p. 56.

[7] "New Coke Wins Round 1, but Can It Go the Distance?" *Business Week* (June 24, 1985), p. 48.

ties to the product, and the decisions and plans based on the flawed research were themselves vulnerable.

Symbolic Value

The symbolic value of Coke was the sleeper. Perhaps this should have been foreseen. Perhaps the marketing research should have considered this possibility and designed the research to map it and determine the strength and durability of these values— that is, whether they would have a major effect on any substitution of a new flavor.

Admittedly, when we get into symbolic value and emotional involvement, any researcher is dealing with vague and nebulous attitudes. But various attitudinal measures have been developed to measure the strength or degree of emotional involvement, such as the *semantic differential,* described in the following box.

INFORMATION BOX

MEASURING ATTITUDES—THE SEMANTIC DIFFERENTIAL

An important tool in attitudinal research, image studies, and planning decisions is the *semantic differential.* It was originally developed to measure the meaning that a concept—perhaps a political issue, a person, or a work of art, or in marketing a brand, product, or company—might have for people in terms of various dimensions. As first presented, the instrument consisted of pairs of polar adjectives with a seven-interval scale separating the opposite members of each pair. For example:

Good —————— Bad

The various intervals from left to right would then represent degrees of feeling or belief ranging from extremely good to neither good nor bad to extremely bad.

This instrument has been refined to obtain greater sensitivity through the use of descriptive phrases. The following are examples of such bipolar phrases for determining the image of a particular brand of beer:

Something special —————— Just another drink

American flavor —————— Foreign flavor

Really peps you up —————— Somehow doesn't pep you up

The number of word pairs varies considerably, but there may be as many as 50 or more. Flexibility and appropriateness to a particular study are achieved by constructing tailor-made word and phrase lists.

Semantic differential scales have been used to compare images of particular products, brands, firms, and stores against competing ones. The answers of all respondents can be averaged and then plotted to provide a "profile," as shown below for three competing beers on four scales (actually, a firm would probably use 20 or more scales in such a study).

(continues)

MEASURING ATTITUDES—THE SEMANTIC DIFFERENTIAL (continued)

In this profile, brand A shows the dominant image over its competing brands in three of the four categories; however, the negative reaction to its price should alert the company to review pricing practices. Brand C shows a negative image, especially regarding the reliability of its product. The old-fashioned image may or may not be desirable, depending on the type of customer being sought; at least the profile indicates that brand C is perceived as being distinctive from the other two brands. Probably the weakest image of all is that of brand B; respondents viewed this brand as having no distinctive image, neither good nor bad. A serious image-building campaign is desperately needed if brand B is to compete successfully; otherwise, the price may have to be dropped to gain some advantage.

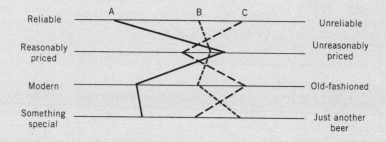

Easy to administer and simple to analyze, the semantic differential is useful in identifying where there might be opportunities in areas presently not well covered by competitors. It is also useful to a well-established firm—such as Coca-Cola—to determine the strength and the various dimensions of attitudes toward its product. Semantic differential scales are also valuable in evaluating the effectiveness of planning changes, such as a change in advertising theme. Here the semantic differential can be administered before and after the campaign, and any changes in perceptions can be pinpointed.

In the example of the three beers, how would you attempt to build up the brand image of beer B? How successful would you expect to be?

Herd Instinct

A natural human phenomenon asserted itself in this case—the herd instinct, the tendency of people to follow an idea, slogan, or concept and to "jump on the bandwagon." At first, acceptance of the new Coke appeared to be reasonably satisfactory. But as more and more outcries were raised—fanned by the press—about the betrayal of the old tradition (somehow Coke became identified with motherhood, apple pie, and the flag), public attitudes shifted vigorously against this perceived unworthy substitute. The bandwagon syndrome was fully activated. It is doubtful that by July 1985 Coca-Cola could have done anything to reverse the unfavorable tide. To wait for it to die down was fraught with danger, for who would be brave enough to predict the durability and possible heights of such a protest movement?

Could such a tide have been predicted? Perhaps not, at least not the full strength of the movement. Coca-Cola expected some resentment, but perhaps it should have been more cautious and considered a worst-case scenario in addition to what seemed the more probable. Coca-Cola would then have been prepared to react to such a *contingency.*

INFORMATION BOX

CONTINGENCY PLANS

Planning involves resource deployment through the use of budgets. Resources to be deployed include both work force and facilities: the number of people to be involved in the particular aspect of the operation, and the amount of money and facilities required to meet planned goals and expectations. Such resource deployment depends on certain assumptions made about both the external and internal environment. When plans are made for major projects, such as new Coke, and resources are committed, the success of the commitment depends greatly on the accuracy of the assumptions that are made. When, as events unfold, it becomes clear that certain assumptions were either overly optimistic or overly pessimistic, then plans and resource deployments need to be revised.

Contingency plans are well used when dealing with a new product or project. Different plans may thereby be developed for the different contingencies, or sets of conditions that may occur. For example, Plan A may assume a certain level of acceptance; Plan B may be developed for better-than-expected circumstances; Plan C may be ready to put to use if early results are discouraging. When such plans are drawn up in advance, a firm is better able to cope with varied outcomes and can either marshal additional resources or cut back to more realistic expectations.

With such contingency plans developed, Coca-Cola would have been better prepared to react to the surprising resistance to its new product. For example, it could have developed plans for different levels of customer acceptance, including the worse scenario that was actually encountered: nonacceptance and public agitation. Although in this case, the decision making under crisis conditions apparently worked out satisfactorily, in another instance it might not have. Carefully thought-out alternative actions generally have a better payoff than decisions made quickly in a crisis situation.

Do you think any contingency plan of Coca-Cola would have anticipated the extent of public agitation? Even if such a worst-case scenario were considered, is it likely that reactions would have been improved? Why or why not?

WHAT CAN BE LEARNED?

Planning and research do not guarantee the best decision. Most decision-making occurs under conditions of uncertainty: the environment ever changing, actions of competitors not always predictable, consumers fickle and illogical. Prudent executives try to decrease the uncertainty by careful planning and diligent research. But this case illustrates that bad decisions can still result. Who could have predicted the belated attachment of consumers to the idea of tradition, or the power of the media in fanning this emotional mindset? With the benefit of hindsight we can see how planning and research efforts could have been improved. But even then the decision might have been faulty.

So, while careful planning and research does not guarantee a correct decision, or the best one, it does improve the "batting average," that is, the probability of making a good decision—sometimes a lot, sometimes only a little. But this is the best we can expect in decision-making under uncertainty, that more good decisions than bad decisions will be made.

Taste is an unreliable preference factor. Taste tests are commonly used in marketing research, but some marketers remain skeptical of their validity. Take beer, for example. Do you know of anybody—despite strenuous claims—who can in blind taste tests unerringly identify which is which among three or four disguised brands of beer? We know that people tend to favor the sweeter in taste tests. But does this mean that such a sweeter flavor will always win out? Hardly. Something else is operating with consumer preference other than the fleeting essence of a taste—unless the flavor difference is extreme. Research and decisions that rely primarily on taste tests tend to be more vulnerable to mistakes.

Brand image is usually a powerful sales stimulant. Advertisers have consistently been more successful by cultivating a desirable image or personality for their brands or the types of people who use them than by standing by such vague statements as "better tasting."

Beware of tampering with the traditional image. Not many firms have a 100-year-old tradition to be concerned with, or even 25, or even 10. Most products have much shorter life cycles. No other product has been so widely used and so deeply entrenched in societal values and culture as Coke.

The psychological components of the great Coke protest make interesting speculation. Perhaps in an era of rapid change, many people wish to hang on to the one symbol of security or constancy in their lives—even if this is only the traditional Coke flavor. Perhaps many people found this protest to be an interesting way to escape the humdrum, by making waves in a rather harmless fashion, and in so doing see if a big corporation might be forced to cry "uncle."

One wonders how many consumers would even have been aware of any change in flavor had the new formula been quietly introduced. But, of course, the advertising siren call of "New!" would have been muted.

So, do we dare tamper with tradition? In Coke's case the answer is probably not, unless it is done very quietly; but, then, Coke is unique.

Tampering with a major product still in high demand may be risky indeed. Conventional wisdom advocates that changes are best made in response to problems, that when things are going smoothly the success pattern or strategy should not be tampered with. This may or may not be a good rule of thumb.

Actually, things were not going all that well for Coke by early 1985. Competitive position had steadily been declining to Pepsi for some years. Vigorous promotional efforts by Pepsi featuring Michael Jackson had increased market share of regular Pepsi by 1.5 percent in 1984, while regular Coke was dropping 1 percent. Moreover, regular Coke had steadily been losing competitive position in supermarkets, dropping almost 4 percent between 1981 and 1985. And foreign business, accounting for 62 percent of total soft-drink volume for Coca-Cola, was showing a disappointing growth rate.[8]

So there was certainly motivation for considering a change. And the obvious change was to introduce a somewhat different flavor, one more congruent with the preference of younger people who were the prime market for soft drinks. We do not subscribe to the philosophy of "Don't rock the boat" or "Don't change anything until forced to." However, Coca-Cola had another option.

Major changes often are better introduced without immediately discarding the present. The obvious alternative was to introduce the new Coke but still keep the old one. The lesson here is, "Don't burn your bridges." Of course, in July Roberto Goizueta brought back the old Coke after some months of turmoil and considerable corporate embarrassment and competitive glee—which soon turned to dismay. The obvious drawback for having two Cokes was dealer resentment at having to stock an additional product in the same limited space and bottler concern at having a more complicated production run. Furthermore, there was the real possibility that Pepsi would emerge as the number one soft drink because of two competing Cokes—and this would be an acute embarrassment for Coca-Cola.

Sheer advertising expenditures does not guarantee effectiveness. Coca-Cola was outspending Pepsi for advertising by $100 million, but its competitive position in the 1970s and early 1980s continued to erode in comparison to Pepsi's. Pepsi's campaign featured the theme of the "Pepsi Generation" and the "Pepsi Challenge." The use of a superstar such as Michael Jackson also proved to be more effective with the youth market for soft drinks than Bill Cosby for Coca-Cola. Any executive has to be left with the sobering realization that the sheer number of dollars spent on advertising does not guarantee competitive success. A smaller firm can still outdo a larger rival.

[8] "Pepsi's High-Priced Sell Is Paying Off," *Business Week* (March 4, 1985), pp. 34–35; "Is Coke Fixing a Coke That Isn't Broken? *Business Week* (May 6, 1985), p. 47.

The power of the media needs to be considered in decisions that are likely to generate widespread interest. The press and broadcast media can be powerful influences of public opinion. With the new Coke, the media undoubtedly exacerbated the herd instinct by publicizing the protests to the fullest. After all, this was news. And news seems to be spiciest when an institution or person can be criticized or found wanting. The power of the press should also be sobering to an executive and ought to be one of the factors she or he considers with certain decisions that may affect the public image of the organization.

CONSIDER

What additional learning insights do you see as emerging from the Coca-Cola case?

CONSEQUENCES

Forced by public opinion into a two-cola strategy, the company found the results to be reassuring. By October 1985 Coke Classic was outselling New Coke by better than 2 to 1 nationwide and by 9 to 1 in some markets. Restaurant chains such as McDonald's, Hardees, Roy Rogers, and Red Lobster had switched back to Coke Classic.

For the full year of 1985, sales from all operations rose 10 percent and profits, 9 percent. In the United States, Coca-Cola soft-drink volume increased 9 percent; internationally it rose 10 percent. Profitability from soft drinks decreased slightly, representing heavier advertising expenses for introducing New Coke and then reintroducing old Coke.

Coca-Cola's fortunes continued to improve steadily, if not spectacularly. By 1988 it was producing 5 of the 10 top-selling soft drinks in the country and had 40 percent of the domestic market to Pepsi's 31 percent.[9]

Because the soft-drink business was generating about $1 billion in cash each year, Roberto Goizueta had made a number of major acquisitions, such as Columbia Pictures and the Taylor Wine Company. However, these did not meet his expectations and were disposed of. Still, by 1988 Coca-Cola had a hoard of $5 billion in new cash and debt capacity, and the enticing problem now was how to spend it.

The most successful diversifications were in the soft-drink area. As recently as 1981 there had been only one Coke, and not too many years before, only one container, the 6½-oz. glass bottle. By 1987 only one-tenth of 1 percent of all Coke was sold in that bottle.[10] Classic Coke was the best-selling soft drink in the United States, and Diet Coke was the third largest selling. New Coke was now being outsold by Classic about 7 to 1. Table 5.2 shows the total sales volume of the Coke family for 1986.

---

[9] John H. Taylor, "Some Things Don't Go Better with Coke," *Forbes* (March 21, 1988), pp. 34–35.

[10] Thomas Moore, "He Put the Kick Back into Coke," *Fortune* (October 26, 1987), pp. 47–56.

Table 5.2   1986 Family of Cokes

Kinds	Millions of Cases
Total of one cola, 1980	1,310.5
1986	
Coca-Cola Classic	1,294.3
Diet Coke	490.8
Coke	185.1
Cherry Coke	115.6
Caffeine-Free Diet Coke	85.6
Caffeine-Free Coke	19.0
Diet Cherry Coke	15.0

Source: "He Put the Kick Back into Coke," *Fortune* (October 26, 1987), p. 48.

Coca-Cola's future looked bright. Per capita soft-drink consumption in the United States had been rising significantly in the 1980s, as shown in the following table:

	Per Capita Consumption	Percent Increase
1980	34.5 gal	
1986	42 gal	22%

Source: Pepsico 1986 Annual Report, p. 13.

The international potential was also great. Per capita consumption outside the United States was only four gallons—yet 95 percent of the world's population lives outside the United States.

CONCLUSION

Some called new Coke a misstep, others a blink. At the time of the fiasco some called it a monumental blunder, the mistake of the century. But it hardly turned out to be that. As sales surged, some competitors accused Coca-Cola of engineering the whole scenario in order to get an abundance of free publicity. Coke executives stoutly denied this and admitted their error in judgment. For who could foresee, as *Fortune* noted, that the episode would "reawaken deep-seated American loyalty to Coca-Cola"?[11]

And who could have foreseen that the widely publicized "mistake" of Coca-Cola would have other positive repercussions? The company would now be viewed as more human and more responsive to the wishes of consumers.

---

[11] *Ibid.*, p. 48.

QUESTIONS

1. How could Coca-Cola's marketing research have been improved? Be as specific as you can.

2. When a firm is facing a negative press, as Coca-Cola was with the new Coke, what recourse does the firm have? Support your conclusions.

3. Do you think Coca-Cola would have been as successful if it had introduced the new Coke as an addition to the line and not as a substitute for the old Coke? Why or why not?

4. "If it's not broken, don't fix it!" Evaluate this statement.

5. Do you think Coca-Cola engineered the whole scenario with the new Coke, including fanning initial protests, in order to get a bonanza of free publicity? Defend your position.

6. Would you, as a top executive at Coca-Cola, have "caved in" as quickly to the protests? Would you have "toughed it out" instead?

HANDS-ON EXERCISES

1. You are the public relations director of Coca-Cola. It is early June 1985, and you have been ordered to "do something" to blunt the negative publicity. What ideas can you offer that might counter or replace the negatives with positive publicity?

2. Assume that you are Robert Goizueta and that you are facing increasing pressure in early July 1985 to abandon the new Coke and bring back the old formula. However, your latest marketing research suggests that only a small group of agitators are making all the fuss about the new cola. Evaluate your options and support your recommendations to the board.

TEAM DEBATE EXERCISE

The decision to go with the new Coke has not been made yet. One group at headquarters is dead set against any change: "if it's not broke, don't fix it." The other group firmly believes that change is not only necessary but long overdue. Debate the two positions as comprehensively and persuasively as you can. (Be sure that you confine your arguments to what was known in early 1985. You cannot use the benefit of hindsight.)

INVITATION TO RESEARCH

What is the current situation with Coca-Cola? Is Coke Classic still the big winner? Is New Coke still being produced? Is Coca-Cola winning the battle with Pepsi? How are the two companies doing in the international arena? What is the status regarding recent diversifications of Coca-Cola?

CHAPTER SIX

Euro Disney: Bungling a Successful Format

With high expectations Euro Disney opened just outside Paris in April 1992. Success seemed ensured. After all, the Disneylands in Florida, California, and, most recently, Japan were all spectacular successes. But somehow all the rosy expectations became a delusion. The opening results cast even the future continuance of Euro Disney into doubt. How could what seemed so right be so wrong? What mistakes were made?

PRELUDE

Optimism

Perhaps a few early omens should have raised some cautions. Between 1987 and 1991, three $150 million amusement parks had opened in France with great fanfare. All had fallen flat, and by 1991 two were in bankruptcy. Now Walt Disney Company was finalizing its plans to open Europe's first Disneyland early in 1992. This would turn out to be a $4.4 billion enterprise sprawling over 5,000 acres 20 miles east of Paris. Initially it would have six hotels and 5,200 rooms, more rooms than the entire city of Cannes, and lodging was expected to triple in a few years as Disney opened a second theme park to keep visitors at the resort longer.

Disney also expected to develop a growing office complex, one only slightly smaller than France's biggest, La Defense, in Paris. Plans also called for shopping malls, apartments, golf courses, and vacation homes. Euro Disney would tightly control all this ancillary development, designing and building nearly everything itself, and eventually selling off the commercial properties at a huge profit.

Disney executives had no qualms about the huge enterprise, which would cover an area one-fifth the size of Paris itself. They were more worried that the park might not be big enough to handle the crowds:

"My biggest fear is that we will be too successful." "I don't think it can miss. They are masters of marketing. When the place opens it will be perfect. And they know how to make people smile—even the French."[1]

Company executives initially predicted that 11 million Europeans would visit the extravaganza in the first year alone. After all, Europeans accounted for 2.7 million visits to the U.S. Disney parks and spent $1.6 billion on Disney merchandise. Surely a park in closer proximity would draw many thousands more. As Disney executives thought more about it, the forecast of 11 million seemed most conservative. They reasoned that since Disney parks in the United States (population of 250 million) attract 41 million visitors a year, then if Euro Disney attracted visitors in the same proportion, attendance could reach 60 million with Western Europe's 370 million people. Table 6.1 shows the 1990 attendance at the two U.S. Disney parks and the newest Japanese Disneyland, as well as the attendance-population ratios.

Adding fuel to the optimism was the fact that Europeans typically have more vacation time than do U.S. workers. For example, five-week vacations are commonplace for French and German employees, compared with two to three weeks for U.S. workers.

The failure of the three earlier French parks was seen as irrelevant. Robert Fitzpatrick, Euro Disneyland's chairman, stated, "We are spending 22 billion French francs before we open the door, while the other places spent 700 million. This means we can pay infinitely more attention to details—to costumes, hotels, shops, trash baskets—to create a fantastic place. There's just too great a response to Disney for us to fail."[2]

TABLE 6.1 Attendance and Attendance/Population Ratios, Disney Parks, 1990

	Visitors	Population (millions)	Ratio
United States			
Disneyland (Southern California)	12.9	250	5.2%
Disney World/Epcot Center (Florida)	<u>28.5</u>	250	<u>11.4%</u>
Total United States	41.4		16.6%
Japan			
Tokyo Disneyland	16.0	124	13.5%
Euro Disney	?	310[a]	?

[a] Within a two-hour flight.

Source: Euro Disney, Amusement Business Magazine.

Commentary: Even if the attendance/population ratio for Euro Disney is only 10 percent, which is far below that of some other theme parks, still 31 million visitors could be expected. Euro Disney "conservatively" predicted 11 million the first year.

[1] Steven Greenhouse, "Playing Disney in the Parisian Fields," *The New York Times* (Feb. 17, 1991); Section 3: 1,6.

[2] Greenhouse, "Playing Disney," 6.

Nonetheless, a few scattered signs indicated that not everyone was happy with the coming of Disney. Leftist demonstrators at Euro Disney's stock offering greeted company executives with eggs, ketchup, and "Mickey Go Home" signs. Some French intellectuals decried the pollution of the country's cultural ambiance with the coming of Mickey Mouse and company: They called the park an American cultural abomination. The mainstream press also seemed contrary, describing every Disney setback "with glee." And French officials in negotiating with Disney sought less American and more European culture at France's Magic Kingdom. Still, such protests and bad press seemed contrived, unrepresentative, and certainly not predictive. Company officials dismissed the early criticism as "the ravings of an insignificant elite."[3]

The Location Decision

In the search for a site for Euro Disney, Disney executives examined 200 locations in Europe. The other finalist was Barcelona, Spain. Its major attraction was warmer weather, but its transportation system was not as good as that around Paris, and it lacked level tracts of land of sufficient size. The clincher for the Paris decision was its more central location. Table 6.2 shows the number of people within 2 to 6 hours of the Paris site.

The beet fields of the Marne-la-Vallee area was the choice. Being near Paris seemed a major advantage, since Paris was Europe's biggest tourist draw. And France was eager to win the project to help lower its jobless rate and also to enhance its role as the center of tourist activity in Europe. The French government expected the project to create at least 30,000 jobs and to contribute $1 billion a year from foreign visitors.

To entice the project, the French government allowed Disney to buy up huge tracts of land at 1971 prices. It provided $750 million in loans at below-market rates,

TABLE 6.2 Number of People Within 2–6 Hours of the Paris Site

Within a 2-hour drive	17 million people
Within a 4-hour drive	41 million people
Within a 6-hour drive	109 million people
Within a 2-hour flight	310 million people

Source: Euro Disney, Amusement Business Magazine.

Commentary: The much more densely populated and geographically compact European continent makes access to Euro Disney much more convenient than it is in the United States.

[3] Peter Gumbel and Richard Turner, "Fans Like Euro Disney But Its Parent's Goofs Weigh the Park Down," *The Wall Street Journal* (March 10, 1994): A12.

and it spent hundreds of millions of dollars on subway and other capital improvements for the park. For example, Paris's express subway was extended out to the park; a 35-minute ride from downtown cost about $2.50. A new railroad station for the high-speed Train a Grande Vitesse was built only 150 yards from the entrance gate. This enabled visitors from Brussels to arrive in only 90 minutes. And when the English Channel tunnel opened in 1994, even London was only 3 hours and 10 minutes away. Actually, Euro Disney was the second largest construction project in Europe, second only to construction of the English Channel tunnel.

Financing

Euro Disney cost $4.4 billion. Table 6.3 shows the sources of financing, in percentages. The Disney Company had a 49 percent stake in the project, which was the most that the French government would allow. For this stake it invested $160 million, while other investors contributed $1.2 billion in equity. The rest was financed by loans from the government, banks, and special partnerships formed to buy properties and lease them back.

The payoff for Disney began after the park opened. The company receives 10 percent of Euro Disney's admission fees and 5 percent of the food and merchandise revenues. This is the same arrangement as Disney has with the Japanese park. But in the Tokyo Disneyland, the company took no ownership interest, opting instead only for the licensing fees and a percentage of the revenues. The reason for the conservative position with Tokyo Disneyland was that Disney money was heavily committed to building the Epcot Center in Florida. Furthermore, Disney had some concerns about the Tokyo enterprise. This was the first non-American and the first cold-weather Disneyland. It seemed prudent to minimize the risks. But this turned out to be a significant blunder of conservatism, because Tokyo became a huge success, as the following box discusses in more detail.

TABLE 6.3   Sources of Financing for Euro Disney (percent)

Total to Finance: $4.4 billion	*100%*
Shareholders equity, including $160 million from Walt Disney Company	32
Loan from French government	22
Loan from group of 45 banks	21
Bank loans to Disney hotels	16
Real estate partnerships	9

Source: Euro Disney.

Commentary: The full flavor of the leverage is shown here, with equity comprising only 32 percent of the total expenditure.

INFORMATION BOX

THE TOKYO DISNEYLAND SUCCESS

Tokyo Disneyland opened in 1983 on 201 acres in the eastern suburb of Urazasu. It was arranged that an ownership group, Oriental Land, would build, own, and operate the theme park with advice from Disney. The owners borrowed most of the $650 million needed to bring the project to fruition. Disney invested no money but receives 10 percent of the revenues from admission and rides and 5 percent of sales of food, drink, and souvenirs.

Although the start was slow, Japanese soon began flocking to the park in great numbers. By 1990 some 16 million a year passed through the turnstiles, about one-fourth more than visited Disneyland in California. In fiscal year 1990, revenues reached $988 million with profits of $150 million. Indicative of the Japanese preoccupation with things American, the park serves almost no Japanese food, and the live entertainers are mostly American. Japanese management even apologizes for the presence of a single Japanese restaurant inside the park: "A lot of elderly Japanese came here from outlying parts of Japan, and they were not very familiar with hog dogs and hamburgers."[4]

Disney executives were soon to realize the great mistake they made in not taking substantial ownership in Tokyo Disneyland. They did not want to make the same mistake with Euro Disney.

Would you expect the acceptance of the genuine American experience in Tokyo to be indicative of the reaction of the French and Europeans? Why or why not?

---

[4] James Sterngold, "Cinderella Hits Her Stride in Tokyo," *The New York Times* (Feb. 17, 1991): 6.

Special Modifications

With the experiences of the previous theme parks, and particularly that of the first cold-weather park in Tokyo, Disney construction executives were able to bring state-of-the-art refinements to Euro Disney. Exacting demands were placed on French construction companies, and a higher level of performance and compliance resulted than many thought possible to achieve. The result was a major project on time, if not completely on budget. In contrast, the Channel tunnel was plagued by delays and severe cost overruns.

One of the things learned from the cold-weather project in Japan was that more needed to be done to protect visitors from such weather problems as wind, rain, and cold. Consequently, Euro Disney's ticket booths were protected from the elements, as were the lines waiting for attractions and even the moving sidewalk from the 12,000-car parking area.

Certain French accents—and British, German, and Italian accents as well—were added to the American flavor. The park has two official languages, English and French, but multilingual guides are available for Dutch, Spanish, German, and

Italian visitors. Discoveryland, based on the science fiction of France's Jules Verne, is a new attraction. A theater with a full 360-degree screen acquaints visitors with a sweep of European history. And, not the least modification for cultural diversity, Snow White speaks German, and the Belle Notte Pizzeria and Pasticceria are right next to Pinocchio.

Disney had foreseen that it might encounter some cultural problems. This was one of the reasons for choosing Robert Fitzpatrick as Euro Disney's president. He is American but speaks French, knows Europe well, and has a French wife. However, he was unable to establish the rapport needed and was replaced in 1993 by a French native. Still, some of his admonitions that France should not be approached as if it were Florida fell on deaf ears.

RESULTS

As the April 1992 opening approached, the company launched a massive communications blitz aimed at publicizing the fact that the fabled Disney experience was now accessible to all Europeans. Some 2,500 people from various print and broadcast media were lavishly entertained while being introduced to the new facilities. Most media people were positively impressed with the inauguration and with the enthusiastic spirit of the staffers. These public relations efforts, however, were criticized by some for being heavy-handed and for not providing access to Disney executives.

As 1992 wound down after the opening, it became clear that revenue projections were, unbelievably, not being met. But the opening turned out to be in the middle of a severe recession in Europe. European visitors, perhaps as a consequence, were far more frugal than their American counterparts. Many packed their own lunches and shunned the Disney hotels. For example, a visitor named Corine from southern France typified the "no spend" attitude of many: "It's a bottomless pit," she said as she, her husband, and their three children toured Euro Disney on a 3-day visit. "Every time we turn around, one of the kids wants to buy something."[5] Perhaps investor expectations, despite the logic and rationale, were simply unrealistic.

Indeed, Disney had initially priced the park and the hotels to meet revenue targets and had assumed demand was there, at any price. Park admission was $42.25 for adults—higher than at the American parks. A room at the flagship Disneyland Hotel at the park's entrance cost about $340 a night, the equivalent of a top hotel in Paris. It was soon averaging only a 50 percent occupancy. Guests were not staying as long or spending as much on the fairly high-priced food and merchandise. We can label the initial pricing strategy at Euro Disney as *skimming pricing*. The following box discusses skimming and its opposite, penetration pricing.

Disney executives soon realized they had made a major miscalculation. Whereas visitors to Florida's Disney World often stayed more than 4 days, Euro Disney—with

---

[5] "Ailing Euro Disney May Face Closure," *Cleveland Plain Dealer* (Jan. 1, 1994): E1.

INFORMATION BOX

SKIMMING AND PENETRATION PRICING

A firm with a new product or service may be in a temporary monopolistic situation, If there is little or no present and potential competition, more latitude in pricing is possible. In such a situation (and, of course, Euro Disney was in this situation), one of two basic and opposite approaches may be taken in the pricing strategy: skimming or penetration.

Skimming is a relatively high-price strategy. It is the most tempting where the product or service is highly differentiated because it yields high per-unit profits. It is compatible with a quality image. But it has limitations. It assumes a rather inelastic demand curve, in which sales will not be appreciably affected by price. And if the product or service is easily imitated (which was hardly the case with Euro Disney), then competitors are encouraged because of the high profit margins.

The penetration strategy of low prices assumes an elastic demand curve, with sales increasing substantially if prices can be lowered. It is compatible with economies of scale, and it discourages competitive entry. The classic example of penetration pricing was the Model T Ford. Henry Ford lowered his prices to make the car within the means of the general public, expanded production into the millions, and in so doing realized new horizons of economies of scale.

Euro Disney correctly saw itself in a monopoly position; it correctly judged that it had a relatively inelastic demand curve with customers flocking to the park regardless of rather high prices. What it did not reckon with was the shrewdness of European visitors: Because of the high prices they shortened their stay, avoided the hotels, brought their own food and drink, and bought only sparingly the Disney merchandise.

What advantages would a lower price penetration strategy have offered Euro Disney? Do you see any drawbacks?

---

one theme park compared to Florida's three—was proving to be a 2-day experience at best. Many visitors arrived early in the morning, rushed to the park, staying late at night, then checked out of the hotel the next morning before heading back to the park for one final exploration.

The problems of Euro Disney were not public acceptance (despite the earlier critics). Europeans loved the place. Since the opening it attracted just under 1 million visitors a month, thus easily achieving the original projections. Such patronage made it Europe's biggest paid tourist attraction. But the large numbers of frugal patrons did not come close to enabling Disney to meet revenue and profit projections and cover a bloated overhead.

Other operational errors and miscalculations, most of these cultural, hurt the enterprise. A policy of serving no alcohol in the park caused consternation in a country where wine is customary for lunch and dinner. (This policy has since been reversed.) Disney thought Monday would be a light day and Friday a heavy one and allocated staff accordingly, but the reverse was true. It found great peaks and valleys in attendance: The number of visitors per day in the high season could be ten times the number in slack times. The need to lay off employees during quiet periods came up against France's inflexible labor schedules.

One unpleasant surprise concerned breakfast. "We were told that Europeans don't take breakfast, so we downsized the restaurants," recalled one executive. "And guess what? Everybody showed up for breakfast. We were trying to serve 2,500 breakfasts at 350-seat restaurants. The lines were horrendous."[6]

Disney failed to anticipate another demand, this time from tour bus drivers. Restrooms were built for 50 drivers, but on peak days 2,000 drivers were seeking the facilities. "From impatient drivers to grumbling bankers, Disney stepped on toe after European toe."[7]

For the fiscal year ending September 30, 1993, the amusement park had lost $960 million, and the future of the park was in doubt (as of December 31, 1993, the cumulative loss was 6.04 billion francs, or $1.03 billion). Walt Disney made $175 million available to tide Euro Disney over until the next spring. Adding to the problems of the struggling park were heavy interest costs. As depicted in Table 6.3, against a total cost of $4.4 billion, only 32 percent of the project was financed by equity investment. Some $2.9 billion was borrowed primarily from 60 creditor banks, at interest rates running as high as 11 percent. Thus, the enterprise began heavily leveraged, and the hefty interest charges greatly increased the overhead to be covered from operations. Serious negotiations began with the banks to restructure and refinance.

ATTEMPTS TO RECOVER

The $921 million lost in the first fiscal year represented a shortfall of more than $2.5 million a day. The situation was not quite as dire as these statistics would seem to indicate. Actually, the park was generating an operating profit, but nonoperating costs were bringing it deeply into the red.

Still, operations were far from satisfactory, although they were becoming better. It had taken 20 months to smooth out the wrinkles and adjust to the miscalculations about demand for hotel rooms and the willingness of Europeans to pay substantial prices for lodging, meals, and merchandise. Operational efficiencies were slowly improving.

By the beginning of 1994, Euro Disney had been made more affordable. Prices of some hotel rooms were cut—for example, at the low end, from $76 per night to $51. Expensive jewelry was replaced by $10 T-shirts and $5 crayon sets. Luxury sit-down restaurants were converted to self-service. Off-season admission prices were reduced from $38 to $30. And operating costs were reduced 7 percent by streamlining operations and eliminating over 900 jobs.

Efficiency and *economy* became the new watchwords. Merchandise in stores was pared from 30,000 items to 17,000, with more of the remaining goods being pure

[6] Gumbel and Turner, "Fans Like Euro Disney." A12.

[7] *Ibid.*

U.S. Disney products. (The company had thought that European tastes might prefer more subtle items than the garish Mickey and Minnie souvenirs, but this was found not so.) The number of different food items offered by park services was reduced more than 50 percent. New training programs were designed to remotivate the 9,000 full-time permanent employees, to make them more responsive to customers and more flexible in their job assignments. Employees in contact with the public were given crash courses in German and Spanish.

Still, as we have seen, the problem had not been attendance, although the recession and the high prices had reduced it. Some 18 million people passed through the turnstiles in the first 20 months of operation. But they were not spending money as people did in the U.S. parks. Furthermore, Disney had alienated some European tour operators with its high prices, and it diligently sought to win them back.

Management had hoped to reduce the heavy interest overhead by selling the hotels to private investors. But the hotels had an occupancy rate of only 55%, making them unattractive to investors. Although the recession was a factor in such low occupancy rates, a significant part of the problem lay in the calculation of lodging demands. With the park just 35 minutes from the center of Paris, many visitors stayed in town. About the same time as the opening, the real estate market in France collapsed, making the hotels unsalable in the short term. This added to the overhead burden and confounded the business plan forecasts.

While some analysts were relegating Euro Disney to the cemetery, few remembered that Orlando's Disney World showed early symptoms of being a disappointment. Costs were heavier than expected, and attendance was below expectations. But Orlando's Disney World turned out to be one of the most profitable resorts in North America.

PROGNOSIS

Euro Disney had many things going for it, despite the disastrous early results. In May 1994 a station on the high-speed rail running from southern to northern France opened within walking distance of Euro Disney. This should help fill many of the hotel rooms too ambitiously built. The summer of 1994, the 50th anniversary of the Normandy invasion, brought many people to France. Another favorable sign for Euro Disney was the English Channel tunnel's opening in 1994, which potentially could bring a flood of British tourists.

Furthermore, the recession in Europe was bound to end, and with it should come renewed interest in travel. As real estate prices become more favorable, hotels can be sold and real estate development around the park spurred.

Even as Disney Chairman Michael Eisner threatened to close the park unless lenders restructured the debt, Disney increased its French presence, opening a Disney store on the Champs Elysees. The likelihood of a Disney pullout seemed remote, despite the posturing of Eisner, since royalty fees could be a sizable source of revenues even if the park only breaks even after servicing its debt. With only a 3.5 percent increase in revenues in 1995 and a 5 percent increase in 1996, these could yield $46 million in royalties for the parent company. "You can't ask, 'What does Euro Disney mean in 1995?' You have to ask, 'What does it mean in 1998?'"[8]

ANALYSIS

Euro Disney, as we have seen, fell far short of expectations in the first 20 months of its operation, so far short that its continued existence was even questioned. What went wrong?

External Factors

A serious economic recession that affected all of Europe undoubtedly was a major impediment to meeting expectations. As noted before, it adversely affected attendance—although still not all that much— but drastically affected spending patterns. Frugality was the order of the day for many visitors. The recessions also affected real estate demand and prices, thus saddling Disney with hotels it had hoped to sell at profitable prices to eager investors to take the strain off its hefty interest payments.

The company assumed that European visitors would not be greatly different from those visitors, foreign and domestic, of U.S. Disney parks. Yet, at least in the first few years of operation, visitors were much more price conscious. This suggested that those within a 2- to 4-hour drive of Euro Disney were considerably different from the ones who traveled overseas, at least in spending ability and willingness.

Internal Factors

Despite the decades of experience with the U.S. Disney parks and the successful experience with the new Japan park, Disney still made serious blunders in its operational planning, such as the demand for breakfasts, the insistence on wine at meals, the severe peaks and valleys in scheduling, and even such mundane things as sufficient restrooms for tour bus drivers. It had problems in motivating and training its French employees in efficiency and customer orientation. Did all these mistakes reflect an intractable French mindset or a deficiency of Disney management? Perhaps both. But Disney management should have researched all cultural differences more thoroughly. Further, the park needed major streamlining of inventories and operations after the opening. The mistakes suggested an arrogant mindset by Disney management: "We were arrogant," concedes one executive. "It was like 'We're building the Taj Mahal and people will come—on our terms.'"[9]

The miscalculations in hotel rooms and in pricing of many products, including food services, showed an insensitivity to the harsh economic conditions. But the greatest mistake was taking on too much debt for the park. The highly leveraged situation burdened Euro Disney with such hefty interest payments and overhead that the breakeven point was impossibly high, and it even threatened the viability of the enterprise. See the following box for a discussion of the important inputs and implications affecting break-even, and how these should play a role in strategic planning.

---

[8] Lisa Gubernick, "Mickey N'est pas Fini," *Forbes* (Feb. 14, 1994): 43.

[9] Gumbel and Turner, "Fans Like Euro Disney," A12.

INFORMATION BOX

THE BREAKEVEN POINT

A breakeven analysis is a vital tool in making go/no go decisions about new ventures and alternative business strategies. This can be shown graphically as follows:

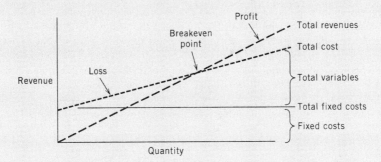

Below the breakeven point, the venture suffers losses; above it, the venture becomes profitable.

Let us make a hypothetical comparison of Euro Disney with its $1.6 billion in high interest loans (some of these as high as 11 percent) from the banks, and what the situation might be with more equity and less borrowed funds.

For this example, let us assume that other fixed costs are $240 million, that the average interest rate on the debt is 10 percent, and that average profit margin (contribution to overhead) from each visitor is $32. Now let us consider two scenarios: (a) the $1.6 billion of debt; and (b) only $0.5 billion of debt.

The number of visitors needed to breakeven are determined as follows:

$$\text{Breakeven} = \frac{\text{Total fixed costs}}{\text{Contribution to overhead}}$$

Scenario (a): Interest = 10% ($1,600,000,000) = $160,000,000
Fixed costs = Interest + $240,000,000
= 160,000,000 + 240,000,000
= $400,000,000

$$\text{Breakeven} = \frac{\$400,000,000}{\$32} = 12,500,000 \text{ visitors needed to breakeven}$$

Scenario (b) Interest = 10% (500,000,000) = $50,000,000
Fixed costs = 50,000,000 + 240,000,000
= $290,000,000

$$\text{Breakeven} = \frac{\$290,000,000}{\$32} = 9,062,500 \text{ visitors needed to breakeven}$$

(continues)

THE BREAKEVEN POINT *(continued)*

Because Euro Disney expected 11 million visitors the first year, it obviously was not going to breakeven while servicing $1.6 billion in debt with $160 million in interest charges per year. The average visitor would have to be induced to spend more, thereby increasing the average profit or contribution to overhead.

In making go/no go decisions, many costs can be estimated quite closely. What cannot be determined as surely are the sales figures. Certain things can be done to affect the breakeven point. Obviously it can be lowered if the overhead is reduced, as we saw in scenario b. Higher prices also result in a lower breakeven because of greater per customer profits (but would probably affect total sales quite adversely). Promotion expenses can be either increased or decreased and affect the breakeven point, but they probably also have an impact on sales. Some costs of operation can be reduced, thus lowering the breakeven. But the hefty interest charges act as a lodestone over an enterprise, greatly increasing the overhead and requiring what may be an unattainable breakeven point.

Does a new venture have to break even or make a profit the first year to be worth going into? Why or why not?

Were such mistakes and miscalculations beyond what we would expect of reasonable executives? Probably not, with the probable exception of the crushing burden of debt. Any new venture is susceptible to surprises and the need to streamline and weed out its inefficiencies. While we would have expected such to have been done faster and more effectively from a well-tried Disney operation, European, and particularly French and Parisian, consumers and employees showed different behavior and attitude patterns than expected.

The worst sin that Disney management and investors could make would be to give up on Euro Disney and not to look ahead 2 to 5 years. A hint of the future promise was Christmas week of 1993. Despite the first year's $920 million in red ink, some 35,000 packed the park most days. A week later on a cold January day, some of the rides still had 40-minute waits.

POSTSCRIPT

On March 15, 1994, an agreement was struck aimed at making Euro Disney profitable by September 30, 1995. The European banks would fund another $500 million and make concessions such as forgiving 18 months' interest and deferring all principal payments for three years. In return, Walt Disney Company agreed to spend about $750 million to bail out its Euro Disney affiliate. Thus, the debt would be halved, with interest payments greatly reduced. Disney also agreed to eliminate for five years the lucrative management fees and royalties it received on the sale of tickets and merchandise.[10]

---

[10] Brian Coleman and Thomas R. King, "Euro Disney Rescue Package Wins Approval," *The Wall Street Journal* (March 15, 1994): A3, A5.

The problems of Euro Disney were not resolved by mid-1994. The theme park and resort near Paris remained troubled. However, a new source for financing had emerged: A member of the Saudi Arabian royal family had agreed to invest up to $500 million for a 24 percent stake in Euro Disney. Prince Alwaleed had shown considerable sophistication in investing in troubled enterprises in the past. Now, his commitment to Euro Disney showed a belief in the ultimate success of the resort.[11]

Finally, in the third quarter of 1995, Euro Disney posted its first profit, some $35 million for the period. This compared with a year earlier loss of $113 million. By now, Euro Disney was only 39 percent owned by Disney. It attributed the turnaround partly to a new marketing strategy in which prices were slashed both at the gate and within the theme park in an effort to boost attendance, and also to shed the nagging image of being overpriced. A further attraction was the new "Space Mountain" ride that mimicked a trip to the moon.

However, some analysts questioned the staying power of such a movement into the black. In particular, they saw most of the gain coming from financial restructuring in which the debt-ridden Euro Disney struck a deal with its creditors to temporarily suspend debt and royalty payments. A second theme park and further property development were seen as essential in the longer term, as the payments would eventually resume.[12]

In August 1995 news broke of Walt Disney Company's proposed $10 billion acquisition of Capital Cities/ABC Inc. Experts said this would be an entertainment behemoth into the next century. Although many growth avenues were now possible, including great international growth in television programming and distribution such as ESPN and the Disney Channel, theme parks were considered very promising. Disney Chairman Michael Eisner announced possibilities of new theme parks in South America, possibly Brazil, as well as in Asia. He noted that Disney executives were scouring the globe looking for potential sites and partners in countries from Spain to China.[13]

In November 1997, *Forbes* magazine updated the situation with Euro Disney—although it had been renamed Disneyland Paris—under the provocative title, "Mickey's Last Laugh (Once Struggling Euro Disney Has Become a Favorite Tourist Destination in Europe)." The article noted that it had 11.7 million visitors in 1996, up from 8.8 million three years before. Cash flow margins had tripled since 1993, and even exceeded those of Tokyo Disneyland, the world's most popular park. The turnaround was credited to lower prices, the big new Space Mountain ride, and the 1994 restructuring that included the cash infusion from Prince Alwaleed.[14]

---

[11] Richard Turner and Brian Coleman, "Saudi to Buy as Much as 24% of Euro Disney," *The Wall Street Journal* (June 2, 1994): A3.

[12] Brian Coleman, "Euro Disney Posts Its First Profit, $35.3 Million for Its Third Quarter," *The Wall Street Journal,* July 26, 1995, p. A9.

[13] Lisa Bannon, "Expanded Disney to Look Overseas for Fastest Growth," *The Wall Street Journal,* August 2, 1995, p. A3.

[14] "Mickey's Last Laugh," *Forbes* (November 3, 1997), p. 16.

WHAT CAN BE LEARNED?

Beware the arrogant mindset, especially when dealing with new situations and new cultures. French sensitivities were offended by Disney corporate executives who often turned out to be brash, insensitive, and overbearing. A contentious attitude by Disney personnel alienated people and aggravated planning and operational difficulties. "The answer to doubts or suggestions invariably was, 'Do as we say, because we know best.'"[15]

Such a mindset is a natural concomitant to success. It is said that success breeds arrogance, but this inclination must be fought against by those who would spurn the ideas and concerns of others. For a proud and touchy people, the French, this almost contemptuous attitude by the Americans fueled resentment and glee at Disney miscues. It did not foster cooperation, understanding, or the willingness to smooth the process. One might almost speculate that had not the potential economic benefits to France been so great, the Euro Disney project might never have been approved.

Great success may be ephemeral. We often find that great successes are not lasting, that they have no staying power. Somehow the success pattern gets lost or forgotten or is not well rounded. Other times an operation grows beyond the capability of the originators. Hungry competitors are always in the wings, ready to take advantage of any lapse. As we saw with Euro Disney, having a closed mind to new ideas or to needed revisions of an old success pattern—the arrogance of success—makes expansion into different environments more difficult and even risky.

While corporate Disney has continued to have strong success with its other theme parks and its diversifications, competitors are moving in with their own theme parks in the United States and elsewhere. We may question whether this industry is approaching saturation, and we may wonder whether Disney has learned from its mistakes in Europe.

Highly leveraged situations are extremely vulnerable. During most of the 1980s, many managers, including corporate raiders, pursued a strategy of debt financing in contrast to equity (stock ownership) financing. Funds for such borrowing were usually readily available, heavy debt had income tax advantages, and profits could be distributed among fewer shares so that return on equity was enhanced. During this time a few voices decried the overleveraged situations of many companies. They predicted that when the eventual economic downturn came, such firms would find themselves unable to meet the heavy interest burden. Most lenders paid little heed to such lonesome voices and encouraged greater borrowing.

The widely publicized problems of some of the raiders in the late 1980s, such as Robert Campeau, who had acquired major department store corporations only to find himself overextended and unable to continue, suddenly changed some expansionist lending sentiments. The hard reality dawned that

---

[15] Gumbel and Turner, "Fans Like Euro Disney," A1.

these arrangements were often fragile indeed, especially when they rested on optimistic projections for asset sales, for revenues, and for cost savings to cover the interest payments. An economic slowdown hastened the demise of some of these ill-advised speculations.

Disney was guilty of the same speculative excesses with Euro Disney, relying far too much on borrowed funds and assuming that assets, such as hotels, could be easily sold off at higher prices to other investors. As we saw in the breakeven box, hefty interest charges from such overleveraged conditions can jeopardize the viability of the enterprise if revenue and profit projections fail to meet the rosy expectations.

Be judicious with the skimming price strategy. Euro Disney faced the classical situation favorable for a skimming price strategy. It was in a monopoly position, with no equivalent competitors likely. It faced a somewhat inelastic demand curve, which indicated that people would come almost regardless of price. So why not price to maximize per-unit profits? Unfortunately for Disney, the wily Europeans circumvented the high prices by frugality. Of course, a severe recession exacerbated the situation.

The learning insight from this example is that a skimming price assumes that customers are willing and able to pay the higher prices and have no lower-priced competitive alternatives. It is a faulty strategy when many customers are unable, or else unwilling, to pay the high prices and can find a way to experience the product or service in a modest way.

CONSIDER

Can you think of other learning insights from this case?

QUESTIONS

1. How could the company have erred so badly in its estimates of the spending patterns of European customers?

2. How could a better reading of the impact of cultural differences on revenues have been achieved?

3. What suggestions do you have for fostering a climate of sensitivity and goodwill in corporate dealings with the French?

4. How do you account for the great success of Tokyo Disneyland and the problems of Euro Disney? What are the key contributory differences?

5. Do you believe that Euro Disney might have done better if located elsewhere in Europe rather than just outside Paris? Why or why not?

6. "Mickey Mouse and the Disney park are an American cultural abomination." Evaluate this critical statement.

7. A deficiency in the planning was neglecting to win over European travel people, such as travel agents, tour guides, even bus drivers. How might this be corrected now?

HANDS-ON EXERCISES

Before

1. It is three months before the grand opening. As a staff assistant to the president of Euro Disney, you sense that the plans for high prices and luxury accommodations are ill-advised. What arguments would you marshal to persuade the company to offer lower prices and more moderate accommodations? Be as persuasive as you can.

After

2. It is six months after opening. Revenues are not meeting target, and a number of problems have surfaced and are being worked on. The major problem remains, however, that the venture needs more visitors and/or higher expenditures per visitor. Develop plans to improve the situation.

TEAM DEBATE EXERCISE

It is two years after the opening. Euro Disney is a monumental mistake, profitwise. Two schools of thought are emerging for improving the situation. One is to pour more money into the project, build one or two more theme parks, and really make this another Disney World. The other camp believes more investment would be wasted at this time, that the need is to pare expenses to the bone and wait for an eventual upturn. Debate the two positions.

INVITATION TO RESEARCH

Has the recent profitability of Euro Disney continued? Are expansion plans going ahead? Have other theme parks been announced? Did the Disney merger with Capital Cities/ABC take place?

CHAPTER SEVEN

Scott Paper, Sunbeam, and Al Dunlap

Al Dunlap was hired in July 1996 by two large Sunbeam investors to turn Sunbeam around. He had gained a reputation as a turnaround artist extraodinaire, most recently from his efforts at Scott Paper. His philosophy was to cut to the bone, and the press frequently called him "Chainsaw Al." He met his comeuppance with Sunbeam. In the process, his philosophy came under bitter attack. But was his strategy all that bad?

ALBERT J. DUNLAP

Dunlap wrote an autobiography, *Mean Business*, of his business philosophy and how it had evolved. He grew up in the slums of Hoboken, the son of a shipyard worker, and was imbued with the desire to make something of himself. He played football in high school and graduated from West Point. A former army paratrooper, he was known as a quick hitter, a ruthless cost cutter, a tough boss. But he got results, at least short-term.

In 1983, he became chief executive of Lily Tulip Co., a maker of disposable cups that was heavily in debt after a buyout. Dunlap quickly exhibited the management philosophy that was to make him famous. He slashed costs, decimating the headquarters staff, closing plants, and selling the corporate jet. When he left in the mid-1980s, the company was healthy. In the latter 1980s, Dunlap became the number-one operations man for Sir James Goldsmith, a notorious raider of corporations. Dunlap was involved in restructuring Goldsmith's acquisitions of Crown-Zellerbach and International Diamond. In 1991, he worked on a heavily debt-laden Australian conglomerate, Consolidated Press Holdings. Two years later, after his "chainsaw approach," Consolidated Press was 100 divisions lighter and virtually free of debt.

By now Dunlap was a wealthy man, having made close to $100 million on his various restructurings. Still, at 56, he was hardly ready to retire. When the board of Scott Paper heard that he was available, they wooed him, even purchasing his $3.2 million house in Florida from him.

SCOTT PAPER—A SICK COMPANY—AND DUNLAP'S RESULTS

An aged Scott Paper was reeling in the early 1990s. Per-share earnings had dropped 61 percent since 1989 on flat sales growth. In 1993, the company had a $277 million loss.

Part of the problem stemmed from Scott's commercial paper division, S. D. Warren. In 1990, the company spent to increase capacity at Warren. Unfortunately, the timing could not have been worse. One of the worst industry slumps since the Great Depression was just beginning. Three subsequent "restructurings" had little positive effect.

Table 7.1 shows the decline in sales from 1990 through 1993. Table 7.2 shows the net income and loss during these four years. Of even more concern was Scott's performance relative to the major competitors Procter & Gamble and Kimberly-Clark during these four years. Table 7.3 shows the comparisons of profits as a percent of sales, with Scott again showing up most poorly. Undoubtedly this was a company needing fixing.

In characteristic fashion, Dunlap acted quickly once he took over as chief executive officer on April 19, 1994. That same day, to show his confidence and commitment, he invested $2 million of his own money in Scott. A few months later, after the stock had appreciated 30 percent, he invested another $2 million.

Only hours on the job, Dunlap offered three of his former associates top positions in the company. On the second day, he disbanded the powerful management committee. On the third day, he fired 9 of the 11 highest-ranking executives. To com-

TABLE 7.1   Sales of Scott, 1990–1993 (billions)

1990	$3.9
1991	3.8
1992	3.9
1993	3.6
Total change, 1990–1993	(7.7%)

Source: Company annual reports.

Commentary: The company's deteriorating sales come at a time of great economic growth and advancing revenues for most firms.

TABLE 7.2   Net Income of Scott and Percent of Sales, 1990–1993

	(millions)	% of sales
1990	$148	3.8%
1991	(70)	(1.8)
1992	167	4.3
1993	(277)	(7.7)

Source: Company annual reports.

Commentary: The company's erratic profit picture, culminating in the serious loss of 1993, deserved deep concern, which it received.

TABLE 7.3 **Profit as a Percentage of Sales: Scott, Kimberly-Clark, and Procter & Gamble, 1990–1993**

	1990	1991	1992	1993
Scott	3.8%	(1.8%)	4.3%	(7.7%)
P & G	6.6	6.6	6.4	(2.1)°
Kimberly-Clark	6.8	7.5	1.9	7.3

Source: Company annual reports.

° Extraordinary charges reflecting accounting changes

Commentary: Scott again shows up badly against its major competitors, both in the low percentage of earnings to sales and their severe fluctuations into earnings losses.

plete his blitzkrieg, on the fourth day he destroyed four bookshelves crammed with strategic plans of previous administrations.

Can such drastic and abrupt changes be overdone? Should change be introduced more slowly and with more reflection? See the following issue box for a discussion of this.

ISSUE BOX

HOW SOON TO INTRODUCE DRASTIC CHANGES?

Some new administrators believe in instituting major changes as quickly as possible. They reason that an organization is expecting this and is better prepared to make the adjustments needed than it ever will be again. Such managers are often referred to as gunslingers, who "shoot from the hip." Other managers believe in moving more slowly, gathering more information, and taking action only when all the pros and cons can be weighed. But sometimes such delays can lull an organization into a sense of false calm, and make for even more trauma when the changes eventually come.

Relevant to the issue of moving swiftly or slowly is the health of the entity. If a firm is sick, in drastic need of help, we would expect a new manager to move more quickly and decisively. A firm doing well, although perhaps not as well as desired, reasonably should not require such drastic and abrupt disruption.

It has always baffled me how a fast-acting executive can acquire sufficient information to make the crucial decisions of who to fire and who to retain and what operations need to be pruned and which supported—all within a few days. Of course, operating statistics can be studied before formally taking charge. But the causes of the problems or successes—the whys—can hardly be understood so soon.

Boards, investors, and creditors want a fast turnaround. Waiting months before taking action to fix a sick company is not acceptable. However, not all companies are easily fixable. For example, Borden, a food and chemical conglomerate, has gone through the fifth restructuring in six years, with little improvement. But maybe Borden needed an Albert Dunlap, the person with a clear vision and a willingness to clean house. And, yes, a supportive board.

Do you think Dunlap acted too hastily in his initial sweeping changes? Playing the devil's advocate (one who takes an opposing view for the sake of debate), support a position that he did indeed act far too hastily.

At the annual meeting in June, barely two months after assuming command, Dunlap announced four major goals for the first year. First, he vowed to divest the company of nonstrategic assets, most notably S. D. Warren, the printing and publishing papers subsidiary, that had received major expansion funding only a few years before. Second he would develop a core team of accomplished senior managers. Third, Scott was to be brought to "fighting trim" through a one-time-only global restructuring. Last, he promised to develop new strategies for marketing Scott products around the world.

In one of the largest relative restructurings in corporate America, more than 11,000 positions out of a total of 25,900 were eliminated around the world. This included 71 percent of the headquarters staff, 50 percent of the salaried employees, and 20 percent of the production workers. Such draconian measures certainly cut costs. But were they overdone? Might such cuts potentially have detrimental long-term consequences? Please see the following issue box for a discussion of this.

In addition to cutting staff, Dunlap sought to reduce other costs, including outsourcing some operations and services. If these could be provided cheaper by other firms, then they should be farmed out. Dunlap announced that with the restructuring completed by year-end, pre-tax savings of $340 million were expected.[1]

By late fall of 1994, Dunlap's plans to divest the company of nonstrategic assets bore fruit. S. D. Warren was sold for $1.6 billion to an international investment group. Other asset sales generated more than $2 billion, with as much as $3 billion expected when completed. This enabled Dunlap to lower debt by $1.5 billion and repurchase $300 million in Scott stock. This led to the credit rating being upgraded.

ISSUE BOX

HOW DEEP TO CUT?

Bloated bureaucratic organizations are the epitome of inefficiency and waste, whether in business corporations or in governmental bodies, including school systems. Administrative overhead might even exceed actual operating costs. But remedies can be overdone, they can go too far. In Scott's case, was the axing of 11,000 employees out of 25,900 overdone?

Although we are not privy to the needed cost/productivity records, we can raise some concerns. Did the massive layoffs go well beyond fat and bloat into bone and muscle? If so, future operations might be jeopardized. Another concern ought to be: Does an organization owe anything to its loyal and long-standing employees, or should they simply be considered pawns in the pursuit of maximizing profits? Where do we draw the line between efficiency and responsibility to faithful employees? And even to the community itself?

You may want to consider some of these questions and issues. They are current in today's downsizing mindset.

---

[1] The New Scott, 1994 Annual Report, p. 5.

The results of Dunlap's efforts were impressive indeed. Second quarter earnings rose 71 percent; third quarter earnings increased 73 percent, the best quarterly performance for Scott in four years. Fourth quarter earnings were 159 percent higher than in 1993, establishing an all-time quarterly record. For the whole year, net income increased 82 percent over the previous year. And the stock price performance since April 19, when Dunlap took over, stood at the top 1 percent of major companies traded on the New York Stock Exchange.[2]

Still, the cost-slashing was not helping market share. In the fiscal year ended April 2, 1995, Scott's bath-tissue sales in key U.S. markets slipped 1 percent, while in paper towels, Scott lost 5.2 percent in sales.[3]

On July 17, 1995, Dunlap's efforts to make Scott an attractive acquisition candidate were capped by Kimberly-Clark's $7.36 billion offer for the firm. In the process, Dunlap himself would be suitably rewarded, leaving far richer than after any of his seven previous restructuring efforts. But Dunlap insisted, "I am still the best bargain in corporate America."[4]

THE SUNBEAM CHALLENGE

Sunbeam is a maker of blenders, electric blankets, and gas grills. These old-line products had shown little growth potential, and revenues and profits languished. After the well-publicized turnaround success of Dunlap, it was not surprising he was courted for the top job at Sunbeam, and he entered the fray with gusto.

The day he was hired, Sunbeam stock rose 50 percent, "on faith." It eventually rose 300 percent. With his customary modus operandi he terminated half of Sunbeam's 12,000 employees and cut back its product offerings. Gone were such items as furniture and bed linens, and efforts were concentrated on things like grills, humidifiers, and kitchen appliances. In 1996, he took massive writeoffs amounting to $338 million, of which almost $100 million was inventory.

In 1997, it looked like Dunlap was accomplishing another of his patented "miracles." Sales were up 22 percent to $1.168 billion, while income had risen from a loss of $196 million the previous year to a gain of $123 million in 1997. For stockholders this translated into earnings per share of $1.41 from $2.37 loss in 1996. Table 7.4 shows the trend in revenues and income of Sunbeam through 1997.

In October 1997, barely a year on the job, Dunlap announced that the turnaround was complete and that he was seeking a buyer for Sunbeam. Stockholders had much to be pleased about. From a low of $12 a share in 1996, the price had risen to $50. Unfortunately, this high price for Sunbeam stock took it out of the range for any potential buyer; $50 gave a market capitalization of $4.6 billion, or four times revenues, a multiple reserved for only a few of the premier companies. So, for the time being the stockholders were stuck with Dunlap.

[2] *Ibid.*, p. 6.

[3] Joseph Weber and Paula Dwyer, "Scott Rolls Out a Risky Strategy," *Business Week* (May 22, 1995), p. 48.

[4] Joann S. Lublin and Steven Lipin, "Scott Paper's 'Rambo in Pin Stripes' Is on the Prowl for Another Company to Fix" *The Wall Street Journal* (July 18, 1995), p. B1.

TABLE 7.4   **Trend of Sunbeam Revenues and Income, 1991–1997**

	1991	1992	1993	1994	1995	1996	1997
				(Millions $)			
Revenues	886	967	1,066	1,198	1,203	964	1,168
Net Income	47.4	65.6	88.8	107	50.5	−196	123

Source: Company annual reports.

Commentary: Dunlap came on the scene in July 1996, the year that Sunbeam incurred $196 million in losses. The $123 million profit for 1997 showed a remarkable and awesome recovery, and would seemingly make Dunlap a hero with his slash-and-burn strategy. Unfortunately, a reaudit did not confirm these figures. The inaccurate figures were blamed on questionable accounting, including prebooking sales and incorrectly assigning costs to the restructuring. The auditors said the company overstated its loss for 1996, and overstated profits for 1997. The revised figures showed a loss of $6.4 million for 1997, instead of the $123 million profit. (*Sources:* Martha Brannigan, "Sunbeam Audit to Repudiate '97 Turnaround," *The Wall Street Journal,* October 20 1998, p. A3; and "Audit Shows Sunbeam's Turnaround Really a Bust," *Cleveland Plain Dealer,* October 21, 1998, pp. 1-C and 2-C.)

Since he was not successful in selling the company, Dunlap went on a buying binge. He began talking about his "vision," with such words as "We have moved from constraining categories to expanding categories. Small kitchen appliances become kitchen appliances. We'll move from grills to outdoor cooking. Health care moves from just a few products to a broad range of products."[5]

So, he bought Coleman Company, Signature Brands and its Mr. Coffee, and First Alert for an aggregate of approximately $2.4 billion in cash and stock. Part of this was financed with $750 million of convertible debentures, as well as $60 million of accounts receivable that were sold to raise cash. Critics maintained he had paid too much for these, especially the $2.2 billion for money losing Coleman. The effect of these acquisitions on Sunbeam's balance sheet was sobering if any stockholders had looked closely.

When Dunlap took over Sunbeam, though it was performing poorly, it had only $200 million in debt. By 1998, Sunbeam was over $2 billion in debt, and its net worth had dropped from $500 million to a negative $600 million.[6]

THE DEBACLE OF 1998, AND THE DEMISE OF DUNLAP

The first quarter of 1998 showed a complete reversal of fortunes. Revenues were down and a first-quarter loss was posted of $44.6 million—all this far below expectations. Sunbeam's stock price plunged 50 percent, from $53 to $25. By midsummer it was to reach a low of $4.62.

Dunlap conceded that he and top executives had concentrated their attention too much on "sealing" the acquisitions of Coleman and the two smaller companies, allow-

[5] As quoted in Holman W. Jenkins, Jr., "Untalented Al? The Sorrows of a One-Trick Pony," *The Wall Street Journal* (June 24, 1998), p. A19.

[6] Matthew Schifrin, "The Unkindest Cuts," *Forbes* (May 4, 1998), p. 45.

ing underlings to offer "stupid, low-margin deals" on outdoor cooking grills. He pointed to glitches with new products, a costly recall, and El Niño. "People don't think about buying outdoor grills during a storm," he said. "Faced with sluggish sales, a marketing executive offered excessive discounts," he further said. More job cuts were promised, through eliminating one-third of the jobs at the newly acquired companies.[7]

On Monday, June 15, after deliberating over the weekend, Sunbeam's board abruptly fired Al Dunlap, having "lost confidence in his ability to carry out the long-term growth potential of the company."[8] Now a legal fight ensued as to what kind of severance package, if any, Dunlap deserved as a consequence of his firing. A severance package for Mr. Dunlap would be "obscene—an obscenity on top of an obscenity, capitalism gone crazy," said Michael Cavanaugh, union leader.[9] Other comments were reported in the media; a sampling is in the following information box.

INFORMATION BOX

THE POPULARITY OF "CHAINSAW" AL DUNLAP

Not surprising, the slashing policy of Dunlap did not bring him a lot of friends, even though he may have been admired in some circles. The following are some comments reported in the press, immediately following his firing:

> He finally got what he's been doing to a lot of people. It was a taste of his own medicine. (union representative)
> I'm happy the son-of-a-bitch is fired. (former supervisor)
> Somebody at that company finally got some sense. (small-town mayor)
> I couldn't think of a better person to deserve it. It tickled me to death. We may need to have a rejoicing ceremony. (small-town mayor)
> I guess the house of cards came tumbling down … when you reduce your workforce by 50 percent, you lose your ability to manage. (former plant manager)

Is there a lesson to be learned from such comments as these? Perhaps it is that the human element in organizations and communities needs to be considered.

Taking a devil's advocate position (one who takes an opposing viewpoint for the sake of argument and full discussion), defend the philosophy of Dunlap.

Sources: Thomas W. Gerdel, "Workers at Glenwillow Plant Cheer Firing of 'Chainsaw' Al," *Cleveland Plain Dealer* (June 16, 1998), 2-C; and "No Tears for a Chainsaw," *The Wall Street Journal* (June 16, 1998), p. B1.

---

[7] James R. Hagerty and Martha Brannigan, "Sunbeam Plans to Cut 5,100 Jobs as CEO Promises Rebound from Dismal Quarter," *The Wall Street Journal* (May 12, 1998), pp. A3 and A4.

[8] Martha Brannigan and James Hagerty, "Sunbeam, Its Prospects Looking Ever Worse, Fires CEO Dunlap," *The Wall Street Journal* (June 15, 1998), pp. A1 and A14.

[9] Martha Brannigan and Joann S. Lublin, "Dunlap Faces a Fight Over His Severance Pay," *The Wall Street Journal* (June 16, 1998), p. B3.

After Dunlap's departure, some accounting irregularities began coming to light. At the end of a three-month audit, the "turnaround" that Dunlap announced for 1997 apparently was tainted. Rather than a turnaround, the good results came from improper accounting moves that adversely affected 1996 and 1998 results, while making 1997, the first full year of Dunlap's leadership, seem far better than it really was. The restated numbers showed that Sunbeam actually had a small operating loss in 1997, while 1996 showed a modest profit.

The inaccurate figures came from dubious accounting, including premature booking sales in 1997 that should have been 1998, incorrectly assigning certain costs to the restructuring, as well as certain other questionable accounting irregularities. Dunlap denied any involvement or knowledge of such matters and that any accounting changes by the auditors were "judgment calls" on matters subject to interpretation.[10]

ANALYSIS

Was Dunlap's Management Style of "Slash and Burn" Appropriate?

We see conflicting evidence in the Scott and Sunbeam cases. Without doubt, he achieved his goal to make Scott an attractive acquisition candidate, and thus reward shareholders and himself. That he did this so quickly seems a strong endorsement of his strategy for turning around sick companies—simply decimate the organization, sell off all ancillary units, cut costs to the bone, and virtually force the company into increased profitability.

The flaw with this reasoning is that it tends to boost short-term performance at the expense of the longer term. Morale and dedication of surviving employees are often devastated. Vision and innovative thinking may be impeded, since the depleted organization lacks time and commitment to deal effectively with more than day-to-day basic operations.

His strategy backfired with Sunbeam. When he couldn't sell the company after massaging the performance statistics for 1997, he was left with a longer-term management challenge, and he was by no means up to this. It is ironic that his reputation for turning around sick companies acted against him with Sunbeam. Investors were so confident of his ability to quickly turn around the company that they bid up the price so high that no one would buy it. And they were stuck with Dunlap.

Yet, many firms have become too bureaucratic, burdened with high overhead and chained to established policies and procedures. Such organizations desperately need paring down, eliminating bloated staff and executive levels, and, not the least, curbing the red tape that destroys flexibility and creativity.

The best answer lies in moderation, cutting the dead wood, but not bone and muscle. The worst scenario is to cut with little investigation and reflection. This cost-

---

[10] Martha Brannigan, "Sunbeam Slashes Its 1997 Earnings in Restatement," *The Wall Street Journal* (October 21, 1998), p. B23.

cutting climate may degenerate to the extent that worthy operations and individuals are pruned regardless of their merit and future promise.

Dunlap's credentials describe a short-term hero, but one with no record of longer-term commitment. We are left to question his staying power, and what we saw with the handling of Sunbeam is damning.

Did the Affliction Require Such Drastic Changes?

Sales of both Scott and Sunbeam were flat, with profit performance deteriorating. Stock prices were falling counter to a bull market, and investors were disillusioned. Did such situations call for draconian measures?

Perhaps, but not necessarily. Neither company was in danger of going belly-up. True, they both were off the growth path, but their brands were still well regarded by consumers. Would less drastic actions have turned around these companies? Maybe, but an ingrained, powerful bureaucracy that is stifling efficiency often requires a complete overhaul if things are to be turned around; moderate efforts just will not do it.

Creeping Bureaucracy

As a firm experiences years of reasonable success and viability, it tends to spawn bureaucratic excesses. The following information box discusses the bureaucratic type of organization.

INFORMATION BOX

THE BUREAUCRATIC ORGANIZATION

The bureaucratic organization is a natural consequence of size and age. Its characteristics include the following:

A clear-cut division of labor

A strict hierarchy of authority

Staffing by technical competence

Formal rules and procedures

Impersonal approaches to decision making[11]

Although a well-structured organization would appear to be best in many circumstances, it tends to be too rigid. It relies heavily on rules and procedures and as a result is often slow to adapt to change. Red tape usually predominates, as do many layers of hierarchy, an abundance of staff, and overspecialization. Consequently, creativity and initiative are stifled, and communication between upper management and lower operations is cumbersome and often distorted. Perhaps even more serious, a bureaucratic

(continues)

THE BUREAUCRATIC ORGANIZATION *(continued)*

organization, with its entrenched administrators and staff positions, has a built-in high overhead that makes it difficult to compete against low-cost competitors.

A bureaucratic organization does not have to be inevitable as a firm attains large size and dominance, as shown in Table 7.5: a firm can still mold itself as an adaptive organization. But the temptation is otherwise.

TABLE 7.5   Contrasts of Bureaucratic and Adaptive Organizations

Organizational Aspects	Bureaucratic	Adaptive
Hierarchy of authority	Centralized	Decentralized
Rules and procedures	Many	Few
Division of labor	Precise	Open
Spans of control	Narrow	Wide
Coordination	Formal and impersonal	Informal and personal

Can you identify the type of person who tends to work best in a bureaucracy? The one who performs worst in this setup?

[11] This section is adapted from John R. Schermerhorn, Jr., *Management* 6th ed. (New York: Wiley, 1999), pp. 75, 223.

We can suspect that Scott fitted this mode. After all, Dunlap eliminated 71 percent of the headquarters staff. Perhaps the cuts were too deep, but maybe this was a bureaucracy grown top heavy and badly needing pruning. The natural consequence of too many administrators and staff people is a company failing to respond well to a changing environment and burdened with overhead too high to enable it to match prices of more lean and aggressive competitors. So while some may disagree with the extent of cost cutting, paring down probably was needed.

Was the same thing true with Sunbeam? Perhaps not to the same extreme, although without detailed records we cannot know for sure. We can suspect, however, that Dunlap, caught up in his success at Scott, simply transferred his strategy to Sunbeam with little consideration of their differences. Can we call this "slashing by formula"? This suggests a rigid mindset devoid of flexibility or compassion.

Paying Too Much for Acquisitions

We see in both Scott and Sunbeam the likelihood that too much was paid for acquisitions. Dunlap quickly sold off the S. D. Warren unit of Scott, and it added $1.6 billion to Scott coffers. But doesn't this mean that someone else thought it was highly attractive with good potential? Could they be right?

Luck can also play a part. Previous Scott management, for example, invested heavily in what seemed a reasonable diversification into commercial paper, only to encounter an unexpected industry downturn. How can you predict this? Was Warren worth keeping? Perhaps sufficient research would have found this out.

With Sunbeam, Dunlap made three questionable acquisitions, and burdened the firm with several billions of dollars of debt. The Coleman acquisition, in particular, caused him grave problems and led to his at least tacitly encouraging some questionable accounting practices to try to bring more revenues into 1997, the year he was hoping to convince investors to buy the company.

WHAT CAN BE LEARNED?

How to jumpstart a languid organization Can we find any keys to stimulating an organization not performing up to potential? or maybe even to inspire it to perform beyond its potential? The challenge is not unlike that of motivating a discouraged and downtrodden athletic team to rise up and have faith in itself and recommit itself to quality of performance.

In both athletics and business, the common notion is that personnel changes have to be made. Dunlap introduced the idea of severe downsizing. But this is controversial, and in view of Dunlap's problems with Sunbeam, almost discredited. So how much should be cut, how quickly should changes be made and how sweeping should they be, and what kind of information is most vital in making such decisions? Furthermore, there is the question of morale and its importance in any restoration.

We find more art than science in this mighty challenge of restoration. In particular, the right blend or degree of change is crucial. Let us look at some considerations:

How much do we trim? In most revival situations, some pruning of personnel and operations is necessary. But how much is too much, and how much is not enough? Is an ax always required for a successful turnaround? One would hope not. Certainly those personnel who are not willing to accept change may have to be let go. And weak persons and operations that show little probability of improvement need to be pruned, just as the athlete who can't seem to perform up to expectations may have to be let go. Still, it is often better to wait for sufficient information as to the "why" of poor performance, before assigning blame for the consequences.

How long do we wait? Mistakes can be made both in taking action before all the facts are known, and in waiting too long. If the changemaker procrastinates for weeks, an organization that at first was psychologically geared to major change might find it more traumatic and disruptive.

What Role Does Strategic Planning Play? Major actions should hardly be taken without *some* research and planning, but strategic plans too often delay change implementation. They tend to be the products of a fumbling bureaucracy and of some abdication of responsibility. (Despite the popularity of strategic planning, it often is a vehicle for procrastination and blame-dilution: "I simply followed the strategy recommendations of the consultants.") Dunlap had an aversion to strategic planning, seeing this as indicative of a top-heavy bureaucratic organization. Perhaps he was right on this, when carried to an extreme. But going into an organization and heedlessly slashing positions without due regard for the individuals involved and the potential is akin to "shooting from the hip," with little regard for careful aiming. Then there is the matter of morale.

Morale considerations. Major restructuring usually is demoralizing to the organizations involved. The usual result is massive layoffs and forced retirements, complete reassignment of people, traumatic personnel and policy changes, and destruction of accustomed lines of communication and authority. This is hardly conducive to preserving stability and morale and any faint spark of teamwork. (You may want to review the Continental Air case for how Gordon Bethune achieved an amazing revitalization of employee morale.)

Moderation is usually best. Much can be said for moderation, for choosing the middle position, for example, between heavy cost-cutting and little cost-cutting. Of course, the condition of the firm is a major consideration. One on the verge of bankruptcy, unable to meet its bills, needs drastic measures promptly. But the problems both of Scott and Sunbeam were by no means so serious. More moderate action could have been taken.

It is better to view the restoration challenge as a *time for building rather than tearing down.* This focuses attention more on the longer view than on short-term results that may come back to haunt the firm, as well as the changemaker, like Dunlap.

Periodic housecleaning produces competitive health. In order to minimize the buildup of dead wood, all aspects of an organization periodically ought to be objectively appraised. Weak products and operations should be pruned, unless solid justification exists for keeping them. Such justification might include good growth prospects or complementing other products and operations or even providing a desired customer service. In particular, staff and headquarters personnel and functions should be scrutinized, perhaps every five years, with the objective of weeding out the redundant and superfluous. Most important, these "axing" evaluations should be done objectively, with decisive actions taken where needed. While some layoffs may result, they might not be necessary if suitable transfers are possible.

CONSIDER

Can you add any additional learning insights?

QUESTIONS

1. "Periodic evaluations of personnel and departments aimed at pruning cause far too much harm to the organization. Such 'axing' evaluations should themselves be pruned." Argue this position as persuasively as you can.

2. Now marshal the most persuasive arguments for such "axing" evaluations.

3. Describe a person's various stages of morale and dedication to the company as it goes through a restructuring, with massive layoffs expected and realized, but with the person finding himself or herself one of the survivors. How, in your opinion, would this affect productivity and loyalty?

4. Is it likely that any decades-old organization will be bloated with excessive bureaucracy and overhead? Why or why not?

5. What decision guides should be used to determine which divisions and subsidiaries are to be divested or sold?

6. What arguments would you make in a time of restructuring for keeping your particular business unit? Which are likely to be most persuasive to an administration committed to a program of heavy pruning?

HANDS-ON EXERCISES

1. You are one of the nine high-ranking executives fired by Dunlap his third day on the job. Describe your feelings and your action plan at this point. (If you want to make some assumptions, state them specifically.)

2. You are one of the two high-level executives kept by Dunlap as he sweeps into office. Describe your feelings and your likely performance on the job.

3. You are one of the three outsiders brought into Scott vice-presidential jobs by Dunlap. You have worked for him before and must have impressed him. Describe your feelings and your likely performance on the job. What specific problems, if any, do you foresee?

TEAM DEBATE EXERCISE

It is early 1996. The board of Sunbeam is considering bringing in a turnaround team. One is the team of Dunlap, which argues for major and rapid change. Another team under consideration is Clarence Ripley's, who advocates more modest immediate changes. Array your arguments and present your positions as persuasively as possible. Attack the recommendations of the other side as aggressively as possible. We are talking about millions of dollars in fees and compensation at stake for the winning team.

INVITATION TO RESEARCH

What is Dunlap up to after being fired by the Sunbeam board in mid-1998? Has he gracefully retired? Is he still fighting for severance pay? Who replaced Dunlap, and how well is he doing? Are his policies much different from Dunlap's?

CHAPTER EIGHT

Contrast—Southwest Airlines: Finding a Strategic Window of Opportunity

In 1992 the airlines lost a combined $2 billion, matching a dismal 1991, and bringing their three-year red ink total to a disastrous $8 billion. Three carriers—TWA, Continental, and America West—were operating under Chapter 11 bankruptcy, and others were lining up to join them. But one airline, Southwest, was profitable as well as rapidly growing, with a 25 percent sales increase in 1992 alone. Interestingly enough, this was a low-price, bare-bones operation run by a flamboyant CEO, Herb Kelleher. Kelleher had found a niche, a strategic window of opportunity, and oh, how he milked it! See the following box for further discussion of a strategic window of opportunity and its desirable accompaniment, a SWOT analysis.

HERBERT D. KELLEHER

Herb Kelleher impresses people as an eccentric. He likes to tell stories, himself often the butt, and many involve practical jokes. He admits he is sometimes a little scatterbrained. In his cluttered office, he displays a dozen ceramic wild turkeys as a testimonial to his favorite brand of whiskey. He regularly smokes five packs of cigarettes a day. As an example of his zaniness, he painted one of his 737s to look like a killer whale to celebrate the opening of Sea World in San Antonio. Another time, during a flight he had flight attendants dress up as reindeer and elves while the pilot sang Christmas carols over the loudspeaker as he gently rocked the plane. Kelleher is a "real maniac," said Thomas J. Volz, vice president of marketing at Braniff Airlines. "But who can argue with his success?"[1]

The son of a Campbell Soup Company executive, Kelleher grew up in Haddon Heights, New Jersey. He graduated from Wesleyan University and New York University Law School. In 1961 he moved to San Antonio, where his father-in-law

---

[1] Kevin Kelly, "Southwest Airlines: Flying High with 'Uncle Herb,'" *Business Week* (July 3, 1989), p. 53.

INFORMATION BOX

STRATEGIC WINDOW OF OPPORTUNITY AND SWOT ANALYSIS

A strategic window is an opportunity in the marketplace, one that is currently neglected by competitors and one that fits well with the firm's competencies. Strategic windows often last for only a short time (although Southwest's strategic window has been much more durable) before they are filled by alert competitors.

Strategic windows are usually found by systematically analyzing the environment, examining the threats and opportunities it holds. The competencies of the firm, its physical and financial resources, and, not the least, its people resources—management and employees and their strengths and weaknesses—should also be assessed. The objective is to determine what actions might be appropriate for that particular enterprise and its orientation. This is commonly known as a SWOT analysis: analyzing strengths and weaknesses of the firm and opportunities and threats in the environment.

Although SWOT analysis may be a formal part of the planning process, it may also be informal and even intuitive. We suspect that Herb Kelleher instinctively sensed a strategic window in short hauls and low prices. While he must have recognized the danger that his bigger competitors would try to match his prices, he believed that with his simplicity of operation he would be able to make a profit while bigger airlines were racking up losses.

Why do you think the major airlines overlooked the possibilities in short hauls at low prices?

helped him set up a law firm, and in 1968, he and a group of investors put up $560,000 to found Southwest. Of this amount, Kelleher contributed $20,000.

In the early years Kelleher was the general counsel and a director of the fledgling enterprise. But in 1978 he was named chairman, although he had no managerial experience, and in 1981 he became CEO. His flamboyance soon made him the most visible aspect of the airline, and he starred in most of its TV commercials. A rival airline, America West, charged in ads that Southwest passengers should be embarrassed to fly such a no-frills airline, whereupon Kelleher appeared in a TV spot with a bag over his head. He offered the bag to anyone ashamed to fly Southwest, suggesting it could be used to hold "all the money you'll save flying us."[2]

Kelleher knew many of his employees by name, and they called him "Uncle Herb" or "Herbie." He held weekly parties for employees at corporate headquarters, and he encouraged such antics by his flight attendants as organizing trivia contests, delivering instructions in rap, and awarding prizes for the passengers with the largest holes in their socks. But such wackiness had a shrewd purpose: to generate a gungho spirit to boost productivity. "Herb's fun is infectious," said Kay Wallace, president

---

[2] *Ibid.*

of the Flight Attendants Union Local 556. "Everyone enjoys what they're doing and realizes they've got to make an extra effort."[3]

THE BEGINNINGS

Southwest was conceived in 1967 on a napkin, according to folklore. Rollin King, a client of Kelleher, then a lawyer, had an idea for a low-fare, no-frills airline to fly between major Texas cities. He doodled a triangle on the napkin, labeling the points Dallas, Houston, and San Antonio.

The two tried to go ahead with their plans but were stymied for more than three years by litigation, battling Braniff, Texas International, and Continental over the right to fly. In 1971 Southwest won, and it went public in 1975. At that time it had four planes flying between the three cities. Lamar Muse was president and CEO from 1971 until he was fired by Southwest's board in 1978. At that point the board of directors tapped Kelleher.

At first Southwest was in the throes of life and death low-fare skirmishes with its giant competitors. Kelleher liked to recount how he came home one day "beat, tired, and worn out. So I'm just kind of sagging around the house when my youngest daughter comes up and asks what's wrong. I tell her, 'Well, Ruthie, it's these damned fare wars.' And she cuts me right off and says, 'Oh, Daddy, stop complaining. After all, you started 'em.'"[4]

For most small firms, competing on a price basis with much larger, well-endowed competitors is tantamount to disaster. The small firm simply cannot match the resources and staying power of such competitors. Yet Southwest somehow survived. Not only did it initiate the cut-throat price competition, but it achieved cost savings in its operation that the larger airlines could not. How long would the big carriers be content to maintain their money-losing operations and match the low prices of Southwest?

In its early years, Southwest faced other legal battles, such as Dallas and Love Field. The original airport, Love Field, is close to downtown Dallas, but it could not geographically expand although air traffic was increasing mightily. A major new facility, Dallas/Fort Worth International Airport, consequently replaced it in 1974. This airport boasted state-of-the-art facilities and enough room for foreseeable demand, but it had one major drawback: It was 30 minutes further from downtown Dallas. Southwest was able to avoid a forced move to the new airport and to continue at Love, but in 1978, competitors pressured Congress to bar flights from Love Field to anywhere outside Texas. Southwest was able to negotiate a compromise, now known as the Wright Amendment, that allowed flights from Love Field to the four states contiguous to Texas. In retrospect, the Wright Amendment forced onto Southwest a key ingredient of its later success: the strategy of short flights.[5]

---

[3] Richard Woodbury, "Prince of Midair," *Time* (January 25, 1993), p. 55.

[4] Charles A. Jaffe, "Moving Fast by Standing Still," *Nation's Business* (October 1991), p. 58.

[5] Bridget O'Brian, "Southwest Airlines Is a Rare Air Carrier: It Still Makes Money," *The Wall Street Journal* (October 28, 1992), p. A7.

GROWTH

Southwest grew steadily but not spectacularly through the 1970s. It dominated the Texas market by appealing to passengers who valued price and frequent departures. Its one-way fare between Dallas and Houston, for example, was $59 in 1987 versus $79 for unrestricted coach flights on other airlines.

In the 1980s Southwest's annual passenger traffic count tripled. At the end of 1989, its operating costs per revenue mile—the industry's standard measure of cost-effectiveness—was just under 10 cents, about 5 cents per mile below the industry average.[6] Although revenues and profits were rising steadily, especially compared with the other airlines, Kelleher took a conservative approach to expansion, financing it mostly from internal funds rather than debt.

Perhaps the caution stemmed from an ill-fated acquisition in 1986. Kelleher bought a failing long-haul carrier, Muse Air Corporation, for $68 million and renamed it TransStar. (This firm had been founded by Lamar Muse after he left Southwest.) But by 1987 TransStar was losing $2 million a month, and Kelleher shut down the operation.

By 1993 Southwest had spread to 34 cities in 15 states. It had 141 planes, and each made 11 trips per day. It used only fuel-thrifty 737s and still concentrated on flying large numbers of passengers on high-frequency, one-hour hops at bargain fares (average $58). Southwest shunned the hub-and-spoke systems of its larger rivals and took its passengers directly from city to city, often to smaller satellite airfields rather than congested major metropolitan fields. With rock-bottom prices and no amenities, it quickly dominated most new markets it entered.

As an example of the company's impact on a new market, Southwest came to Cleveland, Ohio, in February 1992, and by the end of the year was offering 11 daily flights. In 1992 Cleveland Hopkins Airport posted record passenger levels, up 9.74 percent from 1991. "A lot of the gain was traffic that Southwest Airlines generated," noted John Osmond, air trade development manager.[7]

In some markets Southwest found itself growing much faster than projected, as competitors either folded or else abandoned directly competing routes. For example, in Phoenix, Arizona, America West Airlines cut back service in order to conserve cash after a Chapter 11 bankruptcy filing. Southwest picked up the slack, as it did in Chicago when Midway Airlines folded in November 1992. And in California, Southwest's arrival led several large competitors to abandon the Los Angeles–San Francisco route, unable to meet Southwest's $59 one-way fare. Before Southwest fares had been as high as $186 one way.[8]

Now cities that Southwest did not serve were petitioning for service. For example, Sacramento sent two county commissioners, the president of the chamber of commerce and the airport director, to Dallas to petition for service. Kelleher consented a few months later. In 1991 the company received 51 similar requests.[9]

---

[6] Jaffe, *op. cit.*, p. 58.

[7] "Passenger Flights Set Hopkins Record," *Cleveland Plain Dealer* (January 30, 1993), p. 3D.

[8] O'Brian, *op. cit.*, p. A7.

[9] *Ibid.*

A unique situation was developing. On many routes Southwest's fares were so low that they competed with buses and even with private cars. By 1991 Kelleher did not even see other airlines as his principal competitors: "We're competing with the automobile, not the airlines. We're pricing ourselves against Ford, Chrysler, GM, Toyota, and Nissan. The traffic is already there, but it's on the ground. We take it off the highway and put it on the airplane."[10]

Tables 8.1, 8.2, and 8.3 and Figure 8.1 depict various aspects of Southwest's growth and increasingly favorable competitive position. Although total revenues of Southwest were still far less than the four major airlines in the industry (five if we count Continental, which has emerged from two bankruptcies), its growth pattern presages a major presence, and its profitability is second to none.

Tapping California

The formidable competitive power of Southwest was perhaps never better epitomized than in its 1990 invasion of populous California. By 1992 it had become the second largest player, after United, with 23 percent of intrastate traffic. Southwest achieved this position by pushing fares down as much as 60 percent on some routes. The big carriers, which had tended to surrender the short-haul niche to Southwest in

TABLE 8.1   Growth of Southwest Airlines: Various Operating Statistics, 1982–1991

Year	Operating Revenues (000,000)	Net Income (000,000)	Passengers Carried (000)	Passenger Load Factor
1991	$1,314	$26.9	22,670	61.1%
1990	1,187	47.1	19,831	60.7
1989	1,015	71.6	17,958	62.7
1988	880	58.0	14,877	57.7
1987	778	20.2	13,503	58.4
1986	769	50.0	13,638	58.8
1985	680	47.3	12,651	60.4
1984	535	49.7	10,698	58.5
1983	448	40.9	9,511	61.6
1982	331	34.0	7,966	61.6

Source: Company annual reports.

Commentary: Note the steady increase in revenues and in numbers of passengers carried. Although the net income and load factor statistics show no appreciable improvement, these statistics are still in the vanguard of an industry that has suffered badly in recent years. See Table 8.2 for a comparison of revenues and income with the major airlines.

[10] Subrata N. Chakravarty, "Hit 'Em Hardest with the Mostest," *Forbes* (September 16, 1991), p. 49.

TABLE 8.2   Comparison of Southwest's Growth in Revenues and Net Income with Major Competitors, 1987–1991

	1991	1990	1989	1988	1987	% 5-yr gain
Operating Revenue Comparisons ($ millions)						
American	$9,309	$9,203	$8,670	$7,548	$6,369	46.0
Delta	8,268	7,697	7,780	6,684	5,638	46.6
United	7,850	7,946	7,463	7,006	6,500	20.8
Northwest	4,330	4,298	3,944	3,395	3,328	30.1
Southwest	1,314	1,187	1,015	860	778	68.9
Net Income Comparisons ($ millions)						
American	(253)	(40)	412	450	225	
Delta	(216)	(119)	467	286	201	
United	(175)	73	246	426	22	
Northwest	10	(27)	116	49	64	
Southwest	27	47	72	58	20	

Source: Company annual reports.

Commentary: Southwest's revenue gains over these five years outstripped those of its largest competitors. Although the percentage gains in profitability are hardly useful because of the erratic nature of airline profits during these years, Southwest stands out starkly as the only airline to be profitable each year.

other markets, suddenly faced a real quandary in competing in this "Golden State." Some described Southwest as a "500 pound cockroach, too big to stamp out."[11]

The California market was indeed enticing. Some 8 million passengers each year fly between the five airports in metropolitan Los Angeles and the three in the San Francisco Bay area, this being the busiest corridor in the United States. It was also one

TABLE 8.3   Market Share Comparison of Southwest and Its Four Major Competitors, 1987–1991 (in $ billions)

	1991	1990	1989	1988	1987
Total Revenues:					
American, Delta, United, Northwest	$29,757	$29,144	$27,857	$24,633	$21,835
Southwest Revenues	$1,314	$1,187	$1,015	$860	$778
Percent of big four	4.4	4.1	3.6	3.5	3.6
Increase in Southwest's market share, 1987–1991: 22%					

Source: Company annual reports.

[11] Wendy Zellner, "Striking Gold in the California Skies," *Business Week* (March 30, 1992), p. 48.

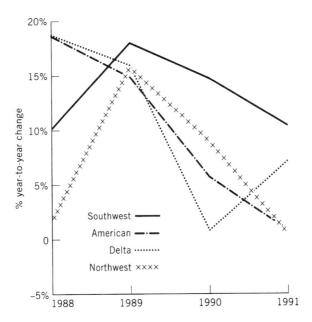

Figure 8.1 Year-to-year percentage changes in revenues, Southwest and three major competitors, 1988–1991.

of the more expensive, because the low fares of AirCal and Pacific Southwest Airlines had been eliminated when these two airlines were acquired by American and US Air.

Southwest charged into this situation with low fares and frequent flights. While airfares dropped, total air traffic soared 123 percent in the quarter Southwest entered the market. Competitors suffered: American lost nearly $80 million at its San Jose hub, and US Air lost money even though it cut service drastically. United, the market leader, quit flying the San Diego–Sacramento and Ontario–Oakland routes where Southwest had rapidly built up service. The quandary of the major airlines was compounded because this critical market fed traffic into the rest of their systems, especially the lucrative transcontinental and trans-Pacific routes. The competitors could hardly abdicate California to Southwest. American, for one, considered creating its own no-frills shuttle for certain routes.[12] Could anyone stop Southwest, with its formula of lowest prices and lowest costs and frequent schedules? And, oh yes, its good service and fun?

INGREDIENTS OF SUCCESS

Southwest's operation under Kelleher had numerous distinctive characteristics contributing to its success pattern and its seizing of a strategic window of opportunity,

[12] *Ibid.*

but the key factors appear to be cost containment, employee commitment, and conservative growth.

Cost Containment

Southwest had been the lowest cost carrier in its markets. Even when its larger competitors tried to match its cut-rate prices, they could not do so without incurring sizable losses, unlike Southwest. Nor did they seem able to trim their costs to match Southwest. For example, in the first quarter of 1991, Southwest's operating costs per available seat mile (i.e., the number of seats multiplied by the distance flown) were 15 percent lower than America West's costs, 29 percent lower than Delta's, 32 percent lower than United's, and 39 percent lower than US Air's.[13]

Many aspects of the operation contributed to these lower costs. Because all its planes were a single aircraft type, Boeing 737s, Southwest had low costs of training, maintenance, and inventory. And since a plane earns revenues only when flying, Southwest worked to achieve a faster turnaround time on the ground than any other airline. While competitors take more than an hour to load and unload passengers and to clean and service the planes, about 70 percent of Southwest's flights have a turnaround time of 15 minutes, and 10 percent have even pared the turnaround time to 10 minutes.

In areas of customer service, Southwest curbed costs as well. It offered peanuts and drinks, but no meals. Boarding passes were reusable plastic cards. Boarding time was saved because no seats were assigned. Southwest subscribed to no centralized reservation service. It did not even transfer baggage to other carriers; that was the passengers' responsibility. Admittedly, such customer service frugalities would be less acceptable on longer flights—and this helped to account for the difficulty competing airlines had in cutting their costs to match Southwest's. Still, if the price is right, many passengers might also opt for no frills on longer flights.

Employee Commitment

Kelleher was able to achieve an esprit de corps unmatched by other airlines despite the fact that Southwest employees were unionized. Unlike the adversarial relationship between unions and, for example, Frank Lorenzo at Eastern and Continental Airlines, Southwest was able to negotiate flexible work rules, with flight attendants and even pilots helping with plane cleanup. Employee productivity continued very high, permitting the airline to carry a lean staff. Kelleher resisted the inclination to hire extravagantly when times were good, necessitating layoffs during leaner times, a policy that contributed to employee feelings of security and loyalty. And the low-key attitude and sense of fun that Kelleher engendered helped, perhaps more than anyone could have foreseen. As Kelleher declared, "Fun is a stimulant to people. They enjoy their work more and work more productively."[14]

---

[13] Chakravarty, *op. cit.,* p. 50.

[14] *Ibid.*

Conservative Growth

Not the least of the ingredients of success was the conservative approach to growth that Kelleher maintained. He resisted the temptation to expand vigorously (for example, to seek to fly to Europe or get into head-to-head competition with larger airlines with long-distance routes). Even in the company's geographical expansion, conservatism prevailed. The philosophy of expansion was to do so only when enough resources could be committed to go into a city with 10 to 12 flights a day, rather than just 1 or 2. Kelleher called this "guerrilla warfare," concentrating efforts against stronger opponents in only a few areas rather than dissipating strength by trying to compete everywhere.

UPDATE

In its May 2, 1994 edition, prestigious *Fortune* magazine devoted its cover story to Herb Kelleher and Southwest Airlines. It raised an intriguing question: "Is Herb Kelleher America's best CEO?" It called him a "people-wise manager who wins where others can't."[15] The operational effectiveness of Southwest continued to surpass all rivals: for example, in such productivity ratios as cost per available seat mile, passengers per employee, and employees per aircraft. Only Southwest remained consistently profitable among the big airlines, by the end of 1996 having been profitable for more than 20 years in a row.

Expansion

Late in October 1996, Southwest launched a carefully planned battle for East Coast passengers that would drive down air fares and pressure competitors to back away from some lucrative markets. It chose Providence, Rhode Island, just 60 miles from Boston's Logan Airport, thus tapping the Boston–Washington corridor. The Providence airport escaped the congested New York and Boston air-traffic-control areas, and from the Boston suburbs was hardly a longer trip than to Logan Airport. Experience had shown that air travelers would drive considerable distance to fly with Southwest's cheaper fares.

As Southwest entered new markets, most competitors refused any longer to try to compete pricewise: they simply could not cut costs enough to compete. Their alternative then was either to pull out of these short-haul markets, or be content to let Southwest have its market share while they tried to hold on to other customers by stressing first-class seating, frequent-flyer programs, and other in-flight amenities.

In April 1997, Southwest quietly entered the transcontinental market. From its major connecting point of Nashville, Tennessee, it began nonstops both to Oakland, California and to Los Angeles. With Nashville's direct connections with Chicago, Detroit, Cleveland, Providence, and Baltimore/Washington, as well as points south,

---

[15] Kenneth Labich, "Is Herb Kelleher America's Best CEO?" *Fortune* (May 2, 1994), pp. 45–52.

this afforded *one-stop,* coast-to-coast service, with fares about half as much as the other major airlines.

Two other significant moves were announced in late 1998. One was an experiment. On Thanksgiving Day, a Southwest 737–700 flew *nonstop* from Oakland, California to the Baltimore–Washington Airport, and back again. It provided its customary no-frills service, but a $99 one-way fare, the lowest in the business. The test was designed to see how pilots, flight attendants, and passengers would feel about spending five hours in a 737, with only peanuts and drinks served in-flight. The older 737s lacked the fuel capacity to fly coast-to-coast nonstop, but with Boeing's new 737–700 series this was no problem. The Thanksgiving Day test seemed a precursor of more nonstop flights as Southwest had firm orders for 129 of the new planes to be delivered over the next seven years. This would enable it to compete with the major carriers on their moneymaking transcontinental flights.

In November 1998, plans were also announced for starting service to MacArthur Airport on Long Island, which would enable Southwest to tap into the New York City market.

WHAT CAN BE LEARNED?

The power of low prices and simplicity of operation. If a firm can maintain prices below those of its competitors, and do so profitably and without sacrificing expected quality of service, then it has a powerful advantage. Southwest was able to do this with its simplicity of operation and no-frills, but dependable, service. Competition on the basis of price is seldom used in most industries (although the airline industry has been an exception), primarily because competitors can quickly match prices with no lasting advantage to anyone. As profits are destroyed, only customers benefit, and then only in the short run.

The effectiveness of the cost control of Southwest, however, points out the true competitive importance of low prices. Customers love the lowest-price producer *if* the producer does not sacrifice too much quality, comfort, and service. While there was some sacrifice of service and amenities with Southwest, most customers found this acceptable because of the short-haul situation; friendly, dependable and reasonable service was still maintained. Whether the same no-frills service would be acceptable on longer transcontinental flights remained to be seen.

Another factor regarding the relationship of customer satisfaction and price will be explored in the following box.

The power of a niche strategy. Directing efforts toward a particular customer segment or niche can provide a powerful competitive advantage. Especially is this true if no competitor is catering directly to such a niche, and if it is fairly sizable. Such an untapped niche then becomes a strategic window of opportunity.

Kelleher revealed the niche strategy of Southwest: while other airlines set up hub-and-spoke systems in which passengers are shunted to a few major hubs

INFORMATION BOX

THE KEY TO CUSTOMER SATISFACTION: MEETING CUSTOMER EXPECTATIONS

Southwest consistently earns high ratings for its customer satisfaction, higher than those of its giant competitors. Yet, these major airlines all offer more than Southwest's food-service; they also provide advance seat assignments, in-flight entertainment on longer flights, the opportunity to upgrade, and a comprehensive frequent-flyer program. Yet Southwest gets the highest points for customer satisfaction.

Could something else be involved here?

Let's call this *expectations*. If a customer has high expectations, perhaps because of a high price and/or the advertising promising high-quality, luxury accommodations, dependable service, or whatever, then if product or service does not live up to these expectations, customer satisfaction dives. Turning to the airlines, customers are not disappointed in the service of Southwest because they don't expect luxury; Southwest does not advertise this. They expect no frills, but pleasant and courteous treatment by employees, dependable and safe flights, and the low price. On the other hand, expectations are higher for the bigger carriers with their higher prices. This is well and good for the first or business class service. But for the many who fly coach...?[16]

Do you think there is a point where a low-price/no-frills strategy would be detrimental to customer satisfaction? What might it depend on?

---

[16] This idea of expectations affecting customer satisfaction was suggested by Ed Perkins for Tribune Media Services and reported in "Hotels Must Live Up to Promises," *Cleveland Plain Dealer* (November 1, 1998), p. 11-K.

from which they are transferred to other planes going to their destination, "we wound up with a unique market niche: we are the world's only short-haul, high-frequency, low-fare, point-to-point carrier. ... We wound up with a market segment that is peculiarly ours, and everything about the airline has been adapted to serving that market segment in the most efficient and economical way possible."[17] The following box discusses the criteria needed for a successful niche or segmentation strategy.

Southwest has been unwavering in its pursuit of its niche. While others have tried to copy, none have fully duplicated it. Southwest remains the nation's only high-frequency, short-distance, low-fare airline. As an example of its virtually unassailable position, Southwest accounts for more than two-thirds of the passengers flying within Texas, and Texas is the second largest market outside the West Coast. Now that Southwest has invaded California, some San Jose residents drive an hour north to board Southwest's Oakland flights, skipping the local airport

[17] Jaffe, *op. cit.*, p. 58.

INFORMATION BOX

CRITERIA FOR SELECTING NICHES OR SEGMENTS

In deciding what specific niches to seek, these criteria should be considered:

1. **Identifiability.** Is the particular niche identifiable so that those persons who constitute it can be isolated and recognized? It was not difficult to identify the short-route travelers, and while their numbers may not have been readily estimated initially, this was soon to change as demand burgeoned for Southwest's short-haul services.

2. **Size.** The segment must be of sufficient size to be worth the efforts to tap. And again, the size factor proved to be significant, with Southwest soon offering 83 flights daily between Dallas and Houston.

3. **Accessibility.** For a niche strategy to be practical, the segment(s) chosen must be such that promotional media can be used to reach it without much wasted coverage. Southwest had little difficulty in reaching its target market through billboards, newspapers, and other media.

4. **Growth potential.** A niche is more attractive if it shows some growth characteristics. The growth potential of short-haul flyers proved to be considerably greater than that for airline customers in general. Partly the growth reflected customers won from other higher cost and less convenient airlines. And some of the emerging growth reflected customers choice of giving up their cars to take a flight that was almost as economical and certainly more comfortable.

5. **Absence of vulnerability to competition.** Competition, both present and potential, must certainly be considered in making specific niche decisions. By quickly becoming the low-cost operator in its early routes, and gradually expanding without diluting its cost advantage, Southwest became virtually unassailable in its niche. The bigger airlines, with their greater overhead and less-flexible operations, could not match Southwest prices without going deeply into the red. And the more Southwest became entrenched in its markets, the more difficult it was to pry it loose.

Assume you are to give a lecture to your class on the desirability of a niche strategy, and you cite Southwest as a classic example. But suppose a classmate asks, "If a niche strategy is so great, why didn't the other airlines practice it?" How do you respond?

where American has a hub. And in Georgia, so many people were bypassing Delta's huge hub in Atlanta and driving 150 miles to Birmingham, Alabama, to fly Southwest that an entrepreneur started a van service between the two airports.[18]

Unlike many firms, Southwest has not permitted success to dilute its niche strategy. It has not attempted to fly to Europe or to get into head-to-head compe-

[18] O'Brian, *op. cit.*, p. A7.

tition with larger airlines on longer domestic flights. And it has not sacrificed growth potential in curbing such temptations: Its strategy still has many cities to embrace.

Seek dedicated employees. Stimulating employees to move beyond their individual concerns to a higher level of performance, a true team approach, was one of many of Kelleher's accomplishments. Such an esprit de corps enabled crews to turn planes around in 15 minutes instead of the hour or more it took competitors; it brought a dedication to serving customers far beyond what could ever be expected of a bare-bones, cut-price operation; and it brought a contagious excitement to the job that was obvious to customers and employees alike.

Having such dedicated employees was not due solely to the nurturing of the extrovertive, zany, and down-home Kelleher, although his personality certainly helped. So did company parties, Kelleher's legendary ability to remember employee names, a sincere company, and Kelleher's interest in the employees. Flying in the face of conventional wisdom, which describes the relationship between management and labor as adversarial with the presence of a union, Southwest achieved its great teamwork while being 90 percent unionized.

Whether such a worker dedication can pass the test of time and the test of increasing size is uncertain. Kelleher himself was 62 in 1993, and retirement looms. A successor will have a different personality, yet it is possible for a large organization to maintain employee commitment. In Chapter 13 we will examine the leadership style of Sam Walton and the growth of Wal-Mart to become the largest retailer.

One factor that encourages a dedicated workforce is company growth. A rapidly growing firm—especially an underdog growing from humble beginnings— has an atmosphere of contagious excitement. Opportunities and advancements depend on growth, and employees can acquire stock in the company and see their shares rising. Success tends to create a momentum that generates continued success, yet we know that eventually all organizations will see slowing growth and possibly even decline. IBM and Sears are witnesses to that scenario.

CONSIDER

Can you identify additional learning insights that could be applicable to firms in other situations?

QUESTIONS

1. In what ways might airline customers be segmented? Which segments or niches would you consider to be Southwest's prime targets? Which segments probably would not be?

2. Do you think Southwest employees' dedication will quickly fade when Kelleher leaves? Why or why not?

3. Discuss the pros and cons of expansion of Southwest beyond short hauls. Which arguments do you see as most compelling?

4. Evaluate the effectiveness of Southwest's unions.

5. On August 18, 1993, a fare war erupted. To initiate its new service between Cleveland and Baltimore, Southwest announced a $49 fare (a sizable reduction from the then standard rate of $300). Its rivals, Continental and US Air, retaliated. Before long, the price was $19, not much more than the tank of gas it would take to drive between the two cities—and the airlines also supplied a free soft drink. Evaluate the implications of such a price war for the three airlines.

6. A price cut is the most easily matched strategy, and usually provides no lasting advantage to any competitor. Identify the circumstances when you see it desirable to initiate a price cut and potential price war.

7. Do you think it is likely that Southwest's position will continue to remain unassailable by competitors? Why or why not?

HANDS-ON EXERCISES

1. Herb Kelleher has just retired, and you are his successor. Unfortunately, your personality is quite different from his: You are an introvert and far from flamboyant, and your memory for names is not good. What would be your course of action to try to preserve the great employee dedication of the Kelleher era? How successful do you think you will be? Did the board make a mistake in hiring you?

2. Herb Kelleher has not retired. He is going to continue until at least age 70. Somehow, his appetite for growth has increased as he has grown older, and he has charged you with developing plans for expanding into longer hauls—maybe to South and Central America, maybe even to Europe. Be as specific as you can in developing such expansion plans.

   Kelleher has also asked for your evaluation of these plans. Be as persuasive as you can in presenting this evaluation.

3. How would you feel personally about a 5-hour transcontinental flight with only a few peanuts, and no other food or movies? Would you be willing to pay quite a bit more to have more amenities?

TEAM DEBATE EXERCISE

The Thanksgiving Day nonstop transcontinental experiment went fairly well, although customers and even flight attendants expressed some concern about the long 5-hour flight with no food and no entertainment. No one complained about the price.

   Debate the two alternatives of going ahead slowly with the transcontinental plan with no-frills, or adding a few amenities, such as some food, reading material, or whatever else might make the flight less tedious. You might even want to debate the third alternative of dropping this idea entirely at this time.

INVITATION TO RESEARCH

What is Southwest's current situation? What is its market share in the airline industry? Is it still maintaining a high growth rate? Has the decision been made to expand the nonstop transcontinental service, and have any changes been made in the no-frills service for this?

PART THREE

EXECUTION FLAWS AND ACCOMPLISHMENTS

CHAPTER NINE

The Travails of Nike

On August 27, 1996, the sports world was intrigued at what was in store for Tiger Woods, the 20-year-old golfer who had just won his third consecutive U.S. Amateur championship. He decided to begin his professional career and dropped out of Stanford in what would have been his junior year.

Tiger's pro-golf career started with a contract with Nike worth $40 million. After the signing he was flown in a Gulfstream IV owned by the founder of Nike, Phil Knight, to play in the Greater Milwaukee Open. All this for a young man who had always flown coach class, and had to count his meal money. He had played amateur golf for the last time. Before the year was over he was to win two tournaments and be named by *Sports Illustrated*, "Sportsman of the Year." This was only the beginning, as next spring he won the prestigious Masters on April 13, 1997 by the biggest margin ever achieved, in the most-watched golf finale in the history of television.

With what some thought was a commodity product, one that could command little brand uniqueness, and one that many others saw as only a short-term fad phenomenon, Phil Knight had fashioned for Nike a strategy that put it in the forefront of growth firms and established it as one of the world's great brand names. Among the 1,200 U.S. brands tracked by Young & Rubicam, Nike ranked among the top ten, alongside Coke, Disney, and Hallmark. In the process, Knight became one of the richest Americans, worth $5.3 billion, behind only Bill Gates of Microsoft, Warren Buffett, the investor supreme, and three others.[1] Unfortunately, his wealth diminished to only $3.5 billion in 1998 as Nike met adversity.[2]

PHIL KNIGHT

The founder of the great Nike running machine was himself only a mediocre runner, a miler of modest accomplishments. His best time was a 4:13, hardly in the same league as the below-4:00 world-class runners. But he had trained under the renowned coach Bill Bowerman at the University of Oregon. In late 1950, Bowerman

---

[1] Randall Lane, "You Are What You Wear," *Forbes* (October 14, 1996), p. 42.
[2] "*Forbes* 400 Richest Americans," *Forbes* (October 12, 1998) p. 227.

had put Eugene, Oregon on the map year after year by turning out world-record-setting long-distance runners.

In completing his MBA at Stanford University, Phil wrote a research paper based on his theory that the Japanese could do for athletic shoes what they were doing for cameras, that is, make a cheaper, better product. After receiving his degree in 1960, Knight went to Japan to seek an American distributorship from the Onitsuka Company for Tiger shoes. Returning home, he took samples of the shoes to Bowerman.

In 1964, Knight and Bowerman went into business. They each put up $500 and formed the Blue Ribbon Shoe Company, sole U.S. distributor of Tiger running shoes. They put their inventory in Knight's father-in-law's basement, and sold $8,000 worth of these imported shoes that first year. Knight worked by days as a Coopers & Lybrand accountant, while at night and on weekends he peddled these shoes mostly to high school athletic teams.

Knight and Bowerman worried that Tiger would find a more established distributor, and so they developed their own shoe and the brand name, Nike, after the Greek winged goddess of victory. At the same time they introduced the "swoosh" logo, described in the following information box. The Nike shoe's first appearance in competition came during the 1972 Olympic trials in Eugene, Oregon. Marathon runners persuaded to wear Nikes placed fourth through seventh, whereas finishers for Adidas—the number-one running footwear-maker in the world—were first, second, and third.

On a Sunday morning in 1975, Bowerman tinkered with his wife's waffle iron and some urethane rubber, and he fashioned a new type of sole, a "waffle" sole whose tiny rubber studs made it more springy than those of other shoes currently on the market. This product improvement—seemingly so simple—gave Knight and Bowerman an initial impetus.

INFORMATION BOX

THE NIKE "SWOOSH" LOGO

The Nike "Swoosh" is one of the world's best-recognized logos. In the very early days of Nike, a local design student at Portland State University was paid $35 for creating it. The curvy, speedy-looking blur turned out to be highly distinctive and has from then on been placed on all Nike products. Phil Knight even had the Swoosh logo tattooed on his left calf. Because it was so familiar, Nike no longer needed to add the name Nike to the logo. (Tiger Woods, in his well-televised charge to win the Las Vegas Invitational Golf Tournament in early October 1996, wore a cap with the swoosh logo discreetly visible.)

The power of the logo made Nike's sponsorship of famous athletes unusually effective as they displayed it in their sports exploits with their shoes and apparel.

In your judgment, do you think Nike could have achieved its present success without this unique but simple logo? In other words, how important is a good logo to a firm?

THE INITIAL CHARGE OF NIKE

The new sole brought 1976 sales to $14 million, up from $8.3 million the year before, and from only $2 million in 1972.

Now Nike was off and running, and was to stay in the forefront of the industry with its careful research and development of new products. By the end of the decade, Nike employed almost 100 people in research and development. It offered more than 140 different models, many of these the most technologically advanced on the market. This diversity came from models designed for different foot types, body weights, running speeds, training schedules, sexes, and levels of skill.

By 1981, Nike led all athletic shoe makers, with 50 percent of the total market. Adidas, the decades-long market leader, saw its share of the market fall well below that of Nike. Demand for Nikes was so great that 60 percent of its 8,000 department stores, sporting goods, and shoe store retailers gave advance orders, often waiting six months for delivery.

In the January 4, 1982 edition of *Forbes* in the "Annual Report on American Industry," Nike was rated number one in profitability over the previous five years, ahead of all other firms in all other industries.

A LETDOWN AND THEN REJUVENATION

By the latter 1980s, however, Reebok had emerged as Nike's greatest competitor, and threatened its dynasty. Nike had underestimated an opportunity. Consequently, it was late with shoes for the aerobic dancing that was sweeping the country, fueled by best-selling books by Jane Fonda and others. Reebok was first with an athletic shoe designed especially for women. Between 1986 and 1987, Nike's sales dropped 18 percent, with profits sinking over 40 percent. Figure 9.1 shows the sales growth of Reebok and Nike from their beginnings to 1995. Of particular note is the great growth of Reebok in the mid-1980s, in only a few years surpassing Nike, which had plateaued as it missed the new fitness opportunity. Then, as can be seen graphically, Reebok began slowing down, while Nike again surged. Table 9.1 shows the net income comparisons. Both firms had somewhat erratic incomes, but the early income promise of Reebok relative to Nike could not be sustained.

Nike counterattacked. Usually when a front runner loses momentum, reversing the trend is difficult. But Phil Knight and Nike were not to be denied.

Knight went for Reebok's weakness: dealer relations. Nike cultivated its customers, especially the larger dealers such as Foot Locker, while Reebok was surprisingly nonchalant and even arrogant in such dealings.

The Struggle to Win Foot Locker

In 1995, Woolworth's Foot Locker, a chain of 2,800 stores, had become the biggest seller of athletic footwear, accounting for $1.5 billion of the $6.5 billion U.S. sales. In

---

[3] *Forbes* (January 4, 1982), p. 246.

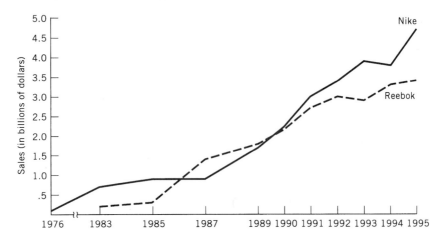

Figure 9.1   Sneaker War: Sales, Nike and Reebok 1976–1995 Billions of Dollars.

Source: Company annual reports.

1993, Nike's sales in Foot Lockers were $300 million, while Reebok was slightly behind with $228 million. Two years later, Nike's Food Locker sales had risen to $750 million, while Reebok's dropped to $122 million.[4]

Reebok was mostly to blame for this. Paul Fireman, CEO of Reebok, seemed to resent the demands of Foot Locker almost from the beginning. For example, in the

TABLE 9.1   Sneaker Wars: Net Income Comparison Nike and Reebok, 1985–1994, In Billions of Dollars

	Nike	Reebok
1985	$10.3	$39.0
1986	59.2	132.1
1987	35.9	165.2
1988	101.7	137.0
1989	167.0	175.0
1990	243.0	176.6
1991	287.0	234.7
1992	329.2	114.8
1993	365.0	223.4
1994	298.8	254.5

Source: Company annual reports.

[4] Joseph Pereira, "In Reebok-Nike War, Big Woolworth Chain is a Major Battlefield," *The Wall Street Journal* (September 22, 1995), p. A1.

1980s when Reebok aerobic shoes faced exuberant demand, Foot Locker wanted exclusivity, that is, special styles solely for itself. It saw exclusive lines as one of its major weapons against discounters, and was getting such protection from other man-ufacturers—but not from Reebok, which persisted in selling its shoes to anybody, including discounters near Foot Locker stores.

In contrast, Nike had worked with Foot Locker for some years, and by 1995 had a dozen items sold only by the chain.

Another aspect of Reebok's poor relationship with Foot Locker was its careless-ness in getting samples on time to Foot Locker buyers. Because of the chain's size, buying decisions had to be made early in the season. Late-arriving samples, or no samples, virtually guaranteed that such new items would not be ordered in any appre-ciable quantity. See the following information box for a discussion of the importance of major customer accounts.

Still, even in 1993, Nike did not look very much a winner though it had wrested market dominance from Reebok. From the high eighties in February of that year, share prices plummeted to the mid-fifties. The reason? Nike's sales were up only 15 percent and earnings just 11 percent, nothing outstanding for what investors consid-ered a growth stock. So Wall Street began questioning: How many pairs of sneakers does the world need? (Critics had earlier assailed McDonald's under the same ratio-nale: How many hamburgers can the world eat?)

Knight responded that the Nike mystique could sell other kinds of goods: out-door footwear from sandals to hiking boots; apparel lines, such as uniforms, for top-

INFORMATION BOX

IMPORTANCE OF MAJOR ACCOUNT MANAGEMENT

Recognizing the importance of major customers has come belatedly to some sellers, probably none more belatedly than Reebok. These very large customers often represent a major part of a firm's total sales volume, and satisfying them in an increasingly com-petitive environment requires special treatment. Major account management should stress developing long-term relationships and service becomes critical in cementing such relations. Understanding and catering to the needs and wants of these customers is a must. If this means giving them exclusivity, and the absolute first right to see new goods and samples, this ought to be done unhesitatingly.

Large account management has resulted in organizational changes in many manu-facturers and suppliers. Separate sales forces are often developed, such as account man-agers, who devote all their time to one or a few major customers, while the rest of the sales force calls on smaller customers in the normal fashion. For a customer the size of Foot Locker, senior executives, even the president of the firm, need to be part of the relationship.

Assume that you think the demands of a major retailer are completely unreasonable. What would you do?

ranked college football and basketball teams—from pants and jerseys to warm-up jackets; even practice gear such as soccer balls. Would not such products associated with athletes be eagerly sought by the general public? Could an athletic shoe company still be a growth company? Apparently so, through wise diversification within the larger athletic goods industry.

In his quest to remain the dominant player, Knight recalled what he learned from his old coach and Nike cofounder, Bill Bowerman: "Play by the rules, but be ferocious."[5]

CREATING AN IMAGE

Knight came to realize that shoes were becoming a disposable consumer good, almost a commodity, with little difference in quality among shoemakers. The challenge for success would come from transforming shoes into status symbols, with frequent model changes. Then if you could combine a fashion image, of being "in" or being "cool," with an aura of entertainment, this ought to powerfully appeal to impressionable consumers, especially those under 30 years old.

So Nike came to introduce new models for every season: baseball shoes in the spring, tennis shoes in the summer, hiking shoes in the fall. Basketball and running shoes were revamped quarterly. Nike averaged more than one new shoe style every day.

The tie-in with entertainment combined with sports heroes suggested a new advertising theme—not promoting shoes as such but what they represented. Knight reasoned that people rooted for a favorite team or courageous athletic, and so Nike would sell not shoes but the athletic ideals of determination, individuality, self-sacrifice, and winning.[6]

Nike had always sponsored athletes, but now it increased that budget to $100 million a year for athletes to use and pitch Nike products. Nike started this in 1973 when it paid star runner Steve Prefontaine to wear Nike shoes—he was brilliant, fiercely competitive, a nonconformist, the model athlete persona Knight was seeking. Unfortunately, Prefontaine died in a car crash in 1975. Eventually Michael Jordan took his place in Nike promotions, and the Chicago Bulls star became recognized as the best basketball player in history and perhaps the most popular athlete in the country.

As Nike sought to rejuvenate itself, Knight recruited other top athletes: John McEnroe, then Andre Agassi in tennis; Nolan Ryan in baseball; Deion Sanders in football; Carl Lewis and Alberto Salazar in track; football/baseball star Bo Jackson; as well as such basketball players as Charles Barkley and Scottie Pippen. Now there was Tiger Woods. Nike headquarters in Beaverton, Oregon became a shrine to athletes, with hundreds of bronze plaques and giant banners.

The use of athletes from different sports enabled Nike to segment the market, all under the umbrella of a single brand. The average American teenager bought ten pairs of athletic shoes a year, six for specific sports, four for fashion, resulting in 6 million teenagers buying more than $1 billion worth of Nike shoes.[7]

[5] Fleming Meeks, "Be Ferocious," *Forbes* (August 2, 1993), p. 41.

[6] "You Are What You Wear," p. 44.

[7] *Ibid.*, p. 45.

"You don't win silver, you lose gold," was the theme of Nike TV spots and billboards throughout Atlanta during the summer Olympics in 1996. Rather than being a sponsor firm and paying up to $40 million to the Olympic committee, Nike furthered its visibility with hundreds of individual athletes and teams wearing the swoosh on their uniforms and shoes.

Knight aimed the company in three new directions as he sought to make Nike a $12 billion company by the end of the century (it was $6.5 billion in the fiscal year ending May 31, 1996). These were women's sports, foreign markets, and Nike Town stores.

Dozens of top women athletes were signed up and heavily promoted. In nonconformist advertising, little girls were depicted imploring their parents to give them a ball instead of a doll.

While Nike had tried to crack international markets, results were far below what might be reasonably expected. For example, in the United States, the average consumer spent $12 a year on Nike products; in Germany only $2. To improve this imbalance, Nike began signing up the best athletes in each country: for example, baseball player Hideo Nomo in Japan; the Boca Juniors soccer team in Argentina; Germany's Formula 1 race car champion, Michael Schumacher.

In 1993, Nike opened a Nike Town superstore in Chicago. It soon ranked with the Navy Pier and the Lincoln Park Zoo as one of the city's top tourist attractions. The seventh Nike Town, a 90,000-square-foot store, opened on 57th Street in New York in November 1996. The landlord was Donald Trump and rent was about $10 million a year.[8]

These huge sports stores featured the broad range of Nike products, as Nike expanded into in-line skates, swimwear, hockey equipment, even sports sunglasses. They also offered sports apparel for toddlers, and of course, hundreds of different shoes. Each sport had its own room in the stores.

Nike Town stores invited hands-on experiencing, such as basketball courts allowing customers to try out various shoes. They also were sports shrines with odes to Nike athletes and displays of their autographed goods. Multiscreen TVs gave a subtle (or perhaps not so subtle) commercial touch. Some customers bought three and four pairs of shoes, as well as other paraphernalia, at a single visit.

Threats to the Image

In the summer of 1996, critical publicity surfaced about U.S. manufacturers operating sweatshops in poor countries of the world, particularly in Asia. Indeed, Nike's footwear, except the Cole Haan label, was produced primarily in Asia by independent subcontractors according to Nike specifications.

In the onslaught of criticisms, even Kathie Lee Gifford was compelled to confess tearfully on her television show that she didn't know that her line of clothes sold by Wal-Mart were made by Honduran girls paid 31 cents an hour.

Hundreds of multinational corporations in almost every industry went overseaes in recent years in order to reduce manufacturing costs, but footwear and apparel makers faced the strongest criticisms.

[8] *Ibid.*, p. 46.

Nike became the target of Made in the U.S.A. Foundation, an organization funded in part by organized labor with the goal of bringing jobs back home. After failing to get a Gifford-like reaction from Michael Jordan, the premier Nike symbol, Made in U.S.A. shifted attention to Phil Knight.

Negative publicity was fueled by prominent exposés of Asian child Labor in *Life* magazine, then by the "Foul Ball" campaign of Labor Secretary Robert Reich, who led an effort to ban soccer balls, including Nike's, stitched by boys and girls in Pakistan. Several members of Congress as well sought to ban imports of all goods made with child labor. Even the enormously popular Jordan was criticized for professing ignorance of the matter by *New York Times* columnist, Ira Berkow.[9] On the night of October 17, 1996, Dan Rather and *Forty-eight Hours* criticized Nike on primetime network TV.

Criticisms of Nike continued into 1997. Activists charged that not only were factory workers in Vietnam paid low wages, but that some were even limited to one trip to the bathroom and two drinks of water per shift, as well as being subjected to verbal abuse, sexual harassment, and such corporal punishment as being forced to stand for long periods in the hot sun. A Nike company executive promised to work to improve working conditions overseas: "Bring us information we can use, and we'll do our damnedest to correct any situations that are wrong."[10]

In early April 1997 came another blow to Nike's image. Thirty-nine members of the Heaven's Gate cult committed suicide in a California mansion. All were wearing new black Nike's, with the swoosh logo readily visible on TV and pictures in the print media. The "Just Do It" slogan of Nike was trumpeted as being entirely apt, and some even spoofed that Nike's slogan should be changed to "Just Did It."

Countercharge

At first, the criticisms seemed to have little impact on sales, with most customers not upset by working conditions in the Far East. The association of Nike with the sordid cult suicides, while misplaced brand loyalty, attested to the pervasiveness of the logo and the slogan.

Early in April 1997, a presidential task force reached an agreement to banish clothing sweatshops worldwide. The eight-month-old White House task force comprised labor unions, human-rights groups, and such apparel and footwear firms as Nike, Reebok, and Liz Claiborne, with other U.S. companies urged to join the crusade.[11]

The greatest boost to Nike's image at first seemed to be young Tiger Woods. His winning of the Masters Tournament before a vast worldwide TV audience and, in the

---

[9] Mark O'Keefe and Jeff Manning, "Firms Find Ways to Share the Guilt," *Cleveland Plain Dealer* (July 28, 1996), pp. 1-I, and 3-I.

[10] "Nike Workers in Vietnam Suffer Abuse, Group Says," *The Wall Street Journal* (March 28, 1997), B15.

[11] Wendy Bounds and Hilary Stout, "Sweatshop Pact: Good Fit or Threadbare?" *The Wall Street Journal* (April 10, 1997), p. A2.

process, breaking or tying nine records including those of being the youngest winner and the first minority to win this most prestigious of all golf tournaments, all while wearing the conspicuous swoosh, focused favorable attention on Nike as perhaps not even Michael Jordan had been able to do. The day after the Masters, ABC News reported that Nike's sales of golf clothing had risen 100 percent since the signing of Tiger.

STORM CLOUDS WON'T GO AWAY

The troubles besetting Nike did not go away. In addition to the continuing bad press about labor conditions in Asia, other environmental factors tormented Nike. First, Asia worked its way deep into recession, or worse. Demand drastically declined and this affected many U.S. firms from mighty airplane builders such as Boeing to sneaker makers the likes of Nike. Estimates were that in Japan alone, two million pairs of Nikes went unsold because of the country's economic problems.[12] Forecasts for how long this malaise would last ranged from months to years.

Another troubling portent was the public's growing disenchantment with athletes. The first inkling hit the media in the fall of 1998, when the great home-run heroes, Mark McGwire and Sammy Sosa, found their exploits were not generating much endorsement money. Reporters now pounced on reports that firms had become skeptical about the cost effectiveness of most athletes in promoting their products: Were they worth it? Fan interest in pro sports seemed to be dropping, perhaps reflecting a growing tide of resentment at overpriced athletes proving to be selfish, arrogant, and decadent—the very role-models that Nike and other firms had spent millions to enlist. Indicative of the "public be damned" attitude of owners and players was the labor strife in the fall and winter of 1998 between the NBA and their multimillionaire players that led to weeks of game cancellations.

Nike slashed its endorsement budget by close to $100 million. Even Tiger Woods was not doing it for Nike. His product line of shoes and apparel introduced in early 1998 met with lukewarm response at best. See the following information box for more discussion of the disappointment of the Tiger Woods product line.

Several other environmental changes bedeviled Nike now. Sporting-goods retailer consolidations closed hundreds of stores and lessened the number of outlets for Nike. The sneaker business was diversifying beyond simply running, basketball, and aerobics shoes into what some called the brown-shoe phenomenon, as demand extended to outdoor brands such as Timberland.

In addition to Timberland, Nike faced increased competition in its basic core business. Adidas, the market leader in Europe that Nike had vanquished from the U.S. market several decades earlier was resurging, with sales increasing 92 percent in North America in one quarter of 1998. Reebok and New Balance were also aggressively pursuing. Furthermore, fashion brands, such as Tommy Hilfiger, intruded into the sneaker market.

---

[12] Bill Saporito, "Can Nike Get Unstuck?" *Time* (March 30, 1998), p. 49.

INFORMATION BOX

WHAT WENT WRONG WITH TIGER'S ENDORSEMENT?

Knight thought the appeal of Tiger Woods would be so universal that he signed him to a $40 million contract when he became a professional in late 1996. Knight predicted that Woods would do nothing less than "change the way people view the game of golf." Early in 1998, Nike introduced the Woods line, which included not only golf shoes but also apparel, with the togs carrying his own logo, a swirling yin-yang emblem designed to reflect his Buddhist beliefs as well as his club speed.

It was soon apparent that Nike's major commitment into golf was a stunning disappointment. The Tiger Woods signature shoe, in particular, fared badly. Retailers blamed the $225 to $250 price tag as well as the gaudy styling. One retailer griped that it looked like a bowling shoe. Other critics complained that golfers tend to be a conservative lot, and Nike designed a shoe that would appeal more to teenagers. While apparel sales were slightly stronger, retailers criticized their high prices, such as $54 and up for polo shorts. "It's a lot of money for a little swoosh," one retailer said.

Tiger himself didn't help. Rather than dominating the PGA tour, he had a decidedly mediocre 1998. Instead of being the man who would break the game's economic and racial barriers, his greatest popularity was in the youth market. Perhaps Nike's product planners did not fully recognize this. They priced their goods for hard-core golfers, but their styling was more for youth.[13]

Do you think the appeal of Tiger Woods will be short-lived, or might it turn out as enduring as Nicklaus and Palmer? Is Tiger likely to replace Michael Jordan in popularity? Does his appeal wholly depend on golf victories?

---

[13] Jeff Manning, "Nike is Landing in the Rough with Tiger Woods Products," *Cleveland Plain Dealer* (August 9, 1998), p. 4-H; Bill Saporito, "Can Nike Get Unstuck?" *Time* (March 30, 1998), p. 53.

Another disturbing possibility was emerging. Had Nike grown too big? Was its logo, the swoosh, too pervasive, to the point that it turned some people off? Even its tag line, "Just Do It," was this becoming counterproductive?

Concerned about such questions, Nike began reassessing. It sought to act smaller by developing categories such as golf, soccer, and women's as separate business units. A new advertising campaign had the softer tag line, "I can." Nike even began toning down its use of the swoosh, removing it from corporate letterheads and most advertising, and substituting a lowercase "nike."

Still, Nike could not escape the vicious comparisons of some critics regarding the rich-man, poor-man image of Knight's wealth—$3.5 billion—and the millions paid Michael Jordan for his endorsements, set against a factory worker's monthly earnings of $20.

Performance results for the fiscal year ending May 31, 1998 showed net income decreasing for the first time in four years, dropping 49.8 percent. This was the lowest net income since 1995.

ANALYSIS

Going back to its beginnings, undoubtedly Nike faced an extraordinarily favorable primary demand in the 1970s. But Nike's success went far beyond simply coasting with the new running movement. Nike outstripped all its competitors, including the heretofore dominant Adidas. This was at a time when foreign brands—for all kinds of goods—had an aura of somehow being better, in fashion and quality and dependability, than American brands.

Product Strategy

Nike, as it reached for its potential, offered an even broader product line than Adidas, the pioneer of the strategy of having many shoe styles. However, a broad product line can have its problems: it can hurt efficiency, create consumer confusion, and greatly add to costs. Most firms are better advised to pare their product lines, to get rid of weak products so that more resources can be allocated to the winners. Here we see the disavowal of such a policy.

Although Nike violated product-mix concepts, we should recognize what it accomplished. By offering a great variety of styles, prices, and uses, Nike appealed to all kinds of runners, and conveyed the image of the most complete running-shoe manufacturer of all. In a rapidly evolving industry in which millions of people of all kinds and abilities were taking up the sport, such an image became very attractive.

Furthermore, in a rapidly expanding market, Nike found that it could tap the widest possible distribution with its breadth of products. It could sell its shoes to conventional retailers, such as department stores and shoe stores, and it could continue to do business with the specialized running-shoe stores. It could even offer some models to discounters since there were certainly enough styles to go around—different models for different types of retail outlets—and everyone could be happy.

Short production runs and many styles generally add to production costs, but in Nike's case this was less of a factor. As we have seen, most of the production was contracted out, some 95 percent to foreign, mostly Far East factories. Short production runs were less of a cost deterrent where many plants were involved.

Research

Early on Nike placed heavy emphasis on research and technological improvement. It sought ever more flexible and lighter-weight running shoes that would be protective but also give the athlete—world-class or slowest amateur—the utmost advantage that technology could provide. Nike's commitment to research and development was evident in the many employees working in this area who had degrees in biomechanics, exercise physiology, engineering, industrial design, chemistry, and related fields. It also engaged research committees and advisory boards, including coaches, athletes, trainers, equipment managers, podiatrists, and orthopedists who met periodically to review designs, materials, and concepts for improved athletic shoes. Activities included high-speed photographic analyses of the human body in motion, the use of athletes on force plates and treadmills, organized wear testing, and continual testing and study of new and modified shoes and materials. Even back in 1981 the budget was about $4 million, a major commitment to research and development for such an apparently simple thing as a shoe.

Doing Things Better

Nike at first attempted no major deviation from the accepted strategy norm of the industry. This norm was established several decades earlier by Adidas. It primarily involved testing and development of better running shoes, a broad product line to appeal to all segments of the market, a readily identifiable trademark or logo prominently displayed on all products, and the use of well-known athletes at prestigious athletic events to show off the products in use. Even contracting out of much of the production to low-cost foreign factories was not unique to Nike. But Nike used these proven techniques far better than its competitors.

This was particularly true in the development of its public image. The great identification of Nike with athleticism, "Just Do It," and its association with the greatest names in sports, maximized the appeal of Nike products. Particularly with a younger customer segment, such identification of its name, logo, and products with those athletes that most looked up to and dreamed of emulating was powerfully effective.

Diversifying to non-shoe products, while still staying in the athletic realm, was a natural evolution for growth. It permitted a positive and effective transference of image.

The Ethics Controversy of Using Foreign Child Labor

Was Nike—and other U.S. manufacturers as well—guilty of violating accepted moral and ethical standards in farming out production to foreign subcontractors in third-world countries using child labor at very low wages? Critics maintained this violated corporate ethics in exploiting underpaid workers to maximize profits back home. But while long hours in a smelly shoe or garment factory may be less than idyllic, others suggested it was preferable to subsistence farming or laboring in even harsher workplaces.

Knight believed that Nike was a force for positive change in Asia: "…good corporations are the ones that lead these countries out of poverty. When we started in Japan, factory labor there was making $4 a day, which is basically what is being paid in Indonesia and being so strongly criticized today. Nobody today is saying, 'The poor old Japanese.' We watched it happen all over again in Taiwan and Korea, and now it's going on in Southeast Asia."[14]

Many of the 120,000 Indonesian workers who produce Nike shoes come from impoverished rural backgrounds. These factories provide a chance not only to earn but to save money and to send the extra cash back to families. The workers are daughters of rural farmers, village schoolteachers, and shop clerks. They live together in factory towns, a dozen to a dormitory room, sleeping on bunk beds. Would they be better off without these jobs? Would some of them be homeless or have to turn to

---

[14] "Nike's Indonesian Operations Facing Scrutiny and Criticism," *Cleveland Plain Dealer* (August 27, 1996), p. 10–C.

prostitution otherwise? Indeed, should we try to impose our value system on other peoples and other nations?

WHAT CAN BE LEARNED?

The right image can bring great psychological product differentiation. Granted that technological differences in running shoes had narrowed so that any tangible advantages of a brand were practically imperceptible, what made Nike stand out? It was the image and the "swoosh" that identified the brand. For something like running shoes and athletic equipment and apparel, the visibility of products in athletic and normal use readily stands out. For many youth, the sight of famous and admired athletes actively using this brand brought the desire to emulate them even if only in using the same brand ... and maybe to dream a little. This is known as *reference group influence,* and is described in the following information box.

Nike fostered this image of celebrity users more than any other firm. With its financial resources it could afford the enormous stipends demanded by the best of these celebrities.

For many people—especially youth—the popularity of the brand became a further attraction. Wearing Nike products was seen as being "cool," belonging to the "in" crowd.

INFORMATION BOX

REFERENCE GROUP INFLUENCE

Reference groups are those individuals and groups with whom an individual identifies. These become a standard or point of reference for forming one's lifestyle and aspirations. Such groups can be ones to which a person would like to belong but does not. They can be ones to which a person does belong. Regardless of whether aspirational or membership, these groups influence product and brand purchases, and even store patronage, under certain circumstances. Nike, by sponsoring famous athletes, provided a potent reference group for many of its youthful customers. With their peers also wearing Nike products, the buying influence was doubly strong.

Two things are necessary for a product or brand to be susceptible to reference group influence. First, the product must be visible so that other people can see it being worn or used. Second, the product must be conspicuous, that is, it must stand out and not be so common that practically everybody has it. Of course, the Nike logo provided both visibility and conspicuousness, and the identification with athletes was unmistakable.

Would you expect a car to be susceptible to reference group influence? a brand of beer? a TV set? Why or why not?

How long is this attraction to athletes and athletics likely to last?—to the end of time? We are seeing today some signs that the appeal of such celebrities is waning. Whether this is a major trend or a short-term phenomenon remains to be seen.

Is Nike's success in building its image transferable to other firms whose products cannot be identified with use by the famous? Do such firms have any possibilities for developing image-enhancing qualities for their brands? They certainly do.

Nike's use of reference group influence represents one way to use image to great advantage. But there are other approaches for image building that can be very effective. Consider the long-advertised lonesome Maytag repairman. Maytag has been highly successful in building a reputation, an image, for dependability and assured quality. In so doing it has been able to sustain a higher price advantage over its competitors. Often, a carefully nurtured image of good quality, dependability, reliable service, or being in the forefront of technology or fashion can bring a firm great success in its particular industry.

No one is immune from mistakes; success does not guarantee continued success. Many executives delude themselves into thinking success begets continued success. It is not so! No firm, market leader or otherwise, can afford to rest on its laurels, to disregard a changing environment and aggressive but smaller competitors. In the mid-1970s, Adidas had as commanding a lead in its industry as IBM once had in computers. But it was overtaken and surpassed by Nike, a rank newcomer, and a domestic firm with few resources in an era when foreign brands (of beer, watches, cars, electronics, and cameras, for example) had a mystique and attraction for affluent Americans that few domestic brands could achieve. But Adidas let down its guard at a critical point. A decade later, Nike then lagged before an aggressive Reebok because it underestimated the growing interest in aerobic dancing. Today, environmental changes, most of which are beyond its control, are savaging Nike. Are these changes only temporary aberrations? With the exception of the economic travails in Asia and other foreign markets, they may not be temporary. If so, Nike must adapt to these changes to remain a market leader.

Growth can be maintained in a saturated industry. Apparently Nike has been able to do this, to continue and even increase its growth trend, while facing the reality of how many running shoes can a market absorb year after year and still be a growth industry. Nike has done this by expanding its horizons from running shoes, to all kinds of athletic and outdoor footwear, to athletic apparel and uniforms, to women's and children's wear. A greater penetration of international markets offers opportunity, as well as the Nike Town superstores.

This is a unique growth plan for Nike; it would not work for every firm. The key element, however, is that diversification into related areas complementing the already strong image of a firm have a higher probability of successful growth. On the other hand, diversification that has little relationship to the strengths and image of the firm are far more questionable, and often unwise. We will see an example of unwise diversification—in the quest for growth—in the Maytag case to come. Often such unwise diversifications come in buyouts in which an unreasonable price is paid along with overreliance on the management resources of the acquired firm. In Nike's case, the diversifications came internally.

Beware of blemishes on the public image; some may not be serious, but others may truly be. The criticisms surfacing in the summer of 1996 about the labor practices in Third World factories at first seemed to have little impact on Nike's fortunes or its image. Partly this was due to Nike being only one of many firms subcontracting production to foreign factories. It also reflected that the typical Nike customer was hardly concerned with underpaid foreign workers who probably would be worse off without Nike's business, and was more interested in getting the best value for his or her money.

However, as the criticisms continued into 1998 a backlash against Nike began developing. Nike even felt it desirable to put a few of the negative letters it had received on the cover of its 1998 annual report. One of them vowed, "No more Nike for me!" Another said, "Your actions so disgust me that I will never buy one of your products again. I hope my attitude proved to be universal." The Associated Press reported a soccer coach at St. John's, who quit rather than wear the swoosh as part of an endorsement deal with Nike: "I don't want to be a billboard for a company that would do these things."[15]

However, such attacks on a firm's reputation or public image often bring far worse consequences, as we will see in several cases to come.

CONSIDER

Can you think of any other insights coming from this case that have transferability to other firms and other situations?

QUESTIONS

1. "The success of Nike was strictly fortuitous and had little to do with great decision making." Evaluate this statement.

2. In the case we offered the possibility that Nike may be becoming too big in its industry, that there are too many "swooshes" to be seen, that its slogan, "Just Do It" may have been advertised too much, that even the name Nike is everywhere you look. Can a firm become too dominant in its industry?

3. "Nike's major problem is that it's too much of a profit monger. It charges obscene prices for shoes and clothing that cost it very little. Unless Knight changes his mindset and offers more modest prices, the glory days of Nike are over." Evaluate this statement.

4. "A great image is very transitory. It can go anytime." Evaluate this statement.

---

[15] William McCall, "Nike Fights Bad Press to Regain Old Image," reported in *Cleveland Plain Dealer* (October 11, 1998), p. 1-H.

5. Do you really think Nike can continue to be a growth stock, or is the end in sight? Give your opinion and rationale.

6. Can celebrity advertising be overdone? How would you attempt to ascertain whether you are getting your money's worth from paying some athlete millions to wear your products?

7. Should Nike be concerned that some ghetto youths have such an attachment to the Nike image that they will strongarm and even kill to get an Air Jordan shoe, for example? If so, how can Nike combat this overzealousness?

8. Donald Trump has claimed that Nike is paying $10 million in rent for its Manhattan store on his premises. Do you think Nike made a mistake with this? Why or why not?

HANDS-ON EXERCISES

1. Phil Knight has charged you with developing a marketing plan to more fully tap the female market for shoes and athletic equipment. Be as specific as you can in your recommendations and defend them as well as you can.

2. The public criticism of Nike's subcontracting most of its production to Asian factories has reached a point where Nike must do something to try to counteract the bad publicity. What would you advise Knight to do about this public image problem? Consider the consequences of your recommendations.

TEAM DEBATE EXERCISES

1. Debate the issue of endorsements of athletes. How much is too much? Where do we draw the line? Should we go only for the few famous? Or should we gamble on lesser stars eventually making it big and offer them long-term contracts? Argue the two sides of the issue: aggressive and conservative.

2. Debate the contentious issue of Nike's use of overseas sweatshop labor in its production.

INVITATION TO RESEARCH

Is the popularity of running and jogging waning today? Has the "sweatshop" issue died out or has it become stronger and more compelling? Are the Nike superstores achieving the success expected?

CHAPTER TEN

Boeing Can't Handle Success

The commercial-jet business had long been subject to booms and busts: major demand for new aircraft and then years of little demand. By the second half of the 1990s, demand burgeoned as never before. Boeing, the world's leading producer of commercial airplanes, seemed in the catbird seat amid the worldwide surge of orders. This was an unexpected windfall, spurred by markets greatly expanding in Asia and Latin America at the same time as domestic demand, helped by deregulation and prosperity, boomed. In the midst of this seeming prosperity, Boeing in 1997 incurred its first loss in 50 years, with longer-term prospects questionable. How could this have happened? How could it have been prevented? How can the situation be corrected?

BACKGROUND OF THE COMPANY

Boeing's was a fabled past, being a major factor in the World War II war effort, and in the late 1950s leading the way in producing innovative, state-of-the-art commercial aircraft. It introduced the 707, the world's first commercially viable jetliner. In the late 1960s, it almost bankrupted itself to build a jetliner twice the size of any other then in service, as critics predicted it could never fly profitably. But the 747 dramatically lowered costs and airfares and brought passenger comfort previously undreamed of in flying. In the mid-1990s, it introduced the high technology 777, the first commercial aircraft designed entirely with the use of computers.

In efforts to reduce the feast-to-famine cycles of the commercial aircraft business, Boeing acquired Rockwell International's defense business in 1996, and in 1997 purchased McDonnell Douglas for $16.3 billion.

In 1997, Boeing's commercial aircraft segment contributed 57 percent of total revenues. This segment ranged from 125-passenger 737s to giant 500-seat 747s. In 1997, Boeing delivered 374 aircraft, up from 269 in 1996. The potential seemed enormous: over the next twenty years, air passenger traffic worldwide was projected to rise 4.9 percent a year, and airlines were predicted to order 16,160 aircraft to expand their fleets and replace aging planes.[1] As the industry leader, Boeing had 60 percent of this market in recent years. At the end of 1997, its order backlog was $94 billion.

---

[1] *Boeing 1997 Annual Report.*

Defense and space operations comprised 41 percent of 1997 revenues. This included Airborne Warning and Control Systems (AWACS), helicopters, B-2 bomber subcontract work, and the F-22 fighter, among other products and systems.

PROBLEMS WITH THE COMMERCIAL AIRCRAFT BUSINESS SEGMENT

Production Problems

Boeing proved to be poorly positioned to meet the surge in aircraft orders. Part of this resulted from drastic layoffs it had made of experienced workers during the industry's last slump, in the early 1990s. Though it hired 32,000 new workers over 18 months starting in 1995, the experience gap upped the risk of costly mistakes. Boeing had also cut back its suppliers in strenuous efforts to slash parts inventories and increase cost efficiency.

But Boeing had other problems. Its production systems were a mess. It had somehow evolved some 400 separate computer systems, and these were not linked. Its design system was labor intensive and paper dependent, and very expensive as it tried to cater to customer choices. A $1 billion program had been launched in 1996 to modernize and computerize the production process. But this was too late: the onslaught of orders had already started. (It is something of an anomaly that a firm that had the sophistication to design the 777 entirely by computers was so antiquated in its use of computers otherwise.)

Demands for increased production were further aggravated by unreasonable production goals and too many plane models. Problems first hit with the 747 Jumbo, and then with a new version of the top-selling 737, the so-called next-generation 737NG. Before long, every program was affected: also the 757, 767, and 777. In 1997, while Boeing released over 320 planes to customers for a 50 percent increase over 1996, this was far short of the planned completion rate. For example, by early 1998 a dozen 737NGs had been delivered to airlines, but this was less than one-third of the 40 supposed to have been delivered by then. Yet, the company maintained through September 1997 that everything was going well, that there was only a month's delay in the delivery of some planes.

Soon it became apparent that problems were much greater. In October, the 747 and 737 assembly lines were shut down for nearly a month to allow workers to catch up and ease part shortages. *The Wall Street Journal* reported horror stories of parts being rushed in by taxicab, of executives spending weekends trying to chase down needed parts, of parts needed for new planes being shipped out to replace defective parts on an in-service plane. Overtime pay brought some assembly-line workers incomes over $100,000, while rookie workers muddled by on the line.[2]

Despite its huge order backlog, Boeing took a loss for 1997, the first in over 50 years. See Table 10.1 for the trend in revenues and net income over the last ten years.

The loss came mostly from two massive writedowns. One, for $1.4 billion, arose from the McDonnell Douglas acquisition and in particular from its ailing commercial

---

[2] Frederic M. Biddle and John Helyar, "Behind Boeing's Woes: Clunky Assembly Line, Price War with Airbus," *The Wall Street Journal* (April 24, 1998), p. A16.

**TABLE 10.1 Boeing's Trend of
Revenues and Income, 1988–1997**

	Revenue	Net Income
	(Million $)	
1988	16,962	614
1989	20,276	675
1990	27,595	1,385
1991	29,314	1,567
1992	30,184	1,554
1993	25,438	1,244
1994	21,924	856
1995	19,515	393
1996	22,681	1,095
1997	45,800	–177

Source: Boeing Annual Reports.

Commentary: Note the severity of the decline in revenues and profits during the industry downturn in 1993, 1994, and 1995. It is little wonder that Boeing was so ill-prepared for the deluge of orders starting in 1995. Then in an unbelievable anomaly, the tremendous increase in revenues in 1997, to the highest ever, resulted in a huge loss.

aircraft operation at Long Beach, California. The bigger writeoff, $1.6 billion, reflected production problems, particularly on the new 737NG. Production delays continued, with more writedowns likely.

As Boeing moved into 1998, analysts wondered how much longer it would take to clear up the production snafus. This would be longer than anyone had been led to expect. Now a new problem arose for Boeing. Disastrous economic conditions in Asia brought major order cancellations.

Customer Relations

Not surprisingly, Boeing's production problems resulting in delayed shipments seriously impacted customer relations. For example, Southwest Airlines had to temporarily cancel adding service to another city because ordered planes were not ready. Boeing paid Southwest millions of dollars of compensation for the delayed deliveries. Continental also had to wait for five overdue 737s.

Other customers switched to Boeing's only major competitor, Airbus Industrie, of Toulouse, France.

Airbus

Airbus Industrie had to salivate at Boeing's troubles. It was a distant second in market share to the 60 percent of Boeing. Now this was changing and it could see achieving a sustainable 50 percent market share. See the following box for a discussion of market share.

INFORMATION BOX

IMPORTANCE OF MARKET SHARE

The desire to surpass a competitor is a common human tendency, whether in sports or business. A measurement of performance relative to competitors encourages this and can be highly motivating for management and employees alike. Furthermore, market share performance is a key indicator in ascertaining how well a firm is doing and in spotting emerging problems, as well as sometimes allaying blame. As an example of the latter, declining sales over the preceding year, along with a constant and improving market share, can suggest that the firm is doing a good job, even though certain factors adversely affected the whole industry.

Market share is usually measured by (1) share of overall sales, and/or (2) share relative to certain competitors, usually the top one or several in the industry. Of particular importance is trend data: Are things getting better or worse? If worse, why is this, and what needs to be done to improve the situation?

Since Boeing and Airbus were the only real competitors in this major industry relative market shares became critical. The perceived importance of gaining, or not losing, market share led to severe price competition that cut into the profits of both firms, as will be discussed later.

How would you respond to the objection that market share data is not all that useful, since "it doesn't tell us what the problem really is"?

Can emphasizing market share be counterproductive? If so, why?

Airbus was positioned to supply planes to airlines whose needs Boeing couldn't meet near term. Some thought it was even producing better planes than Boeing.

United Airlines chose Airbus's A320 twinjets over Boeing's 737s, saying passengers preferred the Airbus product. Several South American carriers also chose A320s over the 737, placing a $4 billion order with Airbus. For 1997, Airbus hacked out a 45 percent market share, the first time Boeing's 60 percent market share had eroded.

The situation worsened drastically in 1998. US Air, which had previously ordered 400 Airbus jets, announced in July that it would buy 30 more. But the biggest defection came in August when British Airlines announced plans to buy 59 Airbus jetliners and take options for 200 more. This broke its long record as a Boeing-loyal customer. The order would be worth as much as $11 billion, the biggest victory of Airbus over Boeing.[3]

Beyond the production delays of Boeing, Airbus had other competitive strengths. While it had less total production capability than Boeing (235 planes vs. Boeing's 550), its production line was efficient and it had done a better job of trimming its costs. This meant it could go head-to-head with Boeing on price. And price seemed to be the name of the game in the late 1990s. This contrasted with earlier days when

---

[3] "British to Order Airbus Airliners," *Cleveland Plain Dealer* (August 25, 1998), p. 6-C.

Boeing rose to world leadership with performance, delivery, and technology more important than cost. "They [the customers] do not care what it costs us to make the planes," Boeing chairman and chief executive Philip Condit admitted. With airline design plateaued, he saw the airlines buying planes today as chiefly interested in how much carrying capacity they can buy for a buck.[4]

WHO CAN WE BLAME FOR BOEING'S TROUBLES?

Was it CEO Philip Condit?

Philip Condit became chief executive in 1996, just in time for the massive emerging problems. He had hardly assumed office before he was deeply involved in the defense industry's merger mania, first buying Rockwell's aerospace operation and then McDonnell Douglas. He later admitted that he probably spent too much time on these acquisitions, and not enough time on watching the commercial part of the operation.[5]

Condit's credentials were good. His association with Boeing began in 1965 when he joined the firm as an aerodynamics engineer. The same year, he obtained a design patent for a flexible wing called the sailwing. Moving through the company's engineering and managerial ranks, he was named CEO in 1996 and chairman in 1997. Along the way, he earned a master's degree in management from the Massachusetts Institute of Technology in 1975, and in 1997 a doctorate in engineering from Science University of Tokyo, where he was the first westerner to earn such a degree.

Was Condit's pursuit of the Rockwell and McDonnell Douglas mergers a major blunder? While analysts do not agree on this, prevailing opinion is more positive than negative, mostly because these businesses could smooth the cyclical nature of the commercial sector.

Interestingly, in the face of severe adversity, no heads have rolled, as they might have in other firms. See the following box for a discussion of management climate during adversity.

Were the Problems Mostly Due to Internal Factors?

The unexpected buying binge by airlines that was brought about by worldwide prosperity fueling air travel maybe should have been anticipated. However, probably even the most prescient decision maker would have missed the full extent of this boom. For example, orders jumped from 124 in 1994 to 754 in 1996. With hindsight we know that Boeing made a grievous management mistake in trying to bite off too much, by promising expanded production and deliveries that were wholly unrealistic. We know what triggered such extravagant promises: trying to keep ahead of arch-rival Airbus.

Huge layoffs in the early 1990s contributed to the problems of gearing up for new business. An early-retirement plan had been taken up by 9,000 of 13,000 eligi-

---

[4] Howard Banks, "Slow Learner," *Forbes* (May 4, 1998), p. 54.

[5] *Ibid.*, p. 56.

ISSUE BOX

MANAGEMENT CLIMATE DURING ADVERSITY: WHAT IS BEST FOR MAXIMUM EFFECTIVENESS?

Management shakeups during adversity can range from practically none to widespread head-rolling. In the first scenario, a cooperative board is usually necessary, and it helps if the top executive(s) controls a lot of stock. But the company's problems will probably continue. In the second scenario, we earlier saw an avowed turnaround expert, Albert Dunlap, come in wielding a mean ax, and indeed seemed to turn around the faltering Scott Paper in a short time. But excessive management changes can destroy a company. And Dunlap's success with Scott did not carry over to Sunbeam. On the other hand, Gordon Bethune turned around Continental Air without wielding a mean ax. So, can we make any conclusions from a sample of cases?

In general, neither extreme—complacency or upheaval—is good. A sick company usually needs drastic changes, but not necessarily widespread bloodletting that leaves the entire organization cringing and sending out resumes. But we need to further define *sick*. At what point is a company so bad off it needs a drastic overhaul? Was Boeing such a sick company? Would a drastic overhaul have quickly changed things? Certainly Boeing management had made some miscalculations, mostly in the area of too much optimism and too much complacency, but these were finally recognized. Major executive changes and resignations might not have helped at all with Boeing.

How do you personally feel about the continuity of management at Boeing during these difficult times? Should some heads have rolled? What criteria would you use in your judgment of whether to roll heads or not?

ble people. This was twice as many as Boeing expected, and it removed a core of production-line workers and managers who had kept a dilapidated system working. New people could not be trained or assimilated quickly enough to match those lost.

Boeing had begun switching to the Japanese practice of lean inventory management that delivers parts and tools to workers precisely as needed so that production costs could be reduced. Partly because of this and also because of the downturn in the early 1990s, Boeing's supplier base changed significantly. Some suppliers quit the aviation business; others had suffered so badly in the slump that their credit was affected and they were unable to boost capacity for the suddenly increased business. The result was serious parts shortages.

Complicating production problems was Boeing's long-standing practice of customizing, thereby permitting customers to choose from a host of options, to fine tune not only for every airline but for every order. For example, it offered the 747's customers 38 different pilot clipboards, and 109 shades of the color white.[6] Such tailor-

---

[6] John Greenwald, "Is Boeing Out of Its Spin?" *Time* (July 13, 1998), p. 68.

ing added significantly to costs and production time. This perhaps was acceptable when these costs could be easily passed on to customers in a more leisurely production cycle, but it was far from maximizing efficiency. Deregulation fare wars made extreme customizing archaic. Boeing apparently got the message with the wide-bodied 777, designed entirely by computers. Here, choices of parts were narrowed to standard options, such as carmakers offer in their transmissions, engines, and comfort packages.

Cut-rate pricing between Boeing and Airbus epitomized the situation by the mid-1990s. Now, costs became critical if a firm was to be profitable. In this climate, Boeing was so obsessed with maintaining its 60 percent market share that it fought for each order with whatever price it took. Commercial airline production had somehow become a commodity business, with neither Boeing nor Airbus having products all that unique to sell. Innovation seemed disregarded, with price the only factor in getting an order. So, every order became a battleground, and prices might be slashed 20 percent off list in order to grab all the business possible.[7] And Boeing did not have the low-cost advantage over Airbus.

Such price competition worked to the advantage of the airlines, and they grew skillful at gaining big discounts from Boeing and Airbus by holding out huge contracts and negotiating hard.

The cumbersome production systems of Boeing—cost inefficient—became a burden in this cost-conscious environment. While some of the problems could be attributed to computer technology not well applied to the assembly process, others involved organizational myopia regarding even such simple things as a streamlined organization and common parts. For example, before recent changes the commercial group had five wing-design groups, one for each aircraft program. Finally it has one. Another example cited in *Forbes* tells of different tools needed in the various plane models to open their wing access hatches.[8] Why not the same tool?

We see a paradox in Boeing's dilemma. Its 777 was the epitome of high technology and computer design, as well as efficient production planning. Yet, much of the other production was mired in a morass with supplies, parts management, and production inefficiency.

Harry Stonecipher, former CEO of McDonnell Douglas before the acquisition and now president and chief operating officer of Boeing, cited arrogance as the mind-set behind Boeing's problems. He saw this as coming from a belief that the company could do no wrong, that all its problems came from outside, and that business-as-usual will solve them.[9]

The Role of External Factors

Adding to the production and cost-containment difficulties of Boeing was increased regulatory demands. These came not only from the U.S. Federal Aviation

[7] "Behind Boeing's Woes ...," pp. A1, A16.

[8] Banks, *op. cit.*, p. 60.

[9] Bill Sweetman, "Stonecipher's Boeing Shakeup," *Interavia Business & Technology* (September 1998), p. 15.

Administration, but also from the European Joint Airworthiness Authority (a loose grouping of regulators from more than 20 European countries). The first major consequence of this increased regulatory climate concerned the new 730NG. Boeing apparently thought it could use the same over-the-wings emergency exits as it had on the older 737. But Europe wanted a redesign. They were concerned that the older type of emergency exits would not permit passengers in the larger version of the plane to evacuate quickly enough. So Boeing had to design two new over-the-wing exits on each side. This was no simple modification since it involved rebuilding the most crucial aspect of the plane. The costly refitting accounted for a major part of the $1.6 billion writedown Boeing took in 1997.

Europe's Airbus Industrie had made no secret of its desire to achieve parity with Boeing and have 50 percent of the international market for commercial jets. This mindset led to the severe price competition of the latter 1990s as Boeing stubbornly tried to maintain its 60 percent market share even at the expense of profits. While its total production capacity was somewhat below that of Boeing, Airbus had already overhauled its manufacturing process, and was better positioned to compete on price. Airbus's competitive advantage seemed stronger with single-aisle planes, those in the 120–200 seat category, mostly 737s of Boeing and A320s of Airbus. But this accounted for 43 percent of the $40 billion expected to be spent on airliners in 1998.[10]

The future was something else. Airbus placed high stakes on a superjumbo successor to the 747, with seating capacity well beyond the 568 people that the 747 carried. Such a huge plane would hold up to a thousand people and operate from hub airports such as New York City's JFK. Airbus was spending $9 billion to develop what it called the A3XX to be debuted by 2004. Meantime, Boeing staked its future on its own 767s and 777s, which could connect smaller cities around the world without the need for passenger concentration at a few hubs.

Have you ever heard of a firm complaining of too much business? Probably not, were it not for Boeing's immersion in red ink trying to cope with too many orders. However, indications began surfacing that Boeing's feast of too much business had abruptly ended. Financial problems in Asia brought cancellations and postponements of orders and deliveries.

In October 1998, Boeing disclosed that 36 completed aircraft were sitting in company storage areas in the desert, largely because of canceled orders. This compared with only 8 such aircraft at the end of 1997 and 19 at the end of the second quarter of 1998.

By December 1998, Boeing warned that its operations may be hurt by the Asian situation for as long as five years, and it announced an additional 20,000 jobs would be eliminated and production cut 25 percent.[11] Of course, it didn't help that Airbus was capitalizing on the production difficulties of Boeing to wrest orders from the stable of Boeing's long-term customers and planned a 30 percent production increase for 1999.

---

[10] Banks, *op. cit.*, p. 60

[11] Frederick M. Biddle and Andy Pasztor, "Boeing May Be Hurt Up to 5 Years by Asia," *The Wall Street Journal* (December 3, 1998), p. A3.

CAN BOEING BE REJUVENATED?

There seems little doubt that Boeing will survive these difficulties and continue to be a major player in the airline, military, and aerospace markets. The acquisitions of Rockwell and McDonnell Douglas should prove long-term advantageous. The Asian crisis will go away, and orders eventually rejuvenate. Competition with Airbus will probably continue strong and even intensify. But the international market has room for two such firms. However, Boeing may have lost its dominant competitive advantage.

Troubling is the time Boeing has taken to cope with its production and efficiency problems. Management mistakes opened the way for an aggressive and hungry competitor. Meantime, severe price competition played havoc with profitability. Boeing badly needed to get its costs under control and develop some uniqueness in products and service over Airbus. At this point in time, its only advantage is higher production capability than Airbus.

WHAT CAN BE LEARNED?

Beware the 3 C's syndrome, again. So many times this mindset rears up and humbles the frontrunner. We saw it earlier with Harley Davidson and IBM. But the firms succumbing are far more than these.

Stonecipher, former CEO of McDonnell Douglas and then president of Boeing, admitted to company self-confidence bordering on arrogance. But it is more than this, this plague that infects successful firms. To review, the 3 C's are conservatism, complacency, and conceit. Complacency is smugness, contentment, self satisfaction. Conservatism is wedded to the past, to tradition. Conceit is disdain for competitors. The current problems of Boeing should have destroyed any vestiges of the 3 C's mindset. But the former "king of the hill" position may be lost.

Growth must be manageable. Boeing certainly showed the fallacy of attempting growth beyond immediate capabilities in a growth-at-any-cost mindset. The rationale for embracing great growth is that we "need to run with the ball" if we ever get that rare opportunity to suddenly double or triple sales. But there are times when a slower, more controlled growth is prudent.

Risks lie on both sides as we reach for these opportunities. When a market begins to boom and a firm is unable to keep up with demand without greatly increasing capacity and resources, it faces a dilemma: (1) stay conservative in fear that the opportunity will be short-lived, but thereby abdicate some of the growing market to competitors, or (2) expand vigorously to take full advantage of the opportunity, but risk being overextended and vulnerable should the potential suddenly fade. Regardless of the commitment to a vision of great growth, a firm must develop an organization and systems and controls to handle it, or find itself in the morass of Boeing, with quality control problems, inability to meet production targets, alienated customers, and costs far out of line. And not the least, having its stock price savaged by Wall Street investors, while its market share tumbles. Growth must not be beyond the ability of the firm to manage it.

Perils of downsizing. Boeing presents a sobering example of the risks of downsizing in this era when downsizing is so much in fashion. With incredibly bad timing, it encouraged many of its most experienced and skilled workers and supervisors to take early retirement, just a few years before the boom began. Boeing found out the hard way that it could replace bodies, but not the skills needed to produce the highly complex planes under severe time pressure for output. It would have been better off to have maintained a core of experienced workers during the downturn, rather than lose them forever. It would have been better to have suffered with higher labor costs during the lean times, disregarding management's typical attitude of paring costs to the bone during such times. Yet, when we look at Table 10.1 and see the severe decreases of revenues and income in 1993, 1994, and lasting well into 1995, we can appreciate the dilemma of Boeing's management.

Problems of competing mostly on price. We have talked about the perils and the rewards of price competition in earlier cases such as Continental and Southwest. Price competition almost invariably leads to price cutting and even price wars to win market share. In such an environment, the lowest-cost, most-efficient producer wins. As we saw in the earlier Southwest Air case, its competitors could not match Southwest's fares and remain profitable, and eventually tried not to even compete with Southwest on the same routes.

More often, all firms in an industry have rather similar cost structures, and severe price competition hurts the profits of all competitors without bringing much additional business. Any initial pricing advantage is quickly matched by competitors unwilling to lose market share. In this situation, competing on nonprice bases has much to recommend it. Nonprice competition emphasizes uniqueness, perhaps in some aspects of product features and quality, perhaps through service and quicker deliveries or maybe better quality control. A firm's reputation, if good, is a powerful nonprice advantage.

Usually new and rapidly growing industries face price competition as marginal firms are weeded out and more economies of operation are developed. The more mature an industry, the greater likelihood of nonprice competition since cutthroat pricing causes too much hardship to all competitors.

Certainly the commercial aircraft production industry is mature, and much has been made of airlines being chiefly interested in how much passenger-carrying capacity they can buy for the same buck, and of their pitting Airbus and Boeing against each other in bidding wars.[11] Nonprice competition badly needs to be reinstated in this industry.

The synergy of mergers and acquisitions is suspect. The concept of synergy says that a new whole is better than the sum of its parts. In other words, a well-planned merger or acquisition should result in a better enterprise than the two separate entities. Theoretically, this would seem possible since operations can be streamlined for more efficiency and since greater management and staff compe-

[12] For example, Banks, *op. cit.,* p. 54.

tence can be brought to bear as greater financial and other resources can be tapped; or in Boeing's case, since the peaks and valleys of commercial demand could be countered by defense and space business.

Unfortunately, such synergy often is absent, at least in the short and intermediate term. More often such concentrations incur severe digestive problems—problems with people, systems, and procedures—that take time to resolve. Furthermore, greater size does not always beget economies of scale. The opposite may in fact occur: an unwieldy organization, slow to act, and vulnerable to more aggressive, innovative, and agile smaller competitors. The siren call of synergy is often an illusion.

The acquisitions of McDonnell Douglas and Rockwell may yet work out well for Boeing. But their assimilation came at a most troubling time for Boeing. The Long Beach plant of McDonnell Douglas alone led to a massive $1.4 billion write-off, and contributed significantly to the losses of 1997. Less easily calculated, but certainly a factor, was the management time involved in coping with these new entities.

CONSIDER

Can you think of additional learning insights?

QUESTIONS

1. Do you think Boeing should have anticipated the impact of Asian economic difficulties long before it did?

2. If it had anticipated sooner the drying up of the Asian market for planes, would this have prevented most of the problems now confronting Boeing? Discuss.

3. Do you think top management at Boeing should have been fired after the disastrous miscalculations in the late 1990s? Why or why not?

4. A major stockholder grumbles, "Management worries too much about Airbus, and to hell with the stockholders." Evaluate this statement. Do you think it is valid?

5. Take an optimistic stance. What do you see for Boeing three to five years down the road?

6. Do you think it likely that Boeing will have to contend with new competitors over the next ten years? Why or why not?

7. Discuss synergy in mergers. Why does it so many times seem to be lacking despite expectations?

8. You are a skilled machinist for Boeing, and had always been quite proud of participating in the building of giant planes. You have just received notice of another lengthy layoff, the second in five years. Discuss your likely attitudes and actions.

HANDS-ON EXERCISES

Before

1. You are a management consultant advising top management at Boeing. It is 1993 and the airline industry is in a slump, but early indications are that things will improve greatly in a few years. What would you advise that might have prevented the problems Boeing faced a few years later? Be as specific as you can, and support your recommendations as to practicality and probable effectiveness.

After

2. It is late 1998, and Boeing has had to announce drastic cutbacks, with little improvement likely before five years, and Boeing's stock has collapsed and Airbus is charging ahead. What do you recommend now? (You may need to make some assumptions; if so, state them clearly and keep them reasonable.)

TEAM DEBATE EXERCISE

A business columnist writes: Boeing could "have told customers 'no thanks' to more orders than its factories could handle. ... It "could have done itself a huge favor by simply building fewer planes and charging more for them."[13] Debate the merits of this suggestion.

INVITATION TO RESEARCH

What is the situation with Boeing today? Has it recovered its profitability? How is the competitive position with Airbus?

---

[13] Holman W. Jenkins Jr., "Boeing's Trouble: Not Enough Monopolistic Arrogance," *The Wall Street Journal* (December 16, 1998), p. A23.

CHAPTER ELEVEN

Toys Я Us: A Category Killer Loses Its Punch

*C*harles Lazarus was generally regarded as a genius who originated the category-killer concept with his Toys Я Us stores. His strategy of offering a huge variety of toys at very good prices, even if service left something to be desired, spawned a host of imitators with other categories of goods. The concept was so potent that it wiped out most other toy stores and even department stores where toys had always been featured at Christmastime. Most department stores gave up their Santas and elves, or else settled for only a few token and hoped-for best-selling items.

With such a powerful concept, how could any non-category-killer stores compete? Yet times were changing.

THE HEADY YEARS

The Beginning

Charles Lazarus, 22 years old, borrowed $2,000 to open a baby furniture store. World War II had ended and a baby boom was beginning. His first store was barely 40 feet by 60 feet. Later, the idea for a toy store came from a customer wanting to buy baby toys.

In 1957, he opened the first toy supermarket. Discount stores were just beginning to emerge on the retail scene and Lazarus's stores brought the discount format to a new category of goods. In the late 1970s, Lazarus took Toys Я Us public.

Toys Я Us (TRU) became both the largest and fastest-growing toy and children's specialty chain in the world. Its earnings grew an astonishing 40 percent a year between 1978 and 1983. Between 1985 and 1992, TRU opened an average of 43 toy stores each year in the United States, 17 more overseas, and 26 Kids Я Us apparel stores. In so doing, it pushed some rivals into bankruptcy and then snapped up their best store sites.

The stores were usually built in uniform dimensions, with this standardization lowering architectural costs, purchasing of fixtures, as well as such other costs as inventory and manpower requirements. Company executives also believed such standardization minimized customer confusion. The stores stocked some 18,000 items throughout the year, in sharp contrast to most competitors who shrunk their toy departments right after Christmas.

The year-round commitment of Toys Я Us not only generated significant sales volume throughout the year, but also had two further advantages: (1) It secured advantageous terms from toy vendors who quickly saw TRU as the major factor in the market that also provided some leveling of the extreme seasonality, and (2) TRU could determine which toys would be hot sellers in the coming peak Christmas selling season, and order accordingly. The competitive advantage over traditional toy retailers was awesome.

The company gained a whopping 25 percent share of toy retailing in the United States by 1990, and now turned its attention overseas. It pulled off a coup in 1991, breaking into the Japanese market, a market notorious for barriers to entry, especially to discount firms. Japanese consumers flocked to Toys Я Us, and in 1992 Michael Goldstein, then vice chairman, predicted that foreign sales would exceed $10 billion by 2000.[1]

The vast buying power of TRU brought prosperity to the major toy manufacturers, in particular, Mattel and Hasbro. For much of the past 15 years, these grew together with TRU. They acquired smaller manufacturers, but cut back on new toy development while funneling more money into movie and TV-licensed products. And they relied on TRU to be the sales engine. In the process, smaller toy departments and stores were spurned.

In these years it seemed that nothing could really compete against the category-killer retailers. See the following box for more discussion of the category-killer phenomenon.

INFORMATION BOX

CATEGORY-KILLER STORES

A category-killer store is the ultimate in specialty stores. It carries only a limited number of product categories, but offers tremendous choice within those categories. Category killers get their name from the strategy of carrying such a huge assortment of merchandise at good prices in a particular category of goods that they destroy the competition.

For example, Sportmart, a Chicago-based sporting goods chain, offered customers a choice of 70 models of sleeping bags, 265 styles of socks, and 15,000 fishing lures. The huge category-killer bookstores of Borders and Barnes & Noble have some 100,000 book titles in stock. Table 11.1 lists major category specialists.

---

[1] Paul Klebnikov, "Trouble in Toyland," *Forbes* (June 1, 1998), p. 60.

TABLE 11.1 Major Category Specialists

Company	Sales (Millions)	Number of Stores
Home Furnishings:		
Bed, Bath & Beyond	$ 601	80
Linens 'N Things	554	145
IKEA US	511	13
Crafts:		
Michaels	1,295	442
Fabri-Centers	835	936
Books:		
Barnes & Noble	1,349	358
Borders	684	116
Sporting Goods:		
Sports Authority	1,046	136
Sports and Recreation	526	80
Pet Supply:		
PETsMART	1,030	262
Office Supply:		
Office Depot	5,300	504
Staples	3,068	443
OfficeMax	2,543	468
Computers		
CompUSA	2,813	96
Computer City	1,800	99
Consumer Electronics:		
Best Buy	7,200	251
Circuit City	7,030	719

Sources: "DSN Top 200," *Discount Store News* (July 1, 1996), and "State of the Industry," *Chain Store Age Executive* (August 1996), Section 2.

Commentary: Why do you suppose there are no apparel category-killer stores? Or are there?

Do you think the category-killer superstores could result in overkill, in that they offer customers too much variety? Do you see any negative implications for a bookstore offering 100,000 different titles, or a sporting goods store with 70 different sleeping bags?

As 1998 began, TRU operated or franchised 1,454 stores that emphasized products for children. The flagship Toys Я Us chain included 698 stores in the United States, and 441 in overseas markets. Its Kids Я Us clothing chain had 215 domestic units. In 1997, the company had purchased a 77-store chain, Baby Superstores. It changed the name to Babies Я Us, and grew this to 98 stores, making it the country's largest baby-store chain. It had also opened two megastores called KidsWorld. These combined a toy store, a baby store, a clothing store, a shoe store, a restaurant, a candy store, as well as a kids' hair salon—two acres of floorspace. But these stores were too big for most customers, and no new ones were opened.

Sales for 1997 (actually fiscal year ending Jan. 31, 1998) reached $11 billion, which was an 11 percent increase over the previous year.

CLOUDS ON THE HORIZON

By the early 1990s the environment for toys began to change, a change not recognized very quickly by TRU management.

In 1994, Charles Lazarus, now 74, handed the reins to Michael Goldstein. Gradually the façade of invincibility began to crumble.

Discount chains such as Wal-Mart, Kmart, and Target starting using toys as loss leaders, pricing them at cost or below in order to attract customer traffic. Warehouse clubs like Sam's Club, Costco, and BJ's Wholesale Club began moving into the toy business. At the other end of the market, small chains emphasizing educational toys and interactive shopping for the smaller fry were growing fast; these included Zany Brainy and Noodle Kidoodle.

Suddenly, TRU was being tormented by price competition more severe than it had ever seen. As a double whammy, it was also beset by competitors' service and decor—aimed at making shopping a desirable experience for both parents and kids—beyond anything that its bare-bones boxy stores had even considered. Its big competitive advantage, vast assortments, was still there. But customers began to be drawn by other shopping considerations, not the least of which were avoiding the long waits at TRU cash registers.

At a Wal-Mart, the merchandise assortment may be one 16-inch bicycle instead of the half dozen at TRU. But the bicycle is less expensive, the store is clean and pleasant, and the sales clerks courteous and usually far more knowledgeable than those at TRU, who may be strained to even direct a customer to the right aisle in the cavernous building.

In efforts not to be too badly outpriced by the discounters, the operating margins of TRU slipped from 12 percent to 8 percent over the four years from 1994 to 1998. But still it could not match the prices of Wal-Mart and other discounters.

Michael Goldstein tried to use his market clout to get the big toy manufacturers such as Mattel and Hasbro not to sell to the warehouse clubs. This brought charges of anticompetitive practices by the Federal Trade Commission.

In 1996 Goldstein tried to react to the nicer decor of his new competitors. He instituted Concept 2000, a remodeling plan for the old utilitarian stores. As much as resources would allow, those stores selected were designed to be less cluttered, to be cleaner and brighter with nicer displays and fixtures, and to have better customer service. Books, videogames, Barbie dolls, and Legos were given separate departments. The cost of such rejuvenation averaged $1.5 million per store.

The new concept didn't work. For the money spent, the return on investment was not positive and most sales gains turned out to be disappointing. Eventually only 15 percent of the stores were remodeled; the rest remained the old warehouse-like boxes.

Even the international operations soured. The seeming coup in 1991 of breaking into the Japanese market, leading to the optimism of Goldstein for foreign sales exceeding $10 billion by 2000, was an acute disappointment. For 1997, foreign sales were only $3 billion. What went wrong?

For one thing, the TRU format needed cheap land and big parking lots, conditions hardly met in most foreign environments, whether Far East or Europe. Furthermore, labor laws and regulations were often stifling. TRU found that its operating margins suffered overseas: 6 percent compared to 8 percent in the United States. So this business proved less profitable than expected.[2]

Results

Things came to a head in March 1998. TRU announced earnings of $490 million, or $1.70 a share, for the year ended January 31, way below analysts' expectations. This reflected a loss in market share of toy retailing from 25 percent in 1990 to 20 percent. TRU soon announced inventory cutbacks, store closings, and work force cuts. In so doing, it took a $495 million charge. Efforts to reduce inventories involved another $500 million.[3]

Profitability problems continued into 1998. In the first half of the year, operating profit fell more than 30 percent. In the third quarter, income fell 50 percent.

Losing the Clout

As the largest toy seller, TRU had enjoyed tremendous clout with its suppliers. It was their largest single customer by far. Now this was changing. With the inventory cutbacks announced in 1998, Hasbro and Mattel faced drastic cutbacks in profits themselves. For example, Mattel's second-quarter 1998 sales to TRU were off $72 million, contributing to an 11 percent fall in second-quarter earnings for Mattel.[4]

Not surprising, Mattel expressed a need to reduce its dependency on TRU. For 1998, TRU was expected to account for 15 percent of Mattel's sales, down from 18 percent in 1997, and 22 percent in 1996. Sales to Wal-Mart, on the other hand, were up to 15 percent in 1997 from 12 percent in 1996.[5]

Hasbro's sales to TRU were down even more: $125 million for the first half of 1998, and expected to be down as much as $200 million for the full year.[6]

---

[2] Klebnikov, *op. cit.*, p. 60.

[3] Joseph Pereira, "Hasbro to Buy Galook, Issues Earnings Warning," *The Wall Street Journal* (September 29, 1998), p. B4.

[4] Lisa Bannon, "Mattel Cuts Forecast for Yearly Profit in Wake of Toys 'R' Us Restructuring," *The Wall Street Journal* (Sept. 25, 1998), p. B8.

[5] *Ibid.*

[6] Pereira, *op. cit.*, p. B4.

Such drastic cutbacks brought on by TRU's weaknesses suggested continuing problems for the company as suppliers were driven into the camps of major competitors, most notably Wal-Mart. The deteriorating market share trend of TRU would hardly be easy to turn around for it had lost its momentum to the most aggressive of competitors.

EFFORTS TO REVITALIZE

Two weeks into 1998, Michael Goldstein relinquished operating command to Robert Nakasone, 50, who had joined the firm in 1985.

Nakasone proposed a major revamping. Inventories would be streamlined and reduced with heavy markdowns to clear out slow-selling goods and overstocks. Some of the problems with inventories were a consequence of TRU stockrooms being a mess. The company averaged less than four inventory turns a year, compared with seven turns at Wal-Mart and eight turns at Target Stores.[7] The following box shows the importance of high inventory turnover for profitability.

Nakasone also announced that the work force would be slashed by as much as 3,000 or 2.8 percent, and 50 underperforming toy stores, mostly in Germany and France, and 9 in the United States, would be closed. Also, 31 of the 214 Kids Я Us clothing stores in the United States were to be closed as well as some distribution centers.

Nakasone pinned hopes for the future on TRU's new C-3 stores, with nine stores being tested for the Christmas season in Georgia, Tennessee, and North Carolina. In 1999 he planned to upgrade 200 of the 697 U.S. toy stores to this format, with most of the rest in 2000. The conversion would cost about $500,000 per store, considerably less than the $1.5 million of the Concept 2000 redesign. The new concept, as of November 1998, had not been truly tested, only strands of the concept had been in different stores. So much was at stake in these nine test stores. (We would expect company executives to be underfoot in these stores.)

The new C-3 stores included a reduction in the back-room space by 18 percent and a reorganization of the store's layout to feature more departmental display of goods. They were touted as being more customer friendly, cost effective, and having a concept with a long-term vision.[8]

To enhance shareholder value, the Board of Directors approved a $1 billion share repurchase program.

Following the company announcement of its charges to restructure its store base and reduce inventory levels, credit-rating agency Standard & Poor's on September 16, 1998 placed the debt of the company on a CreditWatch with negative implications for borrowing and interest rates.

---

[7] Klebnikov, *op. cit.*, p. 56.

[8] William M. Bulkeley, "Toys 'R' Us to Take Big Charge, Cut Jobs and Close 59 Stores," *The Wall Street Journal* (Sept. 17, 1998), p. A4; and Laura Liebeck, "Toys 'R' Us Shakes It Up," *Discount Store News* (October 5, 1998), p. 1.

INFORMATION BOX

IMPACT OF MERCHANDISE TURNOVER ON PROFITABILITY

Let us compare a Toys Я Us store with a Target store of the same sales volume. The TRU store has a turnover of 4, while Target has 8 turns.

Toys Я Us:
Sales	$ 12,000,000
Net profit percentage	5%
Net profit dollars	$600,000
Stock turnover	4
Average stock investment	

$$\frac{12,000,000}{4} = \quad \$ 3,000,000$$

Profitability as measured by return on investment, without considering investment in store and fixtures)

$$\frac{600,000}{3,000,000} = \quad 20\%$$

Target:
Sales	$ 12,000,000
Net profit percent	5%
Net profit dollars	$600,000
Stock turnover	8
Average stock investment	

$$\frac{12,000,000}{8} = \quad \$ 1,500,000$$

Return on investment

$$\frac{600,000}{1,500,000} = \quad 40\%$$

Therefore, the store with the higher stock turnover will be more profitable; it can also lower prices and still be as profitable (or more so) than its competitor with the lower turnover.

Note: To simplify this example, inventory investment is figured at retail price, rather than cost, which would technically be more correct. However, the significance of increasing turnover is more easily seen here.

Why does a store like Target (or Wal-Mart) have so much higher a merchandise turnover than Toys Я Us? What could TRU do to improve its turnover?

Standard & Poor's was also concerned about the company's use of excess cash flow and short-term borrowing to aggressively repurchase shares.[9]

ANALYSIS

Disregard for Environmental Changes

Toys Я Us never detected significant changes in its environment. This is another example of the unfortunate mindset that success guarantees continued success, that nothing needs to change.

So, for a crucial decade and a half it changed neither its stores nor its way of doing business. Sure, it opened more stores, all the same boxy warehouses. Sure, it diversified into babies and kids apparel stores, again with the same type of store. And it reached for overseas markets, as most firms were wont to do. But its operational strategy remained basically the same.

In particular, it ignored changes in

Competition

Consumer tastes

By the 1990s, new competitors were emerging. They were nothing like the small independents or the underfinanced imitators of TRU of the 1970s and 1980s or the department stores for whom toys were only a seasonal sideline. Now TRU faced the might of a Wal-Mart or a Target or warehouse clubs enlarging their toy departments, as well as the creative merchandising of slick toy chains such as Zany Brainy. It had become a victim of its own success. The profits piling up at TRU brought all these rivals salivating to get a piece of the action. And TRU had become flabby and inefficient.

With more attractive shopping alternatives, more and more consumers were becoming dissatisfied with the poor service and the lack of amenities at TRU. In an era of prosperity, greater choice (which TRU still offered, the major competitive advantage it had managed to hold onto) became not as strong a patronage factor as better prices, nicer decor, better service, and excitement/entertainment.

Inability to Be Competitive with Prices

TRU's operating efficiency had worsened over the years. The caliber of employees in its stores was not particularly high, reflecting a misguided cost containment. Undoubtedly, operating procedures and computer technology were not on the cutting edge. As a result, TRU was vulnerable when aggressive and very efficient competitors came on the scene. The inefficiency of TRU was most evident in inventory control and a much lower turnover than these new competitors. Many store stockrooms were a mess, and control inadequacies led to huge overstocks of some goods and stockouts of others. The efficient inventory control technology of firms like Wal-

---

[9] Bulkeley, *op. cit.*, p. A4.

Mart enabled them to sell profitably at lower prices than TRU could match without straining profit margins.

The Burden of Older Facilities

Half of the TRU toy stores in the United States were built before 1989 (358 of the total of 698 in 1998), and more than half of the Kids Я Us stores (112 of the total of 215 in 1998).[10] Many of these were much older than ten years. Its stores were consequently more dated than most of the newer competitors. In retrospect, we can criticize TRU management for not having established a systematic program for rejuvenating older facilities. But in the eagerness to open ever more new stores, it is easy to understand how older ones were given low priority for attention and funding. Still, this was a crucial flaw in the competitive struggle, and one that brought the need for a major catch-up program, but with it a dilemma in allocating scarce resources.

Defense

TRU instituted a major buyback program for its common stock. The motivation for buybacks of this kind is that profits can be distributed over fewer shares, thus making earnings per share higher to the benefit of investors. However, this is a temporary palliative at best. While it suggests that current stock market valuations of the firm are too low, it also raises the suspicion that management sees less payoff in investing for future growth.

THE ANSWER TO TRU'S PROBLEMS

At this stage in the life cycle of TRU, it appears to face three alternatives if it is to overcome what seems like a pervasive declining trend in market position and profits.

1. *Stronger expansion abroad.* It already has, as of the beginning of 1998, 441 stores overseas or 30 percent of all stores. This is a substantial overseas presence, but these stores have lower operating profits—6 percent versus 8 percent—than the domestic stores, primarily because of labor and other regulations and land expenses. Furthermore, as we near 2000, the economic situation in many countries remains less promising.

2. *Meet discount stores on price.* Given the relative inefficiencies of TRU compared to Wal-Mart and the other major competitors, it is unlikely that it can achieve this without a revolution in its inventory control and operating procedures. Even if it can do this, TRU will most likely only be matching the efficiency of competitors, and not be gaining a competitive advantage. With major discount competitors using toys as loss leaders, at least during the peak Christmas selling season, a price advantage for TRU can probably never be achieved.

---

[10] *1998 Toys Я Us Annual Report,* p. 2

3. *Upscaling.* This option on a large scale would have severe cost consequences. Profits would be drastically affected. But TRU may have no choice
but to do some modest scaling up. It must consider getting away from the
worst features of the drab warehouse box stores, and the poor service of low-
paid employees.

Finally

TRU may have to recognize that its category-killer concept was great in its time, but
now has become rusty as a vehicle for continued growth in toy retailing. Should this
experience be sobering for other category-killer stores?

WHAT CAN BE LEARNED?

Vulnerability of original masters. We see this time and again. Success does not
assure continued success. Harley Davidson and IBM exhibited this in Part I,
although both of these firms eventually made great comebacks. (Perhaps in
another edition Toys Я Us may also make a great comeback, but it seems doubtful now.) The three C's mindset of conservatism, complacency, and conceit
appears to be as operative for Toys Я Us as for these other firms.

Now with its aging and unattractive stores, slumping efficiency that results in
high overhead and higher prices, as well as poorer service than competitors, for
many consumers it is no longer the first choice for toy shopping.

Often, organizational malaise confronts a long-established frontrunner, malaise
not only of workers but also of management. It is difficult to detect such letting
down, until a competitive position starts to crumble. In the case of Toys Я Us, the
competitive position worsened rather insidiously. Other toy category-killer chains
had been vanquished by the stronger TRU. But the big general merchandise discounters gradually upped their toy assortments, while smaller creative toy chains
expanded with nice success. Nothing sudden, nothing traumatic—perhaps this is
the worst kind of competitive climate, since it is so lulling to the frontrunner.

How can frontrunners stay sharp? TRU needed to keep in the forefront of
the industry in its stores, in technology (primarily computers for information and
inventory control), and in procedures for handling operations as efficiently as possible. Stores should have been refurbished and updated on a regular schedule.
TRU should have led in the development of inventory control systems and efficient stockroom and warehouse handling and storage of goods to assure lean and
adequate stocks. Constant efforts should have been made to assure that procedures were streamlined, that demands on suppliers were reasonable while extract-
ing from them maximum efficiency in providing goods promptly at lowest prices.
TRU had the clout to demand the same efficiency from suppliers as it did for itself.

Then there were the employees and management people. Higher caliber,
more motivated people were sorely needed. To attract such people was perhaps
the most difficult problem of all. Profit-sharing, better advancement opportuni-

ties, incentive pay, a specific program to lure higher caliber people—such could have made TRU a more attractive place to work. To the defensive argument that this would cost too much, we know that Wal-Mart and Target have achieved far better employees. At the least it would seem that TRU could have done a much better job of hiring, training, and motivating its people.

Can consumers have too much choice? The premise of category-killer stores is that the more choice offered, the greater the appeal. This may be true for books. But is it true for toys, and everything else? For many consumers, so much choice is confusing, makes decisions difficult, and is time-consuming. For those consumers not altogether thrilled at unlimited choice, the only competitive advantage of Toys Я Us is lost.

The Concept of Value

The management guru, Peter Drucker, recently discussed in *Forbes* the need for managers to change their thinking from old assumptions of the past. One of his paradigms concerns the importance of value to a customer, and how this may differ drastically from what management thinks it is.[11]

We can consider what value really is to a mother buying toys. Is a mind-boggling assortment to choose from really the value she is looking for?—especially when checkout lines are four and five deep? or might ease of shopping, good prices, reasonable assortment, and some interactive things for her kids to do in the store while she shops be of far more value?

CONSIDER

Can you think of additional learning insights that could be applicable to other firms in other situations?

QUESTIONS

1. Do you think a consumer can have too much choice in shopping? What might this depend on?

2. Do you think the absolute lowest price for an item is most important for many consumers? What percent would you say comparison shop for the lowest price? What implications, if any, do you see from your estimate?

3. Compare the future promise of Borders, the book superstore, and Toys Я Us. What in your judgment accounts for the difference in their prospects?

4. "Let's face it. Toys Я Us has seen its heyday. It will never come again. It should be content with a smaller share of the market, and not worry so much about Wal-Mart, and making all kinds of drastic and expensive changes." Evaluate this statement from a stockholder.

---

[11] Peter F. Drucker, "Management's New Paradigms," *Forbes* (October 5, 1998), pp. 169–170.

5. Would you be content to work as a management trainee at Toys Я Us today? If not, what would it take to attract you?

6. In its early decades, Toys Я Us ran roughshod over all competitors. Yet today, bigger, with more resources and experience, it is faltering. How do you explain this?

7. In what way does inventory turnover affect profitability? How can inventory turnover be increased?

HANDS-ON EXERCISES

1. It is 1990 and you are a senior assistant to the general merchandise manager of TRU. You sense that the toy environment is changing and you are concerned that TRU is not changing. You have repeatedly told your boss about your concerns, but to no avail. What might you do at this point? Discuss your rationale for whatever decision (or no decision) you take. Also consider the implications.

2. You are a staff assistant to the new CEO, R.C. Nakasone. He has assigned you to develop a proposal to improve the "shopability" of existing TRU stores. He wants you to consider all aspects of this, from some remodeling—but probably not to exceed $500,000 per store—to better customer service, better employees, better layout, as well as what ever other aspects you may come up with. In addition to the recommendations, he wants you to consider the cost/benefit implications. (You may need to make some assumptions on costs.)

TEAM DEBATE EXERCISE

Debate the whole general issue of drastic change versus moderate change for TRU. In arguing the two sides, consider both short-term and long-term aspects. Try to be as specific as you can, including cost consequences, with the less-than-complete information that is available. Be as persuasive in presenting your position as possible, and attack the others' position.

INVITATION TO RESEARCH

1. Try to find out as much about TRU's management development program as you can, such as educational and experiential requirements, starting pay and future expectations, most likely career path, and so on.

2. How is TRU doing today? Has the stock market price come back? How are the newest "C-3 format" stores doing? What has happened to market share?

CHAPTER TWELVE

Saturn's Problems in Japan

*I*n many ways General Motors' Saturn subsidiary had been a success. It was the first really effective effort by a U.S. automaker to emulate and even surpass Japanese cars, offering low prices, reliability, and good looks. In addition, the Saturn was the vanguard of enlightened customer service.

Sales during the first years exceeded company expectations, as well as production capability, with customers waiting up to 2 months for their Saturns. But in these early years, the Saturn was only a dubious success as it was not profitable until 1994.

In its sixth year of sales, 1996, Saturn was the second-best-selling retail car in the United States, behind only Honda Accord. It had a 60 percent customer loyalty rating—meaning that 60 percent of its car buyers bought their next car from Saturn, too. On the J. D. Power & Associates Customer Satisfaction Index, it still routinely outperformed all other manufacturers except the many times more expensive Lexus and Infiniti.

Perhaps it was only natural that Saturn turned its sights overseas, to Japan. In 1997 it came to Japan, seeking to disprove the notion that U.S. carmakers were not trying hard enough to sell their cars there.

BACKGROUND

The beginnings of Saturn stretch to 1982. Originally, it represented an ambitious effort by General Motors to make small cars in the United States as cheaply and well as they could be made overseas. Roger Smith, the CEO of GM at the time, called the $5 billion undertaking "the key to GM's long-term competitiveness."[1]

The project represented GM's attempt to rethink every aspect of automaking. It was hoped that production innovations could save $2,000 from the cost of building a subcompact car. Initial plans called for selling 400,000 units yearly.

So important was the project deemed to be in the total GM scheme that by 1985 Saturn had become a new GM subsidiary. A new factory was to be built from scratch,

---

[1] William J. Hampton, "Will Saturn Ever Leave the Launchpad? *Business Week* (March 16, 1987), p. 107.

and in the search for a new site, bids flooded in from dozens of states. GM finally chose a site near Spring Hill, Tennessee.

Hardly had work begun on the new factory in early 1986 before some company goals began changing. As new models of lowest price imports began coming in from Korea and Yugoslavia, GM executives abandoned the idea of competing on price. Now they began targeting the car for the middle of the import pack, where prices were several thousand dollars higher. As a result the car had grown larger, now positioned between subcompacts such as the Chevrolet Cavalier and midsize cars such as the Oldsmobile Ciera. Sales estimates were downsized. A "first-phase" plant was opened with a capacity for 250,000 cars, with a second factory to be added if sales were strong enough.

By early 1987 pessimists were predicting that the Saturn was doomed. Although production was at least several years away, already demand seemed to be slackening for small cars, and GM was experiencing difficulty with high-tech factories. The more optimistic rumors were that GM might try to save face by folding the separate Saturn subsidiary into the Chevrolet or Pontiac division.

THE EARLY YEARS

As the 1980s drew to a close, GM's share of the U.S. passenger-car market slumped to 33 percent, a loss of 11 points in only five years. At the same time, Japanese car makers had a seven-point gain in market share, to 26 percent. Consumer surveys were even bleaker: A study by J. D. Powers & Associates found that 42 percent of all new-car shoppers would not even consider a GM car.[2] Saturn now began to assume a position of greater importance to GM. Its new fundamental goal was to sell 80 percent of its cars to drivers who otherwise would not have bought a GM car.

Saturn's ascendancy on the eve of its production inauguration had the full support of GM chairman Roger Smith, although his term of office was soon to end. Smith saw the Saturn as having a bigger role than simply appealing to import buyers. He saw it as an example for the rest of GM as to how to reform its own ponderous and tradition-ridden culture. Indeed, Saturn had created an innovative blend of enlightened labor relations, participatory management, and new technology for the latest manufacturing operations. GM was especially interested in the manufacturing and labor breakthroughs that Saturn had initiated. Just as innovative, but not to be recognized for another year or so, was the great change in traditional passenger-car marketing, customer relations, and servicing.

The company was now becoming so optimistic of Saturn's competitiveness that one marketing strategy under consideration was to have dealers place a Honda Civic, a Toyota Corolla, and an Acura Integra in the same show-room with a Saturn and let customers make their own direct comparisons.

Admittedly, the final version of the Saturn was not the 60-mile-per-gallon, $6,000 subcompact originally envisioned, but it was a gem nevertheless. Dealers were

[2] James B. Treece, "Here Comes GM's Saturn," *Business Week* (April 9, 1990), p. 57.

allowed to drive prototypes at GM's Mesa, Arizona, proving grounds, and they were enthusiastic about the car's power train and handling: "We went 100 miles per hour, and it was still going strong," said a Saturn dealer from St. Louis. "It was going through curves at 75 to 80 that imports couldn't."[3] Another dealer who also sold Hondas remarked that a Saturn, besides having the quickness and nimbleness of a Honda, "doesn't have the vibrations that the current domestic models have."[4]

The first Saturns were ready for sale in November 1990. In that first month, 641 were sold. Sales more than doubled to 1,520 by January 1991. The rush was on, limited only by the production capabilities of the single factory. Table 12.1 shows the growth in units sold from the beginning through July 1992. Table 12.2 shows comparative figures of the sales and market share of Saturn to other GM units and also to major Japanese competitors and the total car market for 1991 and 1992. Saturn's surge was awesome.

AFTER TWO YEARS

As demand outstripped supply, dealers were staring at empty lots. In July 1992 Saturn dealers sold 22,305 cars—an average of 115 apiece, twice the rate per dealer for the

TABLE 12.1   Selected Monthly Sales, Saturn, November 1990 through July 1992

Month	Units	Percent Increase
November 1990	641	
January 1991	1,520	137.1%
March 1991	3,302	117.7
May 1991	6,832	106.9
July 1991	8,538	25.0
November 1991	8,355	(2.1)
January 1992	10,757	28.7
March 1992	16,757	55.8
May 1992	18,031	7.6
July 1992	22,305	23.7

Source: David Woodruff, "Saturn: GM Finally Has a Real Winner, but Success Is Bringing a Fresh Batch of Problems," *Business Week* (August 7, 1992), pp. 86–87.

Commentary: Note the steady increase in monthly sales during this time period. Table 12.2 shows further statistics on Saturn's growth. A winner of major proportions for a U.S. automaker seemed to be emerging.

[3] *Ibid.*, p. 58.
[4] *Ibid.*

TABLE 12.2   **Saturn Sales and Market Share Comparisons**

	August		Year to Date	
	1991	1992	1991	1992
Retail Sales (units):				
Saturn	7,000	12,039	40,858	129,753
All GM Subcompacts	33,387	36,322	224,127	306,952
All Subcompacts	171,089	153,936	1,152,287	1,212,509
Total GM	221,547	198,172	2,012,599	1,992,835
Total Industry	690,442	644,808	5,601,704	5,584,494
Market Share:				
Saturn	1.0%	1.9%	0.7%	2.3%
All GM Subcompacts	4.8	5.6	4.0	5.5
Total Detroit Subcompacts	10.0	10.6	8.8	10.0
Total Toyota	5.0	4.3	4.0	4.2
Total Nissan	1.9	2.8	1.9	2.2
Total Honda	4.1	3.5	2.8	2.6
Total Japanese Nameplates	13.0	12.3	10.3	10.8
Total Subcompacts	24.8	23.9	20.6	21.7

Source: Industry statistics.

Commentary: Noteworthy are the substantial Saturn gains, both in sales and market share, from 1991 to 1992 against all other makes, domestic and foreign. Note in particular the market share gains against Japanese competitors: Toyota, Nissan, and Honda. The GM charge for Saturn to take business away from the Japanese imports appeared to be fully realized as 1992 drew to a close, yet Saturn had still to make a profit.

nearest competitor, Toyota.[5] Foreign rivals continued to flood the market with new models, but Saturn was meeting them head on. It had become the highest quality American-made brand, with as few defects as Hondas and Nissans. In customer-satisfaction ratings, according to a survey by J. D. Power & Associates, buyers rated the Saturn ahead of all American-made cars and most imports. Only Lexus and Infiniti— much higher priced cars—were ranked higher. (See Table 12.3.)

The success of Saturn, however, was causing some problems at GM headquarters. To bring plant capacities in line with the demand, GM would have to pump in more money at a time when the auto giant was facing serious financial problems. In 1991 its North American operations had a devastating $7.5 billion loss. Every dollar spent on Saturn meant that struggling divisions such as Chevrolet, which badly needed to update its outmoded models, would receive less. And at a time when GM was closing assembly plants to the anguished consternation of union workers and local governments, the arena was politically not conducive for a still-money-losing Saturn to receive funds to fully capitalize on its burgeoning customer demand.

[5] David Woodruff, "Saturn," *Business Week* (August 17, 1992), p. 86.

**TABLE 12.3   1992 Customer-Satisfaction Ratings
(Score on J. D. Power's Survey of New Car Buyers)**

Lexus	179
Infiniti	167
Saturn	160
Acura	148
Mercedes-Benz	145
Toyota	140
Industry Average	129

Source: J. D. Power's Survey of New Car Buyers, 1992, as reported by
David Woodruff, "Saturn," *Business Week* (August 17, 1992), pp. 86–87;
and Raymond Serafin and Cleveland Horton, "Automakers Focus on
Service," *Advertising Age* (July 6, 1992), pp. 3, 33.

Commentary: Nissan's Infiniti and Toyota's Lexus have established new
industry benchmarks for coddling luxury car buyers. Compared with that
elite group, Saturn has surprisingly placed a close third by redefining the
standard for treatment of buyers of lower priced mass-volume cars. This
high rating is credited to Saturn's elimination of price haggling, high commitment to quality-control, and trail-blazing example of replacing 1,800
cars after a coolant mixup. Saturn's customer-satisfaction commitment is
not lost on Chrysler: All Chrysler brands finished below industry averages, and Chrysler announced a $30 million massive training effort to
improve the way its dealerships handle shoppers and owners.

A GM decision to delay any new investment would seriously jeopardize Saturn.
At the end of July 1992, Saturn dealers had only a 10-day supply of cars on hand; one-
sixth of normal stock. Dealers worried that customers would switch to competing
brands because of unacceptable delays in servicing their orders, which could devas-
tate Saturn's momentum and make it easy for the great GM bureaucracy to downplay
an innovative but unprofitable new division.

Several options short of massive new plant investments were possible. GM
Chairman Robert C. Stempel, who replaced Smith, thought it possible to up the productivity at the single Spring Hill plant. Saturn President Richard G. LeFauve was
rightly concerned about the dangers of pushing too hard for production at the
expense of quality. During a visit by Stempel, after production goals had been
increased along with the number of defects, line workers staged a slowdown, resulting in an easing of production goals. LeFauve saw a temporary solution in adding a
third shift, which could boost capacity by 44 percent.[6]

Rather than adding another plant, LeFauve proposed an additional $1 billion
investment in Spring Hill, which would bring its capacity to 500,000 and enable the
division to meet demand for new models. Increased production would permit expansion beyond the 195 original Saturn dealers so that all states could be covered.

---

[6] Woodruff, p. 88.

Saturn executives worried how to keep their value-conscious buyers as the buyers grew older and wanted to upgrade to bigger cars with more comfort and features. Plans for larger cars and new models depended on further GM investment.

Stempel argued that current Saturn buyers would easily move up to existing GM brands that traditionally cater to older buyers, such as Oldsmobile, Buick, and Cadillac. Still, it was doubtful that Saturn buyers would readily fall into such a trade-up mode, given that most of them were former import buyers who would not have purchased a GM product other than a Saturn.

If GM top management could be convinced to expand Saturn, it was more likely that an older plant would be retooled, rather than a new one built from scratch, regardless of the technological advantages a new facility would offer. Rejuvenating an older plant would save several hundred million dollars and would be more palatable to unions and communities that had experienced the trauma of plant shutdowns. The following issue box discusses the decision problems in allocating scarce resources among competing claims.

ISSUE BOX

HOW SHOULD WE PARCEL OUT INVESTMENT FUNDS?

By mid-1992 the GM executive suite was facing a dilemma of mean consequences. Record multibillion-dollar losses had strapped the company financially, yet never before had the demands for additional investment been so compelling. Saturn, although yet to turn a profit, was a bright star that needed substantial additional production facilities to fully tap its potential. But other divisions, ones dating to the beginnings of GM, needed substantial expenditures either to keep them competitive or to bring them back from the brink. Chevrolet in particular needed funds:

> This flagship division of GM two decades ago was selling one-fifth of all cars in the United States. Now its market share had fallen to only 12.1%. Accentuating the seriousness of Chevrolet's decline, it had long served as GM's entry-level division, the one whose customers often "graduated" to bigger, more expensive GM cars. Chevy dealers were convinced that the aging, hard-to-sell cars in their showrooms were the direct result of GM's generosity to Saturn.[7]

How should problems like this be resolved? Should the nascent star receive whatever it takes to fulfill its promise? Should scarce dollars be committed to resurrecting and sustaining deprived divisions? Should some sort of compromise be worked out, satisfying no one but creating the most equitable solution? Stakeholders in such allocation decisions are more than employees and managers; dealers, communities where plants are located, suppliers, and even customers, have a stake.

How would you resolve this dilemma? Explain your rationale, and support it as persuasively as you can.

---

[7] Kathleen Kerwin, "Meanwhile, Chevy Is Sulking in the Garage," *Business Week* (August 17, 1992), pp. 90–91.

The unique relations of Saturn with its autoworkers will be described more fully in the next section. All workers were given a voice in management decisions, and 20 percent of their pay was linked to quality, productivity, and profitability. In late 1992, dissident union workers forced a vote on the teamwork-oriented labor contract that had been approved in November 1991 by a 72 percent margin. They claimed that this innovative contract ignored some seniority rights earned at other GM plants. On January 13, 1993, workers voted 2-to-1 to keep their teamwork-oriented labor contract, with the vote "reflecting strong endorsement of the partnership between union and management, which works hand in hand with Saturn's mission, philosophy, and values."[8]

INGREDIENTS OF SUCCESS

A New Labor-Management Climate

A large part of Saturn's success has been an enlightened labor-management relationship, one unique among U.S. carmakers in its sharing of responsibility, although a similar approach has been used by Japanese firms.

At first the Saturn plant was conceived as a high-tech operation with robots and automated guided vehicles. But GM's experiences in a joint venture with Toyota Motor corporation in Fremont, California, suggested that a change in labor-management relations could be more important for productivity and quality.

LeFauve, the president of the new subsidiary, was convinced that factory floor workers could make a difference, and he led the way for GM management and the United Auto Workers to work closely together almost from the beginning. Saturn employees and managers eat in the same cafeterias. Under a "team concept," workers are split into groups of 6 to 15 and are headed by a supervisor chosen jointly by workers and managers. Each team is responsible for meeting its own training and production goals. Workers start at a base pay equal to about 90 percent of the average pay at GM and other major U.S. automaker plants. Then they earn bonuses if specific production levels and quality targets are met.

In 1988 Saturn began visiting GM plants and UAW halls in search of workers. Recruiters sought current and laid-off workers willing to shed old habits and work as a team. The choice was not easy for some: They would have to quit their union locals and give up all seniority rights, and there would be no going back. Those who accepted the challenge developed a cultlike commitment.

Training was rigorous. New arrivals faced five days of "awareness training" to teach them how to work in teams and build consensus. Beyond that, workers received 100 to 750 hours of training that even included learning to read a balance sheet, since Saturn opened its books internally and wanted employees to know how much their operations were adding to the cost of a car.

Integration of Production

In contrast to other GM assembly plants, Spring Hill went beyond the usual paint shop and body and assembly plant. Its highly integrated facility includes a power train

---

[8] "Saturn Workers Keep Contract," *Cleveland Plain Dealer* (January 15, 1993), p. E1.

factory that casts, machines, and assembles engines and transmissions. A plastic-molding plant and a shop for assembling the instrument panel and dash into a single unit are also on site. Saturn consequently did not have to rely on key components supplied by factories hundreds of miles away, thus saving on freight costs and shipping delays. Still, some glitches can occur, and a minor delay can shut down the whole operation, but these delays have become increasingly rare.[9]

Quality Control

From the beginning Saturn sought to emphasize quality and freedom from defects. If it was ever to have a chance with its target customers, former buyers of imports, this was essential. The customer-satisfaction ratings (see Table 12.2) confirmed that Saturn had indeed achieved this objective, and while many buyers of imports were skeptical of any American car at first, the durability of Saturn's reputation for quality was converting more and more of them back to an American car.

Buyers' complaints had been quite limited, but Saturn strove to correct those received. Early on there were two recalls: one for defective seats and another for corrosive engine coolant. Some early complaints were of insufficient headroom and noisy, vibrating engines. The company addressed these complaints rather quickly, lowering rear seats half an inch below the initial design, redesigning engine mounts, and adding more insulation under the hood. However, the company's handling of the necessary recalls epitomized a unique approach to customer relations and to the commitment to quality. The information box details an almost unbelievable innovation in the treatment of recalls.

Most often credited for the high quality ratings was the revolutionary labor agreement. This agreement made partners of Saturn's blue-collar and white-collar workers and gave everyone the authority to solve quality problems, from phoning suppliers for corrective action to rearranging machinery to improve quality and productivity. Motivation was spurred by bonuses for meeting specific production levels and quality targets.

Worker comfort was considered in design of the final assembly line, the theory being that less strain on workers translates into fewer mistakes. Consequently, the whole facility was air conditioned. The floor of the assembly line was wood instead of concrete—a first in North America—thus making standing all day less tiresome. And the line itself was designed with the worker in mind: Car bodies moved on pallets that could be raised or lowered for the worker's ease, and workers rode with the body they were working on rather than walking to keep up with the body as on other assembly lines.

Dealer Strategy

While the success of Saturn left many dealers with insufficient cars even to come close to meeting demand, dealers had to be pleased when their monthly sales of 115 apiece in July 1992 were twice the rate per dealer of their nearest competitor, Toyota.

---

[9] Woodruff, p. 88.

INFORMATION BOX

RECALL MAGIC IN FOSTERING QUALITY CREDIBILITY

Only a few months after production commenced for the Saturn, the company was forced to send out 1,836 letters to customers, telling them that the car's radiator had been supplied with a faulty coolant and that the cars must be recalled. Such recalls are rather common in the industry, and car owners grudgingly put up with the inconvenience, but Saturn's recall was different. It offered to replace the cars, not just repair them. Consequently, regardless of odometer readings, each customer was supplied with a brand new Saturn at no cost. One couple, unwilling to wait three weeks for Saturn to deliver a replica of their old car, chose a red model from the lot. It had a sunroof, unlike their old car, but they were given this $530 option for free. Saturn also paid for a rental car for a day and even drove the couple to the rental company's lot.[10] Not surprisingly, Saturn's actions converted the recall into a major coup in customer relations and initiated the image—as no words alone could ever have—of an overwhelming commitment to quality and customer satisfaction.

In the process of handling the recall, Saturn broke other new ground. It publicly named Texaco as the supplier of the bad coolant. When Texaco learned that it would be identified in the Saturn recall, it rushed its explanation to customers: a freak accident, in which a special order of coolant contained too much sodium hydroxide, making it much more caustic and corrosive, especially for Saturn's aluminum engines. In light of the unfavorable publicity focused on the supplier, Texaco prepared to bear the costs associated with this mistake.

Saturn thus placed new responsibilities on its suppliers, that they provide parts meeting specifications without requiring Saturn inspectors to assure quality. At risk was severe damage to a supplier's reputation.

Assess the pros and cons of such drastic handling of recalls in other situations and with other firms. On balance, can we as consumers expect such liberalization in any other recalls of the auto industry?

---

[10] James B. Treece, "Getting Mileage from a Recall," *Business Week* (May 27, 1991), p. 38.

Saturn had been slow in opening new dealerships, especially with demand outstripping production capability. With only 195 dealers by late 1992, these dealers were virtually assured of no close competition from other Saturn dealers. This strategy of maintaining fewer dealers flies in the face of the traditional practice of having many dealerships in each market.

Initially most dealerships were on the east and west coasts, the heart of import demand. California's Santa Clara county imports, for example, had more than 65 percent of the market. Many of the chosen dealers had also sold imports, because Saturn management believed they would know best how to appeal to such buyers.

The decision to concentrate initially on the coasts left some states without any dealerships. It also left the populous midwest undercovered. The midwest was the heart of the "buy American" sentiments, however, and was the area where GM was already strongest. It was believed that aggressive Saturn efforts here could take more sales away from other GM makes than from foreign automakers.

Advertising

The company turned to San Francisco's Hal Riney & Partners for folksy, offbeat advertising. The target customer was similar to a target Honda Civic buyer: median age 33; 68 percent female; 52 percent married; 60 percent with college degrees; 46 percent holding managerial or professional jobs; and with median household income over $40,000.[11] Ads focused on buyers' lifestyles, playing up product themes that baby boomers could easily relate to, such as safety, utility, and value. The approach did much to create an image for Saturn as an unusual car company, and the pricing practices further advanced this theme.

Innovation in Pricing and the Selling Process

Saturn initiated a new approach to pricing and the car-selling process that was a revolution in the auto industry. A variable price policy had long been traditional, with a customer attempting to drive the best bargain possible and in the process participating in an adversarial contest with the car sales person and his or her sales manager. Since the consumer lacked sufficient knowledge about costs and markups and was often uncomfortable and inexperienced with haggling, many car buyers disliked having to negotiate and were never sure if they were getting a reasonable deal.

Saturn cars carried no rebates and were priced at a set bottom price, with no haggling or negotiating needed or accepted. In late 1992, prices started at $9,195, even after an average 8 percent hike for 1993 models. Customers loved the change in automobile retailing, and they knew they were not paying more than a neighbor for the same car.

Other automakers began to emulate Saturn. Ford started selling its subcompact Escort models at one low price. Chrysler was testing the concept. Even Japanese companies were closely watching the acceptance of the innovation. Somehow GM appeared slow to embrace the one-price policy elsewhere in the organization.

Ruling out haggling was only one part of the Saturn innovation in retailing. In formal courses in Spring Hill, managers and salespeople were instructed in low-pressure selling techniques. The theme of the training was that pampering customers could create word-of-mouth advertising that would be particularly effective in such high-priced and even traumatic purchases as cars.

Combining a good product and top-notch service was bound to lead to happy Saturn customers. But good customer relations went even further. Both dealerships and Saturn headquarters followed up with customers to ascertain their satisfaction.

---

[11] Larry Armstrong, "If It's Not Japanese, They Wouldn't Bother Kicking the Tires," *Business Week* (April 9, 1990), p. 6.

Such followup even went so far as special Saturn newsletters, Saturn clubs, and famous homecoming weekends in Spring Hill, Tennessee. In spring 1995, 44,000 people were drawn to this small town and its Saturn plant.

GM'S DILEMMA

Saturn's apparent success was not a particular cause for rejoicing at corporate head-quarters in late 1992. Undoubtedly it would have been if the new venture were proving profitable, but several years and billions of dollars of new investment were thought to be necessary before Saturn turned the corner. Meanwhile, General Motors faced a serious cash crunch, all the more serious after a $7.5 billion loss from North American operations in 1991.

Former chairman Roger B. Smith conceived the Saturn project as a laboratory in which to reinvent his company. When he retired, the firm's commitment cooled despite Saturn having initiated notable innovations in American carmaking. Most of all, it had achieved quality levels deemed impossible by U.S. firms still bedeveled by defects and by an uncomplimentary image compared with foreign imports.

By late 1995, Saturn's unique character was endangered as GM took away its autonomy and brought it under the corporate organization umbrella. This, in spite of Saturn having achieved its first profitable year in 1994. Donald Hudler, then head of Saturn sales and marketing, estimated eventual sales of about 500,000 cars a year, with about 100,000 coming from overseas. To achieve this would require additional investment in production and engineering as well as additional dealers.

In its sixth year of sales, 1996, Saturn was the second-best-selling car in the United States. It also began introducing its innovative marketing to used cars. For used Saturns as well as other "extensively checked-out makes," it offered limited warranties, a 30-day/1,500 miles trade-in policy, as well as a 3-day money-back guarantee. All this with a haggle-free, high-pressure-free selling environment.

THE JAPANESE INVASION

In 1997, Saturn invaded Japan, but on a much more modest scale than Japan had invaded the United States decades earlier. There was ample incentive for such conservative efforts. Since 1996, all three U.S. automakers had tried and failed in this market. These included Chrysler's Neon, Ford's right-hand drive Taurus, and GM's Cavalier.

Saturn wanted to compete with the Japanese rivals as an everyday car, not some novelty item. It installed right-hand steering, a necessity where people drove on the left side of the road. But it also added such features as folding side mirrors to better cope with Japan's narrow streets. It priced its cars around $14,000, below most foreign imports and competitive with Japanese models.

In contrast to the other U.S. cars that distributed through giant importers that sold many different makes of cars, Saturn set up its own dealerships, some nineteen by the middle of 1998. It advertised itself as a friendly company, showing scenes of Saturn's bucolic U.S. headquarters in Tennessee, and its salespeople instead of wearing suits were attired more casually. In an effort to attract parents, every showroom had a play area with toys. Radically departing from traditional selling methods in Japan, Saturn brought its no-haggling policy without high pressure as it sought to reinforce a reputation as a user-friendly company.

Unfortunately, the results were not good. In its first 16 months, Saturn sold only 1,400 cars.

As it turned out, the timing could not have been much worse. The government in the midst of the deepest recession since World War II instituted a consumption tax that depressed all auto sales by nearly 13 percent. A weak yen also hurt profitability, as Keith Wicks, the general director of Saturn Japan, ruefully declared that Saturn can't raise prices "in a deader-than-a-doornail market."[12]

What Went Wrong?

Aside from the bad economy and abysmal timing, can Saturn eventually crack this market that has been so difficult for U.S. manufacturers? Admittedly, the price of Saturn placed it in the most highly competitive sector. It was in direct competition with Japanese cars whose quality levels U.S. manufacturers had been trying to emulate for decades, and Saturn had come closest to achieving. The only U.S. cars that have done at all well in Japan have been the Cadillac Seville and Chrysler's Jeep Cherokee, all much higher priced and appealing to a different customer. The three models of Saturn—four-door sedan, two-door coupe, and station wagon—provided customers little choice and nothing distinctive against the dozens of different models in a similar price range.

Saturn's decision to develop its own dealership network undoubtedly slowed its inroads, since 19 in all of Japan provided poor market coverage, leaving who knows how many potential customers unable to find a dealership. But with the economic conditions and slow sales, attracting more dealers proved difficult, to the point that Saturn was even considering offering financing to any who might be interested.

With Saturn unable to differentiate its cars much from competing cars, its selling environment was its major uniqueness: no-haggle, nonpushy, with cars priced as marked, thereby avoiding the negotiation confrontations of other dealers. It was thought that younger customers and women in particular disliked negotiating.

Still, it sought to provide some uniqueness to its cars, offering limited edition cars. Some of these were equipped with special trimmings and accessories, such as CD and Minidisk players, and built-in navigation systems, which were popular in Japan. Saturn also introduced some of the U.S. dealer promotional efforts, such as community flea markets and owners' parties.[13]

Prognosis

Success in Japan is not assured for Saturn. If, however, GM gives Saturn a long enough leash for its creativity, as well as a time frame of 4 to 7 years to get into the

---

[12] Lisa Shuchman, "How Does GM's Saturn Sell Cars in Japan? Very Slowly," *The Wall Street Journal* (August 25, 1998), p. B4.

[13] *Ibid.*, pp. B1 and B4.

black, it may still achieve reasonable market penetration. But it desperately needs more dealers, although this should come as economic conditions in Japan improve. It also needs more models, particularly a sports utility vehicle (which Saturn also badly needs in the United States).

Regarding its innovative no-haggle policy, should this prove popular with Japanese consumers, it certainly should be easy enough to imitate. Some Toyota dealers are already testing this approach to selling.[14] So Saturn' efforts to differentiate may not be enduring.

WHAT CAN BE LEARNED?

A good reputation must be zealously safeguarded. Saturn gained a notable reputation for quality, unique among U.S. cars, and one of the best among all cars. Such a reputation for being defect-free was an invaluable asset, both in keeping current customers who were likely to buy another Saturn and in attracting new customers by word-of-mouth publicity.

However, one of the realities of a good reputation or public image is that it can quickly be destroyed. In the case of Saturn, if the company lapses a bit on its commitment to quality—especially in pursuit of the profit demands of the parent—then the good reputation will be lost. And Saturn will reside with the other U.S. cars: just another domestic car unable to match the imports in workmanship and quality.

In large firms, politics may work to the detriment of the newcomer. With its untapped and growing consumer demand in its first years of operation, Saturn seemed worthy of substantial additional funding. But GM found itself with limited financial resources and consequent allocation problems. Long-established divisions such as Chevrolet and Oldsmobile competed with Saturn for needed funds. In the presence of such corporate power relations, Saturn, the upstart, found itself thwarted by internal jealousies and entrenched interests.

Is there a moral here? Perhaps it is that huge organizations have profound difficulty in breaking from their traditional patterns (might we even call these ruts?). For some it may be impossible; for others, great adversity may sweep a new climate of change into a moribund organization.

Imitation is not a dirty word. Many organizations shun imitation; nothing else will do but to be innovators. Executive pride is often at stake. Innovation suggests a leader; imitation denotes a follower.

However, imitation has much to recommend it. Successful practices deserve to be imitated. Adopting such practices lessens risks from striking out on your own and often hastens profitability.

Saturn represented innovation with General Motors, but most of the Saturn ideas were borrowed liberally from Japan. For example, just-in-time parts ship-

---

[14] *Ibid.*, p. B4.

ments were holding manufacturing costs down, but not without some danger of slowing the assembly line. Saturn workers were trying to eliminate bottlenecks and reduce costs, just as workers did at factories run by Toyota and Honda. Management and union relations likewise were Japanese in style. The result became a commitment to quality unique among U.S. carmakers but imitative of Japanese imports.

The problems of gaining and holding uniqueness. As desirable as uniqueness or differentiation can be, it is often not easily attained, and more often not maintained. We have seen Saturn's efforts in Japan to gain uniqueness when its product is little different in quality, price, appearance, and targeted customers from entrenched competitors. Saturn brought to Japan its uniqueness in selling and promotional efforts, but if successful this uniqueness may not last. However, if Saturn can develop a mystique with certain consumer segments, this will give it the uniqueness it needs so badly. Just being another foreign car probably will not do it.

Imitation may be contagious. In Japan, if Saturn's selling and promotional efforts turn out to be popular with consumers, Japanese carmakers are bound to quickly imitate.

What lessons can we gain from this? First, that uniqueness is certainly not limited to products. It can come from customers targeted, selling and promotional methods, from enlightened customer service and, not the least, a good reputation, and at the extreme in desirability, a mystique.

CONSIDER

What additional learning insights do you see as emerging from this case?

QUESTIONS

1. What problems might GM management face if it tried to transplant the Saturn concept to other divisions?

2. Do you fault top GM management for pressuring Saturn to turn a profit at the critical juncture of its growth? Why or why not?

3. What problems do you see for Saturn in maintaining its quality and customer relations? Can these problems be resolved?

4. Evaluate the Saturn policy of having relatively few dealers, each with a wide sales territory. What pros and cons do you see for this?

5. How do you personally feel about the haggling that is involved in most car purchases? Do you prefer a one-price policy?

6. How serious do you see the eroding of Saturn's mystique to be with the 1995 corporate policy changes?

7. Do you think Saturn can make it big in Japan? What does this depend on in your estimation?

HANDS-ON EXERCISES

1. You are one of the biggest and most successful Chevy dealers, and you are incensed at the investment dollars given Saturn at the expense of Chevrolet. What will you do? How effective do you think your actions will be?

2. What arguments would you present to corporate top management to be more patient with Saturn, even though for five years they have been reasonably patient, and that such patience will eventually be rewarded, maybe big, if the mystique can be maintained?

3. What arguments would you present for GM to be patient with the Japanese experiment?

TEAM DEBATE EXERCISE

It is the early 1980s. CEO Roger Smith has asked for a briefing to the executive committee on whether Saturn should be set up as a separate division or as part of Chevrolet. He wants both viewpoints presented and given the full persuasive treatment.

INVITATION TO RESEARCH

What is the current situation of Saturn, with regard to production and sales, consumer attitudes regarding satisfaction and quality, the labor force, and top management's commitment? What about the Japanese venture? How profitable is Saturn? Has it yet introduced a sports utility vehicle? Does it still appear to have a mystique?

CHAPTER THIRTEEN

Contrast—Wal-Mart: The Unstoppable

*I*n March 1992 Sam Walton passed away after a two-year battle with bone cancer. Perhaps the most admired businessman of his era, he had founded Wal-Mart Stores with the concept of discount stores in small towns and had brought it to lofty stature as the biggest retailer in the United States—ahead of the decades-long leader, Sears, ahead of another great discount-store success, Kmart, and ahead of a charging J.C. Penney Company.

THE EARLY YEARS OF SAM WALTON

Samuel Moore Walton was born in Kingfisher, Oklahoma, on March 29, 1917. He and his brother James, born three years later, were reared in a family that valued hard work and thrift. They grew up in Missouri in the depths of the Great Depression.

By the time Sam had entered eighth grade in Shebina, Oklahoma, he was already exhibiting the character traits that would dominate his future life: quiet and soft-spoken, but a natural leader who became class president and captain of the football team. He even became the first Eagle Scout in Shebina's history.

At the University of Missouri, Sam excelled in academics and athletics. He worked his way through college by delivering newspapers, working in a five-and-dime store, lifeguarding, and waiting tables at the university.

After his graduation in 1940, Sam went to the J.C. Penney Company and became a management trainee at the Des Moines, Iowa, store. There he applied his work ethic, competed to become Penney's most promising new man, and became imbued with the Penney philosophy of catering to smaller towns and having "associates" instead of employees or clerks. He also met J.C. Penney himself and was intrigued with his habit of strolling around stores and personally meeting and observing customers and salespeople. After 18 months Walton left Penney's to enter the U.S. Army, but what he had learned in the Penney store in Des Moines was to shape his future ideas.

GROWTH OF WAL-MART

Sam Walton was discharged from the Army in August 1945. By chance he stumbled on an opportunity to buy a Ben Franklin variety store franchise in Newport, Arkansas, and he opened it a month later. The lease arrangement with the building's owner did not work out, so he eventually relocated in Bentonville, Arkansas, in 1950. During the 1950s and early 1960s, Walton increased the number of Ben Franklin franchises to 15. In the winter of 1962 he proposed at a Ben Franklin board meeting that the company should aggressively turn its efforts to discounting, citing the great potential of discount stores. The company refused to consider such an innovative idea, so Sam and his brother went ahead anyway and opened a Discount City in Rogers, Arkansas, in 1962; they opened a second store in Harrison, Arkansas, in 1964. The company was incorporated as Wal-Mart Stores on October 31, 1969, and became a publicly held company a year later. In 1970 Walton also opened his first distribution center and general office: a 72,000-square-foot complex in Bentonville, Arkansas. In 1972 Wal-Mart was listed on the New York Stock Exchange.

In 1976 Walton severed ties with Ben Franklin in order to concentrate on the expansion of Wal-Mart. His operations had extended to small towns in Arkansas, Missouri, Kansas, and Oklahoma.

The essence of Walton's management philosophy during these building years was that of an old-fashioned entrepreneur; Walton personally roamed through his own stores, as well as those of competitors, always looking for new ideas in mass-merchandising (i.e., maximizing sales at attractive prices).

But rather than confronting the major retailers—department stores, chains such as Penney's and Sears, and the strong discounters such as Kmart—he confined his efforts to the smaller cities, ones deemed to have insufficient market potential by the major retailers. He saw these towns as a strategic window of opportunity, untapped by competitors. (Review the Southwest Airlines case for a similar seizing of a strategic window.)

Growth accelerated. By the end of 1975 Walton had 104 stores with nearly 6,000 employees and annual sales of $236 million, which generated $6 million net profit. The next year, the number of stores had increased to 125, employees to 7,500, and sales to $340 million, with $11.5 million in profit.

Table 13.1 compares the growth of sales and number of stores of Wal-Mart with that of Kmart, its major competitor, from 1980 to 1990, the decade in which Wal-Mart forged ahead to become the biggest retailer. By the end of fiscal 1991, Wal-Mart had 1,573 stores in 35 states.

Some of these new stores were Wal-Mart SuperCenters, considerably larger than the regular Wal-Marts, having a warehouse-style food outlet under the same roof as the discount store. While such food stores carried items comparable to products in a regular urban supermarket, the assortment and service were superior to those in most direct competitors in the smaller cities. And the key motivation for adding food stores to the general merchandise discount store was the greater frequency of customer shopping: Customers shop weekly for groceries, and such patronage exposes

TABLE 13.1   Comparison of Growth in Sales and
Number of Stores, Wal-Mart and Kmart, 1980–1990

	Kmart		Wal-Mart	
	Sales (millions)	Number of Stores	Sales (millions)	Number of Stores
1980	$14,204	1,772	$1,643	330
1981	16,527	2,055	2,445	491
1982	16,772	2,117	3,376	551
1983	18,597	2,160	4,667	642
1984	20,762	2,173	6,401	745
1985	22,035	2,332	8,451	859
1986	23,035	2,342	11,909	980
1987	25,627	2,273	15,959	1,114
1988	27,301	2,307	20,649	1,259
1989	29,533	2,361	25,810	1,402
1990	32,070	2,350	32,602	1,573

Source: Company annual reports.

Commentary: Several of these statistics are of particular interest. The comparison of the sales from 1980 to 1990, slightly more than one decade, of Wal-Mart and Kmart, show the tremendous growth rate of Wal-Mart, starting at little more than 10% of Kmart sales figures to forge ahead by 1990. And Kmart was no slouch during this period.

Second, Wal-Mart achieved its leadership in total sales with almost 800 fewer stores than Kmart had. This means that Wal-Mart's stores were achieving much higher sales volume than Kmart's, a fact that is further borne out by the statistics in Table 13.3.

them to the other merchandise in the discount store far more frequently than would otherwise be the case.

Wal-Mart by now was also opening another category of stores: Sam's Wholesale, also known as Sam's Clubs. First introduced in 1984, by 1991 there were 148. This wholesale club concept came about as regular discount stores seemed to be reaching saturation in some locations. The wholesale warehouse went a step further in discounting.

Sam's Club stores are large, ranging up to 135,000 square feet. Each store is a membership-only operation, with qualified members including businesses and individuals who are members of certain groups, such as government employees and credit union members. Although the stores are huge, they carry less than 5 percent of the items carried by regular discount stores. Assortments are limited to fast-moving home goods and apparel, generally name brands, with prices 8 to 10 percent over cost but well under those of discount stores and department and specialty stores. Sam's Clubs provided the initial entry for Wal-Mart into the big metropolitan markets that it had avoided in most of its great growth.

In December 1987 Wal-Mart opened its newest merchandising concept, Hypermart USA, in Garland, Texas, a suburb of Dallas. The hypermart offers a combination of groceries and general merchandise in over 200,000 square feet of selling space. The stores also include a variety of fast-food and service shops, such as a beauty shop, shoe repair, and dry cleaners. Thus, a mall atmosphere is created to achieve one-stop shopping.

In spite of optimistic beginnings, the hypermarket idea was not as successful as expected. A scaled-down version was the supercenter. Plans were suspended for building more hypermarkets in favor of the supercenter concept.

For a comparison of sales and profitability of Wal-Mart with Kmart, Sears, and Penney, see Table 13.2. Note that profitability comparisons include operating profit as a percentage of sales and the more valid measure of profitability, the return of equity (i.e., the return on the money invested in the enterprise). From this table we see that the growth of Wal-Mart in sales and profitability compared with its nearest competitors is awesome. Table 13.3 shows another operational comparison, this time in the average sales per store for Wal-Mart and Kmart. And again, the comparison shows the great growth performance of Wal-Mart.

The Future

Sam Walton received the Medal of Freedom from President Bush on March 17, 1992. Unfortunately, he did not live long to enjoy this high honor bestowed on him (among many honors, such as Man of the Year, Horatio Alger Award in 1984, and "Retailer of the Decade" in 1989); he died of cancer nine days later, on March 26, 1992.

David Glass, 53 years old, assumed the role of president and chief executive officer. Glass was known for his hard-driving managerial style. He had gained his retail experience at a small supermarket chain in Springfield, Missouri, and had joined Wal-Mart as executive vice president for finance in 1976. He had been named president and chief operating officer in 1984, while Sam Walton had kept the position of chief executive officer. About the transition of executives, Glass had said

> There's no transition to make, because other principles and basic values he (Walton) used in founding this company were so sound and so universally accepted. … We'll be fine as long as we never lose our responsiveness to the customer.[1]

AFTER SAM WALTON

The behemoth that Sam Walton created rolled irresistibly ahead without him. He had indeed built an enduring concept and organization. Table 13.4 shows operating results for 1993–95. Particularly to be noted is the amazing sales growth in these years, up well over 20 percent each year to more than $82 billion by 1995. The com-

---

[1] Susan Caminiti, "What Ails Retailing," *Fortune* (January 30, 1989), p. 61.

TABLE 13.2 10-Year Comparison of Gross Revenues, Percentage of Operating Margin, and Return on Equity for Wal-Mart and its Competitors[a]

| | Wal-Mart | | | Kmart | | | Sears | | | J.C. Penney | | |
| | % Operating | | | % Operating | | | % Operating | | | % Operating | | |
Year	Gross Revenue	Profit Margin	Equity Return %	Gross Revenue	Profit Margin	Equity Return %	Gross Revenue	Profit Margin	Equity Return %	Gross Revenue	Profit Margin	Equity Return %
1981	$2,445.0	5.6	25.6	$16,527.0	2.2	9.0	$27,357	7.2	8.2	$11,860	7.5	13.2
1982	3,376.3	7.8	25.4	17,040.0	4.3	10.1	30,020	8.8	10.1	11,414	8.3	13.3
1983	4,666.9	8.3	26.6	18,878.9	6.0	16.7	35,883	9.7	14.4	12,078	8.7	13.1
1984	6,400.9	8.5	27.5	21,095.9	6.7	15.4	38,828	10.5	14.1	13,451	7.8	11.4
1985	8,451.5	7.2	25.6	22,420.0	6.2	14.4	40,715	9.5	11.5	13,747	7.7	9.8
1986	11,909.1	7.1	26.6	23,812.1	5.7	14.5	44,282	9.1	10.4	15,151	8.6	11.0
1987	15,959.3	6.8	27.8	25,626.6	5.8	15.7	48,439	8.5	12.1	15,747	9.1	14.6
1988	20,649.0	6.4	27.8	27,301.4	6.5	16.0	50,251	9.2	3.0	15,296	8.3	20.4
1989	25,810.7	6.5	27.1	29,532.7	5.8	6.5	53,794	9.2	10.6	16,405	9.2	18.4
1990	32,601.6	6.0	24.1	32,070.0	5.4	14.0	55,971	7.4	7.0	16,365	2.4	15.6

[a] Gross revenue is in $ billions.

Source: Company annual reports.

Commentary: The comparison with major competitors shows Wal-Mart far exceeding its rivals in revenue growth. The operating profit percentage exceeds Kmart's for most years, but Sears and Penney look better here. However, the true measure of profitability is return on equity, and here Wal-Mart shines: It indeed is a very profitable operation, while offering consumers attractive prices.

TABLE 13.3 Average Sales Per Store, Wal-Mart and Kmart, 1980–1990

	Kmart	Wal-Mart
1980	$8,015,801	$4,978,788
1981	8,042,338	4,979,633
1982	7,922,532	6,127,042
1983	8,609,722	7,269,470
1984	9,554,533	8,591,946
1985	9,448,970	9,838,184
1986	9,835,611	12,152,040
1987	11,274,527	14,325,852
1988	11,833,983	16,401,111
1989	12,508,682	18,409,415
1990	13,646,808	20,726,001

Source: Computed from Table 13.1

Commentary: The great increase in sales per store for Wal-Mart is particularly noteworthy. In 1980 Wal-Mart's average store's sales was hardly one-half that of an average Kmart. By 1990 the average Wal-Mart store was generating more than 50% more sales than an average Kmart.

pany in its 1995 annual report confidently projected 1996 sales would be approximately $96 billion. Only three Fortune 500 companies have higher sales: General Motors, Ford Motor, and Exxon. And Exxon's sales of $97 billion in 1994 are within striking distance.

Major accomplishments in fiscal 1995 included:

- Opening 111 new Wal-Mart discount stores and relocating or expanding 60 additional stores
- Entering the Canadian market through the purchase of 122 Woolco stores
- Opening 75 supercenters, more than doubling the total to 143
- Expanding 75 selectively into international markets, including 24 stores in Mexico and 3 in Hong Kong

INGREDIENTS OF SUCCESS

Management Style and Employee Orientation

Sam Walton cultivated a management style that emphasized individual initiative and autonomy over close supervision. He constantly reminded employees that they were vital to the success of the company, that they were essentially "running their own business," that they were "associates" or "partners" in the business, rather than simply employees.

TABLE 13.4   Operating Performance, 1993–1995

(Dollar amounts in millions except per share data.)	1995	1994	1993
Operating Results			
Net sales	$82,494	$67,344	$55,484
Net sales increase	22%	21%	26%
Comparative store sales increase	7%	6%	11%
Other income—net	918	641	501
Cost of sales	65,586	53,444	44,175
Operating, selling, and general and administrative expenses	12,858	10,333	8,321
Interest costs:			
Debt	520	331	143
Capital leases	186	186	180
Provision for federal and state income taxes	1,581	1,358	1,171
Net income	2,681	2,333	1,995
Per share of common stock:			
Net income	1.17	1.02	.87
Dividends	.17	.13	.11

Source: 1995 Wal-Mart Annual Report.

In such employee relations philosophy, he borrowed from James Cash Penney, the founder of the J.C. Penney Company, and his formulation of the "Penney idea" in 1913. This Penney idea also stressed the desirability of constantly improving the human factor, of rewarding associates through participation in what the business produces, and of appraising every policy and action as to whether it squares with what is right and just.

Walton emphasized bottom-up communication, thereby providing a free flow of ideas from throughout the company. For example, the "people greeter" concept (described in the following information box) was implemented in 1983 as a result of a suggestion received from an employee in a store in Louisiana. This idea proved so successful that it has since been adopted by Kmart, some department stores, and even shopping malls.

Another example of listening to employees' ideas came when an assistant manager in an Alabama store ordered too many marshmallow sandwiches, or Moon Pies. The store manager told him to use his imagination to sell the excess, so John Love came up with an idea to create the first World Championship Moon Pie Eating Contest. It was held in the store's parking lot. The event was so successful that it is now held every year, drawing spectators not only from the community but from all over Alabama and surrounding states.[2]

---

[2] Example described in Don Longo, "Associate Involvement Spurs Gains (Wal-Mart Employees Are Encouraged to Suggest Ideas for Promotions)," *Discount Store News* (December 18, 1989), p. 83.

INFORMATION BOX

GREETERS

All customers entering Wal-Mart stores encounter a store employee assigned to welcome them, give advice on where to find things, and to help with exchanges or refunds. These "greeters" also thank people exiting from the store, while unobtrusively observing any indications of shoplifting.

Staffing exits and entrances is not uncommon by retailers; what makes Wal-Mart's greeters unique is their friendliness and patience. Wal-Mart has found that retirees supplementing pensions usually make the best greeters and are most appreciated by customers. As noted earlier, the greeter idea originated as a suggestion from an employee (associate): Sam Walton liked the idea, and it became a company-wide practice.

Do you personally like the idea of having a store employee greet you as you enter and leave an establishment? On balance, do you think the greeter idea is a plus or a minus? Explain.

Wal-Mart has a profit-sharing plan dating back to 1972 in which all associates share in a portion of the company's yearly profits. As one celebrated example of the benefits of such profit sharing, Shirley Cox had worked as an office cashier earning $7.10 an hour. When she decided to retire after 24 years, the amount of her profit sharing in 1988 was $220,127.[3] In addition, associates may participate in the payroll stock purchase plan in which Wal-Mart contributes part of the cost.

The Sam Walton philosophy of business and management was to create a friendly, "down-home" family atmosphere in his stores. He described it as a "whistle while you work philosophy," one that, as he saw it, stressed the importance of having fun while working because you can work better if you enjoy yourself.[4] He was concerned about losing this attitude or atmosphere: "The bigger Wal-Mart gets, the more essential it is that we think small. Because that's exactly how we have become a huge corporation—by not acting like one."[5]

Another incentive is given to all employees in stores that manage to reduce shrinkage (that is, the loss of merchandise due to shoplifting, carelessness, and employee theft). Employees are given $200 each a year if shrinkage limits are met. This causes associates to become detectives by watching shoppers and each other. In 1989 Wal-Mart had a shrinkage rate of 1 percent of sales, below the industry rate of 2 percent.[6]

---

[3] Example cited in Vance H. Trimble, *Sam Walton: The Inside Story of America's Richest Man* (New York: Dutton, 1990), p. 233.

[4] *Ibid.*, p. 105.

[5] *Ibid.*, p. 104.

[6] Charles Bernstein, "How to Win Employee and Customer Friends," *Nation's Restaurant News* (January 30, 1989), p. F3.

A rather unusual way of making employees feel vital to the Wal-Mart operation is information sharing, which amplifies the idea that employees are associates of the business. Management shares the good news and the bad news about the company's performance. In each store managers share operating statistics with employees, including profits, purchases, sales, and markdowns. Every person, from assistant managers to part-time clerks, see this information on a regular basis. The result: Employees tend to think of Wal-Mart as truly their own company.

Not the least of the open and people-oriented management practices fostered by Sam Walton is what he called MBWA, Management By Walking Around. Managers, from store level to headquarters, walk around the stores to stay familiar with what is going on, to talk to the associates, and to encourage associates to share their ideas and concerns. Such interactions permit a personal touch usually lacking in large firms but so far still dominant as Wal-Mart grows large.

And how have unions fared in such an environment? Not surprisingly, they have had no success. Walton argued that in his "family environment," associates had better wages, benefits, and bonuses than any union could get for them. In addition, the bonuses and profit sharing were inducements far better than those a union could negotiate. As partners in a business operation, how could employees turn to a union?

State-of-the-Art Technology

Sam Walton's decentralized management style led to a team approach to decision making. But this approach would have been difficult to achieve without a heavy commitment to supporting technology. A huge telecommunications system permits Wal-Mart executives to broadcast and communicate to store managers. In addition, home-office management teams, using the company's 11 turboprop planes, fly to various stores to assess their operations. Coming back to headquarters for Friday and Saturday meetings, they assess any problems and coordinate needed merchandise transfers among stores. Through the use of a six-channel satellite, messages can be broadcast to all stores, and a master computer tracks the company's complex distribution system.

Small Town Invasion Strategy

Adopting a strategy similar to that of the J.C. Penney Company of more than half a century before, Wal-Mart shunned big cities and directed its store openings to smaller towns where competition consisted only of local merchants and small outlets of a few chains, such as Woolworth, Gamble, and Penney.

These merchants typically offered only limited assortments of merchandise, had no Sunday or evening hours, and charged substantially higher prices than they would charge in the more competitive environments of larger cities. Other larger retailers, especially discounters, had shunned such small towns as not offering enough potential to support the high sales volume needed for the low-price strategy.

But Wal-Mart found potential in abundance in these small-town markets, as customers flocked from all the surrounding towns and rural areas for the variety of goods and the prices. (In the process of captivating small town and rural con-

ISSUE BOX

IMPACT OF WAL-MART ON SMALL TOWNS

In most of its growth years, Wal-Mart pursued a policy of opening stores on the outskirts of small rural towns, usually with populations between 25,000 and 50,000. Attractive both in prices and assortment of goods, its stores often became beacons in drawing customers from miles around. Wal-Mart also was likely to be the biggest employer in the town, with 200 to 300 local employees.

But the dominating presence of Wal-Mart was a mixed blessing for many communities. Small-town merchants were often devastated and unable to compete. Downtowns in many of these small towns became decaying vestiges of what perhaps a few months previously had been prosperous centers. But consumers benefited.

Wal-Mart brought tradeoffs and controversy: Was rural America better or worse off with the arrival of Wal-Mart? On balance, most experts saw the economic development brought on by Wal-Mart as more than offsetting the business destruction it causes. But few could dispute the sociological trauma.[7]

What is your assessment of the desirability of Wal-Mart coming into a rural small town? How might your assessment differ depending on your particular position or status in that community?

[7] For more discussion of the impact of Wal-Mart, see Karen Blumenthal, "Arrival of Discounter Tears the Civic Fabric of Small Town Life," *The Wall Street Journal* (April 14, 1987), p. 1 ff; Hank Gilman, "Rural Retailing Chains Prosper by Combining Service, Sophistication," *The Wall Street Journal* (July 2, 1984), p. 1 ff.

sumers, Wal-Mart wreaked havoc on the existing small-town merchants. See the issue box above for a discussion of the sociological impact of Wal-Mart on small-town America.) The company honed its skills in such small towns, isolated from aggressive competitors, and found enough business to become the world's largest retail enterprise. Then, flexing its muscles, it began moving confidently into the big cities, whose competitors were as fearful of Wal-Mart as had been the thousands of small-town merchants.

Controlling Costs

Sam Walton was a stickler for holding costs to a minimum in the quest to offer customers the lowest prices. Cost control started with Wal-Mart vendors. Wal-Mart has gained a reputation of being hard to please, of constantly pressuring its suppliers to give additional price breaks and cooperative advertising.[8] In further efforts to buy

[8] Toni Apgar, "The Cash Machine," *Marketing and Media Decisions* (March 1987), p. 82.

goods at the lowest possible prices, Wal-Mart has attempted to bypass middlemen and sales reps and buy all goods direct from the manufacturer. In so doing, a factory presumably would save money on sales representatives' commissions of 2 to 6 percent of the purchase order and thus be able to pass this savings on to Wal-Mart. Understandably, this has aroused a heated controversy by groups representing sales representatives.

Wal-Mart has been able to achieve great savings in distribution. Its sophisticated use of distribution centers and its own fleet of trucks enable it to negotiate lower prices when it buys in bulk directly from suppliers. More than three-fourths of the merchandise sold in a Wal-Mart store is processed through one of the company's 16 distribution centers. Each center serves 150 to 200 stores with daily delivery. For example, the distribution center in Cullman, Alabama, is situated on 28 acres with 1.2 million square feet. Some 1,042 employees load 150 outbound Wal-Mart trailers a day and unload 180. On a heavy day, laser scanners will route 190,000 cases of goods on an 11-mile conveyor.[9]

Each warehouse uses the latest in optical scanning devices, automated materials-handling equipment, bar coding, and computerized inventory. With all of the stores using the satellite network, messages can be quickly flashed between stores, distribution centers, and corporate headquarters in Bentonville, Arkansas. Hand-held computers assist store employees in ordering merchandise. The result is a distribution system that provides stores with on-time delivery at the lowest possible cost. By using the most advanced technologies, Wal-Mart's distribution expenses are only 3 percent of total sales, which is about one-half that of most chains.[10]

Wal-Mart has previously been able to achieve great savings in advertising costs compared with major competitors. Although discount chains typically spend 2 to 3 percent of sales for advertising, Wal-Mart has been able to hold advertising to less than 1 percent of sales. Much of this difference reflects low media rates in most of its markets, the smaller towns. As Wal-Mart moves into larger metropolitan markets, the advertising cost advantage may diminish.

Finally, Wal-Mart's operating and administrative costs reflect a spartan operation that is rigidly enforced. A lean headquarters organization and a minimum of staff assistants compared with most other retailers completes the cost-control philosophy and reflects the frugal thinking of Sam Walton that dates back to his early days.

"Buy American" and Environmental Programs

As foreign manufacturers increasingly began taking market share away from American producers—and in the process, destroying some American jobs—sentiment began mounting for import restrictions to save jobs. And as the amount of imports grew, so did the trade deficit, with consequences not fully understood by most people but generally understood to be something very bad. However, the idea of restricting free world trade is highly controversial: Many experts question whether

---

[9] John Huey, "America's Most Successful Merchant," *Fortune* (September 23, 1991), p. 54.

[10] *Facts about Wal-Mart Stores*, Company publication (Bentonville, Arkansas, n.d.), p. 4.

tariffs, quotas, and other restrictions are in the general best interest. Some say the best scenario is to induce American consumers to "buy American," or at least to give preferential treatment to products produced in this country by American workers; such a policy would eliminate import restrictions but enhance consumer support of American workers and factories.

In March 1985 Sam Walton became very concerned with what seemed to him to be a serious national situation. He sent a message to his buyers to find products that American manufacturers have stopped producing because they couldn't compete with foreign imports. This was the beginning of Walton's "Buy American" program, which had the long-range objective of strengthening the free enterprise system. The program is essentially a cooperative effort between retailers and domestic manufacturers to reestablish the competitive position of American-made goods in price and quality.

This program showcased the power of the huge retailer. Magic Chef, 3M, Farris Fashions, and many other manufacturers joined Walton's crusade, as Wal-Mart pledged to support domestic production for items ranging from film to microwave ovens to flannel shirts and other apparel.

Wal-Mart has been a leader in challenging manufacturers to improve their products and packaging in order to protect the environment. As a result, manufacturers have made great improvements in eliminating excessive packaging, converting to recyclable materials, and eliminating toxic inks and dyes.

The company participates in Earth Day events, with tree plantings, information booths and videos to show customers how to improve the environment. It has also been active in fund raising for local environmental groups, and in "adopt-a-highway" programs, in which store personnel volunteer at least one day every month to collect trash and clean up local highways and beaches.

UPDATE

As now the biggest retailer by far, Wal-Mart is looking for expansion opportunities beyond the United States. As of April 1998, it operated stores in Germany (21 units), Argentina (11), Brazil (9), and China (3). In North America, Wal-Mart operated 1,908 Wal-Mart stores, 456 supercenters, and 444 Sam's Clubs in the United States and 404 in Mexico and 14 in Puerto Rico. Revenues for 1998 reached $117.9 billion, with net income $3.5 billion. The tremendous growth can be compared with its closest competitors left in the dust:

Sears, Roebuck had sales of $40.4 billion and net income of $1.2 billion.

Kmart, the closest discount competitor and one-time biggest retailer, had sales of $32.1 billion and a net loss of $101 million.

J. C. Penney was next in size, with sales of $29.2 billion and net profit of $565 million.

As we saw in the Toys Я Us case in Chapter 11, the irresistible force of Wal-Mart was even destroying the supreme category-killer retailer in toys.

Wal-Mart was surviving well after Sam Walton. He had laid the groundwork well for a superb operation.

WHAT CAN BE LEARNED?

Take good care of people. Sam Walton was concerned with two groups of people: his employees and his customers. By motivating and even inspiring his employees, he found that customers were also well served. Somehow in the exigencies of business, especially big business, this emphasis on people tends to be pushed aside. Walton made caring for people common practice.

By listening to his employees, by involving them, by exhorting them, and by giving them a real share of the business—all the while stressing friendliness and concern for customers—Walton fostered a business climate unique in almost any large organization. In addition to providing customers with the friendliest of employees, his stores also offered honest values and great assortments and catered to the concerns of many middle-income Americans for the environment and American jobs.

Go for the strategic window of opportunity. Strategic windows of opportunity sometimes come in strange guises. They always represent areas of overlooked or untapped potential business by existing firms. But in the formative and early growth years of Wal-Mart, no window could ever have seemed less promising than the one Sam Walton milked to perfection and to great growth. Small towns and cities in many parts of rural America were losing population and economic strength, partly because of the decline in family farms and the accompanying infrastructure of small businesses. It was therefore not surprising that the major discount chains focused their growth efforts on large metropolitan areas. Although many small cities had Penney's and Sears outlets as well as such other chains as Woolworth, Gamble, and Coast to Coast stores, these were usually small stores, often old, marginal, and rather in the backstream of corporate consciousness. This retail environment was one of small stores with limited assortments of merchandise and relatively high prices.

In this environment Sam Walton seized his opportunity. He saw something that no other merchants had: that the limited total market potential meant a dearth of competition. He also saw that the potential was far greater than the population of the small town and its immediate surrounding population. Indeed, a large Wal-Mart store in a rather isolated rural community could draw customers from many miles away.

Do such windows of opportunity still exist today? You bet they do for the entrepreneur with vision, an ability to look beyond the customary, and the courage to follow up on his or her vision.

The marriage of old-fashioned ideas and modern technology can be a potent strategy. Sam Walton embraced this strategy with more success than any other entrepreneur in modern business, and he made it work throughout his organization, despite its growth to great size. In the forefront of retailers in the use of communications technology and computerized distribution, he still was able to motivate his employees to offer friendly and helpful customer services to a degree that few large retailers have been able consistently to achieve.

Other firms can benefit from the example of Wal-Mart in cultivating homespun friendliness with awesome technology, and competitors are trying to emulate. The particular difficulty that many are finding, however, is in achieving consistency.

Showing environmental concern can pay dividends. Today, as perhaps never before, many people are concerned about the environment, and it seems high time that we have such concern, while much of the environment can still be salvaged and protected from the abuses of a modern industrial age. Given such sentiment, the firm that takes a leadership position for environmental protection stands to benefit from improving customer relations and, not the least, from positive media attention.

Another issue important to many Americans involves foreign inroads to the detriment of many U.S. manufacturers and jobs. Regardless of the great controversy over the desirability of free trade, many middle-class Americans have applauded the leadership of Wal-Mart in its widely publicized "Buy American" policy.

What is the moral for other businesses? Be alert to the increasing concerns of the public, and where possible, act on them to achieve a leadership role.

CONSIDER

Can you identify additional learning insights that could be applicable to firms in other situations?

QUESTIONS

1. How might you attempt to compete with Wal-Mart if you were
   (*a*) a small hardware merchant?
   (*b*) a small clothing store for men?
   (*c*) a Woolworth?
2. Do you think Wal-Mart is vulnerable today, and if so, in what way? If you do not think it is vulnerable, do you see any limits to its growth?
3. Why do you think the hypermarket idea failed to meet expectations? Was Wal-Mart too quick to table expansion plans for its hypermarkets?
4. What weaknesses do you see Wal-Mart as either having now or potentially? How can the company overcome them?
5. Wal-Mart is now entering urban areas. What new challenges does this present? Will Wal-Mart need to change? Can "the Wal-Mart way" work only in rural and exurban areas?

6. Can discounting go on forever? What are the limits to growth by price competition?

7. Discuss Wal-Mart's business practice (especially in regard to unions, invading small towns, and supplier relations) in terms of their ethical ramifications for the industry and for society. Should students be encouraged to emulate these practices?

HANDS-ON EXERCISES

1. You are an ambitious Wal-Mart store manager. Describe how you might design your career path to achieve a high executive position with this growing company. Be as creative as you can.

2. You are the principal adviser to David Glass, who has replaced Sam Walton as chief executive. He is very interested in making greater inroads in international markets. He challenges you to design a strategy to successfully invade these markets. What do you advise, and why?

TEAM DEBATE EXERCISES

1. Debate the notion of Wal-Mart aggressively seeking to enter small communities, such as in rural New England, where many people oppose this. Should Wal-Mart bow to the public pressure (which the company deems to be from a small minority of vehement agitators), or should it carry on with "right on its side."

2. Can the great growth of Wal-Mart continue indefinitely? Debate the pros and cons of this.

INVITATION TO RESEARCH

Investigate the continued onslaught of Wal-Mart. Are there any dangers on the horizon?

PART FOUR

CONTROL WEAKNESSES AND STRENGTHS

CHAPTER FOURTEEN

United Way: Where Were the Controls?

*T*he United Way, the preeminent charitable organization in the United States, celebrated its 100-year anniversary in 1987. It had evolved from local community chests, and its strategy for fund-raising had proven highly effective: funding local charities through payroll deductions. The good it did seemed unassailable.

Abruptly in 1992, the persona of honesty and integrity that United Way had built was jeopardized by investigative reporters' revelations of free-spending practices and other questionable deeds of its greatest builder and president, William Aramony. A major point of public concern was Aramony's salary and uncontrolled perks in a lifestyle that seemed inappropriate for the head of a charitable organization that depended mostly on contributions from working people.

In 1993 another paragon of not-for-profit social enhancement organizations came under fire: the venerable Girl Scouts. Contentions were that multimillion-dollar profits of Girl Scout cookies were found to be used mostly to support bureaucracy instead of the Girl Scout troops that provided the labor in the first place. (This is discussed in an information box later in the chapter.)

We are left to question the operations and lack of controls of our major charitable and not-for-profit entities. Business firms have to report to shareholders and creditors, but not-for-profit organizations have been permitted to operate largely without the checks and balances that characterize most other organizations.

THE STATURE AND ACCOMPLISHMENTS OF THE UNITED WAY

For its 100th anniversary, then President Ronald Reagan summed up what the United Way stood for:

December 10, 1986

United Way Centennial, 1887–1987
By The President Of The United States Of America
A Proclamation

Since earliest times, we Americans have joined together to help each other and to strengthen our communities. Our deep-roots spirit of caring, of neighbor helping neighbor, has become an American trademark—and an American way of life. Over the years, our generous and inventive people have created an ingenious network of voluntary organizations to help give help where help is needed.

United Way gives that help very well indeed, and truly exemplifies our spirit of voluntarism. United Way has been a helping force in America right from the first community-wide fund raising campaign in Denver, Colorado, in 1887. Today, more than 2,200 local United Ways across the land raise funds for more than 37,000 voluntary groups that assist millions of people.

The United Way of caring allows volunteers from all walks of life to effectively meet critical needs and solve community problems. At the centennial of the founding of this indispensable voluntary group, it is most fitting that we Americans recognize and commend all the good United Way has done and continues to do.

The Congress, by Public Law 99–612, has expressed gratitude to United Way, congratulated it, and applauded and encouraged its fine work and its goals.

NOW, THEREFORE, I RONALD REAGAN, President of the United States of America, by virtue of the authority vested in me by the Constitution and laws of the United States, do hereby proclaim heartfelt thanks to a century of Americans who have shaped and supported United Way, and encourage the continuation of its efforts.

IN WITNESS WHEREOF, I have hereunto set my hand this tenth day of December, in the year of our lord nineteen hundred and eighty-six, and of the Independence of the United States of America the two hundred and eleventh.

Ronald Reagan

Organizing the United Way as the umbrella charity to fund other local charities through payroll deduction established an effective means of fund-raising. It became the recipient of 90 percent of all charitable donations. Employers sometimes used extreme pressure to achieve 100 percent participation of employees, which led to organizational bonuses. The United Way achieved further cooperation of business organizations by involving their executives as leaders of annual campaigns, amid widespread publicity. It would consequently cause such an executive acute loss of face if his or her own organization did not go "over the top" in meeting campaign goals. A local United Way executive admitted that "if participation is 100 percent, it means someone has been coerced."[1]

For many years, outside of some tight-lipped gripes of corporate employees, the organization moved smoothly along, with local contributions generally increasing every year and with the needs for charitable contributions invariably increasing even faster.

The national organization, United Way of America (UWA), is a separate corporation and has no direct control over the approximately 2,200 local United Way offices. Most of the locals voluntarily contributed one cent on the dollar of all funds they collected, however, and in return, the national organization provided training and promoted local United Way agencies through advertising and other marketing efforts.

Much of the success of the United Way movement in becoming the largest and most respected charity in the United States was due to the 22 years of William Aramony's leadership of the national organization. When he first took over, the United Ways were not operating under a common name. He built a nationwide network of agencies, all operating under the same name and using the same logo of outstretched hands, which became nationally recognized as the symbol of charitable giving. Unfortunately in 1992 an exposé of Aramony's lavish lifestyle and questionable dealings led to his downfall and burdened local United Ways with serious difficulties in fund-raising.

WILLIAM ARAMONY

During Aramony's tenure United Way contributions increased from $787 million in 1970 to $3 billion in 1990. Aramony built up the headquarters staff to 275 employees and increased his headquarters budget from less than $3 million to $29 million in 1991. Of this amount, $24 million came from the local United Ways, with the rest coming from corporate grants, investment income, and consulting.[2] Figure 14.1 shows the organizational chart as of 1987.

Aramony moved comfortably among the most influential people in our society. He attracted a prestigious board of governors, including many top executives from America's largest corporations, but only 3 of the 37 came from not-for-profit organizations. The board was chaired by John Akers, chairman and CEO of IBM. Other board members included Edward A. Brennan, CEO of Sears; James D. Robinson III, CEO of American Express; and Paul J. Tagliabue, commissioner of the National Football League. The presence of such top executives on the board brought United Way prestige and spurred contributions from some of the largest and most visible organizations in the United States.

Aramony was the highest paid executive in the charity field. In 1992 his compensation package was $463,000, nearly double that of the next highest paid execu-

---

[1] Susan Garland, "Keeping a Sharper Eye on Those Who Pass the Hat," *Business Week* (March 16, 1992), p. 39.

[2] Charles E. Shepard, "Perks, Privileges and Power in a Nonprofit World," *The Washington Post* (February 16, 1992), p. A38.

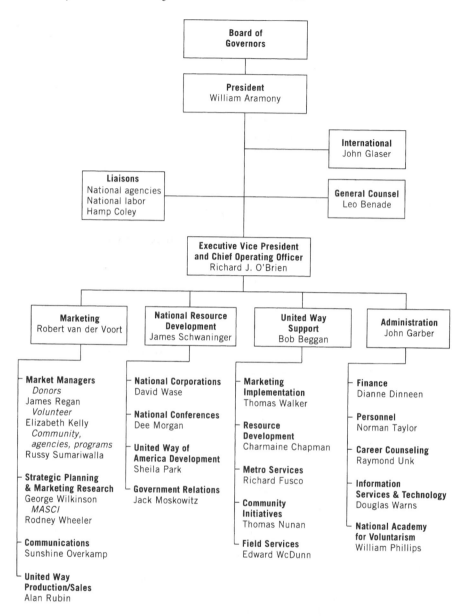

Figure 14.1

tive in the industry, Dudley H. Hafner of the American Heart Association.[3] The board fully supported Aramony, regularly giving him 6 percent annual raises.[4]

[3] Shepard, "Perks, Privileges, and Power," A38; and Charles E. Shepard, "United Way of America President Is Urged to Resign," *The Washington Post* (February 27, 1992), p. A1.

[4] Joseph Finder, "Charity Case," *The New Republic* (May 4, 1992), p. 11.

Investigative Disclosures

The Washington Post began investigating Aramony's tenure as president of United Way of America in 1991, raising questions about his high salary, travel habits, possible cronyism, and dubious relations with five spin-off companies. In February 1992 it released the following information on Aramony's expense charges:[5]

- Aramony had charged $92,265 in limousine expenses to the charity during the previous five years.
- He had charged $40,762 on airfare for the supersonic Concorde.
- He had charged more than $72,000 on international airfare that included first-class seats for himself, his wife, and others.
- He had charged thousands more for personal trips, gifts, and luxuries.
- He had made 29 trips to Las Vegas between 1988 and 1991.
- He had expensed 49 journeys to Gainesville, Florida, the home of his daughter and a woman with whom he had had a relationship.
- He had allegedly approved a $2 million loan to a firm run by his chief financial officer.
- He had approved the diversion of donors' money to questionable spin-off organizations run by long-time aides and provided benefits to family members as well.
- He had passed tens of thousands of dollars in consulting contracts from the UWA to friends and associates.

United Way of America's corporate policy prohibited the hiring of family members within the actual organization, but Aramony skirted the direct violation by hiring friends and relatives as consultants and within the spin-off companies. He paid hundreds of thousands of dollars in consulting fees, for example, to two aides in vaguely documented and even undocumented business transactions.

The use of spin-off companies provided flexible maneuvering. One of the spin-off companies Aramony created to provide travel and bulk purchasing for United Way chapters purchased a $430,000 condominium in Manhattan and a $125,000 apartment in Coral Gables, Florida, for Aramony's use. Another of the spin-off companies hired Aramony's son, Robert Aramony, as its president. Loans and money transfers between the spin-off companies and the national organization raised questions. No records showed that the board of directors had been given the opportunity to approve such loans and transfers.[6]

---

[5] Shepard, "Perks, Privileges, and Power"; Shepard, "President Is Urged to Resign"; Kathleen Telstch, "United Way Awaits Inquiry on its President's Practices," *The New York Times* (February 24, 1992), p. A12 (L); Charles E. Shepard, "United Way Report Criticizes Ex-Leader's Lavish Lifestyle," *The Washington Post* (April 4, 1992), p. A1.

[6] Shepard, "Perks, Privileges, and Power," p. A38.

CONSEQUENCES

When the information about Aramony's salary and expenses became public, reaction was severe. Stanley C. Gault, chairman of Goodyear Tire & Rubber Co., asked, "Where was the board? The outside auditors?"[7] Robert O. Bothwell, executive director of the National Committee for Responsive Philanthropy, said, "I think it is obscene that he is making that kind of salary and asking people who are making $10,000 a year to give 5 percent of their income."[8] At this point let us examine the issue of executive compensation. Are many executives overpaid? The following issue box addresses this controversial topic.

ISSUE BOX

EXECUTIVE COMPENSATION: IS IT TOO MUCH?

A controversy is mounting over multimillion-dollar annual compensations of corporate executives. In 1992, for example, the average annual pay of CEOs was $3,842,247; the 20 highest salaries ranged from over $11 million to a mind-boggling $127 million (for Thomas F. Frist, Jr., of Hospital Corporation of America).[9]

Activist shareholders, including some large mutual and pension funds, began protesting pay practices, especially for top executives of firms that were not doing well financially. New disclosure rules imposed in 1993 by the Securities and Exchange Commission (SEC) spotlighted questionable executive pay practices. In the past, complacent board members, themselves well paid and often closely aligned with the top executives of the organization, condoned liberal compensations, but this may be changing. The major argument supporting high executive compensations is that compared with salaries of some entertainers and athletes, they are modest. And are not their responsibilities far greater than those of any entertainer or athlete?

In light of the for-profit executive compensations, Aramony's salary was modest. And results were on his side: He made $369,000 in basic salary while raising $3 billion; Lee Iacocca, on the other hand, made $3 million while Chrysler lost $795 million. Where is the justice?

Undoubtedly Aramony, as head of a large for-profit corporation could have earned several zeros more in compensation and perks, with no raised eyebrows. But is the situation different for a not-for-profit organization, when revenues are derived from donations of millions of people of modest means? This is a real controversy. On one side, shouldn't a charity be willing to pay for the professional competence to run the organization as effectively as possible? But on the other side, how do revelations of high compensation affect the public image and fund-raising ability of such not-for-profit organizations?

What is your position regarding Aramony's compensation and perks, relative to the many times greater compensation of for-profit executives?

---

[9] John A. Byrne, "Executive Pay: The Party Ain't Over Yet," *Business Week* (April 26, 1993), pp. 56–64.

---

[7] Susan Garland, p. 39.

[8] Felicity Barringer, "United Way Head Is Forced out in a Furor over His Lavish Style," *The New York Times* (February 28, 1992), p. A1.

As a major consequence of the scandal, some United Way locals withheld their funds, at least pending a thorough investigation of the allegations. John Akers, chairman of the board, noted that by March 7, 1992, dues payments were running 20 percent behind the previous year, saying "I don't think this process that the United Way of America is going through, or Mr. Aramony is going through, is a process that's bestowing a lot of honor."[10]

In addition to the decrease in dues payments, UWA was in danger of having its not-for-profit status revoked by the Internal Revenue Service due to the relationship of loans made to the spin-off companies. For example, it loaned $2 million to a spin-off corporation of which the chief financial officer of UWA was also a director, which is a violation of not-for-profit corporate law. UWA also guaranteed a bank loan taken out by one of the spin-offs, another violation of not-for-profit corporate law.[11]

The adverse publicity benefited competing charities, such as Earth Share, an environmental group. United Way, at one time the only major organization to receive contributions through payroll deductions, now found itself losing donations to other charities able to garner contributions in the same manner. All the building that William Aramony had done for the United Way as the primary player in the American charitable industry was now in danger of disintegration because of his uncontrolled excesses.

On February 28, amid mounting pressure from local chapters threatening to withhold their annual dues, Aramony resigned. In August 1992 the United Way board of directors hired Elaine Chao, the Peace Corps director, to replace Aramony.

Elaine Chao

Chao's story is one of great achievement for one aged only 39. She is the oldest of six daughters in a family that came to California from Taiwan when Elaine was 8 years old. She did not know a word of English. The family prospered through hard work. "Despite the difficulties ... we had tremendous optimism in the basic goodness of this country, that people are decent here, that we would be given a fair opportunity to demonstrate our abilities," she told an interviewer.[12] Chao's parents instilled in their six daughters the conviction that they could do anything they set their minds to, and all the daughters went to prestigious universities.

Elaine Chao earned an economics degree from Mount Holyoke College in 1975, then went on for a Harvard MBA. She was a White House fellow, an international banker, chair of the Federal Maritime Commission, deputy secretary of the U.S. Transportation Department, and director of the Peace Corps before accepting the presidency of the United Way of America.

Her salary is $195,000, less than one-half of Aramony's. She has cut budgets and staffs: no transatlantic flights on the Concorde, no limousine service, no plush condominiums. The board of governors has been expanded to include more local repre-

---

[10] Felicity Barringer, "United Way Head Tries to Restore Trust," *The New York Times* (March 7, 1992), p. 8L.

[11] Shepard, "Perks, Privileges, and Power"; Charles E. Shepard, "United Way Chief Says He Will Retire," *The Washington Post* (February 28, 1992), p. A1.

[12] "United Way Chief Dedicated," *Cleveland Plain Dealer* (March 28, 1993), p. 240A.f.

sentatives and has established committees on ethics and finance. Still, Chao has no illusions about her job: "Trust and confidence once damaged will take a great deal of effort and time to heal."[13]

Local United Way's Concerns

In April 1993, for the second time in a year, United Way of Greater Lorain County (Ohio) withdrew from the United Way of America. The board of the local chapter was still concerned about the financial stability and accountability of the national agency. In particular, it was concerned about Aramony's retirement settlement. The national board and Aramony were negotiating a significant "golden parachute" retirement package in the neighborhood of $4 million.

News of this triggered the Lorain County board's decision to again withdraw from UWA. There were other reasons as well for this decision. The national agency was falling far short of its projected budget because only 890 of the 1,400 affiliates that had paid membership dues two years before were still paying. Roy Church, president of the Lorain agency, explained the board's decision: "Since February ... it has become clear that United Way of America's financial stability and ability to assist locals has been put in question. The benefit of being a United Way of America member isn't there at this time for Lorain's United Way."[14]

Elaine Chao's task of resurrecting United Way of America would not be easy.

See the following information box for a discussion of a related example of nonprofit callousness to its parties.

ANALYSIS

Executives' lack of accountability of expenditures was a major contributor to the UWA's problems. This lack of controls encouraged questionable practices, since there was no one to approve or disapprove, and it made executives, especially Aramony, vulnerable to great shock and criticism when their practices became known. The fact that voluntary donations were the principal source of revenues made the lack of accountability all the more scandalous.

Where controls and financial reporting are deficient, and where a system of checks and balances is lacking, two consequences tend to prevail, neither one desirable or totally acceptable. The worst case scenario is outright "white-collar theft," when unscrupulous people find it an opportunity for personal gain. The absence of sufficient controls and accountability can make even normally honest persons succumb to some temptation. Second, insufficient controls tend to promote a mindset of arrogance and allow people to play fast-and-loose with the system. Aramony seemed to fall into this category with his spending extravagances, cronyism, and other conflict-of-interest activities. (Some of the Girl Scout Councils, too, perceived them-

---

[13] *Ibid.*

[14] Karen Henderson, "Lorain Agency Cuts Ties with National United Way," *Cleveland Plain Dealer* (April 16, 1993), p. 7C.

INFORMATION BOX

ANOTHER CONTROVERSY: GIRL SCOUTS AND THEIR COOKIES

The main funding source for the nation's 2.6 million Girl Scouts is the annual cookie sale, estimated to generate $400 million in revenue.[15] The practice goes back some 70 years, although in the 1920s the girls sold homemade cookies. Now each regional council negotiates with one of two bakeries that produce the cookies, sets the price per box, which ranges from $2 to $3, and divides the proceeds as it sees fit. Typically, the Girl Scout troops get 10 to 15 percent, the council takes more than 50 percent, and the rest goes to the manufacturer.

Criticisms have emerged and received public attention regarding the dictatorial handling of these funds by the councils. There are 332 regional councils in the United States, each having an office and a paid staff overseen by a volunteer board. Some councils have dozens of employees, with most serving mainly as policy enforcers and supervisors. At the troop level, volunteer leaders, often women with daughters in the troop, guide their units in the true tradition of scouting, giving their time tirelessly. For the cookie drives, the girls are an unpaid sales force—child labor, as critics assail—that supports a huge bureaucratic structure. Little of the cookie revenue comes back to the local troops.

The bureaucracy does not tolerate dissent well. *The Wall Street Journal* cites the case of a West Haven, Connecticut, troop leader, Beth Denton, who protested both the way the Connecticut Trails council apportioned revenue and the $1.6 million in salaries and benefits paid to 42 council employees. After she complained to the state attorney general, the council dismissed her as leader.[16]

Admittedly, the individual salaries in the bureaucracy were not high by corporate standards or even by not-for-profit standards. Council administrators' salaries ranged up to about $90,000. Perhaps more disturbing was that volunteer leaders saw no annual financial statements of their council's expenditures and activities.[17]

Evaluate the council's position that annual financial records of their council's activities should be entirely confidential to full-time staff.

---

[15] Ellen Graham, "Sprawling Bureaucracy Eats up Most Profits of Girl Scout Cookies," *The Wall Street Journal* (May 13, 1992), p. A1.

[16] *Ibid.*, p. A4.

[17] *Ibid.*

selves as aloof from the dedicated volunteer troop leaders, tolerating no criticism or questioning, dictating and enforcing all policies without consultation or participation, and preventing scrutiny of their own operation.)

The UWA theoretically had an overseer: the boards, similar to the board of directors of business corporations. But when such boards act as rubber stamps, where they are closely in the camp of the chief executives, they are not really exercising control. This appeared to be the case with United Way of America during the "reign" of Aramony; similarly, as discussed in the preceding box, with the regional councils of the Girl Scouts, many of the volunteer boards appear to have exercised little or no control.

Certainly a board's failure to fulfill its responsibility is not unique to not-for-profits. Corporate boards have often been notorious for promoting the interests of the incumbent executives. Although this is changing today, it still prevails. See the following issue box for a discussion of the role of boards of directors.

ISSUE BOX

WHAT SHOULD BE THE ROLE OF THE BOARD OF DIRECTORS?

In the past, most boards of directors have tended to be closely allied with top executives and even composed mostly of corporate officials. In some organizations today this is changing, mostly in response to critics concerned about board tendencies to support the status quo and perpetuate the "establishment."

More and more, opinion is shifting to the idea that boards must assume an active role:

> The board can no longer play a passive role in corporate governance. Today, more than ever, the board must assume an activist role—a role that is protective of shareholder rights, sensitive to communities in which the company operates, responsive to the needs of company vendors and customers, and fair to its employees.[18]

Incentives for more active boards have been the increasing risks of liability for board decisions as well as liability insurance costs. Although the board of directors has long been seen as responsible for establishing corporate objectives, developing broad policies, and selecting top executives, these duties are no longer viewed as sufficient. Boards must also review management's performance—acting as a control mechanism—to ensure that the company is well run and that stockholders' interests are furthered. And, today, they must ensure that society's best interests are not disregarded.

But the issue remains: To whom should the board owe its greatest allegiance—the entrenched bureaucracy or the external publics? Without having board members representative of the many special interests affected by the organization, the inclination is to support the interests of the establishment.

Do you think a more representative and activist board will prevent a similar scenario from damaging United Way in the future? Why or why not?

---

[18] Lester B. Korn and Richard M. Ferry, *Board of Directors Thirteenth Annual Study* (New York: Korn/Ferry International, February 1986), pp. 1–2.

UPDATE

William Aramony was convicted of defrauding the United Way out of $1 million. He was sentenced to seven years in prison for using the charity's money to finance a lavish lifestyle.

Despite this, a federal judge ruled in late 1998 that the charity must pay its former president more than $2 million in retirement benefits. "A felon, no matter how despised, does not lose his right to enforce a contract," U.S. District Judge Shira Scheindlin in New York ruled.[19]

WHAT CAN BE LEARNED?

Beware the arrogant mindset. A leader's attitude that he or she is superior to subordinates and even to concerned outsiders is a formula for disaster, both for an organization and even for a society. Such an attitude promotes dictatorship, intolerance of contrary opinions, and an attitude that "we need answer to no one." We have seen the consequences with William Aramony: moving over the edge of what is deemed by most as acceptable and ethical conduct, assuming the role of the final authority who brooks no questions or criticisms. The absence of real or imagined controls or reviews seems to bring out the worst in people. We seem to need periodic scrutiny to avoid falling into the trap of arrogant decision making devoid of responsiveness to other concerns. The Girl Scout bureaucracy's dealings with its volunteers suggests the inclination toward arrogance and dictatorship in the absence of sufficient real controls.

Checks and balances—controls—are even more important in not-for-profit and governmental bodies than in corporate entities. For-profit organizations have "bottom-line" performance (i.e., profit and loss performance) as the ultimate control and standard. Not-for-profit and governmental organizations do not have this control, so they have no ultimate measure of their effectiveness.

Consequently, not-for-profit organizations should be subject to the utmost scrutiny of objective outsiders. Otherwise, abuses seem to be encouraged and perpetuated. Often these not-for-profit organizations are sheltered from competition, which usually also demands greater efficiency. Thus without objective and energetic controls, not-for-profit organizations have a tendency to be out of hand, to be run as little dynasties unencumbered by the constraints that face most businesses. Fortunately, investigative reporting and increasing litigation by allegedly abused parties today act as the needed controls for such organizations. In view of the revelations of investigative reporters, we are left to wonder how many other abusive and reprehensible activities have not as yet been detected.

Nonprofits are particularly vulnerable to bad press. Nonprofits depend on donations for the bulk of their revenues. Unlike most businesses, they depend on

[19] Reported in *Cleveland Plain Dealer* (October 25, 1998), p. 24-A.

people to give without receiving anything tangible in return. Consequently, any hint or semblance of waste or misdealings with donated money can quickly dry up contributions or cause them to be shunted to other charities.

With governmental bodies, of course, their perpetuation is hardly at stake with bad publicity, but the administrators can be recalled, impeached, or not reelected with enough adverse publicity.

CONSIDER

Can you add to these learning insights?

QUESTIONS

1. How do you feel, as a potential or actual giver to United Way campaigns, about the "high living" of Aramony? Would these allegations affect your gift giving? Why or why not?

2. What prescriptions do you have for thwarting arrogance in nonprofit and/or governmental organizations? Be as specific as you can, and support your recommendations.

3. How do you personally feel about the coercion that some organizations exert for their employees to contribute substantially to the United Way? What implications, if any, do you see as emerging from your attitudes about this?

4. Given the information supplied about the dictatorial relationships between Girl Scout councils and the local volunteers—and recognizing that such anecdotal information may not be truly representative—what do you see as the pros and cons of Girl Scout cookie drives? On balance, is this market-ing fund-raising effort still desirable, or might other alternatives be better?

5. "Since there is no bottom-line evaluation for performance, nonprofits have no incentives to control costs and prudently evaluate expenditures." Discuss.

6. How would you feel, as a large contributor to a charity, about its spending $10 million for advertising? Discuss your rationale for this attitude.

7. Do you think the action taken by UWA after Aramony was the best way to salvage the public image? Why or why not? What else might have been done?

INVITATION TO ROLE PLAY

1. You are an advisor to Elaine Chao, who has taken over the scandal-ridden United Way. What advice would you give her for as quickly as possible restoring the confidence of the American public in the integrity and wor-thiness of this preeminent national charity organization?

2. You are a member of the board of governors of United Way. Allegations have surfaced about the lavish life style of the highly regarded Aramony. Most of the board, being corporate executives, see nothing at all wrong with his perks and privileges. You, however, feel otherwise. How would you convince the other members of the board of the error of condoning Aramony's activities? Be as persuasive as you can in supporting your position.

3. You are the parent of a girl scout, who has assiduously worked to sell hundreds of boxes of cookies. You now realize that the efforts of your daughter and thousands of other girls are primarily supporting a bloated central and regional bureaucracy, and not the local troops. You feel strongly that this situation is an unacceptable use of child labor. Describe your proposed efforts to institute change.

TEAM DEBATE EXERCISE

Debate this issue: Should top executives of large charitable organizations be compensated comparable to corporate executives responsible for similar-size organizations?

INVITATION TO RESEARCH

What is the situation with United Way today? Are local agencies contributing to the national? Have donations matched or exceeded previous levels? Was Elaine Chao able to restore confidence? Is she still with United Way, or has she gone on to other challenges?

CHAPTER FIFTEEN

Met Life: Deceptive Sales Tactics—Condoned or Ill-Controlled?

*I*n August 1993, the state of Florida blew the whistle on giant Metropolitan Life, a company dating back to 1868, and the country's second largest insurance firm. Met Life agents based in Tampa, Florida, were alleged to have duped customers out of some $11 million. Thousands of these customers were nurses, lured by the sales pitch to learn more about "something new, one of the most widely discussed retirement plans in the investment world today."[1] In reality, this was a life-insurance policy in disguise, and what clients were led to think were savings deposits were actually insurance premiums.

As we will see, the growing scandal rocked Met Life, and brought it millions of dollars in fines and restitutions. What was not clear was the full culpability of the company: Was it guilty only of not monitoring agent performance sufficiently to detect unethical and illegal activities, or was it the great encourager of such practices?

RICK URSO: THE VILLAIN?

The first premonitory rumble that something bad was about to happen came to Rick Urso on Christmas Eve 1993. Home with his family, he received an unexpected call from his boss, the regional sales manager. In disbelief he heard there was a rumor going around the executive suites that he was about to be fired. Now, Urso had known that the State of Florida had been investigating, and that company auditors had also been looking into sales practices. And on September 17, two corporate vice-presidents had even shown up to conduct the fourth audit that year, but on leaving they had given him the impression that he was complying with company guidelines.

Urso often reveled in his good fortune and attributed it to his sheer dedication to his work and the company. He had grown up in a working-class neighborhood, the son of an electrician. He had started college, but dropped out before graduating.

---

[1] Suzanne Woolley and Gail DeGeorge, "Policies of Deception?" *Business Week*, January 17, 1994, p. 24.

His sales career started at a John Hancock agency in Tampa, in 1978. Four years later, he was promoted to manager. He was credited with building up the agency to number two in the whole company.

He left John Hancock in 1983 for Met Life's Tampa agency. His first job was as trainer. Only three months later he was promoted to branch manager. Now his long hours and overwhelming commitment were beginning to pay off. In a success story truly inspiring, his dedication and his talent as a motivator of people swept the branch from a one-rep office to one of Met Life's largest and most profitable. In 1990 and 1991, Urso's office won the company's Sales Office of the Year award. By 1993 the agency employed 120 reps, seven sales managers, and 30 administrative employees. And Urso had risen to become Met Life's third-highest-paid employee, earning $1.1 million as manager of the branch. With such a performance history, the stuff of legends, he became the company's star, a person to look up to and to inspire trainees and other employees.

His was the passion of a TV evangelist: "Most people go through life being told why they can't accomplish something. If they would just believe, then they would be halfway there. That's the way I dream and that's what I expect from my people."[2] He soon became known as the "Master Motivator," and increasingly was the guest speaker at Met Life conferences.

On the Monday after that Christmas, the dire prediction came to pass. He was summoned to the office of William Groggans, the head of Met Life's Southeast territory, and was handed a letter by the sober-faced Groggans. With trembling hands he opened it and read that he was fired for engaging in improper conduct.

The Route to Stardom

Unfortunately, the growth of his Tampa office could not be credited to simple motivation of employees. Urso found his vehicle for great growth to be the whole-life insurance policy. This was part life insurance and part savings. As such, it required high premiums, but only part earned interest and compounded on a tax-deferred basis; the rest went to pay for the life insurance policy. What made this so attractive to company sales reps was the commission: A Met whole-life policy paid a 55 percent first-year commission. In contrast, an annuity paid only a 2 percent first-year commission.

Urso found the nurses' market to be particularly attractive. Perhaps because of their constant exposure to death, nurses were easily convinced of the need for economic security. He had his salespeople call themselves "nursing representatives." And his Tampa salespeople carried their fake retirement plan beyond Florida, eventually reaching 37 states. A New York client, for example, thought she had bought a retirement annuity. But it turned out to be life insurance even though she didn't want such coverage because she had no beneficiaries.[3]

As the growth of the Tampa agency became phenomenal, his budget for mailing brochures was upped to nearly $1 million in 1992, ten times that of any other Met Life office. This gave him national reach.

[2] Weld F. Royal, "Scapegoat or Scoundrel," *Sales & Marketing Management* (January 1995), p. 64.

[3] Jane Bryant Quinn, "Yes, They're Out to Get You," *Newsweek* (January 24), 1994, p. 51.

Urso's own finances increased proportionately because he earned a commission on each policy his reps sold. In 1989, he was paid $270,000. In 1993, as compensation exceeded $1 million, he moved his family to Bay Shore Boulevard, the most expensive area of Tampa.

End of the Bonanza

A few complaints began surfacing. In 1990, the Texas insurance commissioner warned Met Life to stop its nursing ploy. The company made a token compliance by sending out two rounds of admonitory letters. But nothing apparently changed. See the following information box about the great deficiency of token compliance without follow-up.

An internal Met Life audit in 1991 raised some questions about Urso's pre-approach letters. The term *nursing representative* was called a "made-up" title. The auditors also questioned the term *retirement savings policy* as not appropriate for the product. However, the report concluded by congratulating the Tampa office for its contribution to the company. Not surprisingly, such mixed signals did not end the use of misleading language at that time.

In the summer of 1993, Florida state regulators began a more in-depth examination of the sales practices of the Urso agency. As a result of this investigation,

---

INFORMATION BOX

THE VULNERABILITY OF COMPLIANCE, IF IT IS ONLY TOKEN

A token effort at compliance to a regulatory complaint or charge tends to have two consequences, neither good in the long run for the company involved:

1. Such tokenism gives a clear message to the organization: "Despite what outsiders say, this is acceptable conduct in this firm." Thus is set the climate for less than desirable practices.

2. Vulnerability to future harsher measures. With the malpractice continuing, regulators, convinced that the company is stalling and refusing to cooperate, will eventually take more drastic action. Penalties will move beyond warnings to become punitive.

Actually, the firm may not have intended to stall, but that is the impression conveyed. If the cause of the seemingly token effort is really faulty controls, one wonders how many other aspects of the operation are also ineptly controlled so that company policies are ignored.

Discuss what kinds of controls Met Life could have imposed in 1990 that would have made compliance actual and not token.

Florida Insurance Commissioner Tom Gallagher charged Met Life with several violations. Now Met Life began more serious investigation.

The crux of the investigations concerned promotional material Urso's office was sending to nurses nationwide. From 1989 to 1993, millions of direct-mail pieces had been sent out. Charges finally were leveled that this material disguised the product agents were selling. For example, one brochure coming from Urso's office depicted the Peanuts character Lucy in a nurse's uniform. The headline described the product as "retirement savings and security for the future a nurse deserves." Nowhere was insurance even mentioned, and allegations were that nurses across the country unknowingly purchased life insurance when they thought they were buying retirement savings plans.

As the investigation deepened, a former Urso agent, turned whistleblower, claimed he had been instructed to place his hands over the words "life insurance" on applications during presentations.

MET LIFE CORRECTIVE ACTIONS

With Florida regulators now investigating, the company's attitudes changed. At first, Met Life denied wrongdoing. But eventually it acknowledged problems. Under mounting public pressure, it agreed to pay $20 million in fines to more than 40 states as a result of unethical sales practices of its agents. It further agreed to refund premiums to nearly 92,000 policyholders who bought insurance based on misleading sales information between 1989 and 1993. These refunds were expected to reach $76 million.

Met Life fired or demoted five high-level executives as a result of the scandal. Urso's office was closed, and all seven of his managers and several reps were also discharged. Life insurance sales to individuals were down 25 percent through September 1994 over the same nine-month period in 1993. And Standard & Poor's downgraded Met's bond rating based on these alleged improprieties.

Shortly after the fines were announced, the Florida Department of Insurance filed charges against Urso and 86 other Met Life insurance agents, accusing them of fraudulent sales practices. The insurance commissioner said, "This was not a situation where a few agents decided to take advantage of their customers, but a concerted effort by many individuals to dupe customers into buying a life insurance policy disguised as a retirement savings plan."[4]

The corporation, in attempting to improve its public image, instituted a broad overhaul of its compliance procedures. It established a corporate ethics and compliance department to monitor behavior throughout the company and audit personal insurance sales offices. The department was also charged to report any compliance deficiencies to senior management and to follow up to ensure the implementation of corrective actions.

In Met Life's *1994 Annual Report*, Harry Kamen, CEO, and Ted Athanassiades, president, commented on their corrective actions regarding the scandal:

---

[4] Sean Armstrong, "The Good, The Bad and the Industry," *Best's Review, P/C* (June 1994), p. 36.

We created what we think is the most effective compliance system in the industry. Not just for personal insurance, but for all components of the company. We installed systems to coordinate and track the quality and integrity of our sales activities, and we created a new system of sales office auditing.

Also, there were organizational changes. And, for the first time in 22 years, we assembled all of our agency and district managers—about a thousand people—to discuss what we have done and need to do about the problems and where we were going.[5]

Meantime, Rick Urso started a suit against Met Life for defamation of character and for reneging on a $1 million severance agreement. He alleged that Met Life made him the fall guy in the nationwide sales scandal.

The personal consequences on Urso's life were not inconsequential. More than a year later he was still unemployed. He had looked for another insurance job, but no one would even see him. "There are nights he can't sleep. He lies awake worrying about the impact this will have on his two teenagers." And he laments that his wife cannot go out without people gossiping.[6]

WHERE DOES THE BLAME LIE?

Is Urso really the unscrupulous monster who rose to a million-dollar-a-year man on the foundations of deceit? Or is Met Life mainly to blame for encouraging, and then ignoring for too long, practices aimed at misleading and even deceiving? Probably the final reckoning will not be reached outside the courtroom. And who can say that the judgment then rendered will be completely valid?

The Case Against Met Life

Undeniably Urso did things that smacked of the illegal and unethical. But did the corporation knowingly provide the climate? Was his training such as to promote deceptive practices? Was Met Life completely unaware of his distortions and deceptions in promotional material and sales pitches? There seems to be substantial evidence that the company played a part; it was no innocent and unsuspecting bystander.

At best, Met Life top executives may not have been aware of the full extent of the hard selling efforts emanating at first from Tampa and then spreading further in the organization. Perhaps they chose to ignore any inkling that things were not completely on the up and up, in the quest for exceptional bottom-line performance. "Don't argue with success" might have become the corporate mindset.

At the worst, the company encouraged and even demanded hard selling and tried to pretend that such could still be accomplished with the highest ethical standards of performance. If such ethical standards were not met, then, company top executives could argue, they were not aware of such wrongdoings.

There is evidence of company culpability (more will undoubtedly be introduced during Urso's suit). Take the training program for new agents. Much of it was

---

[5] *Met Life 1994 Annual Report*, p. 16.
[6] Royal, p. 65.

designed to help new employees overcome the difficulties of selling life insurance. In so doing, they were taught to downplay the life insurance aspects of the product. Rather, the savings and tax-deferred growth benefits were to be stressed.

In training new agents to sell insurance over the phone, they were told that people prefer dealing with specialists. It seemed only a small temptation to use the title *nursing representative* rather than *insurance agent.*

After the scandal, Met Life admitted that the training might be faulty. Training had been decentralized into five regional centers, and the company believed that this may have led to a less standardized and less controlled curricula. Met Life has since reorganized so that many functions, including training and legal matters, are now done at one central location.[7]

The company's control or monitoring was certainly deficient and uncoordinated during the years of misconduct. For example, the marketing department promoted deceptive sales practices while the legal department warned of possible illegality but took no further action to eliminate it.

An Industry Problem?

The Met Life revelations focused public and regulatory attention on the entire insurance industry. The Insurance Commissioner of Florida also turned attention to the sales and marketing practices of New York Life and Prudential. The industry itself seems vulnerable to questionable practices. With millions of transactions, intense competition, and a widespread and rather autonomous sales force, opportunity exists for misrepresentation and other unethical dealings.

For example, just a few months after the Tampa office publicity, Met Life settled an unrelated scandal. Regulators in Pennsylvania fined the company $1.5 million for "churning." This is a practice of agents replacing old policies with new ones, in which additional commissions are charged and policyholders are disadvantaged. Class-action suits alleging churning have also been filed in Pennsylvania against Prudential, New York Life, and John Hancock.

But problems go beyond sales practices. Claims adjusters may attempt to withhold or reduce payments. General agents may place business with bogus or insolvent companies. Even actuaries may create unrealistic policy structures.

With a deteriorating public image, the industry faces further governmental regulation, both by states and by the federal government. But cynics, both within and outside the industry, wonder whether deception and fraud are so much a part of the business that nothing can be done about them.[8]

ANALYSIS

We could also have placed this case under the Ethics section. The choice to include it under Control assumed a lapse in complete feedback to top executives. But maybe

---

[7] "Trained to Mislead," *Sales & Marketing Management,* January 1995, p. 66.

[8] Armstrong, p. 35.

they did not want to know. After all, nothing was life-threatening here, no product safety features were being ignored or disguised, nobody was in physical danger.

This raises a key management issue. Can top executives hide from less than ethical practices—and even illegal ones—under the guise that they did not know? The answer should be *No!* See the following information box for a discussion of management accountability.

So, we are left with top management of Met Life grappling with the temptation to tacitly approve the aggressive selling practices of a sales executive so successful as to be the model for the whole organization, even though faint cries from the legal staff suggested that such might be subject to regulatory scrutiny and disapproval.

The harsh appraisal of this situation is that top management cannot be exonerated for the deficiencies of subordinates. If controls and monitoring processes are defective, top management is still accountable. The pious platitudes of Met Life management that they have now corrected the situation hardly excuse them for permitting this to have developed in the first place.

Ah, but embracing the temptation is so easy to rationalize. Management can always maintain that there was no good, solid proof of misdeeds. After all, where do aggressive sales efforts cross the line? Where do they become more than simply puffing, and become outright deceptive? See the following information box regarding puffing, and this admittedly gray area of the acceptable. Lacking indisputable evidence of misdeeds,

---

INFORMATION BOX

THE ULTIMATE RESPONSIBILITY

In the Maytag case in Chapter 16 we examine a costly snafu brought about by giving executives of a foreign subsidiary too much rein. With Met Life the problem was gradually eroding ethical practices. In both instances, top management still had ultimate responsibility and cannot escape blame for whatever goes wrong in an organization. Decades ago, President Truman coined the phrase, "The buck stops here," meaning that in this highest position rests the ultimate seat of responsibility.

Any manager who delegates to someone else the authority to do something will undoubtedly hold them responsible to do the job properly. Still, the manager must be aware that his or her own responsibility to higher management or to stockholders cannot be delegated away. If the subordinate does the job improperly, the manager is still responsible.

Going back to Met Life, or to any corporation involved with unethical and illegal practices, top executives can try to escape blame by denying that they knew anything about the misdeeds. This should not exonerate them. Even if they knew nothing directly, they still set the climate.

In Japan, the chief executive of an organization involved in a public scandal usually resigns in disgrace. In the United States, top executives often escape full retribution by blaming their subordinates and maintaining that they themselves knew nothing of the misdeed. Is it truly fair to hold a top executive culpable for the shortcomings of some unknown subordinate?

INFORMATION BOX

WHERE DO WE DRAW THE LINE ON PUFFING?

Puffing is generally thought of as mild exaggeration in selling or advertising. It is generally accepted as simply the mark of exuberance toward what is being promoted. As such, it is acceptable business conduct. Most people have come to regard promotional communications with some skepticism—"It's New! The Greatest! A Super Value! Gives Whiter Teeth! Whiter Laundry!…" and so on. We have become conditioned to viewing such blandishments as suspicious. But dishonest, or deceptive? Probably not. As long as the exaggeration stays mild.

But it can be a short step from mild exaggeration to outright falsehoods and deceptive claims. Did Met Life's "nursing representatives," "retirement plans," and hiding the reality of life insurance cross the line? Enough people seemed to think so, including state insurance commissioners and the victims themselves. This short step can tempt more bad practices than if the line between good and bad were more definitive.

Do you think all exaggerated claims, even the mild and vague ones known as puffing, should be banned? Why or why not?

---

why should these executives suspect the worst? Especially since their legal departments, not centralized as they were to be later, were timid in their denunciations?

Turning to controls, a major caveat should be posed for all firms: In the presence of strong management demands for performance—with the often implicit or imagined pressure to produce at all costs, or else—the ground is laid for less than desirable practices by subordinates. After all, their career paths and even job longevity depend on meeting these demands.

In an organizational climate of decentralization and laissez faire, such abuses are more likely to occur. Such a results-oriented structure suggests that it's not how you achieve the desired results, but that you meet them. So, while decentralization is, on balance, usually desirable, it can, in the right environment of top management laxity of high moral standards, lead to undesirable—and worse—practices.

At the least, it leads to opportunistic temptation by lower- and middle-level executives. Perhaps this is the final indictment of Met Life and Rick Urso. The climate was conducive to his ambitious opportunism. For a while it was wonderful. But the clinks and the abuses of accepted practices could not be disguised indefinitely.

And wherever possible, top management will repudiate its accountability responsibilities.

WHAT CAN BE LEARNED?

Unethical and illegal actions do not go undetected forever. It may take months, it may take years, but a firm's dark side will eventually be uncovered. Its reputation may then be besmirched, it may face loss of customers and competitive position, it may face heavy fines and increased regulation.

The eventual disclosure may come from a disgruntled employee (a whistle-blower). It may originate from a regulatory body or an investigative reporter. Or it may come from revelations emanating from a lawsuit. Eventually, the deviation is uncovered, and retribution follows. Such a scenario should be—but is not always—enough to constrain those individuals tempted to commit unethical and illegal actions.

What made the Met Life deceptive practices particularly troubling is that they were so visible, and yet were so long tolerated. A clear definition of what was acceptable and what was not seemed lacking by much of the sales organization. Something was clearly amiss, both in the training and in the controlling of agent personnel.

The control function is best centralized in any organization. Where the department or entity that monitors performance is decentralized, tolerance of bad practices is more likely than when centralized. The reason is rather simple. Where legal or accounting controls are decentralized, the people conducting them are more easily influenced and are likely to be neither as objective nor as critical as when they are more at an arm's length. So, reviewers and evaluators should not be close to the people they are examining. And they should only report to top management.

A *strong sales incentive program invites bad practices.* The lucrative commission incentive for the whole-life policies—55 percent first-year commission—was almost bound to stimulate abusive sales practices, especially when the rewards for this type of policy were so much greater than for any other. Firms often use various incentive programs and contests to motivate their employees to seek greater efforts. But if some are tempted to cross the line, the end result of public scrutiny and condemnation may not be worth whatever increases in sales might be gained.

Large corporations are particularly vulnerable to public scrutiny. Large firms, especially ones dealing with consumer products, are very visible. This visibility makes them attractive targets for critical scrutiny by activists, politicians, the media, regulatory bodies, and the legal establishment. Such firms ought to be particularly careful in any dealings that might be questioned, even if short-term profits have to be restrained. In Met Life's case, the fines and refunds approached $100 million. Although the firm in its 1994 annual report maintained that all the bad publicity was behind, that there were no ill effects, still we can wonder how quickly a besmirched reputation can truly be restored, especially when competitors are eager to grab the opportunity.

The following box describes criticisms of another kind regarding a competitor of Met Life.

CONSIDER

What additional learning insights do you see?

INFORMATION BOX

CRITICISMS OF PRUDENTIAL INSURANCE COMPANY

Prudential has long cultivated its image as the "Rock," using a logo of the Rock of Gibraltar, symbol of permanence and stability. But like Met Life, it faced investigations and litigation over deceptive sales practices that affected millions of policyholders in the 1980s and early 1990s, and its sales of life-insurance policies slowed markedly. The company set aside more than $2 billion to cover the costs of litigation, and took a $1.64 billion charge against 1997 earnings. To try to resurrect its tarnished image, it increased advertising expenditures to $130 million in 1996 and 1997.

In August 1998 it came under fire of another kind, with disclosures of hefty compensations paid its executives, this despite the performance downturn: the top 100 executives averaged $820,000 in 1997, up 30 percent from 1994. By contrast, Met Life's top hundred executives averaged $600,000 in 1997, and State Farm had less than three dozen earning $350,000 or more.[9]

The compensation criticisms probably would not have surfaced had Prudential not sought to end its mutual status and move to public ownership, which would enable it to raise money more easily for purposes such as acquisitions. But demutualization exposed Prudential to critical scrutiny by huge institutional investors, notably the California Public Employees' Retirement System, and TIAA-CREF, a giant pension fund. These major shareholders regularly examine executive-compensation records of publicly traded companies.

Should executives be richly compensated when their firms are not doing well? Is it right to criticize a firm whose executives are far more richly rewarded than others in the same industry? Is it right for institutional investors to criticize and try to change policies in firms they invest in?

---

[9] Scot J. Paltrow, "As a Public Company Prudential May Find Pay Scales Draw Fire," *The Wall Street Journal* (August 14, 1998), pp. A1 and A8.

QUESTIONS

1. Do you think Rick Urso should have been fired? Why or why not?

2. Do you think Met Life CEO and president should have been fired? Why or why not?

3. Why was the term *life insurance* seemingly so desirable to avoid? What is wrong with life insurance?

4. Given the widespread publicity about the Met Life scandal, do you think the firm can regain consumer trust in a short time?

5. "This whole critical publicity has been blown way out of proportion. After all, nobody was injured. Not even in their pocketbook. They were sold something they really needed. For their own good." Evaluate.

6. "You have to admire that guy, Urso. He was a real genius. No one else could motivate a sales organization as he did. They should have made him president of the company. Or else he should become an evangelist." Evaluate.

7. Do you think the arguments are compelling that the control function should be centralized rather than decentralized? Why or why not?

HANDS-ON EXERCISES

Before

1. It is early 1990. You are the assistant to the CEO of Met Life. Rumors have been surfacing that life insurance sales efforts are becoming not only too high-pressure but also misleading. The CEO has ordered you to investigate. You find that the legal department in the Southeast Territory has some concerns about the efforts coming out of the highly successful Tampa office of Urso. Be as specific as you can about how you would investigate these unproven allegations, and how you would report this to your boss, assuming that some questionable practices seem apparent.

2. It is 1992. Internal investigations have confirmed that Urso and his "magnificent" Tampa office are using deceptive selling techniques in disguising the life insurance aspects of the policies they are selling. As the executive in charge in the Southeast, describe your actions and rationale at this point. (You have to assume that the later consequences are completely unknown as this point.)

After

3. The ⚬ ⚬ ⚬ ⚬ has hit the fan. The scandal has become well-publicized, especially with such TV programs as *Dateline* and *20/20*. What would you do as top executive of Met Life at this point? How would you attempt to save the public image of the company?

TEAM DEBATE EXERCISE

The publicity is widespread about the "misdeeds" of Met Life. Debate how you would react. One position is to defend your company and rationalize what happened and downplay any ill-effects. The other position is to meekly bow to the allegations and admit wrongdoing and be as contrite as possible.

INVITATION TO RESEARCH

How is Met Life faring after this extremely bad publicity? Do sales seem to be rebounding? Can you find any information on whether the image has improved, whether the situation has virtually been forgotten by the general public? Can you find out whether Rick Urso has found another job? Are Kamen and Athanassiades still the top executives of Met Life? What conclusions can you draw from your research?

CHAPTER SIXTEEN

Maytag: Leaving a Foreign Subsidiary Free as a Bird

In an unbelievable blunder, Maytag's foreign subsidiary in the United Kingdom accomplished a horror story of decentralized management. This might also be called abdication of authority, and the consequences of such abdication.

The atmosphere at the annual meeting in the little Iowa town of Newton had turned contentious. As Leonard Hadley faced increasingly angry questions from disgruntled shareholders, a thought crossed his mind: "I don't deserve this!" After all, he had been CEO of Maytag Corporation for only a few months, and this was his first chairing of an annual meeting. But the earnings of the company had been declining every year since 1988, and in 1992 Maytag had had a $315.4 million loss. No wonder the stockholders in the packed Newton High School auditorium were bitter and critical of their management. But there was more. Just the month before, the company had suffered the public embarrassment and costly atonement resulting from a monumental blunder in the promotional planning of its United Kingdom subsidiary.

Hadley doggedly saw the meeting to its close and limply concluded, "Hopefully, both sales and earning will improve this year."[1]

THE FIASCO

In August 1992, Hoover Limited, Maytag's British subsidiary, had launched this travel promotion: Anyone in the United Kingdom buying more than £100 (UK pounds) worth of Hoover products (about $150) before the end of January 1993 would get two free round-trip tickets to selected European destinations. For £250 worth of Hoover products, buyers could get two free round-trip tickets to New York or Orlando.

A buying frenzy resulted. Consumers had quickly figured out that the value of the tickets easily exceeded the cost of the appliances necessary to be eligible for them. By the tens of thousands, Britons rushed out to buy just enough Hoover prod-

---

[1] Richard Gibson, "Maytag's CEO Goes Through Wringer at Annual Meeting," *The Wall Street Journal* (April 28, 1993), p. A5.

ucts to qualify. Appliance stores were emptied of vacuum cleaners. The Hoover factory in Cambuslang, Scotland, that had been making vacuum cleaners only 3 days a week was suddenly placed on a 24-hour, 7-days-a-week production schedule—an overtime bonanza for the workers. What a resounding success for a promotion! Hoover managers, however, were unhappy.

Hoover had never expected more than 50,000 people to respond. And of those responding, it expected far fewer would go through all the steps necessary to qualify for the free trip and really take it. But more than 200,000 not only responded but qualified for the free tickets. The company was overwhelmed. The volume of paperwork created such a bottleneck that by the middle of April only 6,000 people had flown. Thousands of others either never got their tickets, were unable to get the dates requested, or waited for months without hearing the results of their applications. Hoover established a special hotline to process customer complaints, and these were coming in at 2,000 calls a day. But the complaints quickly spread, and the ensuing publicity brought charges of fraud and demands for restitution.

Maytag dispatched a task force to try to resolve the situation without jeopardizing customer relations any further. But it acknowledged that it was "not 100% clear" that all eligible buyers would receive their free flights.[2] The ill-fated promotion was a staggering blow to Maytag financially. It took a $30 million charge in the first quarter of 1993 to cover unexpected additional costs linked to the promotion. Final costs were expected to exceed $50 million, which would be 10 percent of UK Hoover's total revenues. This was especially damaging for a subsidiary acquired only 4 years before, that had yet to produce a profit.

Adding to the costs were problems with the two travel agencies involved. The agencies were to obtain low-cost space-available tickets and would earn commission selling "packages," including hotels, rental cars, and insurance. If consumers bought a package, Hoover would get a cut. However, despite the overwhelming demand for tickets, most consumers declined to purchase the package, thus greatly reducing support money for the promotional venture. So Hoover had greatly underestimated the likely response and overestimated the amount it would earn from commission payments. This raises the issue of loss leaders. How much should we use loss leaders as a promotional device? This topic is discussed in the following box.

If these cost overruns had added greatly to Maytag and Hoover's customer relations and public image, the expenditures would have seemed more palatable. But with all the problems the best that could be expected would be to lessen the worst of the agitation and charges of deception. And this was proving to be impossible. The media, of course, salivated at the problems and were quick to sensationalize them:

> One disgruntled customer, who took aggressive action on his own, received the widest press coverage, and even became a folk hero. Dave Dixon, claiming he was cheated out of a free vacation by Hoover, seized one of the company's repair vans in retaliation.

---

[2] James P. Miller, "Maytag U.K. Unit Finds a Promotion Is Too Successful," *The Wall Street Journal* (March 31, 1993), p. A9.

ISSUE BOX

SHOULD WE USE LOSS LEADERS?

Leader pricing is a type of promotion with certain items advertised at a very low price—sometimes even below cost—in which case they are known as *loss leaders*—in order to attract more customers. The rationale is that such customers are likely to purchase other regular-price items as well, increasing total sales and profits. If customers do not purchase enough other goods at regular prices to more than cover the losses incurred from the attractively priced bargains, then the loss leader promotion is ill advised. Some critics maintain that the whole idea of using loss leaders is absurd: The firm is just "buying sales" with no regard for profits.

While UK Hoover did not think of its promotion as a loss leader, in reality it was: The company stood to lose money on every sale if the promotional offer was taken advantage of. Unfortunately for its effectiveness as a loss leader, the likelihood of customers purchasing other Hoover products at regular prices was remote, and the level of acceptance was not capped, so losses were permitted to multiply. The conclusion has to be that this was an ill-conceived idea from the beginning. It violated these two conditions of loss leaders: They should stimulate sales of other products, and their losses should be limited.

Do you think loss leaders really are desirable under certain circumstances? Why or why not?

Police were sympathetic: they took him home, and did not charge him, claiming it was a civil matter.[3]

Heads rolled. Initially, Maytag fired three UK Hoover executives involved, including the president of Hoover Europe. At the annual meeting Mr. Hadley also indicated that others might lose their jobs before the cleanup was complete. He likened the promotion to "a bad accident ... and you can't determine what was in the driver's mind."[4]

Receiving somewhat less publicity was the fact that corporate headquarters allowed executives of a subsidiary such wide latitude that they could saddle parent Maytag with tens of millions of dollars in unexpected costs. Did not top corporate executives have to approve ambitious plans? A company spokesman said that operating divisions were "primarily responsible" for planning promotional expenses. Although the parent may review such outlays, "if they're within parameters, it goes through."[5] This raises the issue, discussed in the following box, of how loose a rein foreign subsidiaries should be allowed.

---

[3] "Unhappy Brit Holds Hoover Van Hostage," *Cleveland Plain Dealer* (June 1, 1993): D1; and Simon Reeve and John Harlow, "Hoover is Sued Over Flights Deal," *London Sunday Times* (June 6, 1993).

[4] Gibson, "CEO Goes Through Wringer," A5.

[5] Miller, "Maytag UK Unit," A9.

HOW LOOSE A REIN FOR A FOREIGN SUBSIDIARY?

In a decentralized organization, top management delegates considerable decision-making authority to subordinates. Such decentralization—often called a "loose rein"—tends to be more marked with foreign subsidiaries, such as UK Hoover. Corporate management in the United States understandably feels less familiar with the foreign environment and more willing to let the native executives operate with fewer constraints than a domestic subsidiary has. In the Maytag/Hoover situation, decision-making authority by British executives was evidently extensive, and corporate Maytag exercised little operational control, being content to judge performance by ultimate results achieved. Major deviations from expected performance goals, or widespread traumatic happenings—both of which happened to UK Hoover—finally gained corporate management attention.

Extensive decentralization has many advantages: First, top management effectiveness can be improved because time and attention is freed for presumably more important matters; second, subordinates are permitted more self-management, which should improve their competence and motivation; and third, in foreign environments, native managers presumably understand their unique problems and opportunities better than corporate management, located thousands of miles away, possibly can. But the drawbacks are as we have seen: parameters within which subordinate managers operate can be so wide that serious miscalculations may not be stopped in time. Because top management is ultimately responsible for all performance, including actions of subordinates, it faces greater risks with extensive decentralization.

"Since the manager is ultimately accountable for whatever is delegated to subordinates, then a free rein reflects great confidence in subordinates." Discuss.

BACKGROUND ON MAYTAG

Maytag is a century-old company. The original business, formed in 1893, manufactured feeder attachments for threshing machines. In 1907 the company moved to Newton, Iowa, a small town 30 miles east of Des Moines, the capital city. Manufacturing emphasis turned to home laundry equipment and wringer-type washers.

A natural expansion of this emphasis occurred with the commercial laundromat business in the 1930s, when coin meters were attached to Maytag washers. Rapid growth of these coin-operated laundries took place in the United States during the late 1950s and early 1960s. The increased competition and soaring energy costs of the 1970s hurt laundromats. In 1975 Maytag introduced new energy-efficient machines and "home style" stores that rejuvenated the business.

The Lonely Maytag Repairman

For years Maytag reveled in a marketing coup, with its washers and dryers enjoying a top-quality image, thanks to ads in which a repairman laments his loneliness because of Maytag's trouble-free products. The result of this dependability and quality image was that Maytag could command a price premium: "Their machines cost the same to make, break down as much as ours—but they get $100 more because of the reputation," grumbled a competitor.[6]

During the 1970s and into the 1980s, Maytag continued to capture 15 percent of the washing machine market and enjoyed profit margins about twice that of competitors. Table 16.1 shows operating results for the period 1974 to 1981. Whirlpool was the largest factor in the laundry equipment market, with a 45 percent share, but this was largely because of sales to Sears under the Sears brand.

Acquisitions

For many years, until his retirement December 31, 1992, Daniel J. Krumm had influenced Maytag's destinies. He had been CEO for 18 years and chairman since 1986, and his tenure with the company encompassed 40 years. In that time the home-appliance business had encountered some drastic changes. The most ominous occurred in the late 1980s with the merger mania, in which the threat of takeovers by hostile raiders often motivated heretofore conservative executives to greatly increase corporate indebtedness, thereby decreasing the attractiveness of their firms. Daniel Krumm was one of these running-scared executives, as rumors persisted that the company was a takeover candidate.

Largely as a defensive move, Krumm pushed through a deal for a $1 billion buyout of Chicago Pacific Corporation (CPC), a maker of vacuum cleaners and other appliances with $1.4 billion in sales. As a result, Maytag was burdened with $500 mil-

TABLE 16.1 Maytag Operating Results, 1974–1981 (in $ millions)

	Net Sales	Net Income	Percent of Sales
1974	$229	$21.1	9.2%
1975	238	25.9	10.9
1976	275	33.1	12.0
1977	299	34.5	11.5
1978	325	36.7	11.3
1979	369	45.3	12.3
1980	346	35.6	10.2
1981	409	37.4	9.1
Average net income percent of sales: 10.8%

Source: Company operating statistics.

Commentary: These years show a steady, though not spectacular, growth in revenues and a generally rising net income, except for 1980. Of particular interest is the high net income percentage of sales, averaging 10.8% over the 8-year period, with a high of 12.3%.

[6] Brian Bremmer, "Can Maytag Clean Up Around the World?" *Business Week* (Jan. 30, 1989), p. 86.

lion in new debt. Krumm defended the acquisition as giving Maytag a strong foothold in a growing overseas market. CPC was best known for the Hoover vacuums it sold in the United States and Europe. Indeed, so dominant was the Hoover brand in England that many people did not vacuum their carpets, but "hoovered the carpet." CPC also made washers, dryers, and other appliances under the Hoover brand, selling them exclusively in Europe and Australia. In addition, it had six furniture companies, but Maytag sold these shortly after the acquisition.

Krumm had been instrumental in transforming Maytag, the number four U.S. appliance manufacturer—behind General Electric, Whirlpool, and Electrolux—from a niche laundry-equipment maker into a full-line manufacturer. He had led an earlier acquisition spree in which Maytag had expanded into microwave ovens, electric ranges, refrigerators, and freezers. Its brands now included Magic Chef, Jenn-Air, Norge, and Admiral. The last years of Krumm's reign, however, were not marked by great operating results. As shown in Table 16.2, revenues showed no gain in the 1989–1992 period, while income steadily declined.

Trouble

Although the rationale for internationalizing seemed inescapable, especially in view of a recent wave of joint ventures between U.S. and European appliance makers, the Hoover acquisition was troublesome. It was a major brand in England and in Australia, but Hoover had only a small presence in Continental Europe. Yet this was where the bulk of the market was, with some 320 million potential appliance buyers.

The probabilities of the Hoover subsidiary capturing much of the European market were hardly promising. Whirlpool was strong, having 10 plants there in contrast to Hoover's two plants. Furthermore, Maytag faced entrenched European competitors such as Sweden's Electrolux, the world's largest appliance maker; Germany's Bosch-Siemens; and Italy's Merloni Group. And General Electric had also entered the market with joint ventures. Europeans' fierce loyalty to domestic brands raised further questions as to the ability of Maytag's Hoover to penetrate the

TABLE 16.2   **Maytag Operating Results, 1989–1992**

	Revenue	Net Income	% of Revenue
	(000,000)		
1989	$3,089	131.0	4.3%
1990	3,057	98.9	3.2
1991	2,971	79.0	2.7
1992	3,041	(315.4)	(10.4)

Source: Company annual reports.

Commentary: Note the steady erosion of profitability, while sales remained virtually static. For a comparison with profit performance of earlier years, see Table 16.1 and the net-income-to-sales percentages of this more "golden" period.

European market without massive promotional expenditures, and maybe not even then.

Australia was something else. Hoover had a good competitive position there, and its refrigerator plant in Melbourne could easily be expanded to include Maytag's washers and dryers. Unfortunately, the small population of Australia limited the market to only about $250 million for major appliances.

Britain accounted for one-half of Hoover's European sales. But at the time of the acquisition, its major appliance business was only marginally profitable. This was to change: After the acquisition it became downright unprofitable, as shown in Table 16.3 for the years 1990 through 1992, as it struggled to expand in a recession-plagued Europe. The results for 1993, of course, will reflect the huge loss for the promotional debacle. Hardly an acquisition made in heaven.

Maytag's earlier acquisitions also were becoming soured. Its acquisitions of Magic Chef and Admiral were diversifications into lower-priced appliances, and these acquisitions did not meet expectations. But they left Maytag's balance sheet and its cash flow weakened (see Table 16.4). Perhaps more serious, Maytag's reputation as the nation's premier appliance maker became tarnished. Meanwhile, General Electric and Whirlpool were attacking the top end of its product line. As a result, Maytag found itself in the number three or number four position in most of its brand lines.

TABLE 16.3 Operating Results of Maytag's Principal Business Components, 1990–1992

	Revenue (000,000)	Income[a] (000)
1990		
North American Appliances	$2,212	$221,165
Vending	191	25,018
European Sales	497	(22,863)
1991		
North American Appliances	2,183	186,322
Vending	150	4,498
European Sales	486	(865)
1992		
North American Appliances	2,242	129,680
Vending	165	16,311
European Sales	502	(67,061)

[a] This is operating income, that is, income before depreciation and other adjustments.

Source: Company annual reports.

Commentary: While these years had not been particularly good for Maytag in growth of revenues and income, the continuing, and even intensifying, losses in the Hoover European operation had to be troublesome. And this was true even before the ill-fated early 1993 promotional results.

TABLE 16.4   Long-Term Debt as a Percent of Capital from Maytag's Balance Sheets, 1986–1991

Year	Long-Term Debt/Capital
1986	7.2%
1987	23.3
1988	48.3
1989	46.8
1990	44.1
1991	42.7

Source: Company annual reports.

Commentary: The effect of acquisitions, in particular that of the Chicago Pacific Corporation, can be clearly seen in the buildup of long-term debt. In 1986 Maytag was virtually free of such commitments; 2 years later its long-term debt ratio had increased almost sevenfold.

ANALYSIS

Flawed Acquisition Decisions

The long decline in profits after 1989 should have triggered strong concern and corrective action. And perhaps it did, but the action was not effective because the decline continued, culminating in a large deficit in 1992 and serious problems in 1993. As shown in Table 16.2, the acquisitions brought neither revenue gains nor profitability. One suspects that in the rush to fend off potential raiders in the late 1980s, the company bought businesses it might never have bought under more sober times and that it also paid too much for these businesses. Further, they cheapened Maytag's proud quality image.

Who Can We Blame in the UK Promotional Debacle?

Corporate Maytag management was guilty of a common fault in its acquisitions. It gave newly acquired divisions a loose rein, letting them continue to operate independently with few constraints: "After all, these executives should be more knowledgeable about their operations than corporate headquarters would be." Such confidence is sometimes misguided. In the UK promotion, Maytag management would seem as derelict as management in England. Planning guidelines or parameters were far too loose and under-controlled. That subsidiary management could burden the parent with $50 million of unexpected charges, and to have such a problem erupt with no warning, borders on the absurd.

Finally, the UK executives' planning for this ill-conceived travel promotion defies all logic. They vastly underestimated the demand for the promotions offer and greatly overestimated paybacks from travel agencies on the package deals. Yet it took no brilliant insight to realize that the value of the travel offer exceeded the price of the appliance—indeed, 200,000 customers rapidly arrived at this conclusion—and that such a sweetheart of a deal would be irresistible to many. Hoover management should have seen that the promotion could prove to be extremely costly to the company. Was it a miscalculation or complete naivete on the part of executives and their staffs, who should have known better?

How Could the Promotion Have Avoided the Problems?

The great problem resulting from an offer that was too good could have been avoided without scrapping the whole idea. A cost-benefit analysis would have provided at least a perspective as to how much the company should spend to achieve certain benefits, such as increased sales, greater consumer interest, and favorable publicity. See the following information box for a more detailed discussion of the important planning tool of a cost-benefit analysis.

INFORMATION BOX

COST-BENEFIT ANALYSIS

A cost-benefit analysis is a systematic comparison of the costs and benefits of a proposed action. Only if the benefits exceed the costs would we normally have a "go" decision. The normal way to make such an analysis is to assign dollar values to all costs and benefits, thus providing a common basis for comparison.

Cost-benefit analyses have been widely used by the Department of Defense in evaluating alternative weapons systems. In recent years such analyses have been sporadically applied to environmental regulation and even to workplace safety standards. As an example of the former, a cost-benefit analysis can be used to determine if it is socially worthwhile to spend $X million to meet a certain standard of clean air or water.

Many business decisions lend themselves to a cost-benefit analysis. It provides a systematic way of analyzing the inputs and the probable outputs of particular major alternatives. While in the business setting some of the costs and benefits can be quantitative, they often should be tempered by nonquantitative inputs to reach the broadest perspective. Schemerhorn suggests considering the following criteria in evaluating alternatives.[7]

- *Benefits.* What are the benefits of using the alternatives to solve a performance deficiency or take advantage of an opportunity?
- *Costs.* What are the costs to implement the alternatives, including direct resource investments as well as any potential negative side effects?
- *Timeliness.* How fast will the benefits occur and a positive impact be achieved?
- *Acceptability.* To what extent will the alternatives be accepted and supported by those who must work with them?
- *Ethical soundness.* How well do the alternatives meet acceptable ethical criteria in the eyes of multiple stakeholders?

What numbers would you assign to a cost-benefit analysis for Maytag Hoover's plan to offer the free airline tickets, under an assumption of 5,000 takers? 20,000 takers? 100,000 takers? 500,000 takers? (Make any assumptions needed as to costs.) What would be your conclusions for these various acceptance rates?

---

[7] John R. Schermerhorn, Jr., *Management*, 6th ed. (New York: Wiley, 1999), p. 61.

A cost-benefit analysis should certainly have alerted management to the possible consequences of various acceptance levels and to the significant risks of high acceptance. However, the company could have set limits on the number of eligibles: perhaps the first 1,000, or the first 5,000. Doing this would have held or capped the costs to reasonably defined levels and avoided the greater risks. Or the company could have made the offer less generous, perhaps by upping the requirements or by lessening the premiums. Such more moderate alternatives would still have made an attractive promotion but not the major uncontrolled catastrophe that happened.

UPDATE—LEONARD HADLEY

In the summer of 1998, Leonard Hadley could look forward and backward with some satisfaction. He would retire the next summer when he turned 65, and he had already picked his successor. Since assuming the top position in Maytag in January 1993, and confronting the mess with the UK subsidiary his first few months on the job, he had turned Maytag completely around.

He knew no one expected much change from him, an accountant who had joined Maytag right out of college. He was known as a loyal but unimaginative lieutenant of his boss, Daniel Krumm, who died of cancer shortly after naming Hadley his successor. After all, he reflected, no one thought that major change could come to an organization from someone who had spent his whole life there, who was a clone so to speak, and an accountant to boot. Everyone thought that changemakers had to come from outside, like Al Dunlap of Scott Paper and Sunbeam. Well, he had shown them, and given hope to all No. 2 executives who resented Wall Street's love affair with outsiders.

Within a few weeks of taking over, he'd fired a bunch of managers, especially those rascals in the UK who'd masterminded the great Hoover promotion that cost the company dearly. He determined to get rid of foreign operations, most of them newly acquired and unprofitable. He just did not see that appliances could be profitably made for every corner of the world, because of the variety of regional customs. Still, he knew that many disagreed with him about this, including some of the board members who thought globalization was the only way to go. Still, over the next 18 months he had prevailed.

He chuckled to himself as he reminisced. He had also overturned the decades-long corporate mindset not to be first to market with new technology because they would "rather be right than be first." His "Galaxy Initiative" of nine top-secret new products was a repudiation of this old mindset. One of them, the Neptune, a front-loading washer retailing at $1,100, certainly proved him right. Maytag had increased its production three times and raised its suggested retail price twice, and still it was selling like gangbusters. Perhaps the thing he was proudest of was getting Maytag products in Sears stores, the seller of one-third of all appliances in the United States. Sears' desire to have the Neptune is what swung the deal.

As an accountant, he probably should be focusing first on the numbers. Well, 1997 was certainly a banner year with sales up 10.9 percent over the previous year, while profitability as measured by return on capital was 16.7 percent, both sales and profit gains leading the industry. And 1998 so far was proving to be even better, with sales jumping 31 percent and earnings 88 percent.

He remembered the remarks of Lester Crown, a Maytag director: "Len Hadley has—quietly, softly—done a spectacular job. Obviously, we just lacked the ability to evaluate him [at the beginning]."

He knew he had surprised everybody in the organization by going outside Maytag for his heir apparent. He is Lloyd Ward, 49, Maytag's first black executive, a marketing expert from PepsiCo, and before that Procter & Gamble.[8]

WHAT CAN BE LEARNED?

Beware overpaying for an acquisition. Hoping to diversify its product line and gain market share overseas, Maytag paid $1 billion for Chicago Pacific in 1989. As it turned out, this was far too much, and the debt burden was an albatross. Chief Executive Leonard Hadley conceded as much: "In the long view, it was correct to invest in these businesses. But the timing of the deal, and the price of the deal, made the debt a heavy load to carry."[9]

Zeal to expand, and/or the desire to reduce the attractiveness of a firm's balance sheet and thus fend off potential raiders, do not excuse foolhardy management. The consequences of such bad decisions remain to haunt a company, and the ill-advised purchases often have to be eventually sold off at substantial losses. The analysis of potential acquisition candidates must be soberly and thoroughly done, and rosy projections questioned, even if this means the deal may be soured.

Beware giving too loose a rein, thus sacrificing controls, especially of unproven foreign subsidiaries. Although decentralizing authority down to lower ranks is often desirable and results in better motivation and management development than centralization, it can be overdone. At the extreme, where divisional and subsidiary executives have virtually unlimited decision-making authority and can run their operations as virtual dynasties, then corporate management essentially abdicates its authority. Such looseness in an organization endangers cohesiveness; it tends to obscure common standards and objectives; and it can even dilute unified ethical practices.

Such extreme looseness of controls is not uncommon with acquisitions, especially foreign ones. It is easy to make the assumption that these executives were operating successfully before the acquisition and have more firsthand knowledge of the environment than the corporate executives.

Still, there should be limits on how much freedom these executives should be permitted—especially when their operations have not been notably successful. In Maytag's case, the UK subsidiary had lost money every year since it was acquired. Accordingly, one would expect prudent corporate management to have condoned less decentralization and insisted on tighter controls than it might otherwise.

[8] Sources include Maytag annual reports, and Carl Quintanilla, "Maytag's Top Officer, Expected to Do Little, Surprises His Board," *The Wall Street Journal* (June 23, 1998), pp. A1 and A8.

[9] Kenneth Labich, "What Companies Fail," *Fortune* (November 14, 1994), p. 60.

In decision planning, consider a worst-case scenario. There are those who preach the desirability of positive thinking, confidence, and optimism, whether it be in personal lives, athletics, or business practices. But expecting and preparing for the worst has much to commend it, since a person or a firm is then better able to cope with adversity, avoid being overwhelmed, and more likely to make prudent rather than rash decisions.

Apparently the avid acceptance of the promotional offer was a complete surprise; no one dreamed of such demand. Yet, was it so unreasonable to think that a very attractive offer would meet wild acceptance?

In using loss leaders, put a cap on potential losses. Loss leaders, as we noted earlier, are items promoted at such attractive prices that the firm loses money on every sale. The expectation, of course, is that the customer traffic generated by such attractive promotions will increase sales of regular profit items so that total profits will be increased.

The risks of uncontrolled or uncapped loss leader promotions is vividly shown in this case. For a retailer who uses loss leaders, the loss is ultimately capped as the inventory is sold off. With UK Hoover there was no cap. The moral is clear: Attractive loss leader promotions should be capped, such as the first 100 or the first 1,000 or for one week only. Otherwise, the promotion should be made less attractive.

The power of a cost-benefit analysis. For major decisions, executives have much to gain from a cost-benefit analysis. It forces them to systematically tabulate and analyze the costs and benefits of particular courses of action. They may find that likely benefits are so uncertain as to not be worth the risk. If so, now is the time to realize this, rather than after substantial commitments have already been made.

Without doubt, regular use of cost-benefit analyses for major decisions improves executives' batting averages for good decisions. Even though some numbers may have to be judgmental, especially as to probable benefits, the process of making this analysis forces a careful look at alternatives and most likely consequences. For more important decisions, input from diverse staff people and executives will bring greater power to the analysis.

CONSIDER

What additional learning insights can you add?

QUESTIONS

1. How could the promotion of UK Hoover have been better designed? Be as specific as you can.

2. Given the fiasco that did occur, how do you think Maytag should have responded?

3. "Firing the three top executives of UK Hoover is unconscionable. It smacks of a vendetta against European managers by an American parent.

After all, their only 'crime' was a promotion that was too successful." Comment on this statement.

4. Do you think Leonard Hadley, the Maytag CEO for only two months, should be soundly criticized for the UK situation? Why or why not?

5. Please speculate: Why do you think this UK Hoover fiasco happened in the first place? What went wrong?

6. Evaluate the decision to acquire Chicago Pacific Corporation (CPC). Do this both for the time of the decision and for now—after the fact—as a post mortem. Defend your overall conclusions.

HANDS-ON EXERCISES

1. You have been placed in charge of a task force sent by headquarters to England to coordinate the fire-fighting efforts in the aftermath of the ill-fated promotion. There is neither enough productive capacity nor enough airline seats available to handle the demand. How do you propose to handle this situation? Be as specific as you can, and defend your recommendations.

2. As a staff vice president at corporate headquarters, you have been charged to develop companywide policies and procedures that will prevent such a situation from ever occurring again. What do you recommend?

TEAM DEBATE EXERCISE

Two schools of thought are emerging after the promotional debacle. One position advocates repudiating the offer, citing the impossibility of fulfilling all the demand. The other position maintains that the promise must be met at all costs, even if private planes have to be leased. Debate the options.

INVITATION TO RESEARCH

Has Hadley retired at 65 as planned? Did Lloyd Ward replace him? Has Maytag entered overseas markets again? How is the Neptune washer doing? Has Maytag brought out any other innovative products?

CHAPTER SEVENTEEN

McDonald's: The Paragon of Controls, But Is This Eroding?

Few business firms anywhere in the world can match the sustained growth of McDonald's. Initially, it grew with one simple product—a hamburger—and although McDonald's today has broadened its product mix somewhat, it still remains uniquely undiversified.

Now, skeptics wonder about McDonald's. Is it nearing the end of its phenomenal growth? Are there chinks in its armor that were not there before, and are these likely to widen?

THE MCDONALD'S GROWTH MACHINE

In its *1995 Annual Report*, McDonald's management was justifiably proud. Sales and profits had continued the long trend upward, and even seemed to be accelerating. See Table 17.1. Far from reaching a saturation point, the firm was opening more restaurants than ever, some 2,400 around the world in 1995, up from 1,800 the year before. "We plan to add between 2,500 and 3,200 restaurants in both 1996 and 1997, with about two-thirds outside of the United States. In other words, we opened more than six restaurants per day in 1995; over the next two years, we plan to open eight a day."[1] And, "Our growth opportunities remain significant: on any given day, 99 percent of the world's population does not eat at McDonald's ... yet."[2]

Company management extolled the power of the McDonald's brand overseas, and how on opening days lines were sometimes "miles" long. "Often our challenge is to keep up with demand. In China, for example, there are only 62 McDonald's to serve a population of 1.2 billion."[3] By the end of 1995, the company had 7,012 out-

[1] *McDonald's 1995 Annual Report*, p. 8.

[2] *Ibid.*, p. 7.

[3]*Ibid.*

TABLE 17.1   Growth in Sales and Profits, 1985–1995

	Sales (millions)	Percent Gain	Income (millions)	Percent Gain
1985	$11,011		$ 433	
1986	12,432	12.9%	480	12.2%
1987	14,330	15.3	549	14.4
1988	16,064	12.1	646	17.7
1989	17,333	7.9	727	12.5
1990	18,759	8.2	802	10.3
1991	19,928	6.2	860	7.2
1992	21,885	9.8	959	11.5
1993	23,587	7.8	1,083	12.9
1994	25,987	10.2	1,224	13.0
1995	29,914	15.1	1,427	16.6

Source: 1995 Annual Report.

Commentary: Of particular interest is how the new expansion policies have brought a burst of revenues and profits in the mid-1990s. How audacious we are to even question these growth policies. But we have.

lets in 89 countries of the world, with Japan alone having 1,482. Table 17.2 shows the top ten countries in number of McDonald's units.

Sometimes in marketing its products in different cultures, adjustments had to be made. The following box describes the changes McDonald's made for its first store in India, which opened October 13, 1996.

TABLE 17.2   Top Ten Foreign Markets in Number of Units at Year End, 1995

Japan	1,482 restaurants
Canada	902
Germany	649
England	577
Australia	530
France	429
Brazil	243
Mexico	132
Netherlands	128
Taiwan	111

Source: 1995 Annual Report.

Commentary: Is the popularity in Japan a surprise?

INFORMATION BOX

McMUTTON BURGERS FOR INDIA

No all-beef patties are to be found in McDonald's packed restaurant in Delhi, India. Ground lamb has been substituted in the "Maharaja Mac" and other 100 percent pure mutton burgers in deference to the Hindu majority's reverence for the cow. The first no-beef McDonald's in the world also serves no pork, since this would offend India's Muslim minority.

Vegetarians can choose between veggie burgers and "Vegetable McNuggets," all cooked by a separate staff who do not handle meat products, conforming to another taboo. Such "Indianizing" has brought heavy crowds—from families, to turbaned Sikhs, to young Western wannabes—to jam the three-floor restaurant. Yet, there are militant critics: "I am against McDonald's because they are the chief killers of cows in the world," said Maneka Gandhi, an animal-rights activist and daughter-in-law of assassinated prime minister Indira Gandhi. "We don't need cow killers in India."[4] But most customers were not concerned about this, and said their only complaint was that the burgers were too small and bland for hearty, spice-loving Indian palates.

A second McDonald's opened in Bombay a week after the Delhi opening. It drew more than 12,000 customers on its first day.

Should the militant activists become more violent about McDonald's "conducting a global conspiracy against cattle," do you think McDonald's should abandon the India market? Why or why not?

[4] "Delhi Delights in McMutton Burgers," *Cleveland Plain Dealer* (November 6, 1996), p. 3-D.

Growth Prospects in the United States

With 11,368 of its restaurants in the United States, wasn't McDonald's rapidly reaching a point of saturation in its domestic market, if not overseas? Top management vehemently disputed this conclusion. Rather, it offered a startling statistical phenomenon to support accelerating expansion. Called "Greenberg's law," after newly appointed McDonald's U.S. chairman Jack Greenberg, it maintained that the more stores McDonald's put in a city the more per capita transactions will result. Thus, with two stores in a city there might be 16 transactions per capita per year. Add two or four more stores and the transactions will not only double, or quadruple, but may even do better than that. The hypothesized explanation for this amazing phenomenon seemingly rested on two factors: convenience and market share. With more outlets, McDonald's increased its convenience to consumers, and added to its market share at the expense of competitors. Hence the justification for the expansion binge.

In the quest for this domestic expansion the company over the last five years had been able to reduce the cost of building a new U.S. traditional restaurant by 26 percent through standardizing building materials and equipment and global sourcing, as well as improving construction methods and building designs. But it had also found abundant market opportunities in satellite restaurants. These were smaller, had lower sales volume, and served simplified menus. This format proved cost efficient in such nontraditional places as zoos, hospitals, airports, museums, and military bases as well as in retail stores such as Wal-Mart, The Home Depot, and some other major stores. For example, such satellite restaurants were in some 800 Wal-Mart stores by the end of 1995, with more planned. In October 1996, a McDonald's Express opened in a 1,200 square-foot space in an office building in Lansing, Michigan, perhaps a harbinger of more such sites to come.

In its eager search for ever more outlets, McDonald's did something it had never done before. It took over stores from weak competitors. In late summer 1996, it bought 184 company-owned Roy Rogers outlets. "Here was an opportunity that was maybe once in a lifetime," Greenberg stated.[5] Earlier the same year, it acquired Burghy's, an 80-store fast-food chain in Italy. And in New Zealand, it added 17 restaurants from the Georgie Pie chain.

The new stores being opened were seldom like the old ones. The popularity of "drive-thru" windows generated 55 percent of U.S. sales, and in the process fewer seats were needed inside. This left more space available for gas stations or for indoor playgrounds—Ronald's Playplaces—to attract families. McDonald's made joint ventures with Chevron and Amoco to codevelop properties. And it signed an exclusive marketing deal with Disney for promoting each other's brands.

McDonald's had always been a big spender for advertising, and this has been effective. Even back in the 1970s, a survey of school children found 96 percent identifying Ronald McDonald, ranking him second only to Santa Claus.[6] In 1995, advertising and promotional expenditures totaled approximately $1.8 billion, or 6 percent of sales.[7]

Factors in the Invincibility of McDonald's

Through the third quarter of 1996, McDonald's could proudly claim 126 consecutive quarters of record earnings. Since its earliest days, the ingredients of success were simple, but few competitors were able to effectively emulate them. The basic aspects were:

- A brief menu, but having consistent quality over thousands of outlets
- Strictly enforced and rigorous operational standards controlling service, cleanliness, and all other aspects of the operation
- Friendly employees, despite a high turnover of personnel because of the monotony of automated food handling
- Heavy mass media advertising directed mostly at families and children

---

[5] Gary Samuels, "Golden Arches Galore," *Forbes* (November 4, 1996), p. 48.
[6]"The Burger That Conquered the Country," *Time* (September 17, 1973), pp. 84–92.
[7] *McDonald's 1995 Annual Report,* p. 9.

- Identification of a fertile target market—the family—and directing the marketing strategy to satisfying it with product, price, promotional efforts, and site locations (at least in the early years, the suburban locations with their high density of families)

However, by the end of 1996, international operations were the real vehicle of growth, providing 47 percent of the company's $30 billion sales and 54 percent of profits. Of no small concern, the domestic operation had not blossomed accordingly.

STORM CLOUDS FOR THE DOMESTIC OPERATION?

Souring Franchisee Relations

In the market-share game, in which McDonald's dominated all its competitors, corporate management concluded that the firm with the most outlets in a given community wins. But as McDonald's unprecedented expansion continued, many franchisees were skeptical of headquarters' claim that no one loses when the company opens more outlets in a community since market share rises proportionately. Still, the franchise holder had to wonder how much his sales would diminish when another McDonald's opens down the street.

The 7,000-member American Franchisee Association, an organization formed to look after franchisees' rights, claimed that McDonald's operators were joining in record numbers.[8] Other franchisees formed a clandestine group called the Consortium, representing dissidents who felt present management was unresponsive to their concerns. They remembered a kinder and gentler company. See the following box for contrasting franchisee views on the high-growth market share policy.

Another concern of franchisees was the new set of business practices developed by corporate headquarters, known as Franchising 2000. The company claimed it instituted this as a way to improve standards for quality, service, cleanliness, and value by giving franchisees better "tools." But some saw this as a blatant attempt to gain more power over the franchised operations. One provision revived a controversial A, B, C, and F grading system, with only franchisees that receive A's and B's eligible for more restaurants. Furthermore, McDonald's began using Franchising 2000 to enforce a single pricing strategy throughout the chain, so that a Big Mac, for example, would cost the same everywhere. The corporation maintained that such uniformity was necessary for the discounting needed to build market share. Those not complying risked losing their franchise.

Franchise relations should not be a matter of small concern to McDonald's. Table 17.3 shows the ratio of franchised restaurants to total restaurants both in the United States and outside the United States. As can be seen, franchises comprise by far the largest proportion of restaurants.

---

[8] Richard Gibson, "Some Franchisees Say Moves by McDonald's Hurt Their Operations," *The Wall Street Journal* (April 17, 1996), pp. A1 and A8.

INFORMATION BOX

THE CONTENTMENT OF TWO MCDONALD'S FRANCHISEES

In 1980, Wayne Kilburn and his wife, Mary Jane, took over the only McDonald's in Ridgecrest, California, a town of 26,000. The Kilburns prospered in the years to come. Then McDonald's instituted its "market-share plan" for Ridgecrest. Late in 1995 it put a company-owned restaurant inside the Wal-Mart. A few months later it built another outlet inside the China Lake Naval Weapons Center. A third new company-owned store went up just outside the naval base. "Basically, they killed me," *Forbes* reports Kilburn saying. And he claimed his volume dropped 30 percent.[9]

In its *1995 Annual Report,* corporate headquarters offered another view concerning franchisee contentment. Tom Wolf was a McDonald's franchisee with 15 restaurants in the Huntington, West Virginia and Ashland, Kentucky markets. He opened his first McDonald's in 1974, had eight by the end of 1993, and opened seven more in the last two years, including two McDonald's in Wal-Mart stores and another in an alliance with an oil company; in addition he added indoor Playplaces to two existing restaurants.

Has all this investment in growth made a difference? The *Annual Report* quotes Tom: "I wouldn't change a thing. Sales are up. I'm serving more customers, my market share is up and I'm confident about the future. Customers say that the Playplaces and Wal-Mart units are 'a great idea.' The business is out there. We've got to take these opportunities now, or leave them for someone else to take."[10]

"The high-growth, market share policy should not bother any franchise. It simply creates opportunities to invest in more restaurants." Evaluate this statement.

---

[9] Samuels, *op. cit.,* p. 48.

[10] *McDonald's 1995 Annual Report,* p. 32.

TABLE 17.3 **Percent of Franchised to Total Traditional Restaurants, Selected Years, 1985–1995**

	1985	1988	1992	1995
Traditional restaurants				
Total	8,901	10,513	13,093	16,809
Operated by franchisees	6,150	7,110	9,237	11,240
Percent franchised to total	69.1%	67.6%	70.5%	66.9%

Source: Calculated from *1995 Annual Report.*

Commentary: While by 1995, the ratio of franchised to total restaurants had dropped slightly, still more than two-thirds are operated by franchisees. Perhaps this suggests that franchisee concerns ought to receive more consideration by corporate headquarters.

Menu Problems

Since 1993, domestic per-store sales slumped from a positive 4 percent to a negative 3 percent by the third quarter of 1996, this being the fifth quarter in a row of negative sales gains. In part this decline was thought attributable to older customers drifting away: "Huge numbers of baby-boomers … want less of the cheap, fattening foods at places like McDonald's. As soon as their kids are old enough, they go elsewhere."[11]

In an attempt to garner more business from this customer segment, McDonald's with a $200 million promotional blitz launched its first "grownup taste" sandwich, the Arch Deluxe line of beef, fish, and chicken burgers. It forecast that this would become a $1 billion brand in only its first year. But before long, some were calling this a McFlop. In September 1996, Edward Rensi, head of U.S. operations, tried to minimize the stake in the new sandwich, and sent a memo to 2,700 concerned franchisees, "the Arch Deluxe was never intended to be a silver bullet."[12] On October 8, Rensi was replaced by Jack Greenberg.

McDonald's domestic troubles were not entirely new. As far back as the late 1980s, competitors, including Pizza Hut and Taco Bell, were nibbling at McDonald's market share, and Burger King was more than holding its own. Even the great traditional strength of McDonald's of unsurpassed controlled standards over food, service, and cleanliness seemed to be waning: A 1995 *Restaurants and Institutions Choice in Chains* survey of 2,849 adults gave McDonald's low marks on food quality, value, service, and cleanliness. Top honors instead went to Wendy's.[13]

In 1991, McDonald's reluctantly tried discounting, with "Extra Value Meals," largely to keep up with Taco Bell's value pricing. But by 1995, price promotions were no longer attracting customers, and per-store sales began slumping. The new, adult-oriented Deluxe line was not only aimed at older adults, but with its prices 20 percent more than regular items, the hope was to parry the discounting.

The company had had previous problems in expanding its line. The McDLT was notably unsuccessful despite heavy promotion. And more recently, the low-fat McLean, an effort to attract weight-conscious adults, was a complete disaster. In fact this beef and seaweed concoction sold so badly that some operators kept only a few frozen patties on hand, while others, as revealed in an embarrassing TV expose, sold fully fatted burgers in McLean boxes to the few customers asking for them.

Some years before, the company had tried but failed to develop an acceptable pizza product. It also was unable to create a dinner menu that would attract evening-hour traffic. Two other experiments were also abandoned: a 1950s-style cafe and a family-type concept called Hearth Express that served chicken, ham, and meatloaf.

---

[11] Shelly Branch, "McDonald's Strikes Out With Grownups," *Fortune* (November 11, 1996), p. 158.

[12]*Ibid.*

[13]*Ibid.*

ANALYSIS

After the many years of uninterrupted growth in sales and profits, and in number of stores opened, the company showed signs of approaching a crossroads with the enduring growth trend endangered.

The international arena still offered tremendous growth possibilities, with more than 8,000 outlets already open. Domestically, however, things were not going as well even though operating statistics looked better than ever. The gains in revenues and income reflected a sharp increase in number of new stores. For example, in 1996 McDonald's opened 2,500 new stores, four times the number of stores opened just four years before. Same-store sales dropped 2.5 percent from 1994 to 1995 for U.S. restaurants—all this despite vigorous discounting and promotional efforts.

Relations with franchisees, formerly best in the industry, deteriorated as corporate management pursued policies more dictatorial and selfish than ever before, policies that signaled the end of the kinder and gentler company they remembered. In particular, the new expansion policy aimed at increased market share regardless of its effect on established franchisees portended worsening relations and the start of an adversarial instead of cooperative climate.

Of course, the cost/benefit consequences of an aggressive expansion policy might seemingly be in the company's best interest, especially with the greater cost efficiencies of recent development. If total market share could be substantially increased, despite same-store sales declining, the accounting analyses might support more stores. But how much is the franchisee to be considered in this aggressive new strategy of McDonald's outlets competing not so much with Wendy's, Burger King, and Taco Bell as with other McDonald's outlets?

A major domestic challenge for a growth-oriented McDonald's was the menu: how to appeal to adults and expand market potential. Corporate executives concluded that the best way to continue growth was to open ever more restaurants in the quest for greater total market share. But another growth alternative was to rejuvenate or diversify menu offerings and thus appeal to more than families and children. This McDonald's had not been able to do in the past, except for introducing the breakfast menu decades ago.

What menu changes should be made? With a history of past failures, confidence in such changes should be modest. Yet, McDonald's, as with any chain organization whether fast food or otherwise, can test different prices and strategies or different menus and different atmospheres in just a few outlets, and only if results are favorable expand further.

Perhaps a poorly recognized trouble spot was McDonald's slackening in its formerly tightest control in any industry over product quality and service. The rigid standards imposed since the days of Ray Kroc were no longer enforced as stringently.

To summarize, is McDonald's in jeopardy? The answer is a resounding *No!* Is it likely to continue its great growth in sales and profits? Probably not; without success in widening the appeal of domestic restaurants, the main engine of growth in future years would be the international operation. Table 17.4 shows the trend in number of

TABLE 17.4   Percent of Non-U.S. to Total Traditional Restaurants, Selected Years, 1985–1995

	1985	1988	1992	1995
Traditional restaurants				
Total U.S. and non-U.S.	8,901	10,513	13,093	16,809
Non-U.S.	1,929	2,606	4,134	6,468
Percent of Total	28.3%	24.8%	31.6%	38.5%

Source: Computed from *1995 Annual Report.*

Commentary: Here we can see the increasing importance of Non-U.S. operations in the decade of the 1990s.

restaurants outside the United States with those in the United States for selected years since 1985. Table 17.5 compares sales and operating income for U.S. and outside-U.S. operations since 1991. Note in particular that income from outside the United States surpassed domestic income by 1995.

Still, the United States is a huge market, and no growth-minded firm would want its luster tarnished here. Whether thousands of new restaurants in the coming years, without some diversification in menus and decor, will fuel the growth needed to continue the trend may be questioned. After all, how many military bases, hospitals, museums, zoos and the like remain untapped? As to outlets in major retail stores, isn't the potential limited?

McDonald's faces a situation that seemingly cries for diversification: perhaps an inspired menu change; maybe a new format to tap different customer segments; perhaps different but related businesses. The great advantage of any chain with many outlets is the opportunity to test different formats and ideas: it can experiment to find better ideas and strategies. But will McDonald's use this opportunity to greatest advantage?

TABLE 17.5   Comparison of U.S. and Non-U.S. Revenue and Income, 1991–1995

	1991	1992	1993	1994	1995
Systemwide sales (billions of dollars)	$19.9	21.9	23.6	26.0	29.9
U. S.	$12.5	13.2	14.2	14.9	15.9
Non-U.S.	7.4	8.6	9.4	11.0	14.0
Operating income (billions of dollars)	1.7	1.9	2.0	2.2	2.6
U. S.	1.0	1.1	1.1	1.1	1.2
Non-U.S.	.7	.8	.9	1.1	1.4

Source: Compiled from *1995 Annual Report.*

Commentary: The growing importance of Non-U.S. operations to McDonald's total sales and income is readily apparent.

LATEST INFORMATION

In late 1998, we can evaluate McDonald's again. Its total growth had increased every year, with 1997 revenues at $11.4 billion, up from $5.5 billion ten years before. Net income was $1.6 billion, having climbed every year from the $646 million of ten years earlier. Still, same-store sales of U.S. restaurants had declined slightly in 1997, and international restaurants had declined more drastically. The insidious problems of the early 1990s were still there.

Jack Greenberg was promoted to CEO in August 1998. He talked about innovating or "reinventing" the category in which they compete, and invited employees and franchisees to a "shared vision" for the company. Greenberg expected hamburgers to diminish as a percentage of total menu items, to be supplemented by more white meat and fish, as well as vegetarian burgers and more efforts to attract health-conscious diners. There was hope that he would improve the alienation felt by many franchisees.

More tangible was the coming introduction of a new way to make sandwiches: "Made for You," delivering sandwiches to order, which also meant fresher with less waste compared with the old system of building sandwich inventories in holding bins. "You don't grow this business by having clean washrooms," Greenberg said. "We will grow this business through food."[14]

Greenberg's successor in the No. 2 position at McDonald's was Alan Feldman. He came on board three years earlier after six years as chief financial officer at Pizza Hut and before that at PepsiCo. Best known for his people skills, he vowed "to embrace franchisees and hear their concerns."[15]

Current Franchisee Requirements

Despite concerns about McDonald's future promise and publicity about franchisee worries, franchisee applications in the United States were more than ten times the number of outlets available. McDonald's could still be very choosy in selecting franchisees. This popularity of franchises meant that retiring franchisees could count on buyers for their stores, while the difficulty of gaining a franchise assured that only highly motivated people would be finalists.

Financial requirements were not for the marginal. Total price tag for a typical full-size McDonald's was around $500,000, with labor, 8 percent of sales, and rent the major expenses after opening. A prospective franchisee trained at least a year, working in restaurants without pay, even performing such tasks as scrubbing bathrooms. Usually when an opportunity finally came it involved pulling up stakes and moving.[16]

---

[14] Kevin Helliker and Richard Gibson, "The New Chief Is Ordering Up Changes at McDonald's," *The Wall Street Journal* (August 24, 1998), p. B4.

[15] Richard Gibson, "New U.S. Chief Orders Changes at McDonald's," *The Wall Street Journal* (May 20, 1998), p. B21.

[16] For other information about gaining a McDonald's franchise, see Richard Gibson, "McDonald's Problems In Kitchen Don't Dim the Lure of Franchises," *The Wall Street Journal* (June 3, 1998), pp. A1 and A6.

WHAT CAN BE LEARNED?

Is it possible to have strong and enduring growth without diversification? For more than four decades, since 1955, McDonald's has grown continuously and substantially. In all this time, the product was essentially the hamburger in its various trappings and accompaniments. Almost all other firms in their quest for growth have diversified, sometimes wisely and synergistically, and other times imprudently and even recklessly. McDonald's has remained undeviatingly focused.

In such a commitment, the product should be something with universal appeal, something frequently consumed, and one having almost unlimited potential. The hamburger probably meets these criteria better than practically any other product, along with beer, soft drinks, and tobacco. And soft drinks, of course, are a natural accompaniment of the hamburger.

But eventually, even the hamburger may not be enough for continued strong growth as the international market becomes saturated and the domestic market oversaturated. Then McDonald's may be forced to seek complimentary diversifications or lose the growth mode.

The insight to be gained, however, is that firms in pursuit of growth often jump into acquisitions far too hastily when the better course of action would be to more fully develop market penetration of their existing products.

Beware the reckless drive for market share. A firm can usually "buy" market share, if it is willing to sacrifice profits in so doing. It can step up its advertising and sales promotion. It can lower its prices, assuming that lower prices would bring more demand. It can increase its sales staff and motivate them to be more aggressive. And sales and competitive position will usually rise. But costs may rise disproportionately. In other words, the benefits to be gained may not be worth the costs.

McDonald's, as we have seen in its domestic operation, has struck a strategy of aggressively seeking market share by opening thousands of new units. As long as the development costs can be kept sufficiently low to permit these new units good profits and not cannibalize or take too much business away from other McDonald's restaurants, then the strategy is defensible. Still, the costs of damaged franchisee relations, the intangibles of lowered morale and cooperation, and festering resentments are difficult to calculate but can be real indeed.

Maintaining the highest standards requires constant monitoring. McDonald's heritage and its competitive advantage have long been associated with the highest standards and controls in the industry for cleanliness, fast service, dependable quality of food, and friendly and well-groomed employees. The following box discusses strategy countering by competitors and the great difficulty in matching non-price strengths.

Alas, in the last few years even McDonald's has apparently let its control of operational standards slip. As mentioned earlier, a 1995 survey of adults gave McDonald's low marks on food quality, value, service, and cleanliness. Wendy's won top honors instead. Why this lapse? Perhaps because the burgeoning inter-

INFORMATION BOX

MATCHING A COMPETITOR'S STRATEGY

Some strategies are easily countered or duplicated by competitors. Price-cutting is the most easily countered. A price cut can often be matched within minutes. Similarly, a different package or a warranty is easily imitated by competitors.

But some strategies are not so easily duplicated. Most of these involve service, a strong and positive company image, or both. A reputation for quality and dependability is not easily countered, at least in the short run. A good company or brand image is hard to match because it usually results from years of good service and satisfied customers. The great controls of McDonald's—the high standards of product quality, service, and cleanliness—would seem to be easily imitated, but they proved not to be, as no other firm fully matched the enforced standards of McDonald's, at least until recently.

Somehow it seems that the strategies and operations that are the most difficult to imitate are not the wildly innovative ones, not the ones that are complex and well researched. Surprisingly, the most difficult to imitate are the very simple ones: simply doing a better job in servicing and satisfying customers and in performing even mundane operations cheerfully and efficiently.

What explanation can you give for competitors' inability to match the standards of McDonald's?

national operation became the focus of attention. But maintaining high standards among thousands of units, company-owned as well as franchised, requires constant monitoring and exhortation. With great numbers of stores this becomes increasingly difficult.

Can controls be too stringent? In a belated attempt to improve standards and tighten up corporate control, McDonald's instituted the controversial Franchising 2000. Among other things this called for grading franchisees, with those receiving the lower grades being penalized. McDonald's also wanted to take away any pricing flexibility for its franchisees: all restaurants must now charge the same prices, or risk losing their franchise. Not surprisingly, some franchisees were concerned about this new "get tough" management.

As with most things, extremes are seldom desirable. All firms need tight controls over far-flung outlets to keep them sufficiently informed of emerging problems and opportunities and maintain a desired image and standard of performance. In a franchise operation this is all the more necessary since we are dealing with independent entrepreneurs rather than hired managers. However, controls can be too harsh and rigid to give any room for special circumstances and opportunities. If the enforcement is too punitive, the climate becomes more that of a police state than a teamwork relationship with both parties cooperating to their mutual advantage.

And this brings us to the next insight for discussion.

Is there room for a kinder, gentler firm in today's hotly competitive environment? Many long-time McDonald's franchisees remembered with sadness a kinder, gentler company. This was an atmosphere nurtured by founder Ray Kroc. To be sure, Kroc insisted that customers be assured of a clean, family atmosphere with quick and cheerful service. To Kroc, this meant strict standards, not only in food preparation but also in care and maintenance of facilities, including toilets. Company auditors closely checked that the standards were adhered to, under Kroc's belief that a weakness in one restaurant could have a detrimental effect on other units in the system. Still, the atmosphere was helpful—the inspectors were "consultants"—rather than adversarial. Kroc could boast in his autobiography that the company was responsible for making more than 1,000 millionaires, the franchise holders.[17]

Many franchisees traced the deterioration of franchiser-franchisee relations to the 1992 death of Gerald Newman, McDonald's chief accounting officer. He spent much of his time interacting with franchisees, sometimes encouraging—he had a reputation for a sympathetic ear—sometimes even giving them a financial break.[18]

So, is it possible and desirable to be a kind and gentle company? with franchisees? employees? suppliers? customers? Of course it is. Organizations, and the people who run them, often forget this in the arrogance of power. They excuse this "get-tough" mindset because of the exigencies of competition and the need to be faithful to their stockholders.

Kind and gentle—is this an anachronism, a throwback to a quieter time, a nostalgia long past its usefulness? Let us hope not.

CONSIDER

Can you add other learning insights?

QUESTIONS

1. How do you account for the reluctance of competitors to imitate the successful efforts of another firm in their industry? Under what circumstances is imitation likely to be embraced?

2. To date McDonald's has shunned diversification into other related and unrelated food retailing operations. Discuss the desirability of such diversification efforts.

3. "Eventually—and this may come sooner than most think—there will no longer be any choice locations anywhere in the world for new hamburger outlets. As a McDonald's stockholder, I'm getting worried." Discuss.

---

[17] Ray Kroc and Robert Anderson, *Grinding It Out: The Making of McDonald's* (New York: Berkley Publishing, 1977), p. 200.

[18] Gibson, *Ibid.*, p. A8.

4. Contrast McDonald's with the previous case involving Maytag's England operation. What insights can be developed from these two cases?

5. What do you think is McDonald's near-term and long-term potential? What makes you think this?

6. Is it likely that McDonald's will ever find a saturated market for its hamburgers?

7. If you ran McDonald's, what changes, if any, would you institute? Please give your rationale for your recommendations.

HANDS-ON EXERCISES

1. You have been given the assignment by Edward Rensi in 1993 to instill a recommitment to improved customer service in all domestic operations. Discuss in as much detail as you can how you would go about fostering this among the 10,000 domestic outlets.

2. As a McDonald's senior executive, what long-term expansion mode would you recommend for your company?

TEAM DEBATE EXERCISES

1. Debate this issue: McDonald's is reaching the limits of its growth without drastic change. (Note: the side that espouses drastic change should give some attention to the most likely directions for such, and be prepared to defend these expansion possibilities.)

2. Debate the issue of a "get-tough" attitude of corporate management toward franchisees even if it riles some, versus involving them more in future directions of the company. In particular, be prepared to address the controversy of unlimited market-share expansion.

INVITATION TO RESEARCH

Is McDonald's becoming more vulnerable to competitors today? Does it have any emerging problems? Has it attempted any major diversifications yet? Is the international operation still overshadowing the domestic?

PART FIVE

ENTREPRENEURIAL
ADVENTURES

CHAPTER EIGHTEEN

Boston Beer: Leading the Microbrewers

*J*im Koch was obsessed with becoming an entrepreneur. He wasn't quite sure where he should do his entrepreneuring—maybe the brewing industry? Years before, his great-great-grandfather, Louis Koch, had concocted a recipe at his St. Louis brewery that was heavier, more full-bodied than such as Budweiser or Miller. However, it was much more expensive to produce than mass-market beers. It involved a lengthy brewing and fermentation process, as well as such premium ingredients as Bavarian hops that cost many times more than those regularly used by other brewers.

Jim had a well-paying job with the prestigious Boston Consulting Group. He had been with them for six-and-a-half years already, but still he was haunted by that dream of becoming his own man. Of late, the thought pursued him that maybe the brewing industry might be ripe for a new type of product and a new approach, a good-tasting brew something like his ancestor's. He wondered if he might have a strategic window of opportunity in a particular consumer segment: men in their mid-twenties and older who were beer aficionados and would be willing to pay a premium for a good-tasting beer. What he couldn't be certain of was how large this segment was, and he knew from his consulting experience that too small a segment doomed a strategy. So, were there enough such sophisticated drinkers to support the new company that he envisioned?

In 1984, he thought he detected a clue that this might indeed be the case: sales were surging for import beers such as Heineken and Beck's with their different tastes. Didn't this portend that enough Americans would be willing to pay substantially more for a full-bodied flavor?

As he studied this more, he also came to believe that these imports were very vulnerable to well-made domestic brews. They faced a major problem in maintaining freshness with a product that goes sour rather quickly. He knew that the foreign brewers, in trying to minimize the destructive influence of the time lag between production and consumption, were adding preservatives and even using cheaper ingredients for the American market.

Some small local brewers offered stronger tastes. But they were having great difficulty producing a lager with consistent quality. And he sensed they were squandering their opportunity. Although they could produce small batches of well-crafted

249

beer, albeit of erratic quality, what they mainly lacked was ability and resources to aggressively market their products.

He decided to take the plunge, and gave up his job.

Amassing sufficient capital to start a new venture is the common problem with almost all entrepreneurs, and so it was with Koch. Still, he was better off than most. He had saved $100,000 from his years with Boston Consulting, and he persuaded family and friends to chip in another $140,000. But while this might be enough to start a new retail or service venture, it was far less than the estimated $10 million or more needed to build a state-of-the-art brewery.

Koch got around this major obstacle. Instead of building or buying he contracted an existing firm, Pittsburgh Brewing Company, to brew his beer. It had good facilities, but more than this, its people had the brewing skills coming from more than 20 years of operation. He would call his new beer Samuel Adams, after a Revolutionary War patriot who was also a brewer.

PROBLEMS

A mighty problem still existed, and the success of the venture hinged on this. Koch would have to sell his great-tasting beer at $20 a case to break even and make a reasonable profit. But this was 15 percent more than even the premium imports like Heineken. Would anyone buy such an expensive beer, and one that didn't even have the cachet of an import? See the following box about the merits of a high-price strategy.

It fell to Koch as the fledgling firm's only salesperson to try to acquaint retailers and consumers with his new beer, this unknown brand with the very high price. "I went from bar to bar," he said. "Sometimes I had to call 15 times before someone would agree to carry it."[1]

He somehow conjured up enough funds for a $100,000 ad campaign in the local market. Shunning the advertising theme of the big brewers that stressed the sociability of the people drinking their brand, Koch's ads attacked the imports: "Declare your independence from foreign beer," he urged. And the name Samuel Adams was compatible with this cry for independence. Foreign brews were singled out as not having the premium ingredients and quality brewing of Samuel Adams. Koch appeared on most of his commercials, saying such things as: "Hi, I'm Jim Koch. It takes me all year to brew what the largest import makes in just three hours because I take the time to brew Samuel Adams right. I use my great-great-grandfather's century-old recipe, all malt brewing and rare hops that cost 10 times what they use in the mass-produced imports."[2]

Gradually his persistence in calling on retailers and his anti-import ads, some of which garnered national attention in such periodicals as *Newsweek* and *USA Today,* induced more and more bartenders and beer drinkers to at least try Samuel Adams. Many liked it, despite the high price. (Or, perhaps, because of it?)

---

[1] Jenny McCune, "Brewing Up Profits," *Management Review,* April 1994, p. 18.

[2] *Ibid.,* p. 19.

INFORMATION BOX

COMPETING ON PRICE, REVISITED: THE PRICE/QUALITY PERCEPTION

In the Southwest Air case, we examined the potent strategy of offering the lowest prices—if this could be done profitably due to a lower expense and overhead structure than competitors.

Here, Boston Beer is attempting to compete while having some of the highest prices in the industry. Is this crazy? Why would anyone pay prices higher than even the expensive imported beers, just for a different taste?

The highest price can convey an image of the very highest quality. We as consumers have long been conditioned to think this. With cars, we may not be able to afford this highest quality, such as an Infiniti, Lexus, or Mercedes convertible. But with beer, almost anyone can afford to buy the highest price brew sometimes, maybe to influence guests or to simply enjoy a different taste that we are led to think is better.

Sometimes such a price/quality perception sets us up. It might be valid, or might not be. Especially is this true where quality is difficult to ascertain, such as with beer and liquor, with bottled water, with perfume, as well as other products with hidden ingredients and complex characteristics.

Do you think you have ever fallen victim to the price/quality misperception? How does one determine quality for an alcoholic beverage such as vodka, gin, and scotch, as well as beer? By the taste? The advertising claims? Anything else?

Now his problem became finding distributors, and this proved particularly troubling for a new firm in an industry where major brands often had a lock on existing wholesalers. The situation was so bad in Boston—no wholesaler would carry Samuel Adams, even though it was a local brand—that Boston Beer bought a truck and delivered the cases itself.

He slowly expanded his distribution one geographical area at a time, from Boston into Washington, D.C., then to New York, Chicago, and California, taking care that production could match the steady expansion without sacrificing quality. He brought in his secretary at Boston Consulting, Rhonda Kaliman, to assist him in building a sales organization. This grew from less than a dozen sales reps in 1989 to 70 nationwide by 1994, more than any other microbrewer and about the same number as Anheuser-Busch, the giant of the industry. Now Samuel Adams salespeople could give more personalized and expert attention to customers than competitors whose sales reps often sold many beverage lines.

Sales soared 63 percent in 1992 when the company went national and achieved distribution in bars and restaurants in 48 states. In a continual search for new beer ideas, Boston Beer added a stout, a wheat beer, and even a cranberry lambic, a type of beer flavored with fruit. Adding to the growing popularity were numerous industry awards and citations Samuel Adams had received since 1984. Not only was it voted the Best Beer in America four times at the annual Great American Beer Festival, but it received six gold medals in blind tastings.

Jim Koch and two of his brewmasters were testing their entry into the Great American Beer Festival—"Triple Bock." They had not yet tried to market this creation, although their expectations were high. But this was so different. It boasted a 17 percent alcoholic content with no carbonation and they planned to package it in a cobalt blue bottle with a cork. It was meant to be sipped as a fine brandy. "It's a taste that nobody has ever put into a beer," Koch said.[3] Too innovative? Jim and his colleagues pondered this as they sipped on this beautiful day in April 1994.

THE BREWING INDUSTRY IN THE 1990S

In 10 years, the company had forged ahead to become a major contender in its industry and the largest U.S. specialty brewer. But a significant change in consumer preferences was confronting the industry in the 1990s. The big brands that had been so dominant, to the extent that smaller brewers could not compete against their production efficiencies, now were seeing their market shares decline. The brand images they had spent millions trying to establish were in trouble. Many were cutting prices in desperate attempts to keep and lure consumers. For example, special price promotions in some markets were offering 12-packs of Budweiser, Coors, and Miller for just $1.99.

The shifting consumer preferences, and the severe price competition with their regular brands, were compelling the big brewers to seek the types of beers that would command higher prices. Imports were still strengthening, growing at an 11 percent rate between 1993 and 1994. But microbrews seemed the wave of the future, with prices and profit margins that were mouth-watering to the big barons of the industry.

Consequently, the major breweries came up with their own craft brands. For example, Icehouse, a name that conveys a microbrewery image, was actually produced in megabreweries by Miller Brewing. So too, Killian's Irish Red, a pseudo-import, was made by Coors in Golden, Colorado. Killian's, stocked in retailer's import cases and commanding a high price, muscled its way abreast of Samuel Adams as the largest specialty beer in the United States.

The brewing industry was desperately trying to innovate. But no one saw anything revolutionary on the horizon, not like the 1970s, when light beer made a significant breakthrough in the staid industry. Now, "ice" beers became the gimmick. First developed in Canada, these are beers produced at temperatures a little colder than ordinary beer. This gives them a slightly higher alcohol content. Whether because of this, or the magic of the name *ice,* these products captured almost 6 percent of total industry sales in 1994, more than all the imports combined. But, still, the potential seems limited.

Anheuser-Busch, with a still dominant 44 percent of U.S. beer sales despite its 9 percent sales volume slide in the early 1990s, asserted its reluctance to change: "The breweries that we have are designed to produce big brands. Our competition can't

---

[3] McCune, p. 20.

compete with big brands. That's why they've had to introduce lots of little brands.[4] But even Anheuser, despite its words, was sneaking into microbrewing by buying into Redhook Ale Brewery, a Seattle microbrewery that sold 76,000 barrels of beer in 1993, versus Anheuser's 90 million. Anheuser's distributors applauded this move as a badly needed step in giving them higher-profit, prestige brands. When Anheuser tiptoed into this market, other giants began to look for microbreweries to invest in.

This troubled Jim Koch: "I'm afraid of the big guys. They have the power to dominate any segment they want." Then he expressed his confidence: "Still, my faith is that better beer will win out."[5]

THE CONTINUING SAGA OF BOSTON BEER

In August 1995, Boston Beer announced an initial public stock offering (IPO) of 5.3 million shares, of which 990,000 shares would be made available directly to the public through a coupon offer. This selling of shares to the general public was unlike any other IPO, and as such caught the fancy of the national press.

The company put clip-and-mail coupons on Samuel Adams six-packs and other beer packages. These offered customers a chance to buy 33 shares of stock at a maximum price of $15, or $495 total. Only one subscription was allowed per customer, and these were honored on a first-come, first-served basis. The success was overwhelming. First distributed in October, by the first of November the offering was oversubscribed. The company expected that the total funds generated from the IPO would be $75 million.[6] But when the new stock offering finally came out on November 20, 1995, heavy demand led to it being priced at $20 a share. Two days later it was selling on the New York Stock Exchange for $30. Interestingly, its stock symbol is SAM.

Boston Beer was riding a high. It reported an impressive 50 percent growth in 1994 over 1993, brewing 700,000 barrels and becoming the largest microbrewery in the country. The entire microbrewing industry was producing more than double the volume in 1990. By now Boston Beer had 12 different beers, including 6 seasonal, and was distributing in all 50 states through 300 wholesalers. Its newest beer, the 17-percent alcohol content Triple Bock, had been introduced to the market.[7]

Most of Boston Beer's production continued to be contract brewed. In early 1995, it did encounter difficulties with Pittsburgh Brewing, the first of the three contract breweries it was now using. Because of an alleged overdraft of $31 million by its owner, Michael Carlow, who was accused of fraud, the brewery was to be auctioned off. Jim Koch stoutly professed having no interest in buying the brewery and that any problems of Pittsburgh Brewery would have no effect on Boston Beer.[8] See the following box for a discussion of contracting out rather than building production facilities.

---

[4] Patricia Sellers, "A Whole New Ballgame in Beer," *Fortune*, September 19, 1994, p. 86.

[5] *Ibid.*

[6] "Boston Beer's Plan for Offering Stock," *New York Times—National Edition* (August 26, 1995), p. 20.

[7] "Little Giants," *Beverage-World* (December 1994), p. 26.

[8] "Sam Adams Brewer May Be On Block," *Boston-Business-Journal* (February 24, 1995), p. 3.

INFORMATION BOX

THE MERITS OF EXPANDING SLOWLY AND KEEPING FIXED COSTS TO A MINIMUM

There is much to be said for any enterprise, new or older, to keep its fixed overhead to a minimum. If it can escape having to commit large sums to physical plant and production facilities, its breakeven point is far less, which means that less sales are needed to cover expenses and interest payments, leaving more to go into profits. In the event of adversity, such a firm can retrench much more nimbly than if burdened with heavy overhead. In every such decision of renting or buying, the economics of the particular situation need to be carefully analyzed.

Arguments against such contracting out usually maintain that efficiency will be sacrificed, since direct control is lacking. So, this argument would maintain that Pittsburgh Brewing could not do as good a job as Boston Beer could have done itself. Yet, the empirical evidence is that Boston's contract brewers were giving it the high standards it wanted. It set the standards and insisted on them being met, or it would find another contract brewery.

Still, the "edifice complex" tantalizes most top executives, as well as hospital and school administrators, who see the stone and mortar of their buildings and factories as conveying tangible evidence of their own importance and accomplishments. They will claim that such is important to the public image of their organization.

Given the approximately $100 million that Boston Beer receives from its IPO, would you predict some of this will go for "stones and mortar"?

ANALYSIS

Entrepreneurial Character

Although many entrepreneurial opportunities come in the retail and service industries, mostly because these typically require less start-up investment, Jim Koch saw the possibility in beer, even without a huge wallet. He started with $100,000 of his own money and $140,000 from friends and relatives. He had the beer recipe and determination. By contracting out the production to an existing brewery with unused production capacity, the bulk of the start-up money could be spent on nonproduction concerns, such as advertising.

His determination to gain acceptance of his beer, despite its high price and nonforeign origin, is characteristic of most successful entrepreneurs. They press on, despite obstacles in gaining acceptance. They have confidence that their product or concept is viable. They are not easily discouraged.

At the same time, Koch believed he had something unique, a flavor and quality that neither domestic nor imported brews could deliver. He had the audacity to further make his product unique by charging even higher prices than the imports, thus conveying an image of highest quality.

His search for uniqueness did not end with the product. He developed an advertising theme far different than that of other beers by stressing quality and aggressively attacking the imports: "Declare your independence from foreign beer." And he was the spokesman on TV and radio commercials, giving them a personal and charismatic touch.

As Boston Beer moved out of regional into national distribution, he developed a salesforce as large as Anheuser-Busch, the giant of the industry. His grasping of uniqueness even went to Boston Beer's initial public stock offering, in which customers were invited to buy into the company through coupons on six-packs. And it was oversubscribed in only a few weeks.

Controlled Growth

The temptation for any firm, but especially for newer, smaller firms, when demand seems to be growing insatiably is to expand aggressively: "We must not miss this opportunity." Such optimism can sow the seeds of disaster, when demand suddenly lessens because of a saturated market and/or new competition. And our firm is left with too much plant and other fixed assets, and a burdensome overhead.

Controlled growth—we might also call this "aggressive moderation"—is usually far better. Now our firm is not shunning growth, even vigorous growth, but is controlling it within its current resources not overextending itself. Boston Beer showed this restraint by expanding within its production capability, adding several more contract brewers as needed. It expanded market by market at the beginning, only moving to a new geographical area when it could supply it. First was Boston, then Washington, D.C., then New York, Chicago, California, and finally all 50 states.

Besides husbanding resources, both material and personnel, aggressive moderation is compatible with the tightness of controls needed to assure high-quality product and service standards. Even more than this, moderation allows a firm to build the accounting and financial standards and controls needed to prevent the dangerous buildup of inventories and expenses.

UPDATE

By 1998, Samuel Adams had become the seventh-largest brewer overall, and was the largest independent craft brewer, in the sector that had grown 39 percent in a five-year period, while U.S. beer total shipments remained virtually flat. Samuel Adams Boston Lager, the company's flagship product, grew faster than the overall craft beer sector, and accounted for the majority of Boston Beer's sales in 1997.

For 1997, revenues were $184 million, down 3.8 percent from the year before, but a major increase from the $77 million in 1994, the year before Boston went public. Net income at $7.6 million was a decline of 9.9 percent from the year before, but this compared with $5.3 million in 1994.

Boston Beer produced more than two dozen styles of beer, and was selling in all 50 states and several foreign countries. Its sales force was still the largest of any craft brewer, and one of the largest in the domestic beer industry.

The acute disappointment had to be the stock market valuation of its shares. An exuberant public reaction to the initial stock offering had bid the price up to $30 a share. Almost immediately, the share price began a slow decline. By late 1998, shares were trading around $8.

WHAT CAN BE LEARNED?

The "price-quality perception." We have a curious phenomenon today regarding price. More consumers than ever are shopping at discount stores because they supposedly offer better prices than other retailers. Airlines competing with lowest prices, such as Southwest and Continental, are greatly increasing airline traffic. Yet for many products, especially those that are complex and have hidden ingredients, a higher price than competitors is the major indicator of higher quality. Boston Beer certainly confirms that higher price can successfully differentiate a firm, especially if the taste is robustly different, and if the theme of highest quality is constantly stressed in advertising.

Perhaps the moral is that both low prices and high prices can be successful. A strategy of lowest prices, however, tends to be more vulnerable, since competitors can easily and quickly match these low prices (not always profitably, of course), while a high-price strategy stressing quality tends to attract less competitors. But it will also attract less customers, as with higher-priced goods such as office furniture. The high-price strategy should be more generally successful with products that are relatively inexpensive to begin with, such as beer, and ones where the image of prestige and good taste is attractive.

The challenge of the right approach to growth. In the analysis section we discussed the desirability of controlled growth or aggressive moderation and noted that Boston Beer practiced this well. There are some who would challenge such a slowness in grabbing opportunities. Exuberant expansion instead is advocated, when and if the golden opportunity is presented (some would call this "running with the ball"). Operations should be expanded as fast as possible in such a situation, some would say. But there are times when caution is advised.

Risks lie on all sides as we reach for these opportunities. When a market begins to boom and a firm is unable to keep up with demand without greatly increasing capacity and resources, it faces a dilemma: stay conservative in the expectation that the burgeoning potential will be short-lived, and thereby abdicate some of the growing market to competitors, or expand vigorously and take full advantage of the opportunity. If the euphoria is short-lived, and demand slows drastically, the firm is then left with expanded capacity, more resource commitment than needed, high interest and carrying costs, and perhaps even jeopardized viability because of overextension. Above all, however, a firm should not expand beyond its ability to maintain organizational and accounting control over the operation. To do so is tantamount to letting a sailing ship brave the uncertainties of a storm under full canvas.

Keep the breakeven point as low as possible, especially for new ventures. Fixed investments in plant and equipment raise the breakeven point of sales needed to cover overhead costs and make a profit. Boston Beer kept its breakeven point low by using contract breweries. Now this would have been a mistake if the quality of production at these breweries was erratic or not up to Boston Beer expectations. These were indeed vital requirements if it were to succeed in selling its high-priced beer. But by working closely with experienced brewers, quality control apparently was no problem.

Certainly the lower breakeven point makes for less risk. Despite research and careful planning, the environment is constantly changing as to customer attitudes and preferences, and particularly in actions of competitors.

When a decision involves high stakes and an uncertain future—which translates into high risks—is it not wiser to approach the venture somewhat conservatively, not spurning the opportunity, but also not committing major resources and efforts until success appears more certain?

The importance of maintaining quality. For a high-priced product, a brief let-down in quality control can be disastrous to the image. The story is told of Jim Koch ordering a draft of his own Samuel Adams at a restaurant across from Lincoln Center in New York City. He was horrified at the taste. He called the manager and they went to the basement and looked at the keg. "It was two-and-a-half months past its pull date." The manager quickly changed the past-its-prime keg, which the distributor, intentionally or not, had sold the restaurant.[9] Sometimes a lapse in quality is not the fault of the manufacturer, but of a distributor or dealer. Whoever is at fault, the brand image is tarnished. And it is difficult to resurrect a reputation of poor or uncertain quality.

For investors, consider the risk of initial public offerings (IPOs). IPOs are often bid up to unreasonable prices in public enthusiasm with new offerings. (We will see more of this in the next chapter.) While Boston Beer has done well as a niche brewer, and indeed dominates its niche, it has to be a major disappointment to its investors who bought in at the beginning. Perhaps the better investor strategy is to wait for public enthusiasm to calm down before taking a stake in a new enterprise.

CONSIDER

Can you think of other learning insights?

QUESTIONS

1. Have you ever tried one of the Boston Beer brews? If so, how did you like the taste? Did you think it was worth the higher price?

2. The investment community evidently thought Boston Beer had great growth probabilities to have bid up the initial price so quickly. Why do you suppose so many fell into this trap? Or was Jim Koch a poor executive in not bringing Boston Beer up to their expectations?

[9] McCune, p. 16.

3. "The myriad specialty beers are but a fad. People will quickly tire of expensive, strong-flavored beer. Much of it is just a gimmick." Discuss.

4. What problems do you see retailers facing with the burgeoning number of different beers today? What might be the implications of this?

5. Playing the devil's advocate (one who takes an opposing view for the sake of argument and deeper analysis), critique the strategy of charging some of the highest prices in the world for your beer.

6. We saw above the detection of a problem with the freshness of a beer at a restaurant by Jim Koch himself. How can Boston Beer prevent such incidents from happening again? Can such distributor negligence or short-sighted actions be totally prevented by Boston Beer?

7. Do you think Boston Beer can continue to compete effectively against the giant brewers who are now moving with their infinitely greater resources into the specialty beer market with their own microbrews? Why or why not?

8. At the last count, Boston Beer produced more than two dozen styles of beer. Do you see any problems with this?

HANDS-ON EXERCISES

1. You are Jim Koch. You have just learned that Michael Feuer, founder of OfficeMax, described in Chapter 20, has grown his entrepreneurial endeavor to a $1.8 billion enterprise in just seven years. It has taken you ten years to grow Boston Beer to a $50 million firm. You are depressed at this but determined to greatly increase your company's growth. How would you go about setting Boston Beer on this great growth path? Be as specific as you can. What dangers do you see ahead?

2. It is 1986 and Boston Beer is beginning its growth after hiring Pittsburgh Brewery to produce its beer. Jim Koch has charged you with coordinating the efforts at Pittsburgh Brewery, paying particular attention to assuring that your quality standards are rigidly maintained. How would you go about doing this?

TEAM DEBATE EXERCISE

Debate how Boston Beer should commit the $100 million it received in late 1995 from the public stock offering. In particular, debate whether the bulk of the proceeds should go to building its own state-of-the-art brewery, or something else.

INVITATION TO RESEARCH

How is Boston Beer faring today? Has its expansion accelerated or stalled? Is it facing any particular problems? Has the stock price risen to the $30 initial issuance price?

Boston Chicken and Planet Hollywood: The Masters of Hype Falter

Boston Chicken and Planet Hollywood have similar turbulent histories. They both seemed to represent entrepreneurship at its best. Their initial public offerings (IPOs) reflected this as they went public with such market hype that investors frantically bid up the prices. But after a few years it became evident that performances did not match the dreams, and both stocks plummeted. How could investors and an ebullient management have been so wrong?

BOSTON CHICKEN

The Promise

Merrill Lynch took Boston Chicken public in late 1993 with an initial public offering of $20 a share. It made a sizzling debut, with the stock price soaring 143 percent on its opening day, the largest first-day jump of any new issue in 1993, and a year later the stock split 2-for-1. Flush with more than $1 billion from its IPO, the company expanded rapidly. It quickly announced plans to open 300 stores a year with a goal of more than 3,000 by 2003. In December 1996, the share price was $41 (equivalent to $82 before the split), and executives and investors alike basked in the heady optimism of becoming another McDonald's.

The product was rotisserie chicken, sold as a full meal in a style reminiscent of those days when mothers stayed home all day to take care of their families. Boston Chicken executives thought this home meal replacement complete with good food and service should appeal to the busy families of today. The only real competitor was Kenny Rogers Roasters, and since it was doing quite well this seemed to confirm the merits of the concept.

The entrepreneurs believed they had to exploit this market with a tremendous expansion before competitors could jump in. Since they had the means to do so with the money raised by the IPO, they decided to capitalize on this and offer their franchisees financing to open stores.

Besides the unique and seemingly attractive concept, investors were also impressed because the chief executive, Scott Beck, had formerly built Blockbuster Video into a major success. In 1994, Beck promised that Boston Chicken sales would reach $3 billion by 1999.[1]

Confusion

Unbelievably, the Boston Chicken concept had not even been proven to work in one store, and now plans were being made for 3,000 stores. Along with its attention given to expansion, the company still groped for the winning food combination. First, it positioned itself as a dinner restaurant; then it experimented with lunch business, introducing Extreme Carver sandwiches that it promoted with coupons. Unfortunately, these discount coupons trimmed profit margins, but worse, the cheaper menu items cannibalized or took sales away from the existing dinner business. (Refer back to Chapter 4 for a discussion of cannibalization.)

In a reversal, the company eliminated the Extreme Carver line and went back to the dinner menu but added meatloaf, ham, and other items for additional choices. It also experimented with salad bars, carryout food, and new desserts.

These menu changes, as well as announced stepped-up advertising and cost cutting, stimulated Wall Street. Stock analysts were still making buy recommendations in late 1996, when the share price reached its zenith. Overlooked by most was that as early as 1994, credit agencies had rated Boston Chicken's debt as junk, because of doubts about the company's ability to repay its debt.

Some analysts still touting the stock worried about financial figures not being adequately disclosed. Steven Kent, at Goldman Sachs, wrote, "At times, management appears to be elusive with information on this complex story."[2] For example, the company provided no information on same-store sales, and this is rather basic information for how well a chain is doing, since more stores can hide deteriorating sales per store. Furthermore, the reported revenues of Boston Chicken did not represent sales from stores at all, but rather royalties and interest on loans the company had made to franchisees to finance the rapid expansion.

The practice of loaning money to franchisees to open their stores was a significant departure from other franchise operations where franchisees put up their own capital to get into the business. Boston Chicken franchisees needed only a minimum of financial resources; thus, more marginal franchisees were attracted. One critic likened Boston Chicken more to a bank than a restaurant company. In defense, the company saw this as a creative strategy for attaining the most rapid growth.[3]

---

[1] Miriam Hill, "There's Plenty of Blame for All in This Tale of Market Hype," *Cleveland Plain Dealer* (April 27, 1998), p. 40-C.

[2] Hill, p. 4-C.

[3] *Ibid.*

Red Flags

Abruptly, ominous storm signals shocked investors. In early 1997, the company disclosed that its franchisees had lost about $150 million. This was the first indication outsiders had that individual outlets were somehow not doing well. The company finally told Wall Street that its weekly per-store sales, which had been growing at a 3 percent to 6 percent yearly rate, had dropped 20 percent from the previous year. Now the company expected to post losses of $1 a share for 1998.

As a result, Boston Chicken's stock plummeted 82 percent in 1997, making it the worst-performing stock of 1,000 tracked by *The Wall Street Journal.* By April 1998, the price per share was down to $4.50; by August 7, 1998, to $1.125; by October 6, 1998, to 50 cents.

Table 19.1 shows the trend of revenues and income through 1997. Things got worse in 1998.

The Year of Disaster (1998)

Early in 1998, Boston Chicken reported a 1997 loss of $223.9 million. Its top three officers resigned: Saad Nadhir, co-chairman and chief executive; Scott Beck, co-chairman and president; and Mark W. Stephens, chief financial officer and vice chairman.

J. Michael Jenkins, 51 years old, was named chairman, president, and chief executive officer. He brought 37 years of experience in the restaurant business. His most recent position was CEO of Vicorp, a chain of 356 family-type restaurants operating as Village Inn and Bakers Square. Before that he turned around the El Chico chain. In an interview, he announced his intentions of focusing on the company's operations "to get it back rockin' and rollin' and growing." He noted Boston Chicken's strong brand, wide market presence, and positioning in a strong niche for casual dining. "We'll get there," he said.[4]

TABLE 19.1 **Trend of Revenues and Profits of Boston Chicken, 1992–1997**

	1992	1993	1994	1995	1996	1997
	(Million $)					
Revenues	8.3	42.5	96.2	159	265	462
Net Income	–5.8	1.6	16.2	33.6	67.0	–223

Source: Boston Chicken annual reports.

Commentary: Looking at these statistics up to 1997, no one could question that this was truly a growth company. This shows, however, the illusion that can accompany insufficient operating information. Individual stores were losing money, and debt buildup was becoming precarious.

Now let us look at two balance sheet statistics:

Long-term Debt	Nil	Nil	130	130	130	739
Cash Flow	–5.6	3.6	22.2	45.0	89.8	–177

The problems have suddenly surfaced in earnest, and Boston Chicken is forced into bankruptcy.

[4] Scott McCartney, "Boston Chicken Officers Resign Top Three Posts," *The Wall Street Journal* (May 4, 1998), p. B10.

The company acquired 527 of its franchisee stores, bringing the number of company-owned stores to 936. It put up for sale its 52 percent stake in a bagel chain, and tried to renegotiate hundreds of millions of dollars of debt on facilities. In order to maintain its credit line, it needed an average revenue per week of $17,500 at each of its Boston Market stores, but was barely meeting that figure in the first quarter of 1998.

The loss for the first quarter of 1998 was $312 million. This, compared with a profit of $21.5 million the year before, raised questions about Boston Chicken's survival in the cutthroat fast-food industry. In late May, the company's auditor, Arthur Andersen, warned that Boston Chicken was facing a liquidity crisis.

Troubles mounted. In August, Boston Chicken faced delisting by the Nasdaq Stock Market, which requires that a listed stock maintain a minimum bid price of $5 a share for 30 consecutive days.

For the second quarter, the company reported a loss of $124.5 million, partly reflecting asset writedowns and provision for loan losses, although revenue for the quarter rose 46 percent from the year earlier.

On October 15, five years after going public in a frenzied IPO, Boston Chicken filed for Chapter 11 bankruptcy protection. (Chapter 11 allows a company to hold off its creditors while it tries to put its finances in order.) It initially closed 178 or 15 percent of its stores, and laid off 500 employees and transferred others.

The company had been testing a new prototype store in Charlotte, North Carolina. It claimed that consumer response was positive, but it planned to test the prototype in other markets before a nationwide conversion. This was a partial hope for the future, if enough financing could be obtained.

Boston Chicken wasn't dead yet, even though its stock price at 50 cents was practically off the board.

What Went Wrong?

Such a great success, at the beginning—how could so much early promise change to disaster? Was fraud or misrepresentation involved? There are no allegations of fraud, although perhaps naive stockbrokers were swayed by the hype, and contributed to runaway expectations.

A lot of condemnation focused on the financing of the franchises. "You had a group of non-restaurateurs operating a restaurant as a finance company," said William H. Moore, an industry analyst.[5] But are these criticisms completely justified?

This strategy could be a vehicle for incredibly rapid expansion, provided the money initially was there, as it was from the public offering. Of course, the risk is far greater than if franchisees are putting up most or all of the investment needed. So, maybe it was a crapshoot, a Vegas experience. But did it have to be?

Not if the franchised outlets were profitable.

But the great majority were not profitable, at least after their overhead charges of interest on loans and franchise fees. Still, many of the outlets had good traffic. *The*

---

[5] Alejandro Bodipo-Memba, "Boston Chicken Inc. Files for Chapter 11, Lays off 500 and Shuts 178 Restaurants," *The Wall Street Journal* (October 6, 1998), p. A4.

Wall Street Journal even reports on the long lines at company restaurants.[6] Another observer, Dennis Amato, chief investment officer with Maxus Investments, said, "The stores I go into are always busy. That's why it seems kind of strange that they're having all these problems."[7]

What was so wrong? Was it poor screening of potential franchisees? Was it poor training and supervision of franchisees and their employees? Maybe. Was it lack of Boston Chicken controls and franchisee guidance and supervision? Probably. Maybe the concept was good, but the execution was abysmal.

Did Boston Chicken expand too far too fast? From May 1992 to 1998, it grew from 34 stores in the Northeast to 1,143 nationwide. Sales jumped from about $21 million in December 1991 to nearly $1.2 billion in 1996, a tremendous growth. One wonders how any central organization could handle all the details and challenges of effectively dealing with and guiding such growth.

Great growth is possible. Witness Wal-Mart, McDonald's, Kmart in its heyday, and many others. But none of these grew as wildly as Boston Chicken. We must have controlled growth. This means growth within the capability of the firm to wisely select its franchisees, give them adequate training, and insist on tight controls over operations, costs, customer service, and locations.

Boston Chicken's problems seem to be not so much emanating from the concepts of family-style restaurants and aggressive financing of franchisees, but in the nitty-gritty of store operations.

Another criticism levied at Boston Chicken was that they had no assured menu and store prototype, that they were still experimenting as they went from 30 stores to more than a thousand. Maybe, but flexibility sometimes is desirable. One would think experimenting with menus and format would lead to better tapping of consumer demand and value satisfaction. Better this than being set in a rigid pattern that allows for no deviations even though some things about the product/service package could be improved.

PLANET HOLLYWOOD

The Vision

Seeking to capitalize on the seemingly universal appeal of celebrities in entertainment and sports—and to blend this with eating out—the restaurant chain, Planet Hollywood, went public in April 1996, and received a stock-market valuation of $3.5 billion that same day. The link with the celebrities, who received stock and options in return for promotional appearances, stimulated strong investor and customer demand, at first.

What was glossed over at the time of the stock offering, and had major implications for successful expansion, was that 43.8 percent of Planet Hollywood's sales came from just four of the company's 14 restaurants in 1995. These four were located in major tourist markets: Las Vegas, Orlando, London, Paris.

[6] Hill, p. 4-C.

[7] Miriam Hill, "Boston Chicken Cooks Up New Menu to Boost Profits," *Cleveland Plain Dealer* (April 27, 1998), p. 4-C.

The investor movie stars—Demi Moore, Bruce Willis, Whoopi Goldberg, Arnold Schwarzenegger among others—at grand openings attracted long lines of fans, and raised expectations of an instant global entertainment phenomenon. To tap this potential, the company organized under five operating divisions: consumer products, food and beverage, lodging and gaming, retail and merchandise, and theaters/entertainment. Paul Westra, Salomon Brothers analyst, wrote: "Planet Hollywood may ultimately become four separate $5 billion businesses: theme restaurants, gaming, lodging and 'other.'" He compared the potential with Starbucks, Disney, and Nike.[8]

In the first few years, most of the concentration was on restaurants. By the end of 1997, the company had grown to 78 Planet Hollywood restaurants, including 46 company-owned and 32 franchised units in 29 countries. Official All Star Cafe, geared to sports celebrities, had nine units in three countries. The company sought to locate in high profile, heavy trafficked areas, thereby being able to attract both destination customers and passers-by.

The company also entered into a number of joint ventures to construct hotels, including casino resort hotels in Las Vegas and Atlantic City. Sales of a broad range of merchandise carrying the company logo also provided revenue. Table 19.2 shows revenue and income figures from 1992 through 1997.

Robert Earl, Co-founder and CEO

British-born Earl, 47, ran the successful Hard Rock Cafe before starting up Planet Hollywood with Keith Barish, a movie producer. With his background, his personality, and his flair for intriguing ideas, he was the consummate promoter/entrepreneur. He easily swayed investors and analysts with grand plans for expanding the company through tantalizing diversifications. Unfortunately, while he also developed a second

TABLE 19.2   Trend of Revenues and Income, Planet Hollywood, 1992–1997

	(Million $)					
	1992	1993	1994	1995	1996	1997
Revenues	20.4	30.7	126	271	373	475
Net Income	−4.5	−5.3	−9.3	20.7	48.1	8.3

Source: Company annual reports.

Commentary: This company went public in April 1995, with a stock-market valuation of $3.5 billion the same day. Looking at the previous three years of losses, it is difficult to understand such investor exuberance. Of course, it did double revenues in 1995 and also made $20 million in profits. But that surely could not have been fully known in April 1995. The increase in revenues of 1994 over 1993 must have contributed to the enthusiasm, but losses almost doubled from 1993 to 1994. We have to think that hype infected stock brokers and investors alike.

[8] Richard Gibson, "Fame Proves Fleeting at Planet Hollywood as Fans Avoid Reruns," *The Wall Street Journal* (October 7, 1998), p. A1.

eating chain, the All Stars Café that had rather modest success, his other projects fizzled.

Marvel Mania, a theme restaurant idea based on Marvel Comic characters, was touted in the stock prospectus, but didn't work out. Nor did a Planet Hollywood Barbie doll promised for Christmas 1997. Cool Planet, joint venture ice-cream parlors, stagnated at two, and the ice cream never made it into supermarkets. Earl had envisioned using for Cool Planet ice cream such movie knockoff names as "Die-Hard Chocolate" and "Termi-Nutter" sundae, but couldn't get the needed permissions.

Another idea intrigued Wall Street: "Chefs of the World," a merchandising and retailing concept. As conceived, renowned chefs would be used, possibly with a TV show. Cookbooks, cookware and utensils, mail order and licensing agreements would follow, along with yet more theme restaurants. But nothing materialized. Still another idea, a chain of live-music locations called "Sound Republic," produced only one restaurant and no ancillary activities.

If it wasn't for his success with Hard Rock Cafe, some would call Robert Earl a dreamer and not a doer. See the following box for a discussion of dreams versus practicality for entrepreneurs.

Problems

Somehow the celebrity theme had no staying power. What did people expect to see? A real live movie star every time they came to a Planet Hollywood?—hardly, except

---

INFORMATION BOX

DREAMS VERSUS PRACTICALITY: WHAT IS THE FORMULA FOR ENTREPRENEURS?

The common notion for success in entrepreneurship is the need for the "great idea." With this great idea, this dream, success is almost guaranteed, some will tell us; without it, one is doomed to mediocrity and failure. Yet, many entrepreneurs dispute such thinking. For example, Nolan Bushnell, founder of Atari, the electronic games company, and several other companies, says that entrepreneurs don't have better ideas than lots of other people, but they have an uncanny ability to translate ideas into practical solutions.[9]

Robert Earl was a consummate idea man, ready to put his dreams to the test. But we can wonder at his ability to tap the practical side of his brain. Can a dreamer make it as a successful entrepreneur? Is perseverance in never giving up dreams a possible substitute for a healthy dose of practicality? Robert Earl may further test the issue.

Many dreamers never escape from their armchair thinking. Earl had no difficulty with this. He was ready to run with his ideas, and also convince other people of their merits. You may want to compare your psyche with his.

---

[9] John Merwin, "Have You Got What It Takes?" *Forbes* (August 5, 1981), p. 60.

in their dreams. They could see celebrities on oversize video screens in the darkened halogen-spotted interior, but never in person. So they ordered an overpriced appetizer, maybe bought Planet Hollywood T-shirts on the way out, perhaps to remember the experience, and never came back. Would they have come back if the food had been better?

Could you blame the celebrities in not patronizing their own restaurants, in not mingling with the common folk? Even if a few might have wanted to, difficult celebrity schedules would have precluded any consistent appearances, even in New York City and Orlando, much less in Minneapolis, Minnesota, St. Louis, Missouri, and Gurnee Mills, Illinois.

For 1996, the year Planet Hollywood went public, same store sales at all restaurants fell 2 percent. In 1997, same store sales fell 11 percent. For the first two quarters of 1998, sales plunged 13 percent and 17 percent respectively. Total second-quarter revenue fell 13.8 percent from the previous year. Not surprisingly, the stock price that was $32.13 the day of the initial offering, plunged to under $4 by October 1998. Westra, the analyst who thought so highly of Planet Hollywood two years before, lamented, "Of all the stocks in my career, I was most wrong with Planet Hollywood."[10]

Now, expansion plans were aborted, with a $44.6 million charge taken to write off some projects. In the summer of 1998, Robert Earl brought in William H. Baumhauer, formerly head of the Fuddruckers hamburger chain, to be president. Baumhauer announced plans to close some restaurants, to reduce employment, to boost pay for restaurant managers to attract better talent, and most important, to fix the food.

Problems worsened. On December 15, 1998, lenders slashed Planet Hollywood's borrowing power and forced the sale of its Orlando, Florida headquarters. A major shareholder, Saudi Prince Alwaleed, sought to sell his 16 percent stake.

What Went Wrong?

We have to wonder at the fickleness of the appeal of celebrities, when the product or service does not match the image or the expectation. Will customers go back to a place in the unreasonable hope that some celebrity might show up, if food compares poorly with other restaurants?

Historical evidence is rather compelling that the use of a celebrity's name without good food is the recipe for failure. Back in the 1960s when fast-food franchises had an early boom, such chains as Minnie Pearl's Chicken, Here's Johnny Restaurants (Johnny Carson), Al Hirt Sandwich Saloon, Broadway Joe's (Joe Namath), Jerry Lucas Beef 'n Shake, and Mickey Mantle's Country Cookin' Restaurants came on the scene with high expectations by investors and franchisees. What soon became apparent, however, was that although the public might pay to see the entertainer or sports figure perform, they would not frequent a fast-food outlet simply because of the famous name, or a picture or poster of the celebrity—unless the food and service warranted their patronage.

[10] *Ibid.*

Things apparently have not changed over the last thirty years. The lure of Planet Hollywood was the possibility of a celebrity appearance, except this was practically nonexistent after the grand opening. Food was ordinary and unexciting and videos of celebrities were not enough to bring back many customers under such circumstances. So we have the great idea—the attraction of celebrities—but abysmal capitalizing on it.

Could Planet Hollywood have done a better job in luring celebrities? Even if it gave celebrities more than a small stake in a restaurant chain, perhaps through stock or options, would these multimillionaires willingly commit time to such an endeavor? They would likely spend any spare time in far more exciting activities than making a personal appearance at a restaurant or store. Besides, in a chain of close to a hundred restaurants how is one going to schedule appearances of such celebrities to assure that each outlet has its fair and frequent share? For the lesser known, or third-rate celebrities, more appearances could be enticed, but would they be that much draw?

So while the concept was interesting, even intriguing at first view, it was a dud in actuality.

With the benefit of hindsight, we wonder why analysts, investors, and management did not foresee that there would be no parade of celebrities except at grand openings, and that after the first few even these would be poorly attended. How could so many have been so myopic about this flawed concept?

WHAT CAN BE LEARNED?

Beware of being swayed by hype and emotional optimism. Especially for new ideas and ventures it is easy to become caught up by enthusiastic forecasts of entrepreneurs and analysts. It is natural to want to believe and be part of an enterprise with golden prospects, and assume the best and ignore any naysayers.

In both of these cases we saw the drastic consequences of such myopia. Critical questions could have been raised at the time of the IPOs about:

1. With Boston Chicken, the use of the moneys generated, primarily to open more outlets and financing franchisees to get started. The strategy implied sacrificing careful selection of franchisees for great growth. The great growth planned also suggested less attention given to store location, training, and controls.

2. With Planet Hollywood, the great dependence on the presence of celebrities. This was the engine that was to drive the company, not the food. How much could Planet Hollywood count on such public appearances? Any sober analysis should have deduced that the restaurants needed to stand on their own without such dependence.

Evaluate ideas for practicality. So we want to be careful not to be swayed by emotionality and hype. But we must be careful not to go to the other extreme, of ignoring creative ideas of high merit. What to do?

Nothing is for sure. But we can make some suggestions. They have worked for many decision-makers, but have sometimes led to discarding promising but uncertain ventures:

1. *Look at the worst scenario.* What is the worst that could happen if we go ahead with this? What would lead to this worst scenario? Could these factors somehow be blunted and overcome? Can we assign probabilities to the various consequences of this decision? Based on our best knowledge, is it worth taking?

2. *Use a devil's advocate.* A devil's advocate is one who takes the opposing position, on the basis of better opening up all sides of a decision. Such a devil's advocate, if well chosen and conscientious, can flesh out the worst scenario and let it stand on its own merits against the proposed action.

Would such techniques have prevented the investor mistakes of Boston Chicken and Planet Hollywood? They might have raised second thoughts to blunt the enthusiasm. Perhaps all would have gained—entrepreneurs and investors alike—from a more sober and objective evaluation of these ideas.

Execution must not be downplayed in the infatuation with euphoric ideas. With proper execution both of these entrepreneurial adventures might have had success. Good execution at Boston Chicken meant satisfactory location research, selecting well-qualified franchisees and training them properly and giving them continuing supervision and control to help achieve profitable enterprises. For Planet Hollywood, it meant making the food service so good and value oriented that people would come back for the food and service, celebrities or no celebrities. Planet Hollywood had a great asset, but it was slipping away: the celebrity theme at first would bring hordes of people to the restaurants during the grand openings. With outstanding food and service they could have been repeat customers. What an opportunity wasted.

Never neglect older operations in the rush to open new ones. The temptation in a strong growth mode is to concentrate most attention and resources on opening new outlets. As a consequence the existing ones are given short shrift in attention and resources needed. The surest indication of such deemphasis is when same store sales decline. Both Boston Chicken and Planet Hollywood faced this, and it led to their comeuppance. Good supervision and controls (i.e., adequate management attention) of older outlets must not be sacrificed in the enthusiasm and rush to open new ones. Yet many firms are guilty of this neglect of their older facilities.

CONSIDER

Can you think of any additional learning insights?

QUESTIONS

1. Do you see any possible way that well-known celebrities can be induced to periodically visit far-flung restaurants or other outlets, except perhaps those in entertainment centers such as New York and Los Angeles?

2. Do you think most well-known celebrities really want to mingle with common folk?

3. Have you eaten in a Boston Chicken (or Boston Market) or Planet Hollywood restaurant? What were your impressions?

4. "The worst thing that could have happened to Boston Chicken was the huge success of their initial public offering." Comment.

5. How do you account for the initial wild investor enthusiasm for both Boston Chicken and Planet Hollywood (and even Boston Beer in the previous case)? Does this mean that all IPOs should be looked at skeptically?

6. Would stronger controls have prevented most of the problems of these two enterprises? How could controls have been more effective?

7. Do you think Boston Chicken can be salvaged?

8. Can Planet Hollywood still be salvaged?

HANDS-ON EXERCISES

Before

1. Design a program for sound growth for Boston Chicken at its beginning, after the IPO.

2. Design a strategy to achieve an enduring customer attraction for Planet Hollywood after the IPO.

After

1. Design a program to salvage Boston Chicken now.

2. Design a program to salvage Planet Hollywood now.

TEAM DEBATE EXERCISE

Debate the two extreme growth orientations: run-with-the-ball versus slow-and-steady-wins-the-race in the Boston Chicken and Planet Hollywood agendas.

INVITATION TO RESEARCH

What is the situation with these two firms today? Have their prospects improved? Have stock prices gone up?

CHAPTER TWENTY

OfficeMax: Grasping the Ring

M ichael Feuer had a passion to be an entrepreneur. He realized this passion was rather late in coming, but by age 42 he was bored with the corporate life. Still, perhaps it had been there all along, this passion.

He had started with Fabri-Centers of America, a 600-store chain, 17 years before, and had quickly rose through the ranks. He liked to describe himself in those days as suffering from the Frank Sinatra syndrome—"I wanted to do it my way." And he got tired of what he called CYB, "covering your backside," which he saw most executives spending too much of their time trying to do, at the expense of total effectiveness. If he only had his own business he could escape these drains on career satisfaction and constraints on his potential. However, he couldn't accept the common notion of the true entrepreneur as one who has enormous self-confidence, enough to give up the security of the paycheck and go off on his or her own. "I'm not a true entrepreneur because I suffer acutely from what I call 'F of F,' the fear of failure."[1]

In his pursuit of entrepreneurship, Feuer turned down a number of big-money corporate jobs and the perks that go with them. Increasingly he felt an overwhelming urge to be his own man, to succeed or fail on his own terms. He soon realized, however, the reality of starting a small business from scratch and the contrast with what might have been if he had chosen the corporate option.

THE START

Feuer found a partner, Robert Hurwitz, and the two recognized a flaw in the way office products were distributed and sold. The traditional channel of distribution for this merchandise was from manufacturers to wholesalers or distributors and finally to stationers, who were usually small retailers. This rather lengthy process imposed markups at each stage of the distribution and resulted in relatively high prices for the

---

[1] Until late 1993, little had been written about the success of OfficeMax. Much of the early material and quotes have come from speeches that Feuer made to various business and graduate business school classes.

end user. Feuer saw this as archaic, akin to the "old-time mom-and-pop groceries on every corner," which were eventually replaced by more efficient and much lower-priced supermarkets. These for the most part bypassed wholesalers and distributors and went directly to manufacturers.

Feuer and Hurwitz (who is no longer active in the firm on a full-time basis) were able to mass $3 million from 50 investors, some friends and family members as well as a number of doctors and lawyers. The two partners did not use any debt financing, nor did they seek venture capitalists. They shunned these most common sources of capital for new firms, not wanting to give up some control of their enterprise; neither did they want to answer to skeptics and defend every major decision. However, for many promising small businesses, venture capital can provide needed startup funds difficult to obtain otherwise. See the following box for more discussion of venture capitalists and their role in fostering small enterprises.

While Feuer and Hurwitz recognized what seemed an attractive opportunity, they were not the only ones to do so. In May 1988 an industry trade paper listed all the embryonic firms in the emerging office products superstore industry. OfficeMax rated number 14 on a list of 15. "We would have been dead last, but another company had started a week later than we did, although neither one of us had any stores."[2]

Feuer and Hurwitz established headquarters offices in a tiny 500-square-foot brick warehouse. It had little heat or air conditioning. The company owned only a few pieces of office furniture, a coffee-marker, and a copy machine, but no fax. The restroom had to be unisex since there was only space for one toilet. They had recruited seven people who were only half-jokingly told that they needed to have small appetites because there was little money to pay them. But Feuer promised that they would share in the financial success of the company, and for these seven their faith and hope for the future was enough. Feuer likes to tell the story of how he reinterviewed a candidate for a vice-president's position who had turned him down in 1988. Had he accepted the job then he would have been a multimillionaire by 1993.

THE FIRST YEAR

Even with $3 million of seed money from the 50 investors, OfficeMax had limited resources for what it proposed to do. A major problem now was to convince manufacturers to do business with this upstart firm in Cleveland. Most manufacturers were satisfied with the existing distribution channels and were reluctant to grant credit to a revolutionary newcomer with hardly a store to its name.

The key to winning the support of these manufacturers lay in convincing them that OfficeMax had such a promising future that it could offer them far more business potential than they would ever have with their present distributors—that OfficeMax would soon be a 30-, 50-, even 300-store chain in a few years. "We explained to them that it was in *their* best interest to help us today—to guarantee a place with us tomorrow."

[2] John R. Brandt, "Taking It to the Max," *Corporate Cleveland* (September 1988), p. 17.

INFORMATION BOX

VENTURE CAPITALISTS: AID TO ENTREPRENEURS

The biggest roadblock to self-employment is financing. Banks tend to be unreceptive to funding unproven new ventures, especially for someone without a track record. Given that most would-be entrepreneurs have limited resources from which to draw, where are they to get the financing needed?

Feuer and Hurwitz bypassed conventional sources of financing by finding 50 willing investors. For many other would-be entrepreneurs venture capitalists may be the answer.

Venture capitalists are wealthy individuals (or firms) looking for extraordinary returns for their investments. At the same time, they are willing to accept substantial risks. Backing nascent entrepreneurs in speculative undertakings can be the route to a far greater return on investment than possible otherwise—provided that the venture capitalist chooses wisely who to stake. This decision is much easier after a fledgling enterprise has a promising start. Then venture capitalists may stand in line for a piece of the action. But until then, the entrepreneur may struggle to get seed money.

How do these sources of funding choose among the many business ideas brought to them? "They look at the people, not the ideas," says Arthur Rock, one of the foremost venture capitalists. "Nearly every mistake I've made has been because I picked the wrong people, not the wrong idea."[3]

For a would-be entrepreneur seeking venture capital, then, the most important step may be in selling yourself, in addition to your idea. Intellectual honesty is sometimes mentioned by venture capitalists as a necessary ingredient. This may be defined as a willingness to face facts rigorously and not be deluded by rosy dreams and unrealistic expectations.

Those who win the early support of venture capitalists will likely have to give away a good piece of the action. Should the enterprise prove successful, the venture capitalists will expect to share in the success. Indeed, the funds provided by a venture capitalist may be crucial to even starting, or they may mean the difference in being adequately funded or so poorly funded that failure is almost inevitable.

Selling a definitive business plan to a prospective venture capitalist is usually a requirement for such financing. In the process, of course, you are selling yourself. You may want to do this exercise. Choose a new business idea, develop an initial business plan, and attempt to persuasively present it to a would-be investor.

---

[3] John Merwin, "Have You Got What It Takes?" *Forbes* (Aug. 3, 1981), p. 61.

To make its message credible, OfficeMax needed to create an image of stability and of a firm poised to jump. To help convey this image, Feuer convinced a major Cleveland bank to grant the company an unsecured line of credit. There was only one condition: OfficeMax had to promise that it would never use it. But this impressive-looking line of credit, bespeaking the faith that a major bank seemingly had in the embryonic firm, brought respect from manufacturers. Then OfficeMax even went so far as to ask them for unheard-of terms of sale—such as 60, 90, even 120 days with a discount.

Xerox was somehow persuaded to grant a year's payment delay for purchases. Many other manufacturers also accepted the outlandish requests. The bold promise of growth was realized, and many manufacturers 5 years later found OfficeMax to be their best customer. OfficeMax became so important at Xerox that the account is now handled by a divisional president and chief financial officer.

The first store was opened July 5, 1988, 3 months after the enterprise itself was started. This was an amazingly short time to fine-tune the concept, find a site, remodel as needed, and merchandise and staff the store. Feuer explains that the firm urgently needed some cash to survive, hence the desperate efforts to bring the first unit on line. In addition to providing needed cash flow, the first store had to confirm the viability and promise of the superstore concept to investors and suppliers alike.

This the first store quickly did. Customers eagerly embraced the great variety yet lowest prices of the superstore, more commonly known today as a category killer store for office products. The only publicity had been a newspaper story 2 days before. Yet, the store racked up $6,400 in sales that first day.

In the next 90 days, stores two and three were opened, also in metropolitan Cleveland. The fourth store opened in Detroit, not far from the executive offices of Kmart, destined a few years later to become a majority shareholder. Within 6 months the company was breaking even before corporate expenses.

As Feuer describes his work schedule in those early days, he typically was in the corporate office from 7:00 A.M. to 7:00 P.M., stopping at his home just long enough to change into nondescript clothing before going to the first store, where he could inconspicuously observe the shopping activity and talk to customers, asking them what they liked and didn't like about the store. He likes to recount how he would even follow customers who left without buying anything out to the parking lot to ask them why OfficeMax did not meet their needs.

Following the example of Feuer, from its inception the company has had a strong commitment to its customers. For example, OfficeMax accepted collect calls from customers. Any complaints had to be resolved in less than 24 hours, complete with an apology from OfficeMax. The company's objective was to build loyalty. "We're not embarrassed to say that we were wrong—and the customer was right."

As the company began making a small profit, Feuer's worst nightmare was that the accounting had been "screwed up," and that OfficeMax was on the verge of bankruptcy without realizing it. With this tormenting thought, he went back to the existing shareholders after 6 months to raise additional capital. The early success of the enterprise enabled them to raise the per share price 75 percent over the original placement.

By the end of the first full year, OfficeMax had 6 stores operational in Ohio and Michigan, with total sales of $13 million. The stores were profitable due to undeviating cost-consciousness.

GROWTH CONTINUES

By early 1990, 2 years into the operation, OfficeMax had 17 stores in operation. Unexpectedly, Montgomery Ward proposed a merger between OfficeMax and Office World, a similar operation that Ward had funded along with a number of venture capitalists. Office World had been started with what seemed to OfficeMax executives as almost a king's ransom. But it proceeded to lose $10 million in a very short time. In the negotiations, OfficeMax was in the power position, and it acquired Office World and its seven Chicago locations on rather attractive terms: Its major concession was to relinquish 2 of its 10 board seats to Montgomery Ward and the venture capitalists, but it acquired along with the stores several million dollars in badly needed cash.

By the summer of 1990, OfficeMax had about $25 million in cash, with 30 stores in operation. It raised another $8 million in a third private placement, at a share price 600 percent higher than the original investors had paid just two years before. Corporate offices were now moved into a building with space for both men's and women's restrooms.

Feuer began an aggressive new expansion program, calling for opening 20 additional stores. Competition was heating up in this new superstore industry, and several competitors had gone public to raise funds for more rapid expansion. Several others had gone bankrupt.

The Kmart Connection

The biggest threat facing OfficeMax now came from news that Kmart was poised to roll out its new Office Square superstore chain, which would be a direct threat to OfficeMax. With all the resources of Kmart—financial, managerial, and real estate expertise and influence—Feuer and company saw themselves being crushed and driven into Lake Erie. Feuer consoled himself that being left penniless would at least be character building.

Mostly as a defensive strategy, Feuer sought to open talks with Kmart. Kmart top executives proved to be receptive, and in November 1990 an agreement was negotiated in which Kmart made an investment of about $40 million in return for a 22 percent equity stake in OfficeMax. As a part of the agreement, the feared Office Square became a possession of OfficeMax, and Kmart received one seat on the OfficeMax board.

Now the expansion program could begin accelerating, with Kmart's full cooperation and support. So good was the rapport that within 10 months of the initial transaction, discussions were started concerning a broader business relationship with Kmart.

As the original goals of the business were being realized, it was perhaps time to cash in some of the chips, Michael Feuer thought. Two options seemed appropriate for the original investors: (1) go public, or (2) structure a new deal with Kmart. The company decided to go with Kmart. Kmart agreed to buy out all of the shareholders, with the exception of 50 percent of the shares of Feuer and partner Hurwitz, for a total market capitalization of about $215 million. This was up from zero just 42 months earlier. What made the deal particularly attractive was the fact that while 92 percent of OfficeMax was sold to a well-heeled parent, it could still retain total autonomy.

Onward and Upward, Without Kmart

By the end of July 1995, OfficeMax had 405 superstores in more than 150 markets in 41 states and Puerto Rico. The typical store was 23,500 square feet and had 6,000 items. Faster growth had been achieved through two major acquisitions: the 46-store Office Warehouse chain and the 105-store BizMart chain.

Sales were primarily to small and medium-sized businesses employing between 1 and 100 employees, home office customers, and individual consumers. But institutions such as school boards and universities were also targets, and the low prices of OfficeMax were a powerful inducement. A new program was established for next-day delivery of office supplies, based on calls to telephone centers with toll-free lines.

The company was planning to open up to 20 new FurnitureMax stores, which were to be 8,000 to 10,000 square feet additions to existing OfficeMax stores devoted to office furniture. It also was testing five to ten new CopyMax stores. Along with a multimedia advertising strategy, the company now had a 220-page merchandise catalog featuring about 5,000 items with toll-free telephone ordering.

Meanwhile, Kmart was seeking additional money to provide badly needed facelifts for its stores in the desperate attempt to hold off the mighty Wal-Mart. This led Kmart to sell its 25 percent share of OfficeMax, as well as some of its other subsidiaries, in order to raise a needed $3 billion in cash. This was finalized in July 1995. OfficeMax sold through underwriters 24,555,375 common shares, including all of the 18,803,526 shares held by Kmart, at $19.875 a share. OfficeMax itself netted $110 million to be used to fund its store expansion. Its future as a public company rather than a subsidiary of Kmart now presented a heady dream to Feuer and his investors. The following box discusses the prescription for great wealth in going public.

By fiscal 1995 (year ending January 31), revenues were over $1.8 billion. Net income was $30.4 million, up 181 percent from the year before. Figures 20.1 and 20.2 show the growth in sales and in number of stores.

INFORMATION BOX

THE PRESCRIPTION FOR GREAT WEALTH FOR ENTREPRENEURS

An entrepreneur often has much to gain by going public with an enterprise after a few years if it shows early success and a promising future. The entrepreneur keeps a portion of the stock and offers the rest to the public. With an attractive new venture, the offering price may be high enough to make the entrepreneur an instant multimillionaire.

Take Office Depot, for example. This is the largest office supply superstore chain in North America, although it is not that much bigger than OfficeMax. It is listed on the New York Stock Exchange and its 94,143,455 shares of common stock sell for about $39 a share, giving a total market value of about $3.7 billion. If OfficeMax went public and had a similar relative market value and if Feuer and Hurwitz held 8 percent of the total capitalization, they would be worth about $296 million or almost $150 million apiece.

What rationale do you see for Feuer's decision to structure a new deal with Kmart rather than go public? Do you agree with his rationale?

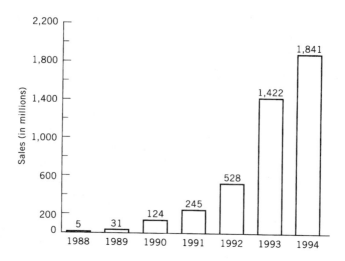

Figure 20.1. Sales growth (fiscal years ending Jan. 31 of the next year). In 1988, OfficeMax projected 1993 sales of less than $100 million; actual 1993 sales were 14 times larger.

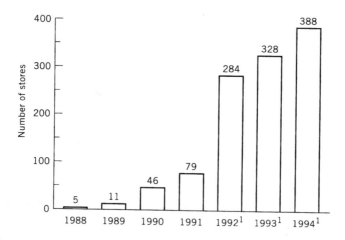

Figure 20.2. Growth in number of stores (fiscal years ending Jan. 31 of the next year). OfficeMax's 1988 business plan called for 50 stores by 1993; the company ended the year with nearly seven times that number.

[1] Includes BizMart stores.

ANALYSIS

Here we see an outstanding entrepreneurial success. The growth rate in only a few years rivals the best we have seen. In the same year that OfficeMax was started, 685,095 other new businesses formed in the United States, but more than half of these eventually failed. Of the survivors only a small percent will ever achieve a value over $50 million. Only a handful will ever reach $200 million. What makes OfficeMax so uniquely successful?

It was not that it had identified a great idea and nurtured it exclusively. While OfficeMax launched on to a business opportunity arising from the archaic distribution structure of the office-supplies industry, it was far from unique in this identification. Indeed, the concept of category killer stores was in the ascendancy for all kinds of different retail goods. Why did OfficeMax succeed brilliantly and most of its competitors fail or succumb to a precarious existence?

Much of the success seems to accrue from the efforts of the principal founder, Michael Feuer. His vision was to retain control of the nascent enterprise by shunning venture capitalists and debt financing. While the money initially raised, $3 million, would seem adequate for most ventures, for a category killer chain it was barely sufficient. But severe austerity with the promise of great rewards in the future satisfied both employees and suppliers. This required optimism and an enthusiastic selling job by Feuer. And it also required a trusting relationship with investors, employees, and suppliers.

Great attention to details—dedication to customer service, to cost containment to the point of austerity, to the myriad details needed for opening stores with adequate employees and merchandise in severe deadline situations—all these were part of the success package.

Building the growth without losing sight of the austerity heritage was perhaps even more important as the enterprise grew from a few stores to 20, 50, and more.

Of particular interest for any growing enterprise is the opportunity to make attractive acquisitions of former competitors who have fallen into desperate straits. The successful firm is in a position to quickly build on the bones of former competitors who could not make it.

UPDATE

By late 1998, analysts attacked OfficeMax: it was showing up more poorly than its two major competitors, Office Depot and Staples. In particular, sales were lagging at the older stores, and OfficeMax warned that third- and fourth-quarter earnings wouldn't hit expectations, mostly because of heavy price-cutting on computers. Critics were quick to point out that Office Depot and Staples were not so adversely affected.[4] Was this just a temporary abberation?

---

[4] For example, Teresa Dixon Murray, "OfficeMax Predicts Shortfall in Earnings," *Cleveland Plain Dealer* (October 7, 1998), pp. 1-C and 2-C; and "OfficeMax Opens New Stores While Sales Lag At Old Ones," *Cleveland Plain Dealer* (October 29, 1998), p. 2-C.

In 1996, OfficeMax became only the fourth company in U.S. history to exceed $3 billion in sales in less than nine years. As of September 1998, it had 769 stores in 48 states and Puerto Rico. Through joint ventures, it also had nine stores in Mexico and a first store in Japan. In addition, there were 129 CopyMax outlets targeting the estimated $9 billion "print for pay" industry, as well as 129 FurnitureMax stores tapping the estimated $12 billion office furniture industry.[5]

In 1999, it planned to open 120 new superstores in the United States on top of 150 opened in 1998. Revenues had steadily climbed to $3.765 billion in 1997, while net income had grown to $89.6 million, an increase of 30 percent from 1996.[6] Over the three-year period from January 31, 1994 to January 31, 1997, OfficeMax's market share compared to Office Depot rose from 30.1 percent to 35.9 percent, as shown below:

	Fiscal Year 1997	**1994**
Office Depot Revenues	$6.716 billion	$4.266 billion
OfficeMax Revenues	3.765	1.841
Market Share of OfficeMax relative to Office Depot	35.9%	30.1%

Yet, OfficeMax's stock price had fallen precipitously to under $10 a share by September 1998.

WHAT CAN BE LEARNED?

Successful entrepreneurship is not easy. Not many who opt for business for themselves expect this to be an easy road, a comfortable and lazy lifestyle. Yet the work ethic of successful entrepreneurs can be awesome, even for those prepared for long hours and worries in the night. Michael Feuer customarily puts in 12- to 18-hour days between working at corporate headquarters and keeping in close touch with stores and customers and suppliers. He admits to waking up at 3 A.M. to stare at the ceiling while wondering if he made the right decision. And he feels a responsibility to his employees, no longer just the seven original ones whose jobs depended on his decisions: By the end of 1993 he admitted to having more than 19,000 reasons to worry in the night.

Would he be less successful with a more moderate work ethic? Perhaps, or perhaps not. But the personal stake in a growing business is a powerful drive for many entrepreneurs to become workaholics even to the point of sacrificing other aspects of their lives, including family.

There is power in a growth image, even if it is only an illusion. In perhaps one of the most crucial moves taken, in the early and most vulnerable months of the

---

[5] *1998 OfficeMax Annual Report.*

[6] *Ibid.*

embryonic enterprise, Feuer and his people were able to sell both bankers and manufacturers on the great growth prospects for the company, that "we would rapidly become a 20-, 50-, or even 300-store chain. We explained that it was in *their* best interest to help us today—to guarantee a place with us tomorrow."

What makes a strong growth company so attractive to investors, creditors, suppliers, and employees? Part of the attractiveness certainly is that everyone likes to be associated with a winner. The greatest appeal of growth companies is their economic promise. This embraces investors, of course, because their investment grows with the business. Creditors and suppliers see more and more business coming their way as the company grows ever larger. And employees see great career opportunities continually opening up in a rapidly growing organization.

Perhaps in creating the image of OfficeMax as a company on the threshold of great growth, Feuer was simply very persuasive. But perhaps many of the people he talked with were so eager to be convinced and to be offered the opportunity to get in on the ground floor of what might be the stuff of dreams that they would accept even grandiose conjecture.

Go the extra miles in customer relations. It is easy for an organization to proclaim its dedication to customer service and good customer relations. Too often, however, it is only lip service, pious pronouncements without real substance. OfficeMax went far beyond lip service. Feuer and his executives, at least in the early years, sought close contact with customers in stores, even to the point of following them to the parking lot to see what might have been lacking in the merchandise or service that discouraged a purchase. The company accepts collect calls from customers, who might have problems or complaints or special needs. A promise of satisfaction of all complaints within 24 hours, the guiding "How can we make you happy?" question in all customer dealings, and readiness to apologize attest to a customer commitment beyond the ordinary. With few exceptions, all businesses depend on customer loyalty and repeat business for their success. Perhaps in office products, where many customers are businesses, customer loyalty is all the more important. But it is easy to delude yourself and an organization that the loss of a single customer is not all that important, and that the firm must guard against being taken advantage of by unreasonable customers. Where should a firm, particularly a retailer, draw the line? Can any retailer be too liberal in handling customer complaints?

Again, the power of "lean and mean." In several earlier cases we noted problems of bloated bureaucracies or inventories, and the dire effect on profitability. We also examined Southwest Airlines and Wal-Mart, both of which followed a policy of flat organizational levels and continued frugality despite increasing size. The temptation with great growth is to let down the barriers and open the spending spigots. OfficeMax so far seems to be resisting this urge.

Again, dedicated employees can give a powerful advantage. As with Southwest Airlines, and also Wal-Mart, OfficeMax was able to stimulate its employees to move beyond individual concerns to a higher level of performance, a true team approach. This dedication, and the vague promise of future great expectations brought employees to OfficeMax for very low wages, some turning down much higher paying jobs for the dream that might or might not come to pass. The dedication of these employees made possible opening the first store from scratch barely 3 months after the company was founded, with other stores quickly following.

The hope for great growth, a trusted leader, and an organization geared to a team effort seem to be most compatible in producing dedicated employees. One suspects there is also a close relationship in lean and mean organizations, where limited bureaucracy and management levels bring ease of communication.

CONSIDER

Can you identify other learning insights coming from this case?

QUESTIONS

1. In the hiring process, how would you identify candidates who are most likely to become dedicated employees?

2. Can a firm be too liberal in handling customer complaints?

3. The two office supply superstore chains closest to OfficeMax in size and growth are Office Depot, mostly located in the west and south, and Staples, predominantly in Florida and the northeast. OfficeMax, on the other hand, has stores coast to cost. Is OfficeMax being sufficiently prudent in spreading itself so widely at this time?

4. Do you think Feuer was being entirely ethical when he sold manufacturers on the desirability of doing business with OfficeMax in the very early day of the company? Why or why not?

5. Do you see any limitations to the future of category-killer stores?

6. Can you think of some types of merchandise where category-killer stores are unlikely to be successful?

7. Feuer puts in 12- to 18-hour days regularly. Do you think he would have been as successful with less of a work ethic? Why or why not?

8. Do a SWOT analysis (see Chapter 8) for OfficeMax. What do you conclude as far as future prospects?

HANDS-ON EXERCISES

1. You own a small office supply store. Business has been steady and sufficient for a good living for you and your family up to now. But an OfficeMax has opened less than a mile away. Discuss how you can possibly compete against such a superstore when you cannot come close to matching the variety of goods or the prices.

2. You are the assistant to Feuer. He wants you to draw up plans for targeting large institutions and businesses. Be as specific as you can be, mak-

ing assumptions where needed, and persuasively support your recommendations.

TEAM DEBATE EXERCISE

On October 25, 1995, the largest office-products retailer, Office Depot, announced that it was planning to open a dozen stores on OfficeMax's home turf, metropolitan Cleveland where OfficeMax has its headquarters and 17 stores. "When we enter a major market, our usual policy is to go in rather quickly and saturate the market with 6 to a dozen to 20 stores within the first couple of years," Office Depot said. Michael Feuer was unfazed. "We think the advantage we have is such a fierce sense and focus of local pride. I don't think there will be much of a test," he said.[7] Debate the challenge OfficeMax now faces: it should be badly worried, because the market already is close to saturation; it should not be worried since the market potential is still increasing and it can outcompete Office Depot.

INVITATION TO RESEARCH

What is the situation with OfficeMax today? Are there any dangers on the horizon? How is the competitive struggle with Office Depot shaping up?

[7] Bill Lubinger, "Office Depot Is Taking on OfficeMax," *Cleveland Plain Dealer* (October 25, 1995), C1.

PART SIX

ETHICAL CONTROVERSIES AND CHALLENGES

CHAPTER TWENTY-ONE

ADM: Price Fixing, Political Cronyism, and a Whistleblower

In June 1995, a whistleblower informed federal agents of the scheme of a giant multinational conglomerate, Archer-Daniels-Midland, to control sales of a widely demanded food additive and thus keep prices high worldwide. For three years, he had been secretly recording meetings of the firm's senior executives with Asian and European competitors. The whistleblower, Mark E. Whitacre, was revealed to ADM by an attorney who was supposedly conferring with him as a possible client.

Repercussions quickly followed. The company charged him with stealing from the firm and fired him. The plot became more complicated. But overhanging all was the role of the corporation and its 77-year-old top executive: Did they truly act unethically and illegally, or were the allegations ballooned out of all proportions? What kind of a person was this whistleblower, a hero or a villain?

THE WHISTLEBLOWER, MARK E. WHITACRE

Mark Whitacre joined Archer-Daniels in 1989, and spent about half his career there helping antitrust investigators. He was a rising star, recruited to head the fledgling BioProducts division, where he rose to become a corporate vice-president and a leading candidate to become the company's next president while still in his thirties.

He had been recruited from Degussa AG, a German chemical company where he was manager in organic chemicals and feed additives. However, his resume inflated his credentials with the title executive vice-president; he was only a vice-president.

While at ADM, he earned a business degree from a home-study school in California. Later ADM issued biographical material crediting him with an MBA from Northwestern University and the prestigious J.L. Kellogg School of Management. In an interview, Whitacre admitted the claims about his MBA were inflated to impress

Wall Street analysts, but he blamed ADM: "I feel bad about it. I, along with other executives that speak at analysts meetings, cooperated … it's a common practice."[1]

His ambition was to become president of ADM, which he claimed was promised him repeatedly.[2] How becoming a governmental informer would help him with this ambition seems murky.

Over three years he secretly helped investigators obtain videotapes revealing two senior executives meeting with Asian and European competitors in various places around the world. The executives were vice-chairman Michael D. Andreas, son and heir apparent of the 77-year-old Dwayne Andreas, chairman and chief executive; and vice-president Terrance Wilson, head of the corn-processing division. Sometimes Whitacre would wear a hidden microphone to obtain the incriminating evidence of price-fixing. We will follow the later travails of Whitacre, but let us examine whistle-blowing in general in the following box.

INFORMATION BOX

WHISTLEBLOWING

A whistleblower is an insider in an organization who publicizes alleged corporate miscon-duct. Such misconduct may involve unethical practices of all kinds, such as fraud, restraint of trade, price-fixing, bribes, coercion, unsafe products and facilities, and violations of other laws and regulations. Presumably, the whistleblower has exhausted the possibilities for changing the questionable practices within the normal organizational channels and, as a last resort, has taken the matter to government officials and/or the press.

Since whistleblowing may result in contract cancellations, corporate fines, and lost jobs, those who become whistleblowers may be vilified by their fellow workers and fired and even framed by their firms. This makes whistleblowing a course of action only for the truly courageous, whose concern for societal best interest outweighs their concern for themselves.

However, there is sometimes a thin line between an employee who truly believes the public interest is jeopardized and the individual who has a gripe or is a fanatic. There are some who believe management is condoning misconduct when in fact such miscon-duct is isolated and without management awareness or acceptance. And some see whistleblowing as a means of furthering their own interests, such as gaining fame or even advancing their careers.

Ralph Nader, in a 1972 book on whistleblowing, suggested that corporate employees have a primary duty to protect society that exists over and above secondary obligations to the corporation. He give examples of whistleblowing heroes, as well as courses of action for other would-be whistleblowers.[3]

Do you think you could ever be a whistleblower? Under what circumstances?

---

[3] Ralph Nader, Peter Petkas, and Nate Blackwell, *Whistleblowing* (New York: Bantam Books), 1972.

---

[1] "ADM Informant Faces Widening Allegations; He Attempts Suicide," *The Wall Street Journal* (August 14, 1995), p. A4.

[2] *Ibid.*

FBI agents on the night of June 27 entered the headquarters of the huge grain-processing company in Decatur, Illinois. They carted off files and delivered grand jury subpoenas seeking evidence of price collusion of ADM and competitors. Whitacre was one of the executives subpoenaed, and met with an attorney recommended by the company's general counsel's office, a common practice when companies face governmental inquiries.

Shortly after this meeting, the attorney disclosed to ADM that Whitacre was the federal informant in their midst, thus imperiling Whitacre's position in the company. This seemed a clear ethical violation of the confidentiality of lawyer/client relations. But the attorney, John M. Dowd of a prominent law firm doing business with ADM, claimed that Whitacre authorized him to do so. Whitacre and his new attorney angrily denied any such authorization.

In any case, now the company had the knowledge to retaliate. They fired him, accused him of stealing $2.5 million, and reported these findings to the Justice Department. Later the company increased the amount it claimed Whitacre had stolen to $9 million. They charged that he had been embezzling money by submitting phony invoices for capital expenditures, then channeling the payments into off-shore bank accounts.

The Justice Department saw the credibility of their key witness being weakened by such allegations, especially since Whitacre acknowledged that he had indeed participated in the bogus invoice schemes, although he said the payments were made with the full knowledge and encouragement of company higher-ups. Nevertheless, he and as many as 12 other ADM executives came under criminal investigation for evading taxes. The Justice Department's criminal fraud section further examined allegations that the off-the-books payments were approved by top management.[4]

A few days later, Whitacre tried to kill himself. At dawn, he drove his car into the garage of his home, closed the door, and left the engine running. On this morning he was supposed to fly to Washington to meet with federal authorities. He had arranged for the gardener to come to work late that morning, but the gardener arrived shortly after seven and found Whitacre unconscious in his car.

Shortly before the suicide attempt, Whitacre had written a letter to *The Wall Street Journal*, acknowledging that he had received money from ADM through unusual means: "Regarding overseas accounts and kick-backs; and overseas payments to some employees, Dig Deep. It's there! They give it; then use it against you when you are their enemy."[5]

On September 13, F. Ross Johnson, an ADM board member, in a talk at Emory University's Goizueta Business School commented on Whitacre's suicide attempt: "You know, he tried to commit suicide. But he did it in a six-car garage, which, I think, if you're going to do it, that's the place to do it. [The audience laughed.] And the gardener just happened to come by. So now he is bouncing around."[6]

Whether the suicide attempt was genuine or contrived, Whitacre apparently faced a traumatic period in his life. He wound up in a suburban Chicago hospital with

---

[4] Ronald Henkoff, "Checks, Lies and Videotape," *Fortune* (October 30, 1995), p. 110.

[5] "ADM Informant Faces…" *Ibid.*, p. A 1.

[6] "ADM and the FBI 'Scumbags'," *Fortune* (October 30, 1995), p. 116

no job and no place to live. He had money problems, being unable to touch any of the funds in his overseas accounts. He and his wife had moved out of their $1.25 million estate near Decatur, Illinois, after contracting to buy a house near Nashville for $925,000. After the suicide attempt, they attempted to back out of the deal, only to be sued for breach of contract.

With all this, somehow Whitacre seemed to have landed on his feet by early October. True, he and his family were living in a rented house in the Chicago area, but he had become chief executive of Future Health Technologies, a startup biotechnology firm, at a six-figure salary comparable to what he earned legally at ADM.

THE ALLEGATIONS AGAINST THE COMPANY

By fall 1995, three grand juries were investigating whether ADM and some of its competitors conspired to fix prices. Three major product lines of ADM were allegedly involved: lysine, high-fructose corn syrup, and citric acid. Lysine is an amino-acid mixed with feed for hogs and chickens to hasten the growth of lean muscles in the animals. High-fructose corn syrup is a caloric sweetener used in soft drinks. Citric acid, like lysine, is a corn-derived product used in the detergent, food and beverage industries.

The importance of these products in the total product mix of ADM is indisputable. For example, while lysine is virtually unknown to the public, it is a key ingredient in the feed industry. About 500 million pounds are produced annually. Prices since 1961 have been averaging more than $1 a pound. So millions of dollars are at stake to manufacturers. With modern facilities at its sprawling complex in Decatur, Illinois, ADM can produce about half the world's purchases of lysine annually. And this is one of the company's highest profit products.

The sweetener, high-fructose corn syrup, is a major product for ADM, with a $3 billion-a-year market worldwide. Soft drinks account for more than 75 percent of annual production.

ADM entered the citric-acid business in 1991 when it acquired a unit of Pfizer. Today it is the primary U.S. maker of this additive. One of the largest customers is Procter & Gamble, which uses it for detergents.

As one example of the seemingly incriminating evidenced of price fixing uncovered in videotapes, Michael Andreas is shown during a meeting he attended with lysine competitors at the Hyatt Regency Hotel at Los Angeles International Airport. There the participants discussed sales targets for each company as a means of limiting supply. This would destroy the free supply/demand machinations of the market and would permit prices to be kept artificially high, thus increasing the profits of the participants.[7] Although the evidence seemed to be substantial, still success at beating the price-fixing charges might well depend on how well ADM could convince that Whitacre, the government's star witness, was a liar and a thief.

With the charges and countercharges of Whitacre and the company, investigations went beyond price-fixing to tax-evasion for high-level executives sanctioned by

---

[7] Reported in "Investigators Suspect a Global Conspiracy In Archer-Daniels Case," *The Wall Street Journal* (July 28, 1995), pp. A1 and A5.

top management. Whitacre may have been the tip of the iceberg. The criminal-fraud division of the Justice Department began investigating whether the company illegally paid millions of dollars in off-the-books compensation to an array of company executives through foreign bank accounts. If so, then the culpability of Whitacre would be muted, and his value as a witness greatly enhanced.

It is worth noting the severity of the penalties if suits successfully come to pass. Fines for price fixing can range into the hundreds of millions of dollars, and some executives could even be given jail sentences. Furthermore, class-action suits by shareholders and customers can result in heavy damage awards. See the following box for a discussion of the famous price-fixing conspiracy of 1959 that set the precedence for jail sentences for executives involved.

ADM AND DWAYNE ANDREAS

The story of Archer-Daniels-Midland Co. is really the story of its chairman, Dwayne O. Andreas. In 1947, ADM chairman, Shreve Archer, died after choking on a chicken bone. Dwayne Andreas was a vice-president at Cargill, a rival firm. For the next 18

INFORMATION BOX

THE FAMOUS PRICE-FIXING CONSPIRACY OF 1959

In 1959, the biggest conspiracy of its kind in U.S. business history impacted the nation's thinking regarding business ethics.

Twenty-nine companies, including such giants as General Electric, Westinghouse, and Allis-Chalmers, were found guilty of conspiring to fix prices in deals involving about $7 billion of electrical equipment. The products involved in the conspiracy included power transformers, power switchgear assemblies, turbine generators, industrial control equipment, and circuit breakers. The companies were fined $1,924,500. Of particular note in this case, 52 executives (none of these top executives) were prosecuted and fined about $140,000. Even more startling, seven of the defendants received jail sentences. This was a first under federal antitrust laws.

On top of all that, almost 2,000 private-action, treble-damage cases were brought as a result of the court findings. In one of these alone, damages of $28,800,000 were awarded.

Incentives for the illegal actions stemmed from several sources. Without doubt, top management was exerting strong pressure on lower executives to improve their performance. Collusion with executives in other firms seemed to be a practical way to do this, especially in an environment rather blasé toward antitrust collusion. This attitude changed with the harsh penalties imposed by Judge J. Cullen Ganey.

Those executives who lost their jobs and went to jail were readily offered equivalent jobs in other corporations. The business community accepted them with open arms. Do you think they deserved such acceptance?

TABLE 21.1   ADM Revenues, 1986–1995

Year ending June 30	Sales (Millions)	Year-to-Year Percent Increase
1986	$5,336	
1987	5,775	10.8
1988	6,798	11.8
1989	7,929	11.6
1990	7,751	(2.2)
1991	8,468	9.3
1992	9,232	9.0
1993	9,811	6.5
1994	11,374	15.9
1995	12,672	11.4
Gain since 1986		137.5%

Source: Adapted from 1995 *ADM Annual Report.*

years he advanced steadily in the industry and became wealthy, while Archer-Daniels showed little growth. In 1966, at age 47, Andreas was asked to become a director at ADM. The founding families sold him a sizable amount of stock and proposed to groom him for the top spot. Four years later, he was named chief executive officer.

In 1995, Andreas was still firmly in command and running the publicly traded company almost as a personal dynasty. In 25 years he had built up the firm into the nation's biggest farm-commodity processor, with $12.7 billion in annual revenue. Table 21.1 shows the steady growth of revenues since 1986, while Table 21.2 shows

Table 21.2   ADM Net Earnings, 1986–1995

Year ending June 30	Earnings (Millions)	Year-to-Year Percent Increase
1986	$230	
1987	265	15.2
1988	353	33.2
1989	425	20.3
1990	484	13.9
1991	467	(3.5)
1992	504	7.9
1993	568	12.7
1994	484	(14.8)
1995	796	64.5
Gain since 1986		246.1%

Source: Adapted from 1995 *ADM Annual Report.*

the growth of earnings, not quite as steady but still almost two and a half times greater than in 1986.

POLITICAL MANEUVERING

Although company headquarters were at Decatur, Illinois, Andreas's influence in Washington was probably unparalleled by any other business leader. ADM led corporate America in political contributions; it contributed hundreds of thousands of dollars to both parties. Furthermore, Andreas supported Jimmy Carter's campaign— ADM even bought his struggling peanut farm in 1981. But Andreas also contributed generously to Ronald Reagan and George Bush. During the Reagan years, when U.S. firms were entering the Soviet market, ADM was in the vanguard. Andreas became close to then-Soviet president, Mikhail Gorbachev. But as a hedge, he also courted Boris Yeltsin, Gorbachev's emerging rival.

Perhaps his greatest political supporter became Senator Robert Dole, who is from the farm state of Kansas. When Dole's wife, Elizabeth Dole, took over administration of the American Red Cross, Andreas donated $1 million to the cause. Dole also was given use of an ADM corporate plane, for which he paid the equivalent of a first-class ticket. An added factor in the friendship and rapport was the proximity of their vacation homes: Dole and his wife own a unit in Sea View, Florida, as do David Brinkley, a renowned TV newsman, and Robert Strauss, an ADM board member, and, of course, Dwayne Andreas.[8] Interestingly, President Clinton also regards Andreas as an ally.

Such political presence has brought great rewards to the company. ADM is a major beneficiary of federal price supports for sugar. Because such supports have kept sugar prices artificially high, ADM's sweetener, high-fructose corn syrup, has been attractive for giant companies such as CocaCola. Estimates are that fructose generates about 40 percent of ADM's earnings.[9]

Archer-Daniels also benefits from the 54-cent-a-gallon excise-tax break on ethanol, being the major producer of this corn-based fuel additive. Indeed, it is doubtful if the ethanol industry would exist without this tax break, and Bob Dole has been its most ardent congressional supporter.

Despite all the campaign contributions and personal rapport with the seats of power in Washington, Andreas and ADM have done little direct lobbying. Rather, such efforts have been done indirectly through various commodity and trade associations. For example, the American Peanut Shellers Association, with ADM support, handles the lobbying on peanut price supports.[10]

The Board of Directors

The investigations and the charges and countercharges drew fire from some of the major institutional holders of ADM stock. For example, the California Public

---

[8] Reported in "How Dwayne Andreas Rules Archer-Daniels By Hedging His Bets," *The Wall Street Journal* (October 27, 1995), p. A8.

[9] *Ibid.*

[10] *Ibid.*

Employees Retirement System—Calpers, as it is known, and owner of 3.6 million shares of Archer-Daniels—complained, charging that the board was too closely tied to Chairman and CEO Dwayne Andreas. "The ADM board is dominated by insiders, many of whom happen to be related to the CEO," Calpers complained. Calpers also criticized the ADM board for approving a 14 percent pay raise for Andreas, "rather than demand the CEO's resignation."[11] Other institutional investors also joined the criticisms: for example, the United Brotherhood of Carpenters, the Teamsters Union, and New York's major pension funds.

Shareholders had several other major criticisms of the board. It was supposed to authorize all capital expenditures above $250,000. The alleged claims for offshore pay were disguised as requests for spending on plant and equipment, and these the board passed with no hesitation. As to the charges of price-fixing and the allegations against major executives, the board was conspicuously uncritical, and finally made some token efforts to look further into the charges.

Brian Mulroney, former prime minister of Canada, co-chaired the special committee charged with coordinating the company's response to the federal investigations. One would think that part of his job was to safegaurd the interests of shareholders. But major institutional shareholders doubted his objectivity, and noted his very close relations to Dwayne Andreas. Critics contended that what was needed was not a rubber-stamp special committee but "a team of experts to lead a full-blown, independent investigation."[12]

Regarding the composition of the board, critics seemed to have a case: the board was hardly objective and unbiased toward company top management; rather, it was highly supportive and dominated by insiders, many of whom were related to the CEO. For example, 4 of Archer-Daniels 17 directors were members of the Andreas family. An additional 6 directors were retired executives or relatives of senior managers. The outside directors also had close connections to Andreas, such as Robert S. Strauss, the Washington lawyer whose firm represented ADM, and Mulroney, who was also with a law firm used by the firm. Even Harvard University Professor Ray Goldberg, a member of the board, had strong ties with Andreas, dating back to his dissertation.

While close bonds of boards with management are not unusual with many companies, such cozy relations can be detrimental to shareholders' best interests.

ANALYSIS

ADM's Conduct

Was ADM guilty of unethical conduct, and even illegalities? At the time this first was written, three grand juries were investigating the price fixing. The Department of

---

[11] Joann S. Lublin, "Archer-Daniels-Midland Is Drawing Fire From Some Institutional Holders," *The Wall Street Journal* (October 11, 1995), p. A8.

[12] Henkoff, p. 110.

Justice was looking into the tax-evasion charges. But nothing had been decided or proven. Perhaps ADM was guilty of price fixing, and perhaps not. Maybe the firm was guilty of nefarious practices to enable its high-level executives to avoid some income taxes through off-the-books compensation. If proven, such practices would not only be unethical, but also illegal and subject to harsh penalties.

Certain other activities of this giant company posed some ethical controversies even if they were not illegal—for example, packing the board with cronies dedicated to preserving the establishment at the expense of stock-holders; the great quest for preferential treatment in the highest corridors of power; and just perhaps, the setting up of Whitacre. Let us examine these ethical issues.

Packing the board so that it is exceptionally supportive of the entrenched management may be condemned as not truly representing the rights of stockholders. But in its 25-years with Andreas at the helm, ADM's stock value rose at an annual average rate of 17 percent over the last decade. Few stockholders could dispute Andreas's contribution to the firm, even though they might fume at his riding roughshod over his critics—especially institutions holding large amounts of stock. Of course, if grand juries do return indictments, the autocratic tactics of Andreas will bring him down if it is proven that he knew of any such illegal activities.

Some would maintain that the courting of favoritism and special treatment from high-level Washington politicians may have gone too far. But should not any organization have the right to do its best to push for beneficial legislation and regulation? Of course, some will be more effective than others in doing so. Is this so much different than competition in the marketplace?

Whitacre's Role

Why did Whitacre choose to be a government mole? Still in his thirties, Whitacre had advanced to high position in the company, with corresponding substantial compensation (enough to afford an estate valued at more than a million dollars), and who was at least one of the top candidates for the presidency of the firm. And yet he had been secretly taping supposedly illegal discussions. Why? What did he have to gain? There was so much to lose.

Added to this, he must have been a very capable executive, yet he was naive enough to leave himself vulnerable by accepting, and maybe even initiating, illegal scams through false invoices and overseas bank accounts. And he apparently naively confessed to a company lawyer his involvement as an informant for the FBI, not just recently but for three years. It doesn't make much sense, does it?

UPDATE

In October 1996, ADM pleaded guilty to criminal price-fixing charges and paid a record $100 million fine and nearly that amount again to settle lawsuits by customers and investors. But ADM's troubles were not ended.

Early in December 1996, a federal grand jury charged Michael Andreas, earning $1.3 million annually as the No. 2 executive at ADM and heir apparent to his father to run the company, and Terrance Wilson, former head of ADM's corn-processing division, with conspiring with Asian makers of lysine to rig the price of the livestock feed additive. Andreas took a leave of absence with full pay, and Wilson retired. It was thought that any conviction or guilty plea by Michael Andreas would destroy his chances of continuing his family's three-decade-long reign over ADM. However, Dwayne Andreas could yet preserve the patrimony: His nephew, G. Allen Andreas, a 53-year-old lawyer, was one of three executives named to share Dwayne Andreas's responsibility in a newly formed office of chief executive.

In a surprising twist to the case, Mark Whitacre, the whistleblower, was also indicted.

The Verdict

The verdicts came in late 1998. After a week of deliberation in a two-month trial, the jury found Andreas, Wilson, and Whitacre guilty in a landmark price-fixing case, thereby giving the Justice Department its biggest convictions in a push against illegal global cartels. The federal prosecutors had been thwarted in how to rebuild the case after their mole, Whitacre, had been convicted of embezzlement and was already serving a 9-year prison sentence. The problem was solved by wringing confessions from Asian executives who were also involved in the conspiracy.

The bizarre behavior of Whitacre, after initially providing documentation of the birth of a price-fixing scheme, was unexpected and almost disastrous, and hard to explain even given that he was a big spender who openly pined to become president of ADM.

WHAT CAN BE LEARNED?

Price fixing is one of the easiest cases to prosecute. Conspiracies to fix prices are direct violations of the Sherman Act. The government does not need to prove that competition was injured or that trade was restrained. All that needs to be proven is that a meeting took place with agreements to fix prices, bids, or allocate market share.

The penalties for price conspiracies have greatly increased since the celebrated electrical equipment industry conspiracy of 1959. Given the ease of prosecution, one would think that no prudent executive would ever take such a risk. Yet, there have been sporadic instances of price-fixing since then, and maybe we have it here with Michael Andreas, the son of Dwayne. Is there no learning experience?

Is political patronage necessary? We know that ADM sought political patronage and preferential treatment to an extraordinary degree—perhaps more than any other firm. Is this so bad?

Purists argue that this distorts the objectivity of our governmental institutions. Others say it is part of the democratic process in a pluralistic society. It might be so vital to our type of government that it cannot be eliminated—at best, can only be curbed.

On the other hand, it simply adds one more dimension to the competitive environment. Other firms can be invited to flex their muscles in the halls of government.

But when it comes to violations of the law, which supposedly reflects the wishes of society, then no firm is immune from the consequences. Even if its political patronage has been assiduously cultivated, it cannot escape the consequences of its illegal actions. The press, and the legal establishment, see to that.

Beware the "shareholder be damned" attitude. Some shareholders of ADM suspect that ADM had this attitude. As a consequence, the company faced at least two dozen shareholder lawsuits. As it approached the 1995 October annual meeting, nine big institutional investors announced plans to vote against reelecting ADM directors. But the move was largely symbolic, since their combined shares represented only 4.9 percent of the 505 million outstanding shares.[13] And their views received little attention in the meeting. Nor, apparently did those of other shareholders. *The Wall Street Journal* reported that at the meeting Andreas squelched criticisms of the issue of the antitrust probe and other allegations as he "summarily cut off a critic by turning off his microphone: 'I'm chairman. I'll make the rules as I go along,' Mr. Andreas said."[14]

A cozy relationship with the board encourages such attitudes. And when operating performance is continually improving, such shareholder criticisms may be seen as merely gnats striving for attention, and thus worthy of being ignored. If the top executive is inclined to be autocratic, then the environment is supportive.

But is this wise? I think not. Should adversity set in, sometime in the future, then such attitudes toward investors can be self-destructive, even with a supportive board. If performance deteriorates, no board can maintain its sheeplike support for incumbent management, not in the face of vehement shareholders (especially large institutional investors) or major creditors.

But does adversity have to come? Only the profoundest optimist can think that success is forever. In ADM's case, adversity may be on the threshhold, if Justice Department investigations result in grand jury indictments.

An organization's ethical tone is set by top management. If top management is unconcerned about ethical conduct, or if it is an active participant in less than desirable practices, this sets the tone throughout the organization. It promotes erosion of acceptable moral conduct in many areas of the operation. It becomes contagious as even those inclined to be more morally scrupulous join their colleagues. Then we have the "follow-the-leader" mindset.

In such an unhealthy environment, a few whistleblowers may arise and attempt to right the situation, often unsuccessfully and at great personal risk. Others who cannot tolerate the decline in moral standards, but don't have the courage to be whistleblowers, will leave the company. Almost inevitably, the misconduct will come to light, and repercussions of the severest kind result. Perhaps top management can escape the blame, though lower-level executives will be sac-

---

[13] "Probe Tears Veil of Secrecy at Archer Daniels Midland," *Cleveland Plain Dealer* (October 18, 1995), p. 3-C.

[14] "How Dwayne Andreas Rules..." p. A1.

rificed. Occasionally, top management also comes under fire, and is forced to resign. Unfortunately, too often with healthy retirement benefits.

CONSIDER

Can you think of other learning insights?

QUESTIONS

1. What is your position regarding top management's culpability for the misdeeds of their subordinates?

2. Do you think ADM's efforts at gaining political favoritism went too far? Why or why not?

3. "If Dwayne's son is found guilty of price-fixing, there's no way that the big man himself cannot be found guilty." Evaluate this statement.

4. "With all the false invoices and persons involved in these millions of dollars of payouts off-the-books, there's no way the company could not have known what was going on." Evaluate.

5. Speculate on what would lead Whitacre to "betray" his company. If a number of possibilities are mentioned, which do you think is most compelling?

6. With the severe penalties and ease of prosecution of price-fixing cases, why would any firm or any executive attempt it today?

7. Why do you suppose, with all its efforts to gain preferential treatment through courting the mighty in government, ADM has not resorted to direct lobbying? Has it missed a golden opportunity to further its causes?

HANDS-ON EXERCISES

Before

1. Assume that Dwayne Andreas wants to maintain high ethical standards in his organization. Describe how he should go about this.

After

2. Assume that several key executives have indeed been found guilty of price-fixing; assume further that there are also indictments of illegal payments to certain executives. Further, the Senate ethics committee is investigating whether there have been improprieties in dealings with some members of Congress. How would you as CEO attempt damage control?

TEAM DEBATE EXERCISE

Debate the ethics of aggressively courting prominent politicians and government administrators. The two extreme positions would be: (1) going as far as you can short of being charged with outright bribery; (2) limiting relationship building to a few token contributions to trade association lobbying efforts.

INVITATION TO RESEARCH

Has ADM's public image been badly tarnished by all this publicity, or can you determine this? Has the firm continued to grow and prosper? Is the Andreas family still in control?

CHAPTER TWENTY-TWO

Tobacco: A Beleaguered but Defiant Industry

Cigarettes are among the world's most profitable consumer products. A cigarette "costs a penny to make, sell it for a dollar, it's addictive, and there's fantastic brand loyalty." So said master investor Warren Buffett as he unsuccessfully sought to take over RJR Nabisco, the tobacco conglomerate.[1] Perhaps because of its profitability, the morality of the business has long been suspect.

Criticisms have accelerated in recent years and bans widely imposed. Still, the tobacco industry remained stubbornly focused on its own best interests. That most critics saw tobacco's best interests as diametrically opposed to society's best interests mattered little to the industry as it aggressively struck back at critics.

In November 1998, a tobacco deal was agreed upon between the industry and 46 states to settle state lawsuits filed to recover Medicaid money spent treating diseases related to smoking. Some said the industry got off far too easy as this ended the largest-ever legal and financial threat to the industry.

CONTROVERSIAL STRATEGIES IN A SHRINKING MARKET

Targeting Minorities

Uptown

This new cigarette was packaged in a showy black-and-gold box and was the first cigarette aimed specifically at African-American smokers. It followed the new strategy of tobacco companies to introduce new brands directed to specific groups, such as women. Now, using careful research and design, everything about Uptown was tailored to black consumers. The results were a surprise.

A storm of protests quickly ensued. Critics maintained that the marketing of Uptown represented a cold-blooded targeting of blacks, who already suffered a

---

[1] "The Tobacco Trade: The Search for El Dorado," *Economist,* May 16, 1992, p. 21.

lung cancer rate 58 percent higher than whites. The protests even reached the office of Louis Sullivan, the Secretary of Health and Human Services. He quickly sided with the critics: "Uptown's message is more disease, more suffering and more death for a group already bearing more than its share of smoking-related illness and mortality." He condemned "the attempts of tobacco merchants to earn profits at the expense of the health and well-being of our poor and minority citizens."[2]

Given the virulence of the protests, R. J. Reynolds abandoned the brand, bitterly decrying the negative attention being focused on it "by a few zealots." The critics had won, this time.

Dakota

Another new cigarette, also targeted to a specific group, was beset with controversy. Dakota was aimed at "virile females." Critics of tobacco's relationship with lung cancer and heart disease were quick to attack this as a nefarious appeal to women.[3]

Another group was especially upset. In some Native American languages, *dakota* means friend. Yet, to a group that already had high rates of smoking addiction, such a brand name seemed a betrayal.

Controversies Over Tobacco Company Sponsorships

Due to the 1971 federal ban on cigarette advertising on TV and radio, tobacco companies desperately sought other media to place their hundreds of millions of advertising dollars. By the early 1990s serious questions were raised about their use of certain media, such as billboards promoting smoking and alcohol in African-American neighborhoods.

Advertising support of black media by tobacco companies also came under fire, even though few other major firms were advertising in black media. Many small minority publications would have folded without the advertising dollars of tobacco companies.

Tobacco company support for minority organizations also began to be questioned. The National Association of Black Journalists turned down a Philip Morris donation: "We couldn't take money from an organization deliberately targeting minority populations with a substance that clearly causes cancer," said the group's president.[4]

The tobacco industry also liberally provided money to women's sports at a time when other money sources were virtually nonexistent. For example, Virginia Slims' funding brought women's tennis into prominence. The controversy concerning this is discussed in the following box.

[2] Ben Wildavsky, "Tilting at Billboards," *New Republic* (August 20, 1990), p. 19.

[3] Paul Cotton, "Tobacco Foes Attack Ads That Target Women, Minorities, Teens and the Poor," *Journal of the American Medical Association* (September 26, 1990), p. 1505.

[4] *Ibid.*, p. 1506.

ISSUE BOX

TOBACCO COMPANY SPONSORSHIP OF ATHLETIC EVENTS

Is it right to allow tobacco companies to sponsor certain athletic events? What seems like a simple question becomes far more complex when we consider tennis tournaments such as Virginia Slims. There is no longer any doubt that smoking causes serious damage to heart and lungs, yet tennis requires top physical fitness and aerobic capacity.

Such sponsorship had particular advantages from the industry's perspective. It created the false association of smoking with vitality and good health, and it directly targeted women. Philip Morris essentially was taking advantage of the inadequate funding of women's sports by making itself a strong presence in this sector.

So we have an unhealthy product sponsoring a prestigious athletic event for women, an event that at least in the early days would probably not have been able to get started without such funding. Do we refuse this funding? Do we ban all cigarette promotions that appear to have some tie-in with health and fitness? Does the evil outweigh the good?

You are a feminist leader with convictions that women's athletic events should be promoted more strongly. The major funding for tennis and golf tournaments has been the tobacco industry, with no alternative major sponsors likely in the near future. Discuss your position regarding accepting such tobacco company sponsorships. Present your rationale as persuasively as you can.

The Old Joe Camel Controversy

In 1988 R. J. Reynolds stumbled upon a promotional theme for its slumping Camel brand. Using a sunglass-clad, bulbous-nosed cartoon camel that it called Joe, it instituted a $75 million-a-year advertising campaign. It featured Joe in an array of macho gear and targeted the campaign to appeal to younger male smokers who had been deserting the Camel brand in droves.

The campaign was an outstanding success. In only three years, Camel's share of sales among the 18- to 24-year age group almost doubled, from 4.4 percent to 7.9 percent.

But the appeal of Old Joe went far beyond the target age group. It was found to be highly effective in reaching children under 13, who were enamored with the character. Six-year-olds in the United States recognized Joe Camel at a rate nearly equal to their recognition of Mickey Mouse. Children as young as three could even identify the cartoon character with cigarettes. Of even more concern to critics, Camel's share of the market of underage children who smoke was nearly 33 percent, up from less than 1 percent before the Old Joe campaign. See Table 22.1 for other results of the survey.

TABLE 22.1   Survey Results of Knowledge and Attitudes Regarding Camel's Old Joe Advertisements

	Students	Adults
Have seen Old Joe	97.7%	72.2%
Know the product	97.5	67.0
Think ads look cool	58.0	39.9
Like Joe as friend	35.0	14.4
Smokers who identify Camel as favorite brand	33.0	8.7

Source: Data from the *Journal of the American Medical Assn.*, as presented in Walecia Konrad, "I'd Toddle a Mile for a Camel," *Business Week* (December 23, 1991), 34. The results are based on a survey of 1,055 students, ages 12 to 19 years, and 345 adults, aged 21 to 87 years.

Controversies Over Billboard Advertising

Critics of Uptown initially focused on its billboard advertising in African-American neighborhoods. They soon expanded their protests to cigarettes in general and to alcohol, and began whitewashing offending billboards. Their only recourse, they argued, was to use civil disobedience to attract attention to their cause.

Reverend Calvin O. Butts III, fiery pastor of Harlem's Abyssinian Baptist Church, led his flock to paint signs with black paint to denote their Afrocentric perspective. Agitation against billboards spread beyond Harlem. In Dallas, County Commissioner John Wiley Price led a group that whitewashed 25 billboards and were arrested on misdemeanor charges. And Chicago priest Michael Pfleger was also arrested for painting billboards. Antismoking and antibillboard activists were having a field day.

Business began heeding the mounting pressure. In June 1990, the Outdoor Advertising Association of America, representing 80 percent of billboard companies, recommended voluntary limits on the number of billboards advertising cigarettes and alcohol near schools, places of worship, and minority neighborhoods.

Targeting Foreign Markets

With increasing restraints on cigarette advertising in the United States and diminishing per capita consumption of cigarettes, the industry turned to foreign markets. But criticisms and restraints surfaced there also.

At least as early as 1984, the Royal College of Physicians in the United Kingdom harshly denounced tobacco usage, stating that smoking killed 100,000 people a year in the U.K. alone. But the Royal College particularly condemned the lack of availability of low-tar cigarettes, "which are practically unknown in the Third World. Developed countries bear a heavy responsibility for the worldwide epidemic of smoking."[5] Most of Europe imposed some bans on advertising by 1991.

---

[5] "Developing Countries: Governments Should Take Action Against Cigarettes before Too Many People Acquire the Potentially Lethal Habit," *New Scientist* (December 1, 1983), p. 42.

With Western Europe's mounting inhospitality to the industry, U.S. tobacco firms eagerly pushed into Asia, Africa, Eastern Europe, and the former Soviet Union. These were big markets and local cigarette makers were vulnerable to the aggressive efforts of U.S. firms.

Countries in the expanding sales area had few marketing or health labeling controls. In Hungary, for example, Marlboro cigarettes were even handed out to young fans at pop music concerts.[6]

ASSESSING THE CONTROVERSIES

Targeting Minorities

Was R. J. Reynolds with its new Uptown brand an ogre, as critics claimed? Without question, inner-city African-Americans had higher usage rates of tobacco and alcohol than their suburban counterparts. There was little doubt that the tobacco firms thought they had developed an effective targeting strategy with brands like Uptown. The dispute hinged on this: Are certain minority groups particularly susceptible to advertising that they need to be protected from potentially unsafe products?

Although proponents of controls argued that certain groups, such as young blacks, needed such protection, others saw that protection as paternalism. Even some black leaders decried the billboard whitewashing and the contentious preaching of certain ministers. Certainly, tempting people was hardly the same as oppressing them. After all, no one had to buy cigarettes and alcohol.

Regardless of the pro and con arguments concerning the susceptibility of inner-city youth to advertisements for unhealthy products, there was more validity to the claims of susceptibility when we consider the vulnerability of children to the attractive models found in most of these commercials and advertisements.

Finally, if legislation should be enacted to ban certain products from billboards, as was done with radio and TV advertising over two decades ago, where should the line be drawn? Should promotions in minority neighborhoods be banned for products that are economically extravagant, such as expensive athletic shoes? Or should promotions be banned for high-cholesterol foods that might cause high blood pressure, or for "muscle" cars?

Assessing Joe Camel

Not surprisingly, criticism abounded after the American Medical Association's disclosure of the study that found Joe Camel so appealing to children. The basis for the concern, of course, was that the popular ads would encourage children to start smoking.

RJR would not yield. It denied that the ads were effective with children: "Just because children can identify our logo doesn't mean they will use the product." It stoutly maintained its right to freedom of speech.[7]

---

[6] "The Tobacco Trade: The Search for El Dorado," *Economist* (May 16, 1992), p. 23.

[7] "Old Joe Must Go," *Advertising Age* (January 13, 1992).

Some advertising people believed RJR's stubbornness was misguided: "By placing Old Joe as a freedom-of-speech issue instead of an unintentional marketing overshoot, [it] risks goading Congress into bans and restrictions on all tobacco advertising … which would shift responsibility for tobacco products to the Food and Drug Administration [which] could regulate the tobacco industry into oblivion."[8]

In 1997, without fanfare, RJR quit using the character.

See the following box for identification of more cigarette issues.

Assessment of Tobacco's Push Overseas

A firm seems entitled to make all the profit it can. If certain markets are being severely constrained, should the firm not have the right to aggressively develop other markets? This is what the tobacco firms are doing.

The issue is clouded because while smoking is generally conceded to be hazardous to health, the risks are a long time in coming. As long as many people are willing to take the risk, should the industry be so negatively judged?

When sophisticated and aggressive promotional efforts are directed to countries where consumers are more easily swayed and far more vulnerable to promotional blandishments, does our perception of what is ethical and what is undesirable change? Should it change?

ISSUE BOX

CONTROVERSIES ABOUT SMOKING

The controversies concerning cigarettes go beyond those detailed in this chapter. For example:

- Should smoking be restricted in the workplace? in restaurants? on airplanes?
- What about some firms not allowing employees to smoke even when they are not at work?
- Should the tobacco industry pay for employee suits concerning their "right to smoke"?
- Should nonsmokers be protected from passive smoke?
- In general, are the rights of smokers being violated?

Discuss and even debate these questions and any other smoking issues you come up with.

---

[8] Craig Stoltz, "RJR Appears Intent on Sticking with Old Joe to the Bitter End," *Adweek Eastern Edition* (March 23, 1992), p. 18.

THE SIEGE INTENSIFIES

Allegations of Rigging Nicotine Levels

A new threat arose to severely test the complacency of the tobacco industry: charges of long-time rigging of nicotine levels to assure that smokers stay hooked. Adding fuel to such allegations were Brown & Williamson Tobacco Corp. internal documents, including a 54-page handbook, obtained by the *Wall Street Journal*, that indicated the tobacco companies had been adding ammonia-based compounds to their cigarettes. Such compounds essentially increase the potency of the nicotine a smoker actually inhales. The B & W documents asserted that Philip Morris's Marlboro, the top brand with a 30 percent share of the U.S. market at the time, may have been the first to use such ammonia technology. Regardless of who was the trailblazer, the practice seemingly had been widely emulated within the tobacco industry.[9]

Nicotine was viewed by most scientists as the active ingredient that caused cigarettes to be addictive. Anything that enhanced the delivery of this into the bloodstream, then, would increase the addictive potential. The industry would not admit this. It maintained that nicotine simply provided better flavor: "The primary purpose for using DAP [an ammonia additive] is to increase taste and flavor, reduce irritation, and to improve body." While admitting that this also increased nicotine delivery, a B & W spokesperson called this "an incidental effect."[10] And tobacco companies at that time still doggedly denied any links between cigarette smoking and heart disease, cancer, or other ailments.

But in 1996, newly disclosed documents suggested that Philip Morris, the nation's foremost tobacco company, had in place as far back as the 1970s a system to hide and destroy potentially damaging data about smoking and health because of liability suits: "These documents appear to be further evidence of the industry's extraordinary effort to keep information secret. These are just the tip of the iceberg of evidence of document destruction."[11]

Repercussions

The industry was already under heavy fire before the latest revelations regarding the ammonia component. The increasing pressure, spearheaded by David Kessler, the Food and Drug Administration's (FDA) commissioner, showed a sharp contrast to the situation when he assumed office in 1990. Then, a few health coalitions were complaining about smoking, but this had been going on for decades. Few people in government paid any attention, mostly because the tobacco industry seemed invulnerable: it had the support of powerful southern congressmen and it also had great monetary resources to provide for the finest legal arsenal and lobbying efforts.

---

[9] Alix M. Freedman, "Tobacco Firm Shows How Ammonia Spurs Delivery of Nicotine," *The Wall Street Journal* (October 18, 1995), pp. A1 and A6.

[10] *Ibid.*, p. A6.

[11] Alix M. Freedman and Milo Geyelin, "Philip Morris Allegedly Hid Tobacco Data," *The Wall Street Journal* (September 18, 1996), p. B11

Though perhaps not obvious to tobacco executives, the climate was subtly changing. In 1985, both Aspen and Vail, Colorado ski resorts, banned smoking in restaurants. Other scattered bans followed. The slow trend abruptly accelerated in 1993 when the Environmental Protection Agency declared smoke a carcinogen. By the end of that year, 436 cities had smoking restrictions. Smoking came to be banned from all domestic air flights regardless of length.

Even the courts were now joining the act. In addition to criminal investigations by the Justice Department in New York and Washington, thirteen other states were seeking reimbursement from the industry for the costs of treating smoking-related illnesses. More, the industry was facing eight class-action suits, filed by smokers claiming they became hooked while the industry concealed the addictive nature of its product. Dr. Kessler also added the resources of the FDA to take up the struggle against cigarettes.

Previous defense strategies of the industry had always been that it was a smoker's free choice to smoke despite an "unproven" risk of lung cancer, so how dare the government interfere. Now Dr. Kessler, given the newest revelations about the ability of the industry to control nicotine with its powerful addictive hold, had a new strategy to present to Capitol Hill. Former Surgeon General C. Everett Koop exhorted him, "Do anything you can" to regulate tobacco. "The country is going to be behind you."[12]

On August 10, 1995 in the White House, President Clinton, with Dr. Kessler standing nearby, unveiled tough proposed regulations on cigarette marketing and sales. This marked the new FDA role against tobacco and one of the most aggressive federal moves ever against the industry.

Even the seemingly fertile overseas markets were rising against tobacco. An aggressive European ad campaign by Philip Morris backfired and had to be abandoned amid a barrage of lawsuits, complaints to regulators, and government criticism. The campaign cited scientific studies to claim that second-hand smoke wasn't a meaningful health risk to nonsmokers. It even suggested that inhaling secondary smoke was less dangerous than eating cookies or drinking milk.[13]

The stakes were high, with Philip Morris's $11.4 billion in European tobacco sales in 1995. But resentment against the tobacco industry was rising by governments struggling to contain burgeoning health-care costs.

Joe Camel was doing somewhat better in Argentina, despite intense criticism by antismoking activists. The first such advertising campaign in Latin America saw sales of the formerly marginal Camel brand shooting up 50 percent, a gain perhaps reflecting that Argentina had no national cigarette age limit.[14]

---

[12] Laurie McGinley and Timothy Noah, "Long FDA Campaign And Bit of Serendipity Led to Tobacco Move," *The Wall Street Journal* (August 22, 1995), p. A4.

[13] Martin Du Dois and Tara Parker-Pope, "Philip Morris Campaign Stirs Uproar in Europe," *The Wall Street Journal* (July 1, 1996), p. B1.

[14] Jonathan Friedland, "Under Siege in the U.S., Joe Camel Pops Up Alive, Well in Argentina," *The Wall Street Journal* (September 10, 1996), p. B1.

THE INDUSTRY FIGHTS BACK

The fight was on. Tobacco firms as well as the advertising industry attacked with lawsuits against the FDA, while tobacco-state legislators desperately worked to replace the proposed regulations with friendlier laws. In the first half of 1996, more than $15 million was spent for lobbying. More millions went to campaign donations to influence lawmakers, and additional millions to defend against lawsuits.[15]

The tobacco industry had been notorious for defending its position aggressively and being confrontational. For example, the professor in Georgia whose study found that Joe Camel was almost as recognizable as Disney characters, thereby calling into question the tobacco industry's claims that their ads were not targeting children, became a target himself. The industry pressured the school administration to fire him. "The only protection he really had was tenure."[16] This saved his job.

Philip Morris has been the most aggressive player in attacking critics. In 1994 it sued the city of San Francisco, trying to overturn one of the nation's toughest anti-smoking ordinances. The ordinance had banned smoking in offices and would shortly also ban it in restaurants. Philip Morris sought to have the court declare the ordinance invalid and unenforceable.

Geoffrey Bible, chairman of Philip Morris, declared an all-out war on tobacco's enemies, with legal attacks and newspaper ads. "We are not going to be anybody's punching bag," he said. "When you are right and you fight, you win."[17] Bible had spent his career pushing Philip Morris around the world, and he practiced what he preached: smoking cigarettes and attacking all critics.

Those struggling to preserve the tobacco industry and its efforts to avoid regulation were by no means limited to cigarette producers. Tobacco was so ingrained in many sectors of our economy that many would suffer were it curbed—for example, local distributors, truckers, people who own and/or replenish vending machines, those involved with billboard ads for cigarettes, and the hundreds of thousands of vendors who saw cigarette sales as a major part of their total business, not to mention those tobacco growers in the southern states who could not countenance switching their crops to lower-yielding alternatives. Against the arguments that alternative employment would replace cigarette dependence, many looked back over decades of such dependence and cringed at the thought of losing it.

Results

Hopes that campaigns against smoking were becoming more effective were dispelled by a study published in the November 1998 *Journal of the American Medical*

---

[15] "Tobacco Lobbyists Spend Millions," *Cleveland Plain Dealer* (September 9, 1996), p. 8A.

[16] Example cited in Maureen Smith, "Tenure," *University of Minnesota Update* (November 1995), p. 4.

[17] Suein L. Hwang, "Philip Morris's Passion to Market Cigarettes Helps It Outsell RJR," *The Wall Street Journal* (October 30, 1995), p. A1.

Association. The research, carried out at 116 four-year colleges, found 28 percent of college students smoking in 1997, up from 23 percent in 1994. The report concluded that this is a cause for national concern.[18]

In 1998, Philip Morris's share of the U.S. cigarette market passed 50 percent for the first time ever. In addition to its aggressive use of the Marlboro Man on billboards and magazine ads, it had a sales-incentive program called Retail Masters that rewarded retailers with payouts based on sales and display of Philip Morris cigarettes. This program was particularly effective with the rapidly expanding cigarette outlet stores, numbering some 5,800 by 1998, that sold nothing but cigarettes at 10 to 15 percent less than convenience stores because of generous manufacturer rebates and display fees. Other tobacco firms also had incentive programs but they were outmuscled by Philip Morris.

Overseas, Philip Morris captured nearly a quarter of the cigarette market in Turkey. It did this by enlisting the help of influential people and lobbying heavily to eliminate the government's control of tobacco prices and distribution. Its prime bargaining chip was the promise that it would invest millions of dollars in the country. True to its word, Philip Morris opened a factory there in 1993, and expanded it into a $230 million facility. Now it could engineer cigarettes to appeal to Turkish tastes but with a stronger kick than local brands. Its salesmen, dressed as cowboys, spread across the country to 130,000 stores with a lavish in-store promotional and incentive plan. Of course, it advertised the Marlboro Man heavily, with cowboy scenes and panoramic vistas. In late 1996, pressured by antitobacco groups, Turkey's Parliament passed one of the strictest cigarette advertising bans in the world. Philip Morris got around this by omitting the word "Marlboro" in its ads and displays, but leaving the easily identifiable red chevron. The company also shrewdly noted that the ban did not cover all nontobacco products and events, and so its Marlboro jeans and other paraphernalia became best sellers and potent promoters of the brand.

Tobacco companies found a new target market for future smokers in women in developing countries. To woo this potential, they sponsored sporting and entertainment events geared to female audiences; they offered cigarettes with free crystal, designer scarves, and silk camisoles; they sent sample cigarettes as congratulatory gifts to new female college graduates. In the Philippines, a devoutly Catholic nation, calendars were even distributed featuring the Virgin Mary and other women saints praying over cigarette packs.[19]

---

[18] H. Wechsler et al., "Increased Levels of Cigarette Use Among College Students: A Cause for National Concern," *Journal of the American Medical Association,* vol. 280, no. 19 (November 18, 1998), pp. 1673–78.

[19] Information for this section has been compiled from a number of sources including Yumiko Ono, "For Philip Morris, Every Store Is a Battlefield," *The Wall Street Journal* (June 29, 1998), B1 and B4; Suein L. Hwang, "How Philip Morris Got Turkey Hooked On American Tobacco," *The Wall Street Journal* (September 11, 1998), pp. A1 and A8; and Stephanie Stapleton, "Tobacco Targeting Third-World Women," *Cleveland Plain Dealer* (November 10, 1998), p. 3-F.

THE TOBACCO DEAL

In spring 1997, new developments portended monumental changes for the tobacco industry in the United States. In late March, the solidarity of the industry was shaken as Liggett Group settled a lawsuit with 22 states, and in the process, finally admitted that smoking was addictive and caused cancer. Further information from Liggett showed that children were targeted for tobacco sales.

In the middle of April 1997, Philip Morris and RJR Nabisco began talks with attorneys general for 25 states suing to recover billions of dollars in public health-care costs for sick smokers. The industry sought protection from all current and future litigation and was willing to contribute an amazing $300 billion over a 25-year period to a settlement fund as well as making certain other concessions. When Congress took up ratifying the agreement in early 1998, it raised the price to $516 billion and cigarette makers were denied the legal immunity they sought in return. Not surprisingly, the industry did not accept this.

In November 1998, a milder deal was negotiated, amounting to $206 billion spread over 25 years. Undoubtedly tobacco's position was bolstered by a major victory that Reynolds scored in a Florida state court on May 5, 1997 where a jury found that the firm wasn't responsible for the death of a three-pack-a-day smoker who died of lung cancer at age 49. The trial had been closely watched as a bellwether for future litigation against the industry.

Forty-six states accepted the new deal. Four other states had already settled their individual suits for a total of $40 billion. The deal put an end to antismoking groups' hopes for a broader agreement that would combat teenage smoking and bring the industry under federal regulation.

WHAT CAN BE LEARNED?

Is it ethically right to vigorously promote a product seen by many as unsafe and even deadly? This issue gets to the heart of the whole matter of tobacco production and marketing. Considered by practically all health experts as dangerous and, in the long term, life threatening, tobacco had been protected by powerful governmental interests, even if such support was eroding.

Even though the industry at last stubbornly admitted some health charges, it refused to soften its aggressiveness in promoting its products. Worse was its aggressive invasion of third-world countries.

The industry is huge with stakeholders: tobacco growers, processors, retailers, tax collectors, influential people in the halls of government, even the lowly paster of billboard ads. Not the least of the supporters of the industry are the users themselves—even though this declines a little from year to year, except on college campuses. Loyal users tend to discount the health dangers as being both far in the future and affecting only a minority of users—"and never me!"

What about morality? It is easy for stakeholders to rationalize that any bad consequences are uncertain at best, that the good outweighs any bad possibilities.

Still, we wonder if the profit motive is not the overriding consideration, far ahead of societal health risks.

Too many times, what is ethical lies in the eyes of the beholder.

Does a militant minority represent acceptable behavior in promoting its own self-interest? In a pluralistic society, minorities are encouraged to present their positions. The issue becomes one of degree. What level of critical behavior—no matter how justified many might see such criticisms—is acceptable? Is white-washing billboards acceptable behavior? What about destroying offending bill-boards or firebombing the stores of opportunistic shopowners? Where do we draw the line? Furthermore, who is to be the judge of what is acceptable and unac-ceptable: a firebrand preacher, a government agency, the police department, the courts?

Is it not perfectly right for any firm, or industry, to pursue its own best inter-ests, as long as it stays within the present law? Ah, this is the rationale that sup-ports tobacco efforts, whether Joe Camel, targeting naive consumers, foreign mar-kets, or nicotine enhancement in pursuit of addiction: these actions formerly were considered entirely legal. Do not laws reflect the majority views on what is moral and ethical? Many would say that they do not reflect prevailing majority views, that they rather reflect the positions of powerful minority interests. Many would see tobacco regulations—or lack thereof—as such.

Perhaps the real issue is whether a firm's best interests should take prece-dence over those of its customers and of society. Either position can be argued. On the one hand, should not a firm seek to foster a better corporate image and bene-fit both society and itself? On the other, should not a firm seek to maximize its profitability to the benefit of stockholders, creditors, suppliers, employees and the like, regardless of outside critics?

Is a firm's public image of little consequence as long as it has a loyal body of customers who support it? This is the position taken by the tobacco industry: defi-ant of critics; secure in the loyalty of a sizable group of addicted customers; aided and abetted by powerful political interests whose constituents have an economic stake in the viability of the industry. For decades this mindset of disregard for the public image has successfully prevailed, despite the cries of critics including most of the medical profession.

Now, finally, could it be that the cigarette makers—and especially Geoffrey Bible of Phillip Morris, the industry's most ardent defender—have miscalculated and that they are mistakenly assuming that the past will ever dictate the future and that attitudes and power positions will remain unchanged?

Perhaps it is high time they seek to develop a more healthy cigarette, even if this lessens the addiction and alienates diehards who demand their nicotine cock-tail. At the least, one would think the prudent action in the face of ever-mounting concern and criticism would be to lower the decibels of their protests and their advertising and promotions, and maybe to embrace some social responsibility before such actions are forced upon them.

In today's litigious environment, callousness regarding society's growing con-cerns may be courting disaster. The tobacco industry proudly boasted that it had never lost a lawsuit accusing it of responsibility for lung cancer and other physical ills and deaths. The industry had always successfully defended itself on the grounds of unproven charges of cigarette smoking contributing to such health hazards, and also on the grounds of individual choice and individual freedom. Now this defense has crumbled. Some at least would see that the industry has capitulated to accept the $206 billion tobacco deal. Others would say that it is the state attorneys general who have capitulated in accepting a deal far milder than the 1997 one. Still, perhaps our litigious environment is on the verge of doing what lawmakers in a pluralistic society with many diverse agendas have been unable to do: bring the tobacco industry to heel. But what about third-world consumers?

In these learning insights we have raised more questions than answers or caveats. But the questions raised ought to be of concern to tobacco executives—and executives of other firms whose products and ways of doing business may not be in the best interests of the general public. A reckoning may be lurking in the wings.

CONSIDER

Can you propose other learning insights or ethical issues?

QUESTIONS

1. Do you actually think Joe Camel leads youngsters to become smokers when they get older? Why or why not?

2. Do you have any problems with the idea of militant ministers leading their followers to whitewash offensive billboards? If not, is tearing down such billboards acceptable? Please discuss as objectively as possible.

3. Do you consider the proof adequate that cigarettes pose a substantial health threat and should be banned or tightly constrained? If you accept this position, should tobacco growers be allowed to continue growing such "unsafe" harvests without restraints?

4. Playing the devil's advocate (one who argues an opposing point for the sake of debate), what arguments would you offer that the cigarette manufacturers should be permitted complete freedom in targeting developing countries?

5. How do you assess the relative merits of the tangible financial contributions that the tobacco industry has made to various minority groups and media, against the negative health consequences of smoking?

6. What is the ethical difference between promoting cigarettes and promoting fatty, cholesterol-laden foods?

7. Do you agree with banning cigarettes from public buildings, workplaces, restaurants, airplanes, and so on? Why or why not?

8. Are the rights of nonsmokers being too highly emphasized? Do smokers have any rights?

HANDS-ON EXERCISES

1. You are the public relations spokesperson for Philip Morris. You have been ordered by Geoffrey Bible to plan a public relations campaign to overturn some of the banning of cigarettes. Be as specific and creative as you can. How successful do you think such efforts would be?

2. You are an articulate young African-American woman who uses Uptown cigarettes and likes them. At a church outing, your minister denounces Uptowns and the company that makes them. Describe how you might respond to such a tirade against your favorite brand.

3. You have been asked by the executive committee of a major tobacco firm to draw up plans for changing the negative public image of the tobacco industry. The hope thereby is to defuse the probability of upcoming federal legislation that would be detrimental. What do you propose? Be as specific as possible.

TEAM DEBATE EXERCISES

1. A great controversy is brewing in the executive offices of Philip Morris. One group led by CEO Bible is strongly in favor of aggressively attacking all critics and defending cigarettes with no holds barred. Still, there is another group supported by some prominent board members who believe the company and the industry should soften its stance. Debate the two sides of this issue.

2. Debate the issue: The rights of nonsmokers are being emphasized too much. Smokers have rights, too.

3. Debate the great $206 billion deal of the tobacco industry. Who won? Should the attorneys general have held stronger against the industry? (You may need to research the provisions of the final agreement compared with what might have been.)

INVITATION TO RESEARCH

1. What is the current situation regarding overseas incursions by U.S. tobacco companies?

2. Has the tobacco industry encountered any new criticisms?

3. Has the Tobacco Deal been advantageous to the industry?

4. Has smoking by college students changed since the *JAMA* report of 1998?

5. Is Geoffrey Bible still alive, or has he died of lung cancer?

CHAPTER TWENTY-THREE

The Classic Contrast— Johnson & Johnson's Magnificent Crisis Management with Tylenol, but Then...

*I*n one of the greatest examples of superb crisis management, James Burke, CEO of Johnson & Johnson, in 1982 handled a catastrophe that involved loss of life in the criminal and deadly contamination of its flagship product, Tylenol. The company exhibited what has become a model for corporate responsibility to customers, regardless of costs.

Yet in a later day, the company showed a lapse in its customer concern, first with alleged price gouging for one of its cancer drugs, then in not disclosing the risk of liver damage from overusing Tylenol.

PRELUDE

It was September 30, 1982. On the fifth floor of the Johnson & Johnson (J & J) headquarters in New Brunswick, New Jersey, Chairman James E. Burke was having a quiet meeting with President David R. Clair. The two liked to hold such informal meetings every two months to talk over important but nonpressing matters that they usually did not get around to in the normal course of events. That day both men had reason to feel good, for J & J's sales and earnings were up sharply and the trend of business could hardly have been more promising. They even had time to dwell on some nonbusiness matters that sunny September morning.

Their complacency and self-satisfaction did not last long. Arthur Quill, a member of the executive committee, burst into the meeting. Consternation and anguish flooded the room as he brought word of cyanide deaths in Chicago that were connected to J & J's most important and profitable product, Extra-Strength Tylenol capsules.

THE COMPANY

Johnson & Johnson manufactures and markets a broad range of health care products in many countries of the world. Table 23.1 shows the various categories of products and their percent of total corporate sales. In 1981 J & J was number 68 on the *Fortune* 500 list of the largest industrial companies in the United States, and it had sales of $5.4 billion. It was organized into four industry categories: professional, pharmaceutical, industrial, and consumer. The professional division included products such as ligatures, sutures, surgical dressings, and other surgery-related items. The pharmaceutical division included prescription drugs, and the industrial area included textile products, industrial tapes, and fine chemicals.

The largest division was the consumer division, consisting of toiletries and hygienic products such as baby care items, first aid products, and nonprescription drugs. These products were marketed primarily to the general public and distributed through wholesalers and directly to independent and chain retail outlets.

Through the years, J & J had assiduously worked to cultivate an image of responsibility and trust. Its products were associated with gentleness and safety—for all customers, from babies to the elderly. The corporate sense of responsibility fully covered the products and actions of any firms that it acquired, such as McNeil Laboratories.

THE PRODUCT

The success of Tylenol, an acetaminophen-based analgesic, in the late 1970s and early 1980s had been sensational. It had been introduced in 1955 by McNeil Laboratories as an alternative drug to aspirin, one that avoided aspirin's side effects. In 1959 Johnson & Johnson had acquired McNeil Laboratories, and the company ran it as an independent subsidiary.

TABLE 23.1 **Contribution to Total Johnson & Johnson Sales of Product Categories, 1983**

Product Classification	Sales (Millions)	Percent of Total Company Sales
Surgical and First-Aid Supplies	$1,268	21%
Pharmaceuticals	1,200	20
Sanitary Napkins and Tampons	933	16
Baby Products	555	9
Diagnostic Equipment	518	9
Tylenol and Variants	460	8
Other (includes hospital supplies, dental products, contraceptives)	1,039	17
Total	$5,973	100%

Source: "After Its Recovery, New Headaches for Tylenol," *Business Week* (May 14, 1984), p. 137.

TABLE 23.2 Market Shares of Major Brands—Over-the-Counter Analgesic Market, 1981

Brand	Percent of Market
Tylenol	35.3
Anacin	13
Bayer	11
Excedrin	10.1
Bufferin	9

Source: "A Death Blow for Tylenol?" *Business Week* (October 18, 1982), p. 151.

By 1974 Tylenol sales had grown to $50 million at retail, primarily achieved through heavy advertising to physicians. A national consumer advertising campaign, instituted in 1976, proved very effective. By 1979 Tylenol had become the largest selling health and beauty aid in drug and food mass merchandising, breaking the 18-year domination of Procter & Gamble's Crest toothpaste. By 1982 Tylenol had captured 35.3 percent of the over-the-counter analgesic market. This was more than the market shares of Bayer, Bufferin and Anacin combined. Table 23.2 shows the competitive positions of Tylenol and its principal competitors in this analgesic market. Total sales of all Tylenol products went from $115 million in 1976 to $350 million in 1982, a whopping 204 percent increase in a highly competitive market. As such, Tylenol accounted for 7 percent of all J & J sales. More important, it contributed 17 percent of all profits.

Then catastrophe struck.

THE CRISIS

On a Wednesday morning in late September 1982, Adam Janus had a minor chest pain, so he purchased a bottle of Extra-Strength Tylenol capsules. He took one capsule and was dead by midafternoon. Later that same day, Stanley Janus and his wife also took capsules from the same bottle—both were dead by Friday afternoon. By the weekend four more Chicago-area residents had died under similar circumstances. The cause of death was cyanide, a deadly poison that can kill within 15 minutes by disrupting the blood's ability to carry oxygen through the body, thereby affecting the heart, lungs and brain. The cyanide had been used to contaminate Extra-Strength Tylenol capsules. Dr. Thomas Kim, chief of the critical care unit of Northwest Community Hospital in Arlington Heights, Illinois, noted, "The victims never had a chance. Death was certain within minutes."[1]

---

[1] Susan Tifft, "Poison Madness in the Midwest," *Time* (October 11, 1982), p. 18.

Medical examiners retrieved bottles from the victims' homes and found another 10 capsules laced with cyanide. In each case the red half of the capsule was discolored and slightly swollen, and its usual dry white powder had been replaced with a gray substance that had an almond odor. One of the capsules had 65 mg of cyanide—a lethal does is considered to be 50 mg.

The McNeil executives learned of the poisonings from reporters calling for comment about the tragedy—calls came from all the media, and then from pharmacies, doctors, hospitals, poison control centers, and hundreds of panicky consumers. McNeil quickly gathered information on the victims, causes of deaths, lot numbers on the poisoned Tylenol bottles, outlets where they had been purchased, dates when they had been manufactured, and the route they had taken through the distribution system.

After the deaths were linked to Tylenol, one of the biggest consumer alerts ever took place. Johnson & Johnson recalled batches and advised consumers not to take any Extra-Strength Tylenol capsules until the mystery had been solved. Drugstores and supermarkets across the country pulled Tylenol products from their shelves; it soon became virtually impossible to obtain Tylenol anywhere.

Those tracking down the mysterious contamination quickly determined that the poisoning did not occur in manufacturing, either intentionally or accidentally. The poisoned capsules had come from lots manufactured at both McNeil plants. Therefore, the tampering had to have happened in Chicago, since poisoning at both plants at the same time would have been almost impossible. The FDA suspected that someone unconnected with the manufacturer had bought the Tylenol over the counter, inserted cyanide in some capsules, then returned the bottles to the stores. Otherwise, the contamination would have been widespread, and not only in the Chicago area.

At this point, Johnson & Johnson was virtually cleared of any wrong-doing, but the company was stuck with having one of its major products publicly associated with poison and death, no matter how innocent it was. Perhaps the task of coping with the devastating impact of the tragedy would have been easier for Johnson & Johnson if the perpetrator were conclusively identified and caught. This was not to be, despite a special task force of 100 FBI agents and Illinois investigators who chased down more than 2,000 leads and filed 57 volumes of reports.[2]

COMPANY REACTION

Johnson & Johnson decided to elevate the management of the crisis to the corporate level and a game plan developed that company executives hoped would ensure eventual recovery. The game plan consisted of three phases: Phase I was to figure out what had actually happened; Phase II was to assess and contain the damage; and Phase III was to try to get Tylenol back into the market.

The company that had always tried to keep a low profile now turned to the media to provide it with the most accurate and current information, as well as to help it pre-

---

[2] "Tylenol Comes Back as Case Grows Cold," *Newsweek* (April 25, 1983), p. 16.

vent a panic. Twenty-five public relations specialists were recruited from Johnson & Johnson's other divisions to help McNeil's regular staff of 15. Advertising was suspended at first. All Tylenol capsules were recalled—31 million bottles with a retail value of more than $100 million. Through advertisements promising to exchange tablets for capsules, through 500,000 telegrams to doctors, hospitals, and distributors, and through statements to the media, J & J hoped to demystify the situation.

With proof that the tampering had not occurred in the manufacturing process, the company moved into Phase II. Financially it experienced immediate losses amounting to over $100 million, the bulk coming from the expense of buying unused Tylenol bottles from retailers and consumers and shipping them to disposal points. The cost of sending the telegrams was estimated at $500,000, and the costs associated with expected product liability suits were expected to run in the millions.

Of more concern to the management was the impact of the poisoning on the brand itself. Many predicted that Tylenol as a brand could no longer survive. Some suggested that Johnson & Johnson reintroduce the product under a new name to give it a fresh start and thus rid itself of the devastated brand image.

Surveys conducted by Johnson & Johnson about a month after the poisonings seemed to buttress the death of Tylenol as a brand name. In one survey 94 percent of the consumers were aware that Tylenol was involved with the poisonings. Although 87 percent of these respondents realized that the maker of Tylenol was not to blame for the deaths, 61 percent said they were not likely to buy Tylenol in the future. Even worse, 50 percent of the consumers said they would not use the Tylenol tablets either. The only promising result from the research was that 49 percent of the *frequent* users answered that they would eventually use Tylenol.[3]

The company found itself in a real dilemma. It wanted so much to keep the Tylenol name; after all, the acceptance had been developed by years of advertising. Now, was it all to be destroyed in a few days of adversity? On the one hand, if J & J brought Tylenol back too soon, before the hysteria had subsided, the product could die on the shelves. On the other hand, if the company waited too long to bring the product back, competitors might well gain an unassailable market share lead. The marketing research results were not entirely acceptable to Johnson & Johnson executives. One manager expressed the company's doubts: "The problem with consumer research is that it reflects attitudes and not behavior. The best way to know what consumers are really going to do is put the product back on the shelves and let them vote with their hands."[4] But what was the right timing?

Johnson & Johnson decided to rebuild the brand by focusing on the frequent users and then to expand to include other consumers. It hoped that a core of loyal users would want the product in both its tablet and capsule forms. In order to regain regular user confidence, J & J ran television commercials informing the public that the company would do everything it could to regain their trust. The commercials featured Dr. Thomas Gates, medical director of McNeil, urging consumers to continue

---

[3] Thomas Moore, "The Fight to Save Tylenol," *Fortune* (November 29, 1982), p. 48.
[4] *Ibid.*, p. 49.

to trust Tylenol: "Tylenol has had the trust of the medical profession and 100 million Americans for over 20 years. We value that trust too much to let any individual tamper with it. We want you to continue to trust Tylenol."[5]

Johnson & Johnson also tried to encourage Tylenol capsule users to switch to tablets, which are more difficult to sabotage. In an advertising campaign it offered to exchange tablets for capsules at no charge. In addition it placed 76 million coupons in Sunday newspaper ads good for $2.50 toward the purchase of Tylenol.

Finally, it designed a tamper-resistant package to prevent the kind of tragedy that occurred in Chicago. Extra-strength capsules were now sold only in new triple-sealed packages. The flaps of the box were glued shut and were visibly torn apart when opened. The bottle's cap and neck were covered with a tight plastic seal printed with the company name, and the mouth of the bottle was covered with an inner foil seal. Both the box and the bottle were labeled, "Do Not Use If Safety Seals Are Broken." This triple-seal package cost an additional 2.4 cents per bottle, but Johnson & Johnson hoped it would instill consumer confidence in the safety of the product and spur sales. In addition the company offered retailers higher-than-normal discounts— up to 25 percent on orders.

Consumers who said they had thrown away their Tylenol after the scare were given a toll-free number to call, and they received $2.50 in coupons too—in effect, a free bottle, since bottles of 24 capsules or 30 tablets sold for about $2.50.

Over 2,000 salespeople from all Johnson & Johnson domestic subsidiaries were mobilized to persuade doctors and pharmacists to again begin recommending Tylenol tablets to patients and customers. This was similar to the strategy initially used when the product was introduced some 25 years before.

The Outcome

Immediately after the crisis, J & J's market share plunged from 35.3 percent of the pain reliever market to below 7 percent. Competitors were quick to take advantage of the situation. Upjohn Company and American Home Products Corporation were seeking Food and Drug Administration permission to sell an over-the-counter version of ibuprofen, a popular prescription pain reliever. Upjohn also granted marketing rights for its brand, Nuprin, to Bristol-Myers Co., maker of Bufferin, Excedrin, and Datril. Upjohn's prescription brand, Motrin—a stronger formulation than Nuprin—was generating some $200 million in 1982, making Motrin the company's biggest-selling drug. And lurking in the wings was mighty Procter & Gamble Company (P&G), the world's heaviest advertiser. P&G was launching national ads for Norwich aspirin and was test-marketing a coated capsule containing aspirin granules.

Yet, there were some encouraging signs for J & J. When *Psychology Today* polled its readers regarding whether Tylenol would survive as a brand name, 92 percent thought Tylenol would survive the incident. This figure corresponded closely with the results of another survey conducted by Leo Shapiro, an independent market

[5] Judith B. Gardner, "When a Brand Name Gets Hit by Bad News," *U.S. News & World Report* (November 8, 1982), p. 71.

researcher, just two weeks after the deaths occurred, in which 91 percent said they would probably buy the product again.

Psychology Today tried to get at the roots of such loyalty and roused comments such as these:

> A 23-year old woman wrote that she would continue to use Tylenol because she felt that it was "tried and true."

> A 61-year old woman said that the company had been "honest and sincere."

> And a young man thought Tylenol was an easy name to say.[6]

Such survey results presaged an amazing comeback: J & J's conscientious actions paid off. By May 1983 Tylenol had regained almost all the market share lost the previous September; its market share reached 35 percent, which it held until 1986, when another calamity struck.

New industry safety standards had been developed by the over-the-counter drug industry in concert with the Food and Drug Administration for tamper-resistant packaging. Marketers under law had to select a package "having an indicator or barrier to entry, which if breached or missing, can reasonably be expected to provide visible evidence to the consumer that the package has been tampered with or opened."[7] Despite toughened package standards, in February 1986, a Westchester, New York, woman died from cyanide-laced Extra-Strength Tylenol capsules. The tragedy of 3½ years before was being replayed. J & J immediately removed all Tylenol capsules from the market and offered refunds for capsules consumers had already bought.

Now the company made a major decision. It decided no longer to manufacture any over-the-counter capsules because it could not guarantee their safety from criminal contamination. Henceforth, the company would market only tablets and so-called caplets, which were coated and elongated tablets that are easy to swallow. This decision was expected to cost $150 million. The president explained: "People think of this company as extraordinarily trustworthy and responsible, and we don't want to do anything to damage that."[8]

By July 1986 Tylenol had regained most of the market share lost in February, and it now stood at 32 percent.

THE INGREDIENTS OF CRISIS MANAGEMENT

Johnson & Johnson was truly a management success in its handling of the Tylenol problem. It overcame the worst kind of adversity, that in which human life was lost in using one of its products, and a major product at that. Yet, in only a few months it recouped most of its lost market share and regained its public image of corporate

---

[6] Carin Rubenstein, "The Tylenol Tradition," *Psychology Today* (April 1983), p. 16.

[7] "Package Guides Studied," *Advertising Age* (October 18, 1982), p. 82.

[8] Richard W. Stevenson, "Johnson & Johnson's Recovery," *The New York Times* (July 5, 1986), pp. 33–34.

responsibility and trust. What accounted for the success of J & J in overcoming such adversity?

We can identify five significant factors:

1. Keeping communication channels open
2. Taking quick, corrective action
3. Keeping faith in the product
4. Protecting the public image at all costs
5. Aggressively bringing back the brand

Effective communication has seldom been better done. Rapport must be gained with the media, to enlist their support and even their sympathy. Alas, this is not easily done, for the press is inclined to sensationalize, criticize, and take sides against the big corporation. Johnson & Johnson gained the needed rapport through corporate openness and cooperation. In the disaster's early days it sought good two-way communication, with the media furnishing information from the field while J & J gave full and honest disclosure of its internal investigation and corrective actions. Important for good rapport, company officials need to be freely available and open to the press. Unfortunately, this goes against most executives' natural bent so that a spirit of antipathy often is fostered.

When product safety is in jeopardy, quick corrective action must be taken, *regardless* of the cost. This usually means immediate recall of the affected product, and this can involve millions of dollars. Even if the fault lies with only an isolate batch of products, a firm may need to recall them all since public perception of the danger likely will transfer to all units of that brand.

Johnson & Johnson kept faith with its product and brand name, despite the counsel of experts who thought the Tylenol name should be abandoned because public trust could never be regained. Of course, the company was not at fault: There was no culpability, no carelessness. The cause was right. Admittedly, in keeping faith with a product there is a thin line between a positive commitment and recalcitrant stubbornness to face up to any problem and accept any blame. But J & J's faith in Tylenol was justified, and without it the company would have had no chance of resurrecting the product and its market share.

Johnson & Johnson strove to protect its public image of being a socially responsible and caring firm. The following information box discusses *social responsibility* and presents the J & J credo regarding this. It is interesting to note that this credo is still prominently positioned in company annual reports ten years later. If there was to be any chance for a fairly quick recovery from adversity, this public image had to be guarded, no matter how beset it was. With the plight of Tylenol well known, with corrective actions prompt and thorough, many people were thus assured that safety was restored. We should note here that for the public image to be regained under adverse circumstances, the corrective actions must be well publicized. Public relations efforts and good communication with the media are essential for this. And, again, it helps when the fault of the catastrophe is clearly not the firm's.

A superb job was done in aggressively bringing back the Tylenol brand. In so doing, coordination was essential. Efforts to safeguard the public image had to be reasonably successful, the cause of the disaster needed to be conclusively established, the likelihood of the event ever happening again had to be seen as virtually impossible. Then aggressive promotional efforts could fuel the recovery.

INFORMATION BOX

SOCIAL RESPONSIBILITY AND THE JOHNSON & JOHNSON'S CREDO REGARDING IT

We can define social responsibility as the sense of responsibility a firm has for the needs of society, over and above its commitment to maximizing profits and stockholders interests. The following credo of J & J illustrates the wide circle of corporate social responsibility that more and more firms are beginning to accept.

Johnson & Johnson's Credo[9]

We believe our first responsibility is to the doctors, nurses, and patients, to mothers and all others who use our products and services. In meeting their needs everything we do must be of high quality. We must constantly strive to reduce our costs in order to maintain reasonable prices. Customers' orders must be serviced promptly and accurately. Our suppliers and distributors must have an opportunity to make a fair profit.

We are responsible to our employees, the men and women who work with us throughout the world. Everyone must be considered as an individual. We must respect their dignity and recognize their merit. They must have a sense of security in their jobs. Compensation must be fair and adequate, and working conditions clean, orderly, and safe. Employees must feel free to make suggestions and complaints. There must be equal opportunity for employment, development, and advancement for those qualified. We must provide competent management, and their actions must be just and ethical.

We are responsible to the communities in which we live and work and to the world community as well. We must be good citizens—support good works and charities and bear our fair share of taxes. We must encourage civic improvements and better health and education. We must maintain in good order the property we are privileged to use, protecting the environment and natural resources.

Our final responsibility is to our stockholders. Business must make a sound profit. We must experiment with new ideas. Research must be carried on, innovative programs developed and mistakes paid for. New equipment must be purchased, new facilities provided, and new products launched. Reserves must be created to provide for adverse times. When we operate according to these principles, the stockholders should realize a fair return.

"Such statements are only pious platitudes. Social responsibility requires more than lip service." How would you answer this?

---

[9] From a company recruiting brochure and annual reports.

Johnson & Johnson's efforts to come back necessarily focused on correcting the problem. Initially it designed a tamper-resistant container to prevent the kind of tragedy that had occurred in Chicago. Extra-strength capsules were now to be sold only in new triple-sealed packages. When another death occurred in 1986, the company dropped capsules entirely and offered Tylenol only in tablet form.

With the safety features in place, J & J then used heavy promotion. This included consumer advertising, with the theme of safety assurance and company social responsibility. J & J offered to exchange capsules for tablets at no charge. It offered millions of newspaper coupons good for $2.50 toward the purchase of Tylenol. Retailers were also given incentives to back Tylenol through discounts, advertising allowances, and full refunds for recalled capsules with all handling costs paid. These efforts, directed to consumers and retailers alike, bolstered dealer confidence in the resurgence of the brand.

ANOTHER SIDE OF JOHNSON & JOHNSON

Ten years later, the customer empathy of J & J seemed to have changed. First there were malpricing allegations concerning a new drug to treat colon cancer. Then Tylenol itself came under critical scrutiny about side-effect coverups.

Levamisole

In May 1992 publicity surfaced that J & J was guilty of "unconscionable" pricing of levamisole, the drug used to treat colon cancer. The charge came from a distinguished physician and cancer expert, Charles G. Moertel of the Mayo Clinic, at the annual meeting of the American Society of Clinical Oncology. Under J & J's brand name, Ergamisol, levamisole cost patients (or their insurance companies) $1,250 to $1,500 for a year's supply.

The controversy arose not so much from the absolute price of the life-saving drug, but from its price relative to a 30-year-old veterinary version of the drug, which farmers used to treat their sheep for parasites. This version cost only $14. The dispute first came to light when an Illinois farmer being treated for cancer noticed that her pills contained the same active ingredients she used to deworm her sheep.

Under sponsorship of the National Cancer Institute, Dr. Moertel and others found that levamisole, combined with a staple chemotherapy drug, was spectacularly effective in patients with advanced colon cancer. Dr. Moertel lauded it: "We now have a therapy with a national impact. We were specifically promised that it would be marketed at a reasonable price."[10]

Johnson & Johnson doggedly defended its pricing of the consumer version of the drug thus: "The price of the product reflects costly research over decades to determine possible uses in humans for other diseases."[11] J & J also pointed out that

[10] Marilyn Chase, "Doctor Assails J & J Price Tag on Cancer Drug," *The Wall Street Journal* (May 20, 1992), pp. B1, B8.

[11] *Ibid.*, p. B1.

sales were less than $15 million a year, a relatively modest amount for a pharmaceutical product. At the same time, the company claimed to have rerun parts of 1,400 studies involving 40,000 patients in seeking new applications of the drug in humans.

Dr. Moertel dismissed J & J's justification for the high prices as being necessary to meet high research and regulatory costs in preparing the drug for human consumption. He maintained that the National Cancer Institute, funded by American taxpayers, sponsored the studies. "The company just supplied the pills, which cost pennies." Moertel raised the question whether a new use for an old drug—a windfall—should justify a price surge. "Just because aspirin was found to improve your risk of heart attack, should you charge more?"[12]

The bad publicity now confronting J & J was not confined to the print media. TV news programs, such as *20/20*, soon featured this controversy along with criticisms of drug pricing of the entire pharmaceutical industry. Compounding the problem, the spokespersons for J & J and the other pharmaceutical firms did not publicly uphold their positions convincingly.

Unwarned Dangers of Using Tylenol

In January 1998, *Forbes* magazine revealed more questions about J & J's drive for profit-maximization at the expense of customers. It cited specific instances of children and adults being grievously affected by overdosing of Tylenol.

For example, Lucy Keele, 5 years old, had the flu and her mother gave her four extra tablets in one day. The overdose of Tylenol destroyed her liver and within a week she was dead. The bitter irony was that the product's advertising slogan was, "Nothing's safer."[13]

Forbes alleged that hundreds of fatalities and serious liver injuries resulted from acetaminophen, the active ingredient of Tylenol, and that J & J had to pay out millions of dollars in legal settlements, most of these under agreements requiring plantiffs not to disclose the terms. Children, drinkers, and those undernourished were most at risk, with consequences even life threatening.

Acetaminophen has all of aspirin's effectiveness with fevers and pain, but without aspirin's tendency to upset the stomach, nor the one-in-a-million chance of aspirin causing Reye's syndrome, a severe nervous system complication for children. Millions of people use Tylenol without ill effects.

The gist of *Forbes'* complaint was that Tylenol labels did not sufficiently spell out liver damage risks. Sure, the labels warned in red letters not to use if the package had been tampered with, a throwback to the cyanide days of 1982. And after cases like Lucy Keele, J & J strengthened the warning label a little at a time. But the severe consequences of overdosing or using if you drank, were downplayed. Why was J & J so reluctant to publicize the hazards? Was it due to an innocent oversight, or because it might scare people away?

---

[12] *Ibid.*, p. B8.

[13] Thomas Easton and Stephen Herrera, "J & J's Dirty Little Secret," *Forbes* (January 12, 1998), p. 42.

Finally, after decades of doing little to reveal the hazards of using Tylenol, now perhaps because of the adverse publicity, the company in early July 1998 announced it was redrafting Tylenol labeling. Now it would include a warning that people who consume three or more alcoholic drinks a day should consult a physician before taking the drug, and heavy drinkers "may be at increased risk for liver damage when taking more than the recommended dose."[14]

UPDATE

Johnson & Johnson's is truly a success story, an enduring growth company. Over the last ten years revenues and profits have steadily risen every year. Revenues reached $22.6 billion in 1997, with net income $3.3 billion. The company ranks as the largest and most diversified health care company in the world. Its products now range from blockbuster prescription drugs, to professional products such as sutures, surgical accessories, and catheters, to a wide list of consumer products such as Tylenol, bandages, and toiletries.

With this broad product mix, how important is Tylenol to J & J today? It is still plenty important. Of the company's $22.6 billion revenues for 1997, it is estimated that $1.3 billion or almost 6 percent came from Tylenol. (In 1982, at the time of the contamination, Tylenol contributed 8 percent of the $5.9 billion total company sales.) J & J has heavily promoted Tylenol to maintain this prominence. *Advertising Age* estimated the company's domestic ad budget for Tylenol at $250 million, more than Coca-Cola spent on Coke.[15] In 1997, Tylenol held an overwhelming share of the acetaminophen market, and 30 percent of the combined market for branded cold, headache, and fever remedies.

Consequently, J & J's reluctance to be truly forthright about the dangers is not surprising. As Easton and Herrera of *Forbes* observed, "It's a tricky business to keep your customers from hurting themselves but not scare them away."[16]

But did J & J owe its customers more disclosure? This reluctant warning of the risks of overdosing in any case represents an about-face in concern for customers from the actions taken in 1982 and 1986 in removing all Tylenol capsules from the market without hesitation.

WHAT CAN BE LEARNED?

Any company's nightmare is having its product linked to death or injury. Such a calamity invariably results in fear and loss of public confidence in the product and the firm. At worst, such disaster can kill a company, as happened with some canned-food firms whose products were contaminated with the deadly botulism toxin. The

---

[14] Thomas Easton and Stephan Herrera, "Better Later Than Never," *Forbes* (August 10, 1998), p. 14.

[15] *Ibid.*, p. 44.

[16] *Ibid.*

more optimistic projections would have a firm losing years of time and money it had invested in a brand, with the brand never able to regain its former robustness. In the throes of the catastrophe, J & J executives grappled with the major decision of abandoning the brand at the height of its popularity or keeping it. The decision could have gone either way. Now with hindsight, we know that the decision not to abandon was unmistakably correct, but at the time it was recklessly courageous.

Faced with a catastrophe, a brand may still be saved, but cost might be staggering. J & J successfully brought back Tylenol, but it cost hundreds of millions of dollars. The company's size at the time, over $5 billion in sales from a diversified product line, enabled it to handle the costs without jeopardy. A smaller firm would not have been able to weather this, especially without a broad product line.

Whenever product safety is an issue, the danger of lawsuits must be reckoned with. In the absence of corporate neglect, the swift constructive reaction, and the fact that the company could hardly have anticipated a madman, J & J escaped the worst scenario regarding litigation. Still, hundreds of millions of dollars in lawsuits were filed. Such suits accused J & J of failing to package Tylenol in a tamper-proof container, and the legal expenses of defending were high. The threat of litigation must be a major consideration for any firm. Even if the organization is relatively blameless, legal costs can run into the millions, and no one can predict the decisions of juries.

Copycat crimes are a danger. Although other firms in an industry stand to gain an advantage in a competitor's crisis, they and firms in related industries need to be alert for copycat crimes. By November, a month after the deaths, the Food and Drug Administration had received more than 270 reports of chemicals, pills, poisons, needles, pins, and razor blades in everything from food to drinks to medications. Fortunately, no deaths resulted from these incidents. But FDA Commissioner Hayes worried: "My greatest fear is that because of the notoriety of the case and the financial damage to the company, someone else will take out his or her grudges on a product and do something similar."[17] Actually, the Tylenol case was not the first time products had been deliberately contaminated. Eyedrops, nasal sprays, milk of magnesia, foods, and cosmetics have all been targets of tampering. An Oregon man was sentenced to 20 years in prison for attempting to extort diamonds from grocery chains by putting cyanide in food products on their shelves.

A firm can come back from extreme adversity with good crisis management. Certainly, one of the major things we can learn from this case is that it is possible to come back from extreme adversity. Before the Tylenol episode, most experts did not realize this. The general opinion was that severe negative publicity resulted in such an image destruction that recovery could take years. The most optimistic predictions were that Tylenol might recover to about a 20 to 21 percent market share in a year; the pessimistic predictions were that the brand would never recover and should be abandoned.[18] Actually, in eight months, Tylenol had regained almost all

---

[17] "Lessons That Emerge from Tylenol Disaster," *U.S. News & World Report* (October 18, 1982), p. 68.
[18] "J & J Will Pay Dearly to Cure Tylenol," *Business Week* (November 20, 1982), p. 37.

of its market share, to a satisfactory 35 percent. For such a recovery, a firm has to manifest unselfish concern, quick corrective action, and unsparing spending, and it must have a good public image before the catastrophe.

Contingency planning can aid crisis management. Although not all crisis possibilities can be foreseen, or even imagined, many can be identified. For example, contingency plans for worse-case scenarios can be developed for the possibility of food and medicine tampering or the loss of major executives in an accident of some sort. Sometimes in such planning, precautionary moves may become evident for minimizing the potential dangers. For example, with food and medicine tampering, different containers and sealed bottle tops might virtually eliminate the danger. And with executive accidents, many firms have a policy that key executives not fly on the same flight or ride in the same car.

Behavior may lapse: good deeds and favorable publicity may not be enduring. Accusations in 1992 of J & J's "unconscionable" drug pricing became widely publicized. Criticisms focused on major price differences for essentially the same drug. Were these the "reasonable prices" that the company credo promised, or the best interest of customers that was so superbly manifested ten years before?

The reluctance to fully disclose the risks on Tylenol labels was not as widely publicized as levamisole. J & J was fairly successful in downplaying the accusations and for a while thought it more worthwhile (that is, profitable) to settle matters in the courts rather than risk scaring other customers. Of course, lawsuits did nothing to bring back damaged livers, and worse. Under new top management, the evidence suggested that J & J was no longer the customer-responsive firm that it was with CEO James Burke in the traumatic days of 1982.

We always hate to see the best interests of customers subordinated to company profitability. J & J had shown a major commitment to customers in the Tylenol tampering catastrophe, and business schools reveled in case studies of this wonderful paragon of corporate responsibility and crisis management. Now our idol appears tarnished by short-sighted self-interest. The company credo talks about the first responsibility being to those "who use our products and services." One wonders whether J & J in recent years has forgotten that responsibility and manifesto.

CONSIDER

Can you think of other learning insights?

QUESTIONS

1. Did J & J move too far in recalling all Extra-Strength Tylenol capsules? Would not a sufficient action have been to recall only those in the Chicago area, thus saving millions of dollars? Discuss.

2. How helpful do you think the marketing research results were in the decision on keeping the Tylenol name?

3. "We must assume that someone had a terrible grudge against J & J to have perpetrated such a crime." Discuss.

4. What justification do you think Johnson & Johnson could offer for its levamisole pricing that would be generally acceptable to the press and public opinion?

5. How do you reconcile the great concern of J & J for its customers during the Tylenol scare, and its seemingly callousness over levamisole pricing and incomplete warning on labels of Tylenol? On balance, what is your assessment of the company regarding (a) its public image, (b) its concern for customers, (c) its ethical commitment?

6. "The Tylenol episode represents great crisis management. Ethics was hardly a factor." Do you agree that this case does not really belong in the ethics section of this book?

HANDS-ON EXERCISES

1. Assume this scenario: It has been established that the fault of the contamination was accidental introduction of cyanide at a company plant. Given this scenario, how will you, as CEO of J & J, direct your recovery strategy? Give your rationale.

2. Assume the role of the person responsible for the pricing of levamisole for treatment of colon cancer. What do you advise the executive committee regarding any pricing changes after the negative publicity in May 1992?

3. It is 1998, and publicity has surfaced of hundreds of deaths and destroyed livers due to the misuse of Tylenol. Lawyers and other critics are hounding the company for its labeling negligence. A hoard of reporters are besieging company headquarters. Describe your actions as chief representative of the company.

TEAM DEBATE EXERCISES

1. Debate both sides of the burning issue, at the height of the crisis, of keeping the Tylenol name and trying to recoup it, or abandoning it. You must not use the benefit of hindsight for this exercise.

2. Debate this dilemma relative to full disclosure on Tylenol packages of risks from overdosing: To keep customers from hurting themselves but not scare them away.

INVITATION TO RESEARCH

1. What is the situation today with levamisole (or Ergamisole) pricing?

2. How complete is the labeling of Tylenol today with full risk disclosure?

CHAPTER TWENTY-FOUR

Conclusions: What Can Be Learned?

*I*n considering mistakes, three things are worth noting: (1) even the most successful organizations make mistakes but survive as long as they maintain a good "batting average," (2) mistakes should be effective teaching tools for avoiding similar errors in the future, and (3) firms can bounce back from adversity and turn around.

We can make a number of generalizations from these mistakes and successes. Of course management is a discipline that does not lend itself to laws or axioms, because exceptions to every principle or generalization can be found. Still, the decision-maker does well to heed the following insights. For the most part they are based on specific corporate experiences and are transferable to other situations and other times.

INSIGHTS REGARDING OVERALL ENTERPRISE PERSPECTIVES

Importance of Public Image

The impact, for good or bad, of an organization's public image was a common thread through a number of cases—for example, Nike, Continental, Harley Davidson, Southwest Airlines, Saturn, United Way, Boston Beer, the tobacco industry, and Johnson & Johnson.

Nike shows the power of an image that was compatible with the product and attractive to the target market. The carefully nurtured association with some of the most esteemed athletes in the world, men and women, whom many of its customers were eager to emulate, if only in their dreams, propelled Nike and its "swoosh" logo to dominance in the athletic apparel industry. Still, we saw a positive image becoming tarnished for Nike.

Continental Airlines is a case for hope. It shows that a reputation in the pits, not only with employees but with the general public, can be resurrected and revitalized, even over a short period of time, but it takes inspired leadership to do this. And this Gordon Bethune, its new CEO, supplied.

Harley Davidson, the cycle maker, showed an image turnaround also, only it took decades to accomplish. The image of the black-jacketed motorcyclist was a disaster, but in the 1980s this turned around to become even a status symbol. Harley executives helped develop the new mystique, and then exploited it.

Southwest's image of friendliness, great efficiency, and unbeatable prices propelled it to an unassailable position among short-haul airlines. Now it seeks to expand its image to longer hauls.

The nonprofit United Way was brought to its knees by revelations about the excesses of its long-time chief executive, William Aramony. Donations dwindled and local chapters withheld funds from the national organization as the reputation of the largest charitable organization was sullied.

As for the tobacco industry, it seems to be forever putting its foot in its mouth in its stubborn quest to maximize profits at any cost.

Johnson & Johnson gained a great image of undeviating concern for its customers, regardless of cost. In recent years, it has let this concern and image slip in a more aggressive pursuit of profit.

Other examples of capitalizing on a positive image are Saturn and Boston Beer. On the other hand, Planet Hollywood's nebulous association with celebrities proved fragile at best.

The importance of a firm's public image is undeniable, yet some firms continue to disregard this and either act in ways detrimental to image or else ignore the constraints and opportunities that a reputation affords.

Power of the Media

We have seen or suspected the power of the media in a number of cases. Coca-Cola, Nike, United Way, IBM, and the tobacco industry are obvious examples. This power is often used critically—to hurt a firm's public image. The media can fan a problem or exacerbate an embarrassing or imprudent action. In particular, this media focus can trigger the herd instinct, in which increasing numbers of people join in protests and public criticism. And the media in their zeal can sometimes cross the line, as in singling out Nike for all the employment abuses in third-world countries.

We can make these generalizations regarding image and its relationship with the media:

1. It is desirable to maintain a stable, clear-cut image and undeviating objectives.

2. It is difficult and time-consuming to upgrade an image.

3. To satisfy negative media mindset, new top management may be needed if image is to be upgraded.

4. A good image can be quickly lost if a firm relaxes in an environment of aggressive competition.

5. Well-known firms, and not-for-profit firms dependent on voluntary contributions, are especially vulnerable to critical public scrutiny and must use great care in safeguarding their reputations.

No Guarantee of Success

That success does not guarantee continued success or freedom from adversity is a sobering realization that must come from examining these cases. Many of the mistakes occurred in notably successful organizations, such as Harley Davidson, IBM, Euro Disney, Nike, Boeing, Toys Я Us, Maytag, Met Life, United Way, even Coca Cola. How could things go so badly for such firms conditioned to success? The three C's mindset offers an explanation for this perversity.

The Three C's Mindset

We can also call this the "king-of-the-hill" syndrome. With such an organizational climate, success actually brings vulnerability. The three C's—complacency, conservatism, and conceit—can blanket leading organizations. To avoid this, a constructive attitude of never underestimating competitors can be fostered by:

- Bringing fresh blood into the organization for new ideas and different perspectives
- Establishing a strong and continuing commitment to customer service and satisfaction
- Conducting periodic corporate self-analyses designed to detect weaknesses as well as opportunities in their early stages
- Continually monitoring the environment and being alert to any changes (more about this later)

The environment is dynamic, sometimes with subtle and hardly recognizable changes, at other times with violent and unmistakable changes. To operate in this environment, an established firm must be on guard to defend its position.

Adversity Need Not Be Forever

Just as a dominant firm can lose its momentum and competitive position, so can a faltering organization be turned around. So significant and even inspiring is this possibility, that we devoted Part I to major comeback firms: Continental Airlines, Harley Davidson, and IBM.

If a faltering firm can at least maintain some semblance of viability, it has hope, although not certainty. We wonder whether Boston Chicken and Planet Hollywood can come back, and whether Toys Я Us can regain its stature as the major factor in the toy industry.

PLANNING INSIGHTS

What Should Our Business Be?

An organization's business, its mission and purpose, should be thought through, spelled out clearly, and well communicated by those involved in policy making.

Otherwise, the organization lacks unified and coordinated objectives, which is akin to trying to navigate without a map.

Good judgment suggests choosing safe rather than courageous goals. The high-risk orientations of such new enterprises as Boston Chicken and Planet Hollywood represented abuses of business and investor judgment.

Determining what a firm's business is or should be gives a starting point for specifying goals. Several elements help with this determination.

The firm's *resources and distinctive abilities and strengths* should play a major role in determining its goals. It is not enough to wish for a certain status or position if resources and competence do not warrant this. To take an extreme example, a railroad company can hardly expect to transform itself into an airline, even though both may be in the transportation business. A Wal-Mart is hardly likely to successfully imitate a Neiman Marcus.

Environmental and competitive opportunities ought to be considered. The initial inroads of foreign carmakers in the United States stemmed from environmental opportunities for energy-efficient vehicles, at a time when U.S. carmakers had ignored this area. Southwest Air similarly found opportunity in lowest prices for short hops that its bigger competitors could not match without losing money.

The Right Growth Orientation

The opposite of a growth commitment is a status-quo philosophy, one uninterested in expansion or the problems and work involved. Harley Davidson was content, despite being pushed around by foreign competitors, until eventually a new management reawakened it decades later.

In general, how tenable is a low-growth or no-growth philosophy? Although at first glance it seems workable, such a philosophy sows the seeds of its own destruction. More than four decades ago the following insight was pointed out:

> Vitality is required even for survival; but vitality is difficult to maintain without growth, at least in the American business climate. The vitality of a firm depends on the vigor and ambition of its members. The prospect of growth is one of the principal means by which a firm can attract able and vigorous recruits.[1]

Consequently, a firm not obviously growth-minded finds it difficult to attract able people. Customers see a growing firm as reliable, eager to please, and constantly improving. As we saw with OfficeMax, suppliers and creditors tend to give preferential treatment to a growth-oriented firm because they hope to retain it as a customer and client when it reaches large size.

But emphasizing growth can be carried too far. Somehow the growth must be kept within the abilities of the firm to handle. Several cases, such as Wal-Mart, McDonald's, and Southwest Air, showed how firms can grow rapidly without losing control. But we also have the bungled growth efforts of Maytag's Hoover Division in

---

[1] Wroe Alderson, *Marketing Behavior and Executive Action* (Homewood, IL: Irwin, 1957), p. 59.

the United Kingdom, and Euro Disney where controls were loosened far too much for foreign subsidiaries. Not to be outdone, we saw the unethical growth climate at Met Life. Good financial judgment and decent ethical behavior must not be sacrificed to the siren call of growth. With relatively new firms, such as Boston Chicken and Planet Hollywood, growth can easily outpace resources and management competence.

We can make these generalizations about the most desirable growth perspectives:

1. Growth targets should not exceed the abilities and resources of the organization. Growth at any cost—especially at the expense of profits and financial stability—must be shunned. In particular, tight controls over inventories and expenses should be established, and performance should be monitored closely.

2. The most prudent approach to growth is to keep the organization and operation as simple and uniform as possible, to be flexible in case sales do not meet expectations, and to seek a low breakeven point, especially for new and untried ventures.

3. Rapidly expanding markets pose dangers from both too conservative and overly optimistic sales forecasts. The latter may overextend resources and jeopardize viability should the demand contract; the former opens the door to more aggressive competitors. There is no right answer to this dilemma, but management should be aware of the risks and the rewards of both extremes.

4. A strategy emphasizing rapid growth should not neglect other aspects of the operation. For example, older stores should not be ignored in the quest to open new outlets, as Toys Я Us was guilty of.

5. Decentralized management is more compatible with rapid growth than centralized, because it puts less strain on home office executives. However, delegation must have well-defined standards and controls as well as competent subordinates. Otherwise, the Maytag Hoover fiasco may be repeated.

6. The integrity of the product and the firm's reputation must not be sacrificed in pursuit of rapid growth. This is especially important when customers' health and safety may be jeopardized.

Search for Uniqueness

Most firms seek some differential advantage or uniqueness over existing competitors. Some never find it, or they rely on gimmicks, such as a new package or some product feature of little consequence to customers. Boston Beer found a genuine measure of uniqueness in its flavor and quality of brewing. Saturn found its uniqueness in a different approach to customers than automakers had ever had: a comfortable and caring relationship, one that developed tremendous customer loyalty and the highest satisfaction ratings of any U.S. car. All the successes we examined had uniqueness: Southwest Air, Johnson & Johnson, Nike, McDonald's, Wal-Mart, even Harley Davidson at last, with its fortuitous mystique.

On the other hand, Toys Я Us lost its attractive uniqueness. Nike is in danger of losing its. Even McDonald's, for decades unique in its control of product quality and service, is no longer unique among its competitors. Saturn's problems, when it tried to bring its uniqueness in the U.S. auto market to the Japanese market, came about because it was no longer unique against Japanese competitors in Japan.

So, uniqueness is widely sought, but not always achieved. It is a mistake to hold the idea that uniqueness has to come from a different product or perhaps a different way of distribution. It can come from simply doing some things better, such as better service, better quality control, greater dependability, or greater efforts toward pleasing customers.

We can make these generalizations regarding finding opportunities and strategic windows:

1. Opportunities often exist when a traditional way of doing business has prevailed in the industry for a long time—maybe the climate is ripe for a change.

2. Opportunities often exist when existing firms are not entirely satisfying customers' needs.

3. Innovations are not limited to products but can involve customer services as well as such things as methods of distribution.

4. For industries with rapidly changing technologies—usually new industries—heavy research and development expenditures are usually required if a firm is to avoid falling behind its competitors. But heavy R & D expenditures do not guarantee being in the vanguard, as shown by the tribulations of IBM despite its huge expenditures.

Power of Judicious Imitation

Some firms are reluctant to copy successful practices of their competitors; they want to be leaders, not followers. But successful practices or innovations may need to be copied if a firm is not to be left behind. Sometimes the imitator outdoes the innovator. Success can lie in doing the ordinary better than competitors.

GM's Saturn achieved its initial success by imitating many of the successful practices of its Japanese competitors. Nike outdid Adidas, with the same marketing strategy. Michael Feuer with OfficeMax took a similar format to other category-killer stores, but did things better. Boston Beer found its distinctiveness in being a more robust-tasting beer, and the highest price of all. On the other hand, many competitors of McDonald's long ignored its successful format, even though the high standards and rigid controls were obvious to all. Admittedly, it is not easy to develop high standards and controls and to insist that they be followed. We can make this generalization:

> It makes sense for a company to identify the characteristics of successful competitors (and even similar but noncompeting firms), and then to adopt these characteristics if they are compatible with its resources. Let someone else do the experimenting and risk

taking. The imitator faces some risk in waiting too long, but this usually is far less than the risk that the innovator faces.

EXECUTION INSIGHTS

The Austerity Mindset

Four of the firms we studied exemplified this philosophy to the fullest. Two are rather new firms, Boston Beer and OfficeMax, and it is possible that with greater size they may release the austerity reins. Another firm, Southwest Air, shows no signs of changing its successful austerity format. And our last firm, Wal-Mart, has grown to great size firmly wedded to the frugality of its founder, Sam Walton.

And we have seen the opposite in the organizational bloat of an IBM, the difficulties of Toys Я Us in competing with the discount stores because of its higher fixed costs and bloated inventories. Likewise, besieged Scott Paper and Sunbeam, reeling from the drastic cuts of Al Dunlap, deserved some of this because their organizations had grown cumbersome.

Lean and mean is the order of the day with many firms. The problem with the lemming-like pursuit of the lean-and-mean goal is knowing how far to downsize without cutting into bone and muscle, which then becomes counterproductive. As thousands of managers and staff specialists can attest, the loss of jobs and destruction of career paths has been traumatic for individuals and society alike. So it is much better not to become bloated in the first place.

Resistance to Change

People, as well as organizations, are naturally reluctant to embrace change. Change is disruptive, it destroys routines and muddies interpersonal relationships with subordinates, coworkers, and superiors. Previously important positions may be downgraded or even eliminated, and persons who view themselves as highly competent may be forced to assume unfamiliar duties, with the fear that they cannot master the new assignments. When the change involves wholesale terminations in a major downsizing, such as the ones Dunlap engineered, the resistance and fear of change can become so great that overall efficiency is seriously jeopardized.

Normal resistance to change can be combatted by good communication with participants about forthcoming changes. Without such communication rumors and fears may be blown far out of proportion. Acceptance of change is facilitated if employees are involved as fully as possible in planning the changes, if their participation is solicited and welcomed, and if assurance can be given that positions will not be impaired, only changed. Gradual rather than abrupt changes also make a transition smoother.

In the final analysis, however, possible negative repercussions should not deter making needed changes and embracing different opportunities. If change is desirable, as it usually is with long-established bureaucratic organizations, it should be initiated. Individuals and organizations can adapt to change—it just takes some time.

Prudent Crisis Management

Crises are unexpected happenings that pose threats, ranging from moderate to cata-strophic, to the organization's well-being. A number of cases involved crises: for example, United Way, Maytag, Euro Disney, Coca-Cola, ADM, Met Life, and of course Johnson & Johnson. Some handled their crisis reasonably well, such as United Way, Euro Disney, and the paragon of crisis management, J & J, although we can question in the first two cases how such crises were allowed to happen in the first place. However, Maytag, ADM, and Met Life either overreacted or else failed badly in salvaging the situation.

Most crises can be minimized if a company practices risk avoidance, has contin-gency plans, and is alert to changes in the environment. For example, it is prudent to prohibit key executives from traveling on the same plane; it is prudent to insure key executives so that their incapacity will not endanger the organization; and it is pru-dent to set up contingency plans for a strike, an equipment failure or plant shutdown, the loss of a major customer, unexpected economic conditions, or a serious lawsuit. With these contingency plans, it is best to work back from a worst-case scenario. Some crises can be anticipated, such as a looming oil embargo, a shortage of certain raw materials, a growing union militancy in the industry.

Insurance usually covers certain risks, but the mettle of any organization can be severely tested by an unexpected crisis not covered adequately by insurance: for example, a major product recall because of serious safety or health risks. Such may have major impact on profits, as Johnson & Johnson found with its Tylenol recall. Crises may necessitate some changes in the organization and the way of doing business, but they need not cause the demise of the company if alternatives are weighed and actions taken only after due deliberation. Firms should avoid making hasty disruptive changes or, the other extreme, making too few changes too late.

Don't Rock the Boat

This philosophy advocates not making changes unless problems warrant it. If things are going well, even if not as well as desired, don't tamper, since the conse-quences might be worse. This is also commonly known as the "if it's not broke, don't fix it" philosophy. The Coca-Cola case is the strongest confirmation of this idea: changing the flavor of Coke slightly did not improve demand but simply aroused condemnation.

As with most things, however, this admonition of not changing that which seems to be satisfactory should not be graven in stone. An operation may be improved through fine-tuning; an alternative may be better. The present-day dilemma of Toys Я Us suggests that unchanging policies and strategies of the past need to be reworked. IBM, Nike, Boeing, and United Way were slow in making changes and severe problems caught up with them, as were Scott Paper and Sunbeam long before Dunlap brought drastic changes. Continuance of the status quo is usually just a wistful dream, one that deludes any organization not geared to the possibility of change.

Environmental Monitoring

A firm should be alert to changes in the business environment: changes in customer preferences and needs, in competition, in the economy, in government regulation, and even in international events such as nationalism in Canada, NAFTA, OPEC machinations, changes in Eastern Europe and South Africa, and economic developments in the Far East. IBM, Harley Davidson, Boeing, and Toys Я Us failed to detect and act upon significant changes in their industries. Disney encountered different customer attitudes in Europe than it had experienced before.

How can a firm remain alert to subtle and insidious or more obvious changes? It must have *sensors* constantly monitoring the environment. The sensor may be a marketing or economic research department, but in many instances such a formal organizational entity is not really necessary to provide primary monitoring. Executive alertness is essential. Most changes do not occur suddenly and without warning. Feedback from customers, sales representatives, and suppliers; news of the latest relevant projections in business journals; and even simple observations of what is happening in stores, advertising, prices, and new technologies can provide information about a changing environment. Unfortunately, in the urgency of handling day-to-day operating problems, managers may miss clues of imminent changes in the competitive environment.

Following are generalizations regarding vulnerability to competition:

1. Initial market advantage tends to be rather quickly countered by competitors.

2. Countering by competitors is more likely when an innovation is involved than when the advantage involves more commonplace effective management, such as superb cost controls or customer service.

3. An easy-entry industry is particularly vulnerable to new and aggressive competition, especially if the market is expanding. In new industries, severe price competition usually weeds out the marginal firms.

4. Long-dominant firms tend to be vulnerable to upstart competitors because of their complacency, conservatism, and conceit. They frequently are resistant to change, and myopic about the environment.

5. Careful monitoring of performance at strategic control points can detect weakening positions needing corrective action before situations become serious. (This will be further discussed shortly.)

6. In expanding markets it is unwise to judge performance by increases in sales rather than by market share; an increase in sales may hide a deteriorating situation as competitors increase sales more.

7. A no-growth policy invites competitive inroads.

The Power of Giving Employees a Sense of Pride and a Caring Management

The great turnaround of Continental from the confrontational days of Lorenzo has to be mainly attributed to the people-oriented environment fostered by Bethune. The marvel is how quickly it was done, started with such a simple thing as an open-door policy to the executive suite, and encouragement of full communication with employees.

Still, Continental is not unique is this enlisting of employees to the team. Other successful firms have done so, although perhaps none so strikingly or so suddenly. Kelleher of Southwest Airlines certainly developed this esprit d'corp, and this helps account for the great cost advantage Southwest has. Ray Kroc of McDonald's fostered this as McDonald's began its great charge, although the relationships with franchisees seem diminished today under new top management. Michael Feuer gained dedicated employees in the early growth years of OfficeMax, as did Sam Walton of Wal-Mart.

Then we have the other extreme, the mechanistic handling of employees by Al Dunlap. Any temporary improvement of profits, through cutting expenses to the bone with vast layoffs, finally came home to roost as he himself was fired at Sunbeam.

Boeing's problems with its peaks and valleys of layoffs and hiring destroyed any hope of widespread pride and esprit d'corp of its employees, except perhaps for a nucleus. This sense of pride was certainly latent with such a national and visible product, but management did not achieve stability of employment, and therefore lost employee morale.

A key factor in cultivating employee morale and teamwork lies in the perceived growth prospects of the firm, in addition to a people-oriented management. Where growth prospects look good, even coming back from the adversity of Continental, then employees can grasp that extra measure of enthusiasm and motivation.

CONTROL INSIGHTS

Delegation Overdone

Good managers delegate as much as possible to subordinates. By giving them some freedom and as much responsibility as they can handle, future leaders of the organization are developed. More than this, delegation frees higher executives to concentrate on the most important matters. Other areas of the operation need come to their attention only where performances deviate significantly from what is expected at *strategic control points.* This is known as *management by exception.*

Management by exception failed, however, with Maytag and its overseas Hoover division. The flaw lay in failing to monitor faulty promotional plans. By the time results were coming in, it was too late. Admittedly, with diverse and far-flung operations it becomes more difficult to closely monitor all aspects, but still there should be strategic control points to warn of impending dangers. Furthermore, home office approval of expenditures above a certain amount must be enforced.

We found similar problems in other cases. The Euro Disney difficulties may have resulted from too much autonomy: the European operation did not adjust well to a somewhat different playing field, in which customers were far more price-conscious than had been experienced before.

At the top executive level, United Way found the excesses of its chief, Aramony, to be unacceptable. Here, the board of directors could be faulted for being far too tolerant of a chief executive's questionable behavior. This raises another issue: How closely should the board exercise control?

Board of Directors Patsies

A board of directors can monitor top management performance closely and objectively. Or it can be completely supportive and uncritical. In the latter situation, the board exercises no controls on top management; in the former, it becomes an important control factor at the highest level.

Given the potential control power of the board, top executives find their own interests best served by packing the board with supporters. Dwayne Andreas of ADM succeeded in doing so and found virtual freedom to run the company as he saw fit. Even large institutional shareholders could not muster enough support to thwart his dictatorship. Aramony of United Way also had a sympathetic and supportive board that permitted his excesses to go unmonitored, until investigative reporters blew the whistle.

Instead of assuming the status of watchdogs for investors' best interests, such patsy boards disserve them.

Systematic Evaluations and Controls

Organizations need feedback to determine how well something is being done, whether improvement is possible, where it should occur, how much is needed, and how quickly it must be accomplished. Without feedback or performance evaluation, a worsening situation can go unrecognized until too late for corrective action.

As firms become larger, the need for better controls or feedback increases, because top management can no longer personally monitor all aspects of the operation. Mergers and diversifications, which often result in loosely controlled decentralized operations—for example, again, Maytag and its overseas Hoover division—all the more need systematic feedback on performance.

Financial and expense controls are vital. After all, if costs and inventories get severely out of line—and worse, if this is not recognized until late—then the very viability of the firm can be jeopardized. At the least, a firm like Toys Я Us is at a cost and price disadvantage compared to its far more efficient competitors.

Performance standards are another critical means of control for large and widespread operations. Unless operating standards are imposed and enforced, uniformity of performance is sacrificed, resulting in unevenness of quality and service and a lack of coordination and continuity among the different units. Even unethical and illegal practices may ensue, as we saw with Met Life. Instead of running a tight ship, managers face a loose and undisciplined one. McDonald's has long been the model of a tight ship, with its enduring insistence on the tightest standards in the industry, although this shows signs of eroding today.

INSIGHTS REGARDING SPECIFIC STRATEGY ELEMENTS
Appeal of Price

In several cases we have seen an anomaly regarding the effective use of price. Southwest Airlines owes its great strategic advantage to offering the lowest prices in its industry, and doing this profitably because of a cost structure lower than other air carriers. Yet, Continental Air found that the low-price strategy of Frank Lorenzo almost destroyed it. Discount stores base their customer appeal on offering lower prices than conventional retailers. Undoubtedly some customers are strongly attracted by low prices, but low prices must not be at the expense of reasonable customer service and product quality.

Yet, we saw several cases where high prices attract. The entrepreneur, Jim Koch, targeted his Boston Beer as having a robust flavor with some of the highest prices in the industry. Nike had long been able to charge premium prices for some of its athletic shoes, bolstered by the image of Michael Jordan and other famous athletes. And Harley Davidson customers are willing to wait months to obtain its high-priced bikes.

On the other hand, high prices did not work to Disney's advantage in Euro Disney. The French and most other Europeans apparently were more frugal than Disney executives had expected; only when prices were cut significantly was the theme park's viability more certain.

With prices it seems that we face the twin appeals to bargains and to highest quality. Although more customers are attracted to bargains and low prices, a significant number are willing to pay a lot more for something they believe is the highest quality. And the great majority of customers believe that high price equates to high quality—which it does sometimes, but not always.

Can Advertising Do the Job?

We are left with contradictions regarding the power and effectiveness of advertising. Boston Beer, despite its larger competitors and rather modest expenditures for advertising, carved a significant niche in the beer market. At the time of Coca-Cola's blunder with its New Coke it was spending $100 million more for advertising than Pepsi, and all the while was losing market share. Does advertising have much relationship with success?

It seems that the right theme can bring success, as witness Nike's great success with celebrity endorsements in creating an image irresistible to many of its customers. And the low-key, homey nonproduct advertising of Saturn succeeded in nurturing "the Saturn family." Maytag Hoover's promotional campaign certainly created great attention and interest, miguided though the plan was. And how can we forget the success of the Joe Camel theme, despite public protests?

Thus we see the great challenge of advertising. One never knows for sure how much should be spent to get the job done, to reach the planned objectives of perhaps increasing sales or market share by a certain percentage. However, despite the inability to measure directly the effectiveness of advertising, it is the brave—or foolhardy—executive who decides to stand pat in the face of aggressive increased promotions by competitors. We draw these conclusions:

- There is no assured correlation between expenditures for advertising and sales success, but the right theme or message can be powerful.

- In most cases, advertising can generate initial trial, but if the other elements of the strategy are relatively unattractive, customers will not be won or retained.

Analytical Management Tools

We identified several of the most useful analytical tools for decision making. In Euro Disney we discussed breakeven analysis, a highly useful means for making go/no-go decisions about new ventures and alternative business strategies. In Maytag, the cost-benefit analysis was described that might have prevented the bungled promotion in England. And we encountered the SWOT analysis in the Southwest Air case. While these analyses do not guarantee the best decisions, they do bring order and systematic thinking into the art of management decision making.

ETHICAL CONSIDERATIONS

A firm tempted to walk the low road in search of greater short-run profits may eventually find that the risks far outweigh the rewards. This holds for industries, too; the tobacco industry has been grudgingly confronting wave after wave of attacks and an eager media quick to publicize them.

We have examined more than a few cases dealing with ethical controversies, for example, ADM's indictment for price fixing and its more subtle efforts to gain special influence in the halls of government. Then there was Met Life's indictment for deceptive sales practices, and the exposés of undesirable practices by United Way. While we cannot delve very deeply into social and ethical issues,[2] some insights are worth noting:

1. A firm can no longer disavow itself from the possibility of critical ethical scrutiny. Activist groups often publicize alleged misdeeds long before governmental regulators will. Legal actions may follow.

2. Public protests may take a colorful path, with marches, picketing, billboard whitewashing, and the like, and may enlist public and media support for their cause.

Should a firm attempt to resist and defend itself? The overwhelming evidence is to the contrary. The bad press, the adversarial relations, and the effect on public image are hardly worth such a confrontation. The better course of action may be to back down as quietly as possible, repugnant though such may be to a management convinced of the reasonableness of its position.

Most of the ethical problems we saw came from a hostile media. Sensationalism, exaggeration, and taking sides against the big corporation usually sell more copies or gain more audience. Many executives are uncomfortable and even hostile toward an inquisitive press. So, they create a bad impression, frequently one of trying to hide something. Even worse is to be confrontational, as the tobacco industry has long practiced.

Johnson & Johnson's secret for gaining rapport with the media was corporate openness and cooperation. After the Tylenol catastrophe, it sought good two-way communication with media furnishing information from the field while J & J gave full

---

[2] For more depth of coverage, see R. F. Hartley, *Business Ethics* (New York: Wiley), 1993.

and honest disclosure of its own investigation and actions. To promote good rapport, company officials were readily available to the press.

Unfortunately, J & J's openness with the media and concern for customers seems to have eroded in recent years, with publicity of overpricing of a vital cancer drug, and reluctance to make full disclosure of risks of Tylenol overdosing.

GENERAL INSIGHTS

Impact of One Person

In many of the cases one person had a powerful impact on the organization. Sam Walton of Wal-Mart is perhaps the most outstanding example, but we also have Ray Kroc of McDonald's, who converted a small hamburger stand into the world's largest restaurant operation; Herb Kelleher of Southwest Air, tormentor of the mighty airlines; Phil Knight of Nike, who could never break the four-minute mile in college, but went on to bring Nike world leadership in running and other athletic gear. Less well known are Jim Koch of Boston Beer and Michael Feuer of OfficeMax.

For turnaround accomplishments, Gordon Bethune, who turned around a demoralized Continental Airlines stands tall, as does Lou Gerstner of IBM, with Vaughan Beals of Harley Davidson no slouch.

One person can also have a negative impact on an organization. Al Dunlap, the decimator of sick companies, who finally got his comeuppance with Sunbeam, is perhaps best known. Then there is William Aramony who almost destroyed United Way by his high living and arrogance. Less well-known are Dwayne Andreas, the long-time CEO of ADM, who set the climate for illegalities both embarrassing and reprehensible, and Geoffrey Bible of Philip Morris, the industry's most aggressive defender. The impact of one person, for good or ill, is one of the recurring marvels of history, whether business history or world history.

Prevalence of Opportunities for Entrepreneurship Today

Despite the maturing of our economy and the growing size and power of many firms in many industries, opportunities for entrepreneurship are still abundant. Opportunities exist not only for the changemaker or innovator, but also for the person who only seeks to do things a little better than existing, and complacent, competition.

Most entrepreneurial successes are unheralded, although dozens are widely publicized. While we dealt specifically with new business ventures in Part V, with such rising stars as Boston Beer and OfficeMax, two other cases are not so many years away from their births: for example, Wal-Mart and Southwest Airlines. Bill Gates of Microsoft is another winner.[3] Opportunities are there for the dedicated. Venture capital to support promising new businesses has helped many fledgling enterprises. As a new business shows early promise, initial public offerings (IPOs) (i.e., new stock

---

[3] This case is described in R. F. Hartley, *Marketing Mistakes,* 7th ed. (New York: John Wiley, 1998), pp. 217–233.

issues) become important sources of capital, as we saw with Boston Beer, Boston Chicken, Planet Hollywood, and OfficeMax.

But entrepreneurship is not for everyone. The great venture capitalists look at the person, not the idea. Typically they distribute their seed money to resourceful people who are courageous enough to give up security for the unknown consequences of their embryonic ventures, who have great self-confidence, and who demonstrate a tremendous will to win.

CONCLUSION

We learn from mistakes and from successes, although every management problem and opportunity seems cast in a unique setting. But there are still common elements. One author has likened business strategy to military strategy:

> Strategies which are flexible rather than static embrace optimum use and offer the greatest number of alternative objectives. A good commander knows that he cannot control his environment to suit a prescribed strategy. Natural phenomena pose their own restraints to strategic planning, whether physical, geographic, regional, or psychological and sociological.[4]

He later adds:

> Planning leadership recognizes the unpleasant fact that, despite every effort, the war may be lost. Therefore, the aim is to retain the maximum number of facilities and the basic organization. Indicators of a deteriorating and unsalvageable total situation are, therefore, mandatory … No possible combination of strategies and tactics, no mobilization of resources … can supply a magic formula which guarantees victory; it is possible only to increase the probability of victory.[5]

Thus, we can pull two concepts from military strategy to help guide business strategy: the desirability of flexibility in an unknown or changing environment and the idea that a basic core should be maintained in crises. The first suggests that the firm should be prepared for adjustments in strategy as conditions warrant. The second suggests that there is a basic core of a firm's business that should be unchanging; it should be the final bastion to fall back on for regrouping if necessary. Harley Davidson stolidly maintained its core position, even though it let expansion opportunities slither away. IBM had a solid core that it was able to maintain and from which it could mount a resurgence. Whether Toys Я Us has such a solid core remains to be seen.

In regard to the basic core of a firm, every viable firm has some distinctive function or "ecological niche" in the business environment:

---

[4] Myron S. Heidingsfield, *Changing Patterns in Marketing* (Boston: Allyn & Bacon, 1968), p. 11.

[5] *Ibid.*

Every business firm occupies a position which is in some respects unique. Its location, the product it sells, its operating methods, or the customers it serves tend to set it off in some degree from every other firm. Each firm competes by making the most of its individuality and its special character.[6]

Woe to the firm that loses its ecological niche.

QUESTIONS

1. Design a program aimed at mistake avoidance. Be as specific, as creative, and as complete as possible.

2. Would you advise a firm to be an imitator or an innovator? Why?

3. "There is no such thing as a sustainable competitive advantage." Discuss.

4. How would you build controls into an organization to ensure that similar mistakes do not happen in the future?

5. Array as many pros and cons of entrepreneurship as you can. Which do you see as most compelling?

6. Do you agree with the thought expressed in this chapter that a firm confronted with strong criticism should abandon the product or the way of doing business? Why or why not?

7. We have suggested that the learning insights discussed in this chapter and elsewhere in the book are transferable to other firms and other times. Do you completely agree with this? Why or why not?

HANDS-ON EXERCISE

Your firm has had a history of reacting to rather than anticipating changes in the industry. As the staff assistant to the CEO, you have been assigned the responsibility of developing adequate sensors of the marketplace. How will you go about developing such sensors?

TEAM DEBATE EXERCISE

Debate the extremes of forecasting for an innovative new product: conservative versus aggressive.

---

[6] Alderson, p. 101.